H. DANIEL-ROPS

THE CHURCH IN THE EIGHTEENTH CENTURY

TRANSLATED FROM
THE FRENCH BY
JOHN WARRINGTON

IMAGE BOOKS

A Division of Doubleday & Company, Inc.
Garden City, New York

Image Books Edition
by special arrangement with E. P. Dutton & Co., Inc.
Image Books edition published February 1966

H. Daniel-Rops: *L'Église des Temps Classiques: L'Ère des Grands Craquements,* first published in France by Librairie Arthème Fayard, 1960.

TRANSLATOR'S NOTE

M. Daniel-Rops dealt with the period 1622–1789, under the general title *L'Église des Temps Classiques*, from the second of which, *L'Ère des Grands Craquements*, this volume has been translated.

CONTENTS

MAPS

CHAPTER I

THE INTELLECTUAL REVOLT

1. A DOUBTFUL HERITAGE

In the course of one among many funeral orations[1] which revealed him as the living conscience of his age, Bossuet uttered a fierce denunciation of what he called 'the intemperance of the mind'. That of the senses, he declared, is not the only nor even perhaps the most insidious form of licence; the intellect has its own instability and temptations. 'Pride that can suffer no legitimate authority, wilful giddiness, temerity that halts at nothing'—such, according to Bossuet, are the true causes of an arrogant revolt, comparable with that of Lucifer, to which such intemperance leads. Its end, the rebel's goal, is 'to become the sole object of his delight, to make himself his own god'. The aged bishop's analysis was sound; he was well acquainted with the human soul and also with his period. Looking into the future he beheld a scene that wrung from him a cry of anguish: what was to become of the Christian faith? Could it withstand the assaults of unleashed pride? Would not the gates of hell prevail against the Word? To his friend Huet, Bishop of Avranches, he wrote: 'I see preparations for a grand assault upon the Church.'

But his lordship of Meaux was mistaken. The great struggle was not in preparation: it had begun two centuries earlier. In order to discover the origins of that arrogant revolt, of that intellectual aberration, we must go back to the heyday of the Italian Renaissance, when the humanist mind, marvelling at its own progress, gradually cut itself adrift from the traditions, the observances and eventually the very dogmas of Christianity. Even during the Quattrocento such men as Poggio, Filefo and Lorenzo Valla,[2] papal officials though they were, vilified monks, priests and nuns with a ferocity far beyond the old spirit of medieval anti-clericalism, assailing the Church herself, her prestige and her organization. They were followed

by the more determined sceptics of the Roman Academy,
Platina and Leto; by the members of Pontana's Academy at
Naples; and at Florence by Marsupini, who had dared to refuse the sacraments on his deathbed. By the end of the fifteenth century the attack had reached unprecedented heights
of animosity with Pomponazzi and then Vicomercato, master
of the Paduan School, who seemed to be little more than
pure materialists. The immortality of the soul, original sin,
the Redemption, the authority of the Church, all the essential
dogmas, had been called in question by these forbears of the
freethinkers.

The sixteenth century witnessed a continuation and development of that trend, which derived added impetus from
the Protestant Reformation. By ousting religious authority in
favour of individual judgment the Reformers involuntarily
undermined the bases of faith and prepared the ground for
irreligion. Luther, towards the end of his life, became aware
of this result, which Calvin sought to avoid through the imposition of a theocratic dictatorship at Geneva by means
identical with those of the Inquisition. How was it possible,
on the other hand, to prevent certain minds, as they watched
the proliferation of sects and the bitter disputes between
contradictory confessions, from concluding that all the
churches without exception were equally at fault? How persuade them that the existence of truth was possible, when
they had been repeatedly assured that the ancient Catholic
Church, guardian of that truth for sixteen centuries, was a
monster of error and corruption? The logical successors of
Luther, Zwingli and Calvin were the Sozzini, uncle and
nephew, two Sienese resident in Poland, whose destructive
handling of Christian dogma led them to stark deism.

Thus the great century of religious dispute was characterized simultaneously by a steady advance of irreligion. The
remarkable progress of physical science was largely responsible for this phenomenon. The human intellect, as it began to
pierce the secrets of nature, experienced a sense of intoxica-
tion with which we are familiar. Francis Bacon, whose thought
was more honest than his life, while exalting 'the dignity and
progress of Science', persuaded others to believe nothing that
was not proved by experimental demonstration; and this view

became widespread. An obscure professor of Caen exclaimed: 'Just fancy the authority of one man, whose teaching rests upon no observation or mathematical proof, serving as an article of faith!' This one man was, of course, the Pope. To leave the future of the world to science was the idea of Giordano Bruno, an errant Dominican, and later of his fellow and rival Campanella; the Church, with her creed, her orthodoxy, appeared to them as the enemy of scientific progress. Lauding the numerous achievements of the human mind and its techniques in recent years—compass, printing press, gunpowder, discovery of new worlds and increased knowledge of the heavens—Campanella ended a short treatise with three little words that herald the triumphant atheism of today: 'We are free.' In other words, we have no need of God.

Intellectual revolt was on the march. Among its violent and fanatical supporters were Étienne Dolet and his small circle at Lyons, where the printing house of Gryphe issued many suspect books; the picturesque Bohemian Jerome Cardan, who explained the mystery of the Incarnation by astrology and declared himself a 'perfidious and envious detractor of religion'; Vanini, an unfrocked Carmelite, who went so far as to treat Christ as an impostor and His miracles as tricks of conjuring; the epicurean poet Théophile de Viau, a complete sceptic, who believed neither in God nor in the Devil, but in passion alone. True, their numbers were not large, perhaps a few hundred; but they were the source of a veritable river. Under the pretext of humanism, freedom of the mind, the new ideas found some strange allies. Vicomercato, the Paduan atheist, was authorized to teach at the Collège de France; Étienne Dolet was for several years protected by Marguerite de Navarre; and Campanella was actually received by the pious King Louis XIII.

Worse still, there were some who did not consider themselves unbelievers, but who laboured, perhaps unwittingly, for the cause of unbelief. Such was Rabelais, whose satirical mind (though he never openly denied the faith) did more than scoff at ecclesiastical absurdities, often sneering at the very dogmas of Christianity. Such too was Montaigne. His *Essais* sparkled with excellent and perfectly orthodox maxims; but his work deserved the strictures of Father Garasse, who said that it ended by 'gently strangling the religious sentiment, as with a silken cord'. Moreover, if we take a look at their disciples we can see to what extent the masters' thought can be considered harmless. Jacques Tabureau, the heir of Rabelais, in his *Dialogues non moins profitables que facétieux*, expected nothing. Pierre Charron, a friend and pupil of Montaigne, rejected the latter's 'What do I know?' in favour of the radical scepticism summed up in the phrase 'I know nothing', whence he inferred that all religions are worthless. About the year 1600 there were few real atheists, but there was an increase in the number of those who were beginning to be known as Libertines.

The early seventeenth century, then, received from its predecessor, together with the rich inheritance of Trent and the great schools of spirituality, another legacy, one that was fraught with danger. Here we have an aspect (surely the fundamental aspect) of that latent crisis whose symptoms are visible, as we have seen,[3] in many corners of that majestic edifice described as the Age of Spiritual Grandeur. The struggle was between the traditional values upon which Christianity had established a world order and those which claimed to represent the future. The neo-classical period marks, in this as in every field, the moment when a still victorious resistance is opposed to the forces of disruption; but the neo-classical system was doomed to weaken and collapse, until the rebellion of the intellect could be waged in the full light of day.

2. THE AFFAIR OF GALILEO

How did the Church react in face of perils she could not ignore? The secular arm, whose aid she had the power to invoke, provided her with a formidable weapon of coercion and repression, and of this she made full use. The Inquisition, devised long ago to withstand the menace of intellectual revolt, took action wherever it continued to exist.[4] It had already struck a number of resounding blows. Giordano Bruno, arrested at Venice and handed over to the papal authorities, was condemned as a heretic and burned on the Campo dei Fiori, where his statue stands today. Vanini too was put to death, his tongue torn out by the executioner. Campanella was more fortunate; he was merely obliged to leave Rome, and died peacefully in the Dominican house of Saint-Honoré at Paris. At the request of the religious authorities, Louis XIII began his reign by signing the decrees of 1617 against irreligion and blasphemy, as a result of which Théophile de Viau suffered imprisonment.

There was thus a decided reaction to the perils with which irreligion was menacing the faith. But these coercive measures were not altogether effective. They were frustrated by the connivance which godlessness found for itself in the most varied circles, not least in high places; even during the Quattrocentro there had been popes who showed remarkable indulgence towards atheistic humanists. Furthermore the Holy Office, though capable of punishing open nonconformity, seems to have been less efficient when called upon to silence men whose scepticism lay beneath the surface of their writings. Rabelais, for instance, was able to publish his works with almost complete impunity, and Montaigne was requested to do no more than revise his own *Essais*. Finally, we may ask whether the steps taken by the Inquisition were well chosen, whether they invariably served the cause of truth and the interests of the Church.

This question is prompted by a famous episode which involved one of the most celebrated figures of the early seventeenth century—Galileo. The affair, as we know, has been tirelessly exploited against the Church; anti-clerical polemists have elected to charge her in this matter with obscurantism and ferocity. We are all familiar with the picture of a brilliant scientist imprisoned for his discoveries and stigmatizing his judges in the eyes of posterity with a few devastating words. That picture, however, is not altogether accurate. Galileo was born at Pisa in 1564. His scientific endowments were manifest from youth upwards, and in 1592 he obtained a chair in the University of Padua. Possessed of a lively mind, curious and keenly interested in the visible world about him, he devoted much of his time to studying the stars, with particular reference to the problem of their movement. At that time the accepted explanation was the Ptolemaic theory derived from Aristotle and propounded some fourteen centuries earlier. According to that theory the earth was at rest in the centre of the universe, and all else, stars and planets alike, revolved about it. The Bible was held to contain numerous passages which confirmed this view; not only the famous episode of Joshua halting the sun, but also several verses of the Psalms (ciii. 5) and Ecclesiastes (i. 4, 6), where the immobility of the earth and the mobility of the sun were expressly stated. During the fifteenth century, however, Cardinal Nicholas of Cusa had advanced the contrary hypothesis, which had been taken up and developed by Canon Copernicus in the sixteenth: the sun does not revolve; the earth and all the planets do. But that was a mere hypothesis, put forward as such by its authors, which science could not as yet confirm by demonstration. In Germany it had been resolutely opposed by the Protestant leaders, Luther and Melanchthon; Pope Clement VII, on the other hand, had treated it more favourably, and none of his eleven successors had seen fit to contradict it.

The young professor at Padua encountered the ideas of Copernicus and made them his own. The telescope had been invented in 1608 by the Dutch optician Lippershey; Galileo constructed one which magnified surfaces 900 times and enabled him to observe the phases of the moon, the satellites of Jupiter, the rings of Saturn and many other striking phenomena of outer space. In 1610, in his *Nuntius Sidereus* (Messenger of the Stars), he informed the public of his astonishing discoveries. In 1611, while studying Jupiter, he believed himself to have hit upon scientific proof of the Copernican theory. He went to Rome and was welcomed with extraordinary marks of favour: Pope, prelates and princes, all were anxious to hear about the wonders of the heavens.

Nothing untoward would have happened if Galileo had confined himself to the field of science. But having been attacked by various adversaries and accused of denying the truths of Holy Scripture, he undertook, with the help of two tactless pupils, to enter the field of biblical exegesis and show that the new system was in perfect accord with the sacred text. His arguments were considered by Pope Paul V to be strongly infected with the principles of free judgment upheld by the Reformers. The Holy Office was alarmed and in 1616 condemned the two fundamental propositions of the system,

that the sun is the centre of the world and the earth is in
motion. Galileo, though not named, was required to abandon
the condemned thesis, and he at once declared his unqualified
readiness to submit to the judgment of authority. None of
his writings was placed on the Index, and the Pope most
generously declared that he himself would protect him against
his detractors.

Years passed. Cardinal Barberini became Pope. He was a
friend and warm admirer of the scientist, and had even dedicated to him a Latin ode. Galileo, haloed thus with glory and
continuing his labours undisturbed, perhaps believed that the
time had come to have the decisions of 1616 revoked. At all
events, he was attacked by a Jesuit, Father Grassi, and replied
with a polemical work: *Il Saggiatore* (The Essayist), which
he dedicated to the Pope and to which Mgr Riccardi, Master
of the Sacred Palace, granted an *imprimatur*. Encouraged by
success, he proceeded to write an enormous work entitled
A Dialogue on the Two Greatest Systems of the World
(1632), in which he formally declared the Copernican view
to be the sole scientific and demonstrated theory. To this
work Mgr Riccardi was not prepared to grant his *imprimatur*
unless it were preceded by a preface that would represent
the system as a mere hypothesis. Galileo refused.

The affair was envenomed not only by the astronomer's
enemies, who denounced him to the Inquisition for having
violated the undertaking he had given in 1616, but also by
his friends and supporters. Campanella, for example, foolishly
involved the Pope by informing all and sundry that
'Simplicius' in the *Dialogue*, the ridiculous opponent of the
Copernican theory, was in fact Urban VIII—which was quite
untrue. The trial before the Holy Office (1633) dragged on
for several months; during which time Galileo, instead of
being detained in prison, was authorized to stay with a friend.
Two charges were brought against him: (1) that he had expounded the condemned thesis, declaring it to be scientifi-
cally established, and (2) that he had adhered to it *in foro
interno*. Despite a threat of torture, he resolutely denied the
second charge, a denial which he still maintained when confronted with his work. Nevertheless he was 'gravely suspect of
heresy', and on 22nd June he received sentence in the Do-

minican Convent of the Minerva. His *Dialogue* was banned; he himself was ordered to read, kneeling, a precise formula of abjuration, to recite the seven penitential psalms each week for three years and to remain in prison for the remainder of his life. This last clause of the sentence, however, was interpreted in the most generous fashion, for until his death (1642) he was allowed to reside either in the *palazzo* of his friends the Piccolomini at Siena, or in his own villa at Florence, where, as he was fond of saying, he 'offered willing sacrifice to Bacchus, without forgetting Venus and Ceres'. He lived as a good Christian, too, never seeking to rebel in public against the judgment that had overtaken him.[5]

The affair of Galileo then was not played out in the atmosphere of inquisitorial terror that some writers have imagined; one cannot even say that the high ecclesiastical authorities posed systematically, *a priori*, as enemies of scientific progress. If Galileo (and this applies even more to many of his supporters) had not implied, or even expressly declared, that the new astronomy negatived the biblical text, the second trial would have been avoided. It is, however, none the less true that the attitude taken by the Holy Office in this matter is open to criticism. It was doubtless impossible, in the climate of that age, for official theologians and exegetes to acknowledge any but the literal meaning of the sacred text, even in its smallest details. The Protestant churches, and the very Synagogue itself, had adopted exactly the same view.[6] But the inquisitorial court, by taking its stand in the realm of scientific fact and presuming to forbid belief in the rotation of the earth, placed the Church in an untenable position and made her look absurd in scientific eyes, even though the doctrine of her infallibility was not in this instance at stake. We shall unfortunately discover the same opposition to scientific progress in the subsequent history of Christian apologetics. On the other hand, it does not seem that Galileo's judges detected the most dangerous threat of his ideas. The whole of his defence was based ultimately upon a formula which can be expressed as follows: 'The Bible says one thing; my eyes have seen something quite different.' He sought to draw a hard and fast line between the domain of faith and that of experience. But such a line was going to hallow the divorce between faith and science, revelation and reason. It was possible to condemn Galileo if he treated Holy Scripture with contempt. But it should also have been explained why the scheme of divine inspiration and that of scientific discovery did not coincide, and how theology was quite compatible with science. No such explanation, however, was forthcoming at that date.

3. LIBERTINES

It is nevertheless important not to exaggerate the peril of unbelief. At the beginning of the seventeenth century genuine scepticism was professed by very few, and even those who in their hearts did not believe were restrained by prudence and desire for tranquillity from public declaration of the fact. Throughout Christian Europe, however, there were men who paid small respect to orthodox views, in Germany as in Sweden, in the Swiss cantons as in the small Italian states, particularly Florence and Venice. Their unbelief assumed different forms according to locality. The English inclined to what was later known as Deism, of which Herbert of Cherbury (1583–1648) was the precursor. The Germans had their 'conscientious' disciples of Mathias Knutzen who completely rejected the supernatural and based the spiritual life upon the *Diktat* of conscience. In France the most active group was that of the Libertines.

This word led to some confusion: the Libertines professed total freedom, but freedom of what kind—intellectual or moral? In the case of many, no doubt, both. A measure of libertinism arose directly from circumstances. The violence of passions unleashed during the Wars of Religion, the troubles of the League and the conspiracies against Richelieu all tended to prejudice men's minds against religion and its restraints. The influence of Montaigne was used, if necessary, to justify a strain of amiable scepticism and playful epicureanism. Not all Libertines, of course, were 'boozers seeking their happiness in a tavern', those rakes and debauchees against whom Father Mersenne directed the heavy salvo of his three great tomes in 1623; but such people did exist, parading vice and prone to blasphemy. Among them were Gaston d'Orléans, at whose mansion was held a 'Council of Matternot', and who may be considered as their leader—Paul de Gondi too, Cardinal de Retz, their brilliant model. Théophile de Viau was their theorist, and his verses reassured them:

> *'On ne saurait dompter la passion humaine,*
> *Contre amour la raison est importune et vaine.'*
>
> ['*Human passion cannot be subdued,*
> *Reason is vain and powerless against love.*']

Other members of the group included Boisrobert, Saint-Amant, Tristan, Mainart and, more notable, two elderly survivors from the reign of Henri IV, Bassompière and Bellegarde, who were in full accord with the youngest recruits. Noble ladies also were Libertines, such as the Duchesse de Chevreuse, whose conversation was full of 'licentious behaviour, riotous living, coquetry and oaths'.[7] It is true that when the rod of authority smote Théophile, their master, in 1623, many moral Libertines judged it wiser to amend their ways, outwardly at least.

Intellectual Libertines were less numerous; as La Bruyère informs us, the majority of people were 'too lazy-minded to tell themselves that God does not exist'. Those who did so were highly educated men who had read Campanella, the Paduans and the atheistic humanists of the Renaissance. Their bedside books were *Secrets de la Nature*, described by Father Garasse as an 'Introduction to the Undevout Life'; *Traité de la Sagesse* by Pierre Charron, a professor of theology who would have been greatly perturbed had he been able to foresee the success of his work; and especially Montaigne's *Essais*, the final editions of which received corrections and additions, tending in every case to scepticism. These people met behind closed doors for the discussion of learning and philosophy. Their leading thinker was Pierre Gassendi (1592–1655), canon of Digne and professor of mathematics in the Collège Royal at Paris; a distinguished scholar and astronomer, he claimed to reconcile the teaching of Christ with that of Epicurus, and has sometimes been looked upon as a kind of Existentialist. Around him, and forming with him a notorious tetrad, were gathered the Swiss pastor Diodati, the bibliographer Naude,[8] and above all François de la Mothe le Vayer (1588–1672), tutor first to the king's brother and then for a time to young Louis XIV himself. La Mothe sang the praises of scepticism as 'the highest degree of human happiness'; he also devised no fewer than thirty-three syllogisms to prove the immortality of the soul, before concluding that they provided no 'geometrical evidence'.

It may be asked whether these Libertines as a whole constituted a grave danger to the Church. Perhaps not; in many cases they were only epicureans, who, so far from turning their backs upon Christianity, sought to combine 'a purified scepticism with pious sentiments' and to make of their lives, as one of them, Samuel Sorbière, expressed it, 'a pleasant and peaceful voyage'. We may likewise recall the famous words with which Bossuet denounced them: 'What have these rare geniuses seen? What more have they seen than others? . . . They have seen nothing, they understand nothing; they are unable even to prove the nothingness to which they aspire.' Nevertheless their tribe did not dissolve in the sunshine of the Great Reign; its virulence went from strength to strength and contributed much to the final overthrow of the neo-classical edifice. In 1661 a distinguished French soldier was obliged to take refuge in London because a highly compromising letter from him had been discovered among Fouquet's papers; but if the ecclesiastical tribunals had been as vigilant as the secular authorities, they might have called him to account for his *Conversation du Maréchal d'Hocquincourt avec le Père Canaye*, in which the conflict between religion and reason was expounded with a wealth of frivolous sarcasm. This talented and witty man was destined to end his long life (1610–1703) in a state of complete libertinism, both moral and intellectual. His name was Saint-Évremond.

4. THE RATIONALISTS: DESCARTES

It was common knowledge that the Libertines were avowed or secret enemies of Christianity, and preachers thundered against them from the pulpit. Far less suspicion was roused by another class of men who were beginning to be known as

Rationalists and who quietly applied themselves to a work that was in many respects more dangerous. St Thomas Aquinas had long ago given reason its true place in the scheme of human life, and distinguished its domain from that of faith; but he had also shown that there were necessarily points of contact between the two, and had laid down the conditions in which they would function harmoniously. For three centuries Christian thought had built the best part of its structure on his *Summa*. But what would happen if the interrelation of faith and reason were denied, or simply overlooked? What path would reason take in its new-found autonomy? Surely to an outright denial of faith.

We have already named Francis Bacon (died 1626) as one of the fathers of scientism, which was now on the increase. Not only in his works on scientific philosophy, but also in his treatises on *Life and Death* and *The Wisdom of the Ancients*, it is possible to detect the outlines of empiricism, a practical variety of rationalism. Reason had no need of faith in order to apply itself to the systematic observation of nature and thus become a marvellous instrument of discovery. Whatever pains the former Lord Chancellor may have taken to place beyond doubt the immortality of the soul and the existence of God, his method tended none the less to breach the walls of Christian thought.

The question arises whether the same was true of René Descartes. To hear it asked would certainly have surprised the holy Cardinal Bérulle. One day in November 1628, having heard the Poitevin, who was as yet unknown, demolish the pretensions of one Chandoux, a drawing-room philosopher, he 'obliged him in conscience to write down what was in his mind', warning him that he would have to answer before the Sovereign Judge 'for the wrong he would do the human race by the depriving it of the fruit of his meditations'. Moreover, Descartes carefully refrained throughout his life from opposing the teaching of the Church. Indeed as a zealous Catholic, devoted to Our Lady and furiously hostile to the Libertines, he often proclaimed in his writings a faith so unshakable that there appears no reason why he should have been suspected. 'Believing most firmly in the infallibility of the Church', declaring that 'Scripture is always truthful', and even claiming to be 'God's champion', why should he be ranked with those who urged the human intellect towards rebellion? Perhaps Dom Poulet was right in saying that 'he is one of those who least intended the harm which they did'.

Descartes is a mysterious figure: he has been called the 'masked philosopher'. The much vaunted brilliance of his mind undoubtedly concealed some curiously dark region; he is far less simple than many of his followers have represented him. Looking out from his fine portrait by Frans Hals, with lean face, rugged features and large brown eyes sparkling with intelligence beneath a low brow, he reminds us of the soldier of fortune that he was for a long time, rather than of an intellectual leader; but the deep-graven lines, and even more the enigmatic smile on those thin, drawn lips, indicate something very different. It may well be that this great thinker caught a glimpse of the final consequences to which his theories would lead, and suffered accordingly as a Christian.

A former pupil of the Jesuits at La Flèche, introduced by them to Thomism, which influenced him profoundly,[9] he had long thumbed the book of nature before shutting himself away in Holland at the age of thirty-three and devoting himself exclusively to intellectual endeavour. He began by making numerous discoveries in many fields—algebra, geometry, physics and astronomy—disputing with Hobbes, Roberval and young Pascal. Later, disturbed by the condemnation of Galileo (upon news of which he thought of burning his papers), he resolved to confine himself to abstract speculation. Thenceforward his whole concern was with that *cogito* which assured him of his own existence, with that mighty effort to create a philosophical synthesis of science, morality, psychology and metaphysics which would explain the essential structure of man's intelligence. Many of his scientific theories were doomed to destruction—those, for instance, on the pineal gland as seat of the soul, on tides and whirlwinds or on animals as machines insensible to pain; but his philosophical method would survive the centuries. In 1641 appeared the *Discourse on Method*, showing the road that must be followed in order not only to appreciate the experience of sense, but also to study the passions of the soul or to demonstrate the existence of God. It was immediately recognized by contemporaries as a work of capital importance, and it remains so to this day.

The starting point of Cartesianism is universal and systematic doubt. It is a form of discipline which frees the mind from intellectual pride as well as from the tyranny of the senses, and herein Descartes is opposed to the sensualism of Bacon. Doubt thus enables a man 'to penetrate beneath the shifting sands and find the rock'. What is this rock? Nothing else than evidence, that which reason shows to be irrefutable. Upon this foundation Descartes erected an enormous edifice of clear ideas and logical deduction, wherein the mind is at ease even though it must ultimately recognize that there are also realities obscure and subtle, intuitive realities, which are not within the province of reason and its evidences. The system is applied in every field: in that of morality, for example, where, since nothing is more evident than man's desire for happiness, we may conclude that in order to attain it he must achieve his psychological equilibrium, in other words that he must control his passions. But are there not cases, it might be asked, where doubt does not enable us to lay hold upon the evidence? The answer is no; for then there operates the principle springing from Descartes's deepest intuition: 'I think, therefore I am'—*Cogito ergo sum*. To doubt is to think; thought is bound up with the existence of the thinking being; therefore to doubt is to exist, to touch reality. Applied to metaphysics, this principle provides a decisive argument in favour of the existence of God, infinite and perfect Being: whether I admit the idea, or whether I doubt it because His existence is not evident, the mere fact that that idea is present to my mind proves that there is a reality extrinsic to my being. God then appears as the starting point and the culmination of the entire Cartesian edifice.

Such a conclusion, however, must not lead us to infer that that edifice is truly Christian. Many aspects of the system, and even more so the general climate in which it was evolved, are foreign if not definitely hostile to Christianity. The God of Descartes—that God whom someone has described as 'demonstrated like the properties of a triangle'—is indeed the 'god of the philosophers and learned', whom Pascal rejected; but is He also the God of mercy, incarnate for love of men and infinitely aware of their misery? Methodical doubt, carried to its extreme, destroys the argument of authority, which is paramount in the spiritual life of a Christian as well as in the organization of the Church. The demand for clear ideas, irrefutable evidence, logical arguments, is surely opposed to the mysteries of faith, and most certainly to miracles. Descartes was at pains to declare in all humility that he excluded revealed truths from the field of reason, because 'they are above our understanding'. Nevertheless his philosophy, which gives no place to faith, severs the link established by St Thomas: 'Truths which depend on faith cannot be proved by natural demonstration'; but in that case, being indemonstrable, are they not absurd? It was a slippery slope upon which the successors of Descartes joyfully took their stand. Other men, less Christian than the founder, would retain nothing of Cartesianism but reliance upon the universal sufficiency of reason. Here we have one of the sources of the modern world's great heresy, the revolt of human reason against all revealed truth and even against God Himself. The logical result of the system is shown clearly in *L'Histoire de Calejava ou de l'Isle des Hommes Raisonnables*, published in 1700 by Claude Gilbert, a fanatical Cartesian: 'In following reason we depend upon ourselves alone, and we become in some sense gods.'

As soon as the system of Descartes became known to the intelligentsia it was welcomed with open arms. Patronized by Condé and many noblemen, this 'bold and attractive' philosophy was quickly adopted in the *salons*. The Duchesse du Maine, the Marquise de Sablé and Mme de Grignan proclaimed themselves enthusiastic Cartesians; Father Mersenne was loud in its praise; Father Ciermans, S.J., of Louvain, exalted it as offering a satisfactory explanation of 'all that is most secret in nature'. Its influence was felt for a moment by Pascal, as well as by Bossuet in his *Traité de la connaissance de Dieu et de soimême*; by Fénelon too and by the leading Jansenists. Father Malebranche of the Oratory dreamed of erecting upon it a Christian philosophy and apologetic. Cartesianism was victorious in England, Italy, Belgium and, of course, despite fierce resistance, in Holland; ten years after his

death Descartes was read and admired by everyone in Europe
who claimed to be educated and intelligent.

Very soon, however, men began to realize the dangers it
concealed; for the Cartesian method was employed just as
quickly by those who were more or less hostile to the faith.
The Libertines used it to support their own views, as Saint-
Évremond openly admitted; while Spinoza's reliance upon it
led him to reject the Scriptures. As early as 1645, during his
lifetime, Descartes had been accused by some Dutch Protestants of favouring atheism, and in Belgium the Society of
Jesus forbade the teaching of his doctrine in their schools.
Pascal, converted in a face-to-face encounter with God,
wherein reason had played no part at all, joined issue with
Descartes; he declared him 'useless and uncertain', and he
added (a little unfairly) that he could not forgive him for
'having wished to bypass God'. Moreover it was with reference
to Cartesianism that Bossuet spoke in prophetic terms of a
'grand assault upon the Church': 'I see emerging from the
womb of its principles (which I think are wrongly understood) more than a heresy; and I foresee that the conclusions
to be drawn from it in opposition to the dogmas held by our
fathers will render it odious and cause the Church to lose all
the fruits which she was able to expect from it with a view to
establishing in the minds of philosophers the divinity and
the immortality of the soul.' Condemned at Louvain and then
by the Sorbonne, the *Discourse on Method* was placed on the
Index by Rome in 1663, though with the mitigating clause
'*donec corrigatur*'. But the influence of Cartesianism steadily
increased.

5. A NEW APOLOGETIC: BLAISE PASCAL

The success of Descartes, even among believers, is attributable largely to the weakness of Catholic apologetics at the
moment of his appearance. Serious minds hesitated to choose
between the anaemia of Aristotelianism and the lethargy of
Fideism. It was not surprising that a course of clear ideas
was welcomed as a tonic.

At that date, however, not all Catholic thought was devoid

of interest. The positive effort of theologians at the end of the previous century, notably in Spain and Portugal, had not been altogether futile. Indeed Francisco Suarez, the master of Evora, had died as recently as 1617, and Lessius in 1623. The mystical theologian Thomas de Vallgornera, while remaining strictly loyal to his scholastic predecessors, tried to rejuvenate Thomism. The Portuguese John of St Thomas (1589–1644), while lecturing at Alcala, compiled his *Cursus Theologicus* and *Compendium Totius Doctrinae Christianae*, which represented the most solid exposition and defence of Thomist thought. In France the Jesuit Denys Petau (1583–1652) endeavoured in his great history of dogmas to emphasize the teaching of Scripture and tradition, opening the way for a theology that would draw its life-blood more than hitherto from history and the Fathers. Louis Thomassin, a young and immensely learned Oratorian, was about to set out upon the same road. But these majestic labours, confined to specialists, could not prevent the progress made by Libertines and Rationalists.

It must be admitted that those who undertook to defend the faith against her adversaries and to evolve an apologetic that would serve as a weapon of offence were not remarkable, their numbers notwithstanding. Bookshops were stacked with apologetic works bearing high-flown or resounding titles: *Rayons de la divinité dans les créatures*; *Les Triomphes de la religion*; *Le Tombeau des athées*; or again, *Le Libertin converti* and *L'impiété battue et renversée*. These last two titles show that the defence of the Gospel was markedly combative. Father Garasse, a polemical expert whose clownish ranting entertained the world at large, hurled insult and invective at the 'self-styled clever people of today'. More moderate was the scholarly Father Mersenne, who proposed to crush them beneath three large octavo volumes. The whole of this work was summary and routine. Garasse's thirty-five proofs of the existence of God were not altogether convincing; nor were Mersenne's thirty-six. Father Richeome and Dom Polycarpe de la Rivière lapsed too frequently into affectation and triviality. So did Yves de Paris; but this famous Capuchin preacher was aware that it was not sufficient to appeal to scholastic syllogisms and to the arguments of authority or of Fideism.

He sometimes invoked moral certitude, the divine voice in man, in a way that reminds us alternately of Pascal and Chateaubriand. Jean Belin, Bishop of Belley, and a few others enable us to feel the trend that was to instil new life into religious psychology and at the same time into the science of apologetics. It made its triumphant appearance with the publication of the *Pensées*.

Pascal.[10] It is impossible to utter the word 'apologetics' without immediately recalling the name of one who, in the eyes of countless men, remains the first if not the only persuasive defender of the faith. When he died in 1662 there were discovered among his papers a number of unpublished fragments. Some of them were fully developed theses, others were casual notes jotted down in the heat of sudden inspiration, often elliptical almost to the point of incomprehensibility; but all were moving and original. His nephew Étienne Périer, believing himself to have lighted upon a treasure that must not be lost, engaged two secretaries familiar with Pascal's handwriting to collect these fragments into a large file and make two copies of its contents. In 1670 Pascal's friends and relations decided that it was time to publish the *Pensées de M. Pascal sur la religion et sur quelques autres sujets*; but because of the irenic atmosphere that then prevailed in consequence of the Clementine Peace,[11] the editors omitted or modified passages that might arouse contention.[12]

It was known that Pascal had had a definite purpose in jotting down all these notes in his almost illegible handwriting. These *disjecta membra* were intended as the raw material of a great work. After his astounding conversion in 1654, when he turned again wholly to God and to the practice of the Catholic religion, he desired to raise a monument to that which henceforward seemed to him the 'one thing necessary'. Intoxicated with the divine, swallowed up by the infinite, he devoted to that labour every moment of the time left to him by his feverish existence, and he tells us that he prepared the work 'on his knees', making of the task a prayer. Death prevented him from forming these preparatory notes into the splendid whole that his genius would undoubtedly have produced. But its plan and general outline are clearly indicated in certain of the fragments:

'Men despise religion; they hate it and fear lest it be true. To cure that sickness one must begin by showing that religion is in no way contrary to reason; next one must show that it is worthy of veneration, and win for it respect; and lastly one must render it lovable, and prove that it is true.'

Pascal's *Apologia* then, had it been completed, would have consisted of two main parts. Its aim would have been first to persuade men, particularly the Libertines and the sceptics of Montaigne's school, to lay aside their doubt and indifference, and secondly to rescue from their torpor those Catholics who, 'though within the body of the true Church, are not in accordance with the purity of the Gospel maxims'. Pascal, however, had no intention of proceeding on the basis of reasoning. What good would that have been? The God of the Christians is not 'the mere author of geometrical truths'; it is vain to demonstrate Him like the properties of a triangle. The new apologist starts from man himself, from man, a speck lost in the immensity of creation, who must become aware of his own littleness; of his interior wretchedness; of his abysmal loneliness which is yet linked with sublime grandeur. In the tradition of Bérulle, Pascal would have the 'nonentity capable of God' understand that while he is nothing he bears within himself the image of Him who is all. Moreover there is in human experience one inescapable reality which inevitably brings a man, if he gives it a thought, face to face with God and the Cross, his only hope—death. Willy-nilly 'it is necessary to make a choice'. We are all 'embarked'; by the very fact of living we have to make election for or against acceptance of life transcending life, for or against God. It is restlessness therefore, holy restlessness, that Pascal seeks to instil into or reawaken in the conscience, which will thus be led to cast itself upon its sole source of strength, the one and only solution.

Having persuaded his adversary to wish that the Christian religion may be true, Pascal proceeds to show that it is in fact true. Alone of all religions it explains the fundamental contradiction in man, his wretchedness as a sinner and his grandeur as one redeemed. 'It has achieved a perfect understanding of mankind' and that is why 'it promises the true good'. To this first line of proof Pascal meant to add others: extrinsic, e.g. prophecies, miracles and the astounding presence of Christianity in the framework of history; intrinsic, derived chiefly from the perfect adaptation of Christian doctrine to human needs. The *Pensées* provide a few indications of the direction he proposed to take, but this part of the work remained almost untouched.

It may be asked whether Pascal's demonstration, had it been completed, would have proved more striking than the imperfect but impassioned outline whose details every reader can fill in by opening the *Pensées* at almost any page. What moves and astonishes us in that inexhaustible collection is not the arguments (not even the celebrated argument of the wager) but the cry which we seem to hear and which re-echoes our most secret anguish. Here we have the self-revelation of a soul, the soul not only of one who stands upon the highest peaks of human genius, but also of a Christian for whom God is a vital experience, the alpha and omega of all. The whole of Pascal's apologetic was born during that night of fire, when, surrounded on all sides by the abyss, he learned that appeal to Jesus is the sole defence against appalling anguish, and realized with invincible certitude that Christ crucified had shed for him as for every man 'such and such a drop of His Blood'. Once that certitude has imposed itself upon the mind, argument and reasoning and all the syllogisms of the Scholastics are of small importance. True apologetic is founded not upon weak reason, but upon the joint force of intuitive knowledge and assent, which lifts a man above himself and which Pascal calls by the mysterious name of heart. 'It is the heart, not the reason, that senses God. This is the meaning of faith: God apprehended by the heart.'

Served by an incomparable style worthy alike of a scholar and of a poet, rich in phrases that pierce the soul like arrows —who can forget 'The eternal silence of infinite space' or 'You would not be seeking Me had you not already found Me'?— Pascal's teaching opened up a new field for Christian apologetic. It matters little that some have sought to discover in the *Pensées* signs of virulent Jansenism; that certain theologians have denounced Pascal for having opened the door to Rousseau's sentimentalism, to Kant's subjectivism and even to Immanentism and Modernism. It is the fate of genius to be betrayed and twisted to suit every whim. In order to be convinced that he brought to the Christian faith an incomparable weapon at a critical hour, it suffices to recall with what vehemence the eighteenth century treated him. 'He makes straight for Pascal', says Sainte-Beuve of Voltaire, 'as the finest representative of Christianity.' It is not the good fortune of everyone to be the chosen target of God's enemies.

6. 'HE WHO REIGNETH IN HEAVEN'

Pascal is unique. A system of apologetics proceeding from the heart cannot move and convince others unless it is expounded by one who has not only thought out its train of argument but has also experienced it as an interior struggle. The drama of human unrest depicted in the *Pensées*, with their broken, breathless and overwhelming phrases, was inimitable, though it is possible to detect the influence of Pascal upon a number of subsequent writers. Among these were Filleau de La Chaise, who tried to prove the truth of the miracles of Moses by supplementing the gaps in the second part of the *Pensées*; the Oratorian Mauduit, who carried the argument of the wager to ridiculous extremes; and, more notable still, the Protestant pastor Abbadie,[13] of whom Mme de Sévigné said: 'I don't think I've ever heard anyone talk about religion as that man does.'

But the apologists of the Great Century were not true heirs of Pascal. Extremely numerous and voluble, they belonged to what has been called the Golden Age of apologetics. Here we cannot hope to name more than a very few from an almost interminable list: Father Beurrier, parish priest of Saint-Étienne-du-Mont, who gave Pascal the Last Sacraments; Father Lescalopier, author of *Humanitas Theologica*, which was much used in the seminaries; Gilbert de Choiseul-Praslin, Bishop of Tournai, whose *Mémoires touchant la religion* were reprinted ten times in fifteen years; Choisy and Dangeau, members of the Académie, whose *Dialogues sur l'immortalité de l'âme et l'existence de Dieu* found favour with men and women of the world. Further, as we have seen,[14] all the great pulpit orators—Fléchier, Mascaron, Massillon, Bourdaloue and many others—were in varying degrees apologists, anxious not only to teach the Christian religion to their hearers and persuade them to observe its precepts, but also to demonstrate its excellence and its truth.

Three such men shone in the eyes of their contemporaries with unequalled brilliance, though they may appear to us very different as regards both intellectual eminence and achievement. First of these, beyond doubt, is Bossuet,[15] who was more admired in his own day as an apologist than as an orator. The Eagle of Meaux, indeed, may justly be described as an apologist by virtue of all his writings, the whole of his life and every phase of his thought. Whether in plain statement or dispute, whether he is teaching or doing battle with others, his aim is always the triumph of Holy Church and of God's cause. Majestically sure of his own proofs, he yields nothing to his adversary, whose arguments appear to him miserably weak. He is an apologist in his little handbook *L'Exposition de la doctrine de l'Église catholique* (1671), where he explains with wonderful clarity the requirements of faith; he is the same in *L'Histoire des variations des églises protestantes* (1688), where he contrasts the unity of the Roman Church with the disorder resulting from the Protestant Reformation; he is the same again, and even more so, in his *Discours sur l'histoire universelle* (an attempt to prove the divine origin of Christianity from the growth of humanity), as well as in his *Politique tirée de l'Écriture Sainte*, which relies solely upon the social utility of religion. Orchestrating a few themes with the utmost skill, Bossuet is the very type of the 'classical' apologist, who does not pretend to add to the traditional arguments, but exploits them to perfection. Only the argument from the beauty of the liturgy escapes him. Elsewhere, into whatever field he ventures, he is supreme.

It is therefore astonishing that some writers of the period ranked another apologist with Bossuet, and even granted him precedence. I refer to Pierre Daniel Huet (1630–1721), Bishop of Avranches,[16] author of a *Démonstration évangélique*, of a treatise on the locality of the earthly paradise and of many other learned works. No one disputes his erudition;[17] but he was clearly no expert either in metaphysics or in theology, and his apologetical works bear witness to these shortcomings. Claiming to refute Hobbes and Spinoza, whom he regarded as 'destroyers' and enemies of society, he undertook to demonstrate the truth of Christianity and the authenticity of Scripture by methods which an embittered contemporary described as 'forced parallelisms, conjuring tricks that savour of mental instability'. He was severely criticized by Racine, Jurieu and the great Arnauld; but he was read in the seminaries, and his *Démonstration* was reprinted five times.

In order to justify dogmas and obtain their acceptance, it is not enough to use the argument of authority or to devise elaborate schemes of impassioned pleading. Such at any rate was the view of Malebranche. More earnestly even than Bossuet and in different circumstances,[18] he desired to construct a serene and sovereign demonstration of their necessary truth. His *Recherche de la verité* (1675) and *Conversations chrétiennes* were a new and important contribution to the science. But the apologetics of Malebranche, which have been described as founded upon order, 'an order which constrains God Himself in His government and Christ in His work of redemption',[19] remained within the same framework as that of Bossuet and poor Huet—neo-classical apologetics in the full sense of the word.

For indeed apologetics, as practised in that golden age, are part and parcel of the neo-classical system;[20] they may even be described as its keystone, since they demonstrate the excellence of the religion which is its mainstay. By strengthening faith they endeavour to justify and uphold the established order, which indeed they resemble. It is no mere accident that the words 'He who reigneth in heaven' flow repeatedly from Bossuet's pen; they remind us by analogy of him who reigned on earth, the 'viceroy' of God. The science of apologetics is essentially authoritarian: it is founded upon the authority of Scripture, of the Church and of tradition. It is also 'reasonable', according to the spirit of the age; to believe is to obey reason, to behave reasonably. Let it not be said that this is impossible, that the mind formulates arguments contrary to faith. St Thomas has already given the answer to all such objections: 'Belief is an act of the intellect moved by assent of the will' (*Summa* II[a] II[ae], q. IV, a. 2). One ought to believe, it is necessary to believe, and it is reasonable to believe. If that is so, intellectual rebellion is surely impossible. Nevertheless it continued to make headway.

7. FISSURES IN THE GLORIOUS EDIFICE

It made headway slowly, unobtrusively, but irresistibly. True, the neo-classical system opposed to the forces of disruption its own solid affirmations of order and certitude; but it was unable to prevent the mind from labouring secretly to overthrow it. Moreover within the neo-classical system itself, such as we have seen it at the height of its power and glory, there were hidden cleavages. It is possible to detect them even in the works of such men as Corneille and Racine, whom we commonly recognize as the most brilliant witnesses. The cult of man which is found underlying every aspect of the Great Century, had an innate tendency to cut man off little by little from God. It may be doubted whether Corneille and Racine, both of them excellent Christians, perceived that their writings were fundamentally unchristian. Corneille almost certainly did not. Yet man as depicted by him never obeys the precepts of gentleness, humility, pardon for offences and love of one's enemies, which belong to the essence of the Gospel. When he seeks to rise above himself and practises the highest virtues, he is moved not so much by Christian ideals as by a Stoic or Nietzschean desire to surpass his natural potentialities. Even Polyeucte, who sacrifices his love and his life for his faith, is hardly superior to Cinna or El Cid. Nor is it certain that Corneille himself grasped the full significance of Pauline's mystical ascent, which appears to me the most profoundly Christian element in that wonderful tragedy; his contemporaries did not appreciate it at all, preferring the passionate scenes between Pauline and Sévère. Racine, on the other hand, Racine the Jansenist, does seem to understand the dangers of a literature centred exclusively upon man and taking human passion as its constant theme. That much is suggested by his sudden abandonment of the theatre at the age of thirty-eight, and by his self-imposed silence which remained unbroken except for the production of two deeply religious plays, *Esther* and *Athalie*. Who knows what horror he experienced in the depths of his being when he looked back, after his conversion, upon such a work as *Phèdre*, which in public he defended. The naked, burning language of passion was hardly such as a faithful soul could allow itself to employ; it was the literature of man, but not the work of a Christian.

And so, bearing within it a secret wound, the neo-classical order could not hope for ever to resist the forces that were about to attack. The exaltation of man without reference to God was destined to result in man's claim to be independent of God. During the reign of Louis XIV there were many signs of what has been called 'the crisis of the European conscience'—European, because France was not its only home. Fissures appeared in the imposing edifice. 'We had contemporaries under Louis XIV,' Diderot afterwards declared in speaking of himself and his fellow philosophers. Indeed a close look at those forerunners of Voltaire, Helvetius and d'Alembert shows them to have been often more audacious and aggressive than their eminent successors. 'The great battle of ideas',[21] says Hazard, 'took place before 1715 and even before 1700.'

A variety of causes underlay the development of the crisis. Some must be sought in the very link whereby the neo-classical system tied Christianity to itself. Tightly bound up with that regime, religion would suffer increasingly from blows delivered by critics who longed for change in the established order. On the other hand, all was far from perfect within the Church; so once again the unworthiness of Christians detracted from the worthiness of Christianity and thus provided the enemies of the faith with an arsenal of weapons. What answer could be given to Pierre Bayle when he wrote: 'It is no more surprising that an atheist should live virtuously than that a Christian should indulge in every sort of crime'? Three grave crises shook the Church and helped to discredit her: Gallicanism with its squabbles between the Most Christian King and the Pope; Quietism with its theological duel between two bishops; and, still worse, Jansenism, not only on account of the disedifying spectacles which it produced, but also because of an excessive recourse to human will and reason on the part of the orthodox theologians in their struggle with the doctrinarians of grace. It is inaccurate to attribute the crisis only to a rebellion of intellect and conscience; believers themselves were in part responsible.

The fact, however, remains that the wind of rebellion continued to gather strength. The symptoms observed at the beginning of the seventeenth century were now confirmed. Libertinism was not extinct: Saint-Évremond lived as an exile in London until 1703. Representative of the moral Libertines was the epicurean Chapelle, whose total immorality preserved an air of elegance and discretion, and who summed up his rule of life in this couplet:

> *'Que j'aime la douce incurie*
> *où je laisse couler mes jours!'*

> [*'I love the care-free spirit*
> *In which I let my days flow by.'*]

The intellectual Libertines, who were beginning to be known in France as *esprits forts*, included Saint-Pavin and des Barreaux, disciples of Théophile de Viau; François Bernier, a follower of Gassendi; and La Mothe le Vayer's pupil Jean d'Hesnault, who expressed his denial in melancholy but emphatic terms:

> *'Tout meurt en nous quand nous mourrons;*
> *la mort ne laisse rien et n'est rien elle-même!'*

> [*'When we die all within us dies;*
> *death leaves nothing, and is itself nothing!'*]

The Rationalists witnessed a rapid increase of their numbers; they were encouraged by the triumph of Descartes, indisputable from about 1685; but more and more of them were rejecting those elements of Cartesianism which safeguarded the rights of faith, and retained only those which enabled them to proclaim the autonomy of reason. The career of unbridled reason knew no bounds; it recognized neither tradition nor authority. 'There is nothing wrong', declared Fontenelle, 'in renouncing everything with a view to studying everything.' Thus the presentiments of Bossuet in his old age were justified. At the end of the seventeenth century it would have been possible to anticipate some words of Caraccioli written in 1735: 'If Descartes returned to the world now, you would see in him the most formidable foe of Christianity.'

If further evidence be required we need only refer to the writings of Baruch Spinoza (1632–77), the most renowned, the most brilliant, but also, as Leibniz said, the most 'immoderate' of Cartesians. His principal work, the Latin *Theologico-Political Treatise*, appeared in the same year as Pascal's *Pensées*; translated into French by Saint-Glain in 1678, it created such a scandal that he refrained from publishing the *Treatise on God, Man and Beatitude* and the *Ethics*, which he circulated in manuscript form and which were not printed until after his death. Descartes's thought was carried to its farthest limits in those coldly impassioned pages. The pale Dutch Jew, who earned a livelihood by polishing lenses, calmly asserted that men must discard all traditional beliefs; must convince themselves that there is no difference, except one's point of view, between *natura naturans* (God) and *natura naturata* (the world); must radically separate morality from faith and metaphysics, and overthrow the 'absurdities' upon which both the 'city of man' and the 'city of God' are founded. Descartes's *Discourse on Method*, then, had led to pantheism and nihilism.

This twofold stream of Libertinism and Rationalism, between which no hard and fast line existed, was swelled from many other sources. Throughout the seventeenth century enormous strides were made by scientism, a philosophy so to speak of scientific progress considered as the measure of advance in every other field. All the sciences, it is true, were marching from one triumph to another; the age of Newton succeeded that of Descartes, and Bossuet himself recognized that man had 'almost changed the face of the world'. The basic science of mathematics was entering a new era with the application of algebra to geometry; with Descartes's use of curves; with the introduction of the calculus of probabilities by Pascal and Fermat, and that of the infinitely small by Leibniz and Newton; not forgetting the general employment of logarithmic tables. All the natural sciences were caught up in this movement. In 1676 Roemer calculated the speed of light, and in 1704 Newton attempted to explain its nature. Following Pascal, Torricelli demonstrated that air has weight, Huyghens established the laws of the pendulum, and Mariotte those of the compression of gas. The 'infinite spaces' which had terrified Pascal were revealing themselves to the human eye, thanks to the invention of ever more powerful telescopes, and the Observatory of Paris, made illustrious by Cassini, shone with unparalleled brilliance. In physiology Harvey's discoveries on the circulation of the blood were followed by those of Pecquet on the formation of chyle, which from 1673 onwards were officially expounded by Dionis at the Jardin du Roi. Nor did the applied sciences lag behind. The balance clock was constructed by Huyghens, the microscope by opticians at Middelburg, and the first steam engine by Denis Papin in 1690. In presence of such vast achievements, how could man have resisted the lure of pride? There were indeed eminent scientists, among them Newton and Leibniz, who felt their faith strengthened by all those wonderful discoveries, and declared that so marvellous a world could not have been devised except by an intelligence far transcending that of man. Others, however, saw in these things nothing but grounds for exalting human reason.

Many causes extrinsic to Christianity, therefore, explain the manifest progress of irreligion in an age when faith appeared to be the cornerstone of society. The impulse was insidious but irresistible. The popularity of travel books—and strange to say, an enthusiastic interest in the missions—gave rise to the famous legend of the 'noble savage' so full of virtue, so superior to civilized man and having no need of the Gospel for his perfection. Protestants who had fled to Holland and Prussia after the revocation of the Edict of Nantes did not hesitate, in the name of tolerance and intellectual rights, to denounce the Catholic Church as beneficiary of terrorism; and although their propaganda, disseminated through an endless flow of pamphlets, did not convert all readers to Calvinism, it did tend to deprive them of respect for established authority and the priesthood. Nonconformity became rampant.

This state of mind, of radical nonconformity, was best reflected in Pierre Bayle (1647–1706), a Frenchman from the county of Foix, whose Protestant convictions had obliged him to seek asylum at Rotterdam. His *Dictionnaire historique et critique*, published in 1697, is an alphabetical indictment of what he considered foolishness, error and superstition; but it was often directed at the same time against Catholicism, and even against Christianity. Notwithstanding his refusal to be ranked as a Cartesian, Bayle was a fanatical devotee of reason, 'the supreme tribunal, the ultimate court, from which there is no appeal'. He made no frontal attack upon religious beliefs, but confined himself to stating the arguments for and against, raising difficulties and throwing doubt into the reader's mind. In one article after another throughout this monumental work all the motives of belief are so carefully undermined that they must inevitably collapse. The philosophers of the eighteenth century—Diderot for the Encyclopaedia, and Voltaire—acquired from Bayle's Dictionary an arsenal of weapons for use in their struggle against the faith.

Irreligion launched its fiercest attack upon those points of Christian dogma where the supernatural appeared to clash with reason. Bayle was an expert at this game. The comet of which there was much talk in 1681, and which was commonly believed to presage disaster, afforded him an opportunity to show that such apprehensions were simply old wives' tales. It was a short step from superstitious fear to miracles and the insinuation that these too were nothing but inventions of disordered minds. Sorcerers, witches and possessed persons likewise were taken to prove that the Devil did not exist, and indeed that the whole supernatural world is an absurdity in the eyes of reason. Fontenelle (1657–1757), whose long life bestrode two centuries, made a speciality of oracles, the possibility of which he denied and was thus able to dismiss the notion of Providence. Some idea of the limits to which this new rationalist criticism was carried may be obtained from an obscure utopian novel, where we read the following decisive argument against the resurrection of the body. The population of France represents more than ten million cubic feet of flesh, and that mass renews itself every sixty years. Calculate then what it will become in ten thousand years: a heap incomparably larger than the planet.

A celebrated dispute which stirred the republic of letters affords a perfect illustration of the intellectual climate at that time. It began in 1657 when Jean Desmarets, Seigneur de Saint-Sorlin, a converted Libertine and an indifferent poet, published an heroic poem entitled *Clovis ou la France chrétienne*. Its originality lay in the fact that its chief character was not a famous figure of the ancient world, as had been customary since the Renaissance, but a modern; it was inspired, moreover, not by pagan legend but by Christianity. The author was severely criticized, and he replied by passing from his own case to general principles. He declared that his *Clovis* was better than the *Aeneid*, because French poetry was superior to Latin, and because Christian subjects alone were suitable to heroic poetry, since true heroism was Christian. Thus began the Quarrel of Ancients and Moderns, in which the greatest literary figures became involved. Boileau, the lawgiver of Parnassus, pronounced in the third canto of his *Art poétique* a formal condemnation of the Moderns, taking his stand upon principle:

> 'De la foi d'un chrétien les mystères terribles
> D'ornements égayés ne sont point susceptibles . . .'

> ['The terrible mysteries of a Christian's faith
> Do not admit of elaborate ornamentation.']

It was disputed whether inscriptions on public monuments should be in Latin or French. For several years elections to the Académie Française were made for or against the Moderns. Bruyère's election was a triumph for the Ancients, but the entry of Fontenelle into that illustrious society spelled their defeat. The quarrel lasted, moreover, until the end of Louis XIV's reign and even longer, for Mme Dacier and Houdar de la Motte were still at loggerheads on the threshold of the eighteenth century.

It may be surprising that so much passion was aroused by differences of opinion as to the use of language or the choice of subjects for tragic drama. In fact, however, the whole dispute moved quickly into a very different field with the advent of Fontenelle. He held that the Moderns must be superior to the Ancients because they had profited by recent discoveries and the march of progress. Herein lies the fundamental issue, the crucial point of debate. Was it right to abide by the customs, traditions and intangible rules bequeathed by the past, or to launch out towards the future in the name of 'progress' and the 'modern spirit'? That was the sum and substance of the dispute, and it was concerned with more than literature alone. In 1715 the Abbé Terrasson, a loyal disciple of Descartes, published his *Dissertation critique sur l'Iliade d'Homère*, in which he wrote: 'My principal aim is to endow polite literature with that spirit of philosophy which has made such great progress in the natural sciences during the past hundred years. By philosophy I mean a superiority of reason which makes us trace back everything to its proper and natural principles, regardless of opinions that other men have held.' Even though such thrusts were not aimed directly at the teaching of the Church and of tradition, that teaching suffered none the less. During the same year Terrasson's thesis was carried a stage further by the Abbé d'Aubignac, who declared that 'nothing should be decided on the strength of authority'. This audacious critic was writing about Homer, upon whose very existence he cast doubt; but his aphorism ranged far beyond the boundaries of literature. Thus the Quarrel of Ancients and Moderns, which began in the narrow field of literary language and subject-matter, went on to swell the waters of intellectual revolt. 'Men refused any longer to admire the great models of antiquity,' says Paul Hazard, 'to follow rules that would make possible a repetition of that achievement; in no time at all authority and tradition were undermined, giving place to a new law—the law of progress. There suddenly emerged a new conception of mankind's advance.' When Terrasson wrote that his religion harmonized with his philosophy, and that he understood no obedience unless it accorded with reason, he may or may not have realized that he was overthrowing the very foundations of his faith, and others would make use of his principles to reject both religion and obedience. At all events he was far removed from the original purpose of Desmarets de Saint-Sorlin in starting the debate.[22]

Thus at the close of the Great Century and the 'Most Christian' reign there were numerous indications of a crisis which, under the imposing masks of order and intellectual conformity, was a source of anxiety to many minds. Religion was openly indicted; nor was France the only country where irreligion spread. In England, Anglicanism was on the way to becoming Deism pure and simple, discarding the supernatural dogma and hierarchy, while believing itself still Christian.[23] In Germany, the fore-runners of *Aufklärung*[24] were engaged upon a task which, though not professedly anti-Christian and still less irreligious, would prove no less harmful to Christianity. In Italy, Giovanni Battista Vico, an unacknowledged genius whose *Scienza Nuova* opened new fields to the philosophy of history, argued that mankind had long since emerged from the 'divine age'.

Spread throughout intellectual Europe, these new ideas penetrated deeper into the masses than did those of the Libertines and Rationalists in the preceding era. That penetration, however, did not amount to much. Certain works through which the new ideas were transmitted, those of Saint-Évremond and Fontenelle, for example, brought handsome profits to the book trade; and 288 out of 500 libraries possessed the heavy folio volumes of Bayle's Dictionary. But the latter cannot have had many readers. The literature that really counted, because it was read by the public at large, was a small number of strictly censored journals which naturally included no seditious theses; at the most they sometimes passed rapidly from hand to hand, as we find, for example, in Molière's *Don Juan*.[25] But until 1715, says Daniel Mornet, 'the new ideas were confined to the literary world; they did not penetrate far into the lives of ordinary men'.[26]

8. FROM MALEBRANCHE TO THE BOLLANDISTS: A CONSTRUCTIVE EFFORT

The danger, however, was none the less real, and believers had good cause to declare its presence. Apologetics therefore remained largely polemical, as it had been in the days of Garasse and Mersenne. Bossuet spent most of his middle life and old age in a titanic struggle, on many fronts, against all whom he regarded as a menace to the integrity of the faith of the Church: Libertines of all colours, rationalist followers of Descartes and Spinoza, and so forth. One of the leading lights in this combat was a Benedictine, Dom François Lamy, a former musketeer who had become a monk and confessed that he retained 'the warlike temperament'. No aspect of irreligion was spared by that theological duellist whose zeal, however, proved greater than his success. Protestants followed the same path, and we shall find among them[27] numerous representatives of polemical apologetic. Thus every protagonist of the new ideas met with determined opposition. Descartes was confronted by Desgabets, by Huet (when he burned the books he had once adored), by Bossuet, and even by the pseudo-mystic Antoinette Bourignon,[28] who claimed that 'God had shown her, and indeed expressly declared, that Cartesianism was the most accursed heresy of all time'. Spinoza was often treated as criminal, subversive, a miserable apostate Jew; that of course did not suffice to refute him, but he was also criticized with more relevance by Bossuet, by Malebranche and, above all, by Fénelon. Bayle aroused the hostility of Protestants such as Elie Benoist, as well as of Catholics. Nevertheless it remained doubtful whether this apologetical offensive, even though supported by a government which hunted down obnoxious books, had much chance of checking the new ideas, or whether some other means would have to be found.

Another attitude of mind began to appear, strongly reminiscent of Christian humanism in the sixteenth century. Instead of opposing the new ideas as a single whole, instead of considering every utterance of irreligious thinkers as a farrago of error and calumny, would it not be better to adopt any useful points their objectionable theses might contain, and at the same time to ward off criticism by eliminating from the teaching of Holy Church whatever might give grounds for attack? In other words, why not substitute a constructive effort for a system of aggressive argument? This tendency can be seen very clearly in Fénelon, who devoted the last ten years of his life to a series of apologetical works, the most important of which, although somewhat dull and insipid, is the *Traité de l'existence et des attributs de Dieu* (1687). While stoutly resisting the pantheism of Spinoza, he paid great attention to the progress of natural science, using it to demonstrate and inspire love for the author of so many marvels: far from resulting in unbelief, scientific progress should help to confirm men's faith. Leibniz and Newton, both Protestants, thought likewise.

It is from this point of view that we must notice the importance of Nicolas Malebranche (1638–1715), an Oratorian. Crowds of attentive hearers, illustrious visitors from all parts of Europe, flocked to his cell, to the *salon* of his niece Mlle de Vailly, to that of his pupil the Marquise de l'Hôpital and above all to the Château de Sceaux, where the Duchesse du Maine welcomed him as a prince of the mind. Fontenelle himself acknowledged that Malebranche's system, 'so intellectual and so shrewd', exercised a powerful attraction; society in the neo-classical age prided itself upon its intellectualism. It was, however, only by slow stages that Malebranche, a sensitive priest with mystical leanings,[29] attained to the realms of intellectualism and philosophy. His fine features, his deep-set eyes which seemed to look inwards, spoke loudly of a temperament far removed from that of a scholastic wrangle. It was through a sense of duty, through an urge to be of service to God's cause, that he turned to philosophy, wherein he employed undeniable gifts as a thinker, simple language and an easy style, all of which enabled him to make the most abstruse subjects crystal clear. What was his goal? We have his own reply; it was 'to place metaphysics at the service of religion and to shed upon the truths of faith that light which helps to reassure the mind and render it in full accord with the heart'. Thenceforward his labours were orientated to this one purpose; his great works, *Recherche de la vérité, Conversations chrétiennes, Traité de la nature et de la grâce* and *Traité de l'Amour de Dieu*—thirty volumes in all—form an impressive whole. Malebranche's aim, in brief, was to accomplish in the seventeenth century what the Fathers and Doctors of the Church had achieved when they absorbed Plato and Aristotle into Christianity. Thinkers had recently appeared who could contribute new wealth to the spiritual treasure of mankind; instead of leaving them in exterior darkness, why not try to adopt them, or at least as much of their offering as was acceptable? Surely the end of revealed truth and the end of reason (itself a gift to man) are identical. Why not borrow from Pascal the support of psychological experience, of the interior life that discovers and 'feels' God? Above all, why not borrow from Descartes his rigorous and highly pertinent method of demonstration? Malebranche became a thorough Cartesian, more thorough perhaps than he realized. 'I owe to Descartes,' he said, 'or to his manner of philosophizing, the opinions that I oppose to his, and the boldness to find fault with him.' Yes, indeed. And what is more, it seems that he wished, by relying chiefly upon St. Augustine, to perfect the work of Descartes, to launch him on the sea of apologetics, to employ him as an instrument capable of reintegrating man with God, in such a way that intellectual activity would become the hallmark of eternity.

Malebranche the mystic, then, was transformed into a resolute partisan of reason. He declared that 'one must never assent to ideas unless they are so evidently true that the withholding of assent causes interior pain and secret reproaches of reason'; and he proclaimed that reason is for men 'as natural a right as that of breathing'. A whole system of apologetics was raised upon these foundations, on the accord of reason and faith. It was intended to solve the great problems confronting the mind: that of miracles, for example, or that of grace and damnation. God is the creator of all, of the material world as well as of human reason; and since the latter is an image of the Divine Word, it must be able to explain and justify whatever on earth seems to us incomprehensible. 'The nature or force of any given thing is nothing but the divine will.'

All this was undeniably splendid and, as part of Malebranche's constant 'vision of God', altogether acceptable. But did he not sometimes go too far? Looking for natural causes everywhere, writing, for instance, that 'the fewer miracles there are the more God is glorified', or again 'it is an act of piety to reduce the number of miracles', did he not come perilously near to playing the enemy's own game? In subordinating God Himself to reason and its order, he deprived Him of freedom, and thus enabled the malicious Bayle to declare that according to Father Malebranche's theology the wisdom of God involved the damnation of many souls. Despite the loftiness of his purpose, it may be that the great Oratorian's endeavour was so far in advance of his time that it could not avoid committing indiscretions not unlike those to which the

Modernists yielded long afterwards. The eighteenth century retained only his rationalism, for which he was praised by Voltaire. It is fairer to see in Malebranche the precursor of an attitude of the Christian mind which does not reject intellectual progress, but seeks to make it part and parcel of the Christian system.

The constructive effort undertaken by Malebranche, with manifest ability but not always with success, in the realm of philosophy, may be seen probing another domain—that of historical criticism—with special reference to documentary evidence. This was one of the points at which the assault of irreligion was most powerful. Du Cange, Treasurer of France at Amiens, revived the study of Latin, particularly of Low Latin, with his two glossaries. Many scholars concentrated upon the best established traditions, in order to test their veracity, and it often happened that accepted beliefs suddenly fell to pieces beneath their scrutiny. These methods were applied to Holy Scripture, to ecclesiastical history and to hagiography, not unfrequently with disastrous results. In order to oppose them it was not sufficient to invoke the argument of authority or to repeat that such-and-such had 'always been admitted'; learned men were no longer satisfied with that line of defence. It was better to take a bold stand on the enemy's own ground, to meet criticism with criticism by ridding the Church and tradition of all that was superfluous, doubtful or erroneous.

Such was the attitude of several great scholars who were about to point the way into the future. The Benedictines of Saint-Maur—the 'Maurists', as they had been called since the beginning of the seventeenth century—had laid the foundations of sound historical criticism through the labours of Dom Tarisse, abbot of Saint-Germain-des-Prés. Next, Dom Luc d'Achéry produced enormous editions of conciliar canons, historical chronicles and lives of the saints. But the decisive impulse was given by Dom Jean Mabillon (1632–1707). A brilliant scholar as well as an exemplary monk, he began by editing the works of St Bernard; then he undertook publication of the *Actes des saints Bénédictins*, omitting all that was evidently mere legend; after which he collaborated in the more comprehensive *Acta Sanctorum*. At the request of Colbert he visited Germany and Italy, examined original manuscripts and profited by his stay at Rome to demand the employment of more scientific precision in the excavation of the catacombs. Among his pupils were Dom Ruinart, author of *Actes sincères des martyrs,* and Dom Denys de Sainte-Marthe, who in 1710 resumed work on *Gallia Christiana,* a general history of the French dioceses, which had been begun by Charles Robert, archdeacon of Chalon-sur-Saône, but had remained incomplete for a hundred years. Catholic erudition was thus firmly established, thanks to Mabillon and some of his rivals. Among the latter was Baluze, Colbert's librarian, compiler of an *Histoire des papes d'Avignon* and of an *Histoire des conciles de la Gaule narbonnaise;* also Father Louis Thomassin, an Oratorian and the first historian of dogma.

Alongside the Maurists, but concerned more with hagiography (a field overgrown with legend), another team of well-trained scholars accomplished a no less fruitful and beneficial work of research. These were Belgian Jesuits who soon became known as Bollandists. Their founder was Father Rosweyde, who in 1616 published a collection entitled *Vie des pères,* remarkable for its critical apparatus. He was succeeded in 1629 by Father de Bolland (1596–1665), who, with the help of Father Papebrock, embarked on a huge series of volumes intended ultimately to include the life of every saint mentioned in the calendar. With courage beyond praise, the Bollandists rooted out everything in those pious narratives that seemed to lack firm historical bases. Their work, despite a number of setbacks,[30] is still in course of completion.[31]

Today all these efforts seem quite remarkable, and they undoubtedly represented for the Church the beginning of a new road into the future. Nevertheless it has to be admitted that they were little appreciated by contemporaries. Those who, like Malebranche, wished to put new life into Catholic apologetics by borrowing elements from modern thought were violently assailed. Bossuet, though he held the Oratorian in high esteem, failed completely to perceive what was valuable in his doctrine notwithstanding its occasional excesses; he treated him with that peculiar loftiness which he knew so well how to assume, hurling at him these few but disdainful and peremptory words: 'Eternal Wisdom is not bound to express itself through the mouths of philosophers.' Dom Henezon, abbot of Saint-Mihiel, who sought to apply the Cartesian method to the problem of grace, was reduced to silence. Men of learning were equally helpless. Mabillon had to brave the ferocity of many foes, particularly that of De Rancé, the 'tempestuous abbot' of La Trappe, who accused him of leading monks astray from their vocation, 'which is to weep and not to teach'. The gentle Benedictine replied, in his *Traité des études monastiques*, by showing that neither St Benedict nor St Bernard had taken such a view.[32] Another attack was launched by one of his brethren at Saint-Germain-des-Prés, who was distressed at his having cast doubt upon the most edifying details in the lives of the Benedictine saints. A third was directed by the excavators of the Roman catacombs; they denounced him to the Congregation of the Index, which, thanks to the intervention of certain bishops (Fléchier among them), refrained from condemning him but required him to revise his writings on the subject. The Bollandists experienced the same sort of difficulties; for the Carmelites, enraged by their having ventured to deny the direct descent of Carmel from the prophet Elias, haled them before the Spanish Inquisition and declared a number of statements taken from their publications to be 'heretical, savouring of heresy, schismatical, scandalous or gravely insulting to several popes, to the sacred Congregation of Rites, to the Breviary and to the martyrology'. This declaration was published in four languages (Latin, Spanish, French and Italian), so that no one throughout the Spanish Netherlands could plead ignorance of its contents; but Rome wisely abstained from giving it official approval. It was no easy matter to remind the Church, however tactfully, that she would do well to deprive her enemies of the weapons they employed against her.

9. THE BATTLE OF THE BIBLE: FROM SPINOZA TO RICHARD SIMON

The struggle, though violent in the field of hagiography and ecclesiastical history, was even more so in that of Holy Scripture. Catholic interest in the Bible had been steadily

increasing for more than a century. Besides the so-called
Louvain edition, which was no longer suited to contemporary
taste, there were the Paris and London polyglot versions for
the learned; while the less learned were satisfied with editions
by the Abbé de Marolles, Father Amelotte and Bishop
Godeau, until the publication of another and superior version
by Father Bouhours, S.J. The most famous was that of Port-
Royal, due in large part to Le Maître de Sacy; accuracy was
not, perhaps, its outstanding quality, but in language and
style it was unrivalled. The edition (20,000 copies) published
by order of Louis XIV after the revocation of the Edict of
Nantes, in order to provide a Catholic Bible for convert
Protestants, was destined to exercise a profound influence
throughout France.

Interest in the sacred books led to a closer study of the text,
and the number of exegetes increased. Extensive work was
done by the hebraists Houbigant, Génébrard and Siméon de
Muis, as well as by such Greek scholars as Morin. Many collections of biblical extracts and maxims appeared, among
them one compiled by Jean de la Haye. Even more notable
were the commentaries on Holy Scripture; those of the Capuchin Bernard de Picquigny on the Epistles of St Paul were
reprinted no fewer than thirty-four times. Considering the
new attitude of mind then evolving, it was inevitable that all
this enthusiasm should lead to differences of opinion. Progress in the study of oriental languages raised textual problems
which seemed hard to solve in the light of traditional teaching. Fresh discoveries appeared to contradict the Bible. Was it
possible that the Chinese existed before Adam, as their annals
and calendars implied? If geological strata had taken millions
of years to form, as men were beginning to recognize, the
Deluge must have occurred at some incredibly remote date.
Nor did the chronology of the royal dynasties of Egypt square
with calculations derived from the Old Testament. But the
New Testament itself was no more immune to criticism. How
account for discrepancies between the four Evangelists? Was
it necessary to place a literal interpretation upon the huge
numbers of peoples and years mentioned in the Apocalypse?
Questions of that kind were raised by the hundred on all
sides. Christian Cartesians tried to suggest that a line must

be drawn between reason and faith in biblical exegesis; but it was clear that the progressive dechristianization of rationalism would ultimately attempt to overthrow the scriptural foundations of religion.

This task of demolition was accomplished with a sort of cold fury by Spinoza. In his famous theologico-political work he treated the Bible as he treated metaphysical faith, the moral order and the political order, that is to say, without the least respect. An inspired book? No, no; simply a tale for ignorant, grown-up children, a clumsy and gaudy puppet-show! The historical narratives of the Old Testament? A tissue of legend. Miracles? Well, when they are not mere inventions they are capable of natural explanation; the crossing of the Red Sea, for example—a gale of wind would have made that possible. The spiritual meaning vanished beneath this furious assault. The Jews were no longer recognized as a chosen people, nor were the prophets heard as foretelling the advent of Christ. Indeed Christianity itself, according to Spinoza, had no right to be called a revealed religion; its appearance and success were due to historical causes easily identifiable. It is not surprising that the Protestant councils of Holland agreed with the heads of the Synagogue in condemning the philosopher and his treatise as 'blasphemous and impious in the highest degree'.

There were many adversaries of this biblical rationalism whose most violent form was embodied in Spinoza. They included Protestants as well as Catholics, and even such militant rationalists as Pierre Bayle. Dom François Lamy and Bishop Huet of Avranches. Malebranche and Fénelon were also of their number. It must, however, be admitted that the defence of strict orthodoxy, though vigorous in tone, was too often miserably weak in reasoning. Proof that Moses was the spiritual teacher of the whole world, declared Huet, lies in the fact that during his sojourn in Egypt he must have known the god Teuth (Thoth), whom all the evidence showed to be identical with the Mexican god Teutl! A miscellany entitled *Questions curieuses sur la Genèse* proved that Eve was formed from Adam's side (his left side, to be exact) from the fact that (*a*) the left side of the human body is weaker than the right, and (*b*) that it is the seat of the heart, an organ which, as everyone knew, causes men to love women! The most ridiculous questions were propounded with the utmost solemnity. To what species of reptiles did the serpent in Genesis belong? Since Our Lady was a virgin, did she produce milk? Some assertions made with all the precision of a hammer blow were no less remarkable. One pious book stated that Adam died on 20th August 2930 B.C., and that Noah released the dove from the ark on 18th February 2305; a second wondered anxiously whether the world began in 6984 or 3740 B.C.; a third gave the chronology of Our Lord's life, from birth to death, almost to a day. More honest was Father Antonio Foresti, who explained that in his works on Holy Scripture he chose dates not for their accuracy but for their convenience.

Fortunately there were a few men who decided that such nonsense could never establish confidence in the Bible. They even thought that the divine inspiration of Scripture did not necessarily exclude the possibility of error in the sacred text, since the latter had been written down, copied and recopied by men. As early as the sixteenth century two great Jesuits, Maldonatus and Salmeron, had proposed solutions in which faith was wedded to good sense. Others of a like nature were advanced about 1585 by Lessius and Corneille de la Pierre (Cornelius à Lapide), who thereby stirred a hornets' nest in the University of Louvain. Some fifty years earlier the Jesuits Bonfrère and Holden, simultaneously with the Protestant Louis Capelle, outlined a theory of inspiration which foreshadowed the definitions of our own day; but reaction was so strong that the Society recoiled, and the learned Father Denys Petau publicly declared, perhaps by way of prudence, that he had never for a moment doubted that each of the six 'days' of creation was actually a period of twenty-four hours and no more.

Now there came upon the scene Richard Simon (1638–1712). He was an Oratorian, a man of fiery temperament but lucid intellect. Keenly interested from youth upwards in all that concerned the Bible and the Jewish people, he began by mastering Greek, Hebrew and other oriental languages, so as to be no longer dependent on the Latin Vulgate; he was also well grounded in philology and history. It was not long before he realized that the 'theological' sense of the Bible must needs rest on the 'grammatical', i.e. literal, sense; 'otherwise', as he pertinently observed, 'everyone will take the liberty of translating Scripture according to his prejudices, and then he will no longer be interpreting the word of God, but explaining it in the light of his own ideas'. This principle underlay the *Histoire critique du Vieux Testament*, which he published in 1678. It created so great a scandal, roused such a chorus of protest, that he was expelled from the Oratory. Having settled in Normandy, he continued his labours, republishing his book in Holland and following it with a dozen more, among them the *Histoire critique du Nouveau Testament*. In course of time his ideas assumed greater certainty and precision. 'God's instruments', he used to say, 'were *men*, and they did not cease to be men for all that they were prophets.' According to Richard Simon inspiration directed them and preserved them from essential error, but did not intervene in every detail of their work. The right way to prevent sceptics from being able to scorn the Bible and make a laughing stock of its most exalted teaching was to throw light upon the Holy Book by means of science, to understand the circumstances in which it was written and to compare scriptural data with those of archaeology.

As for the apologetical system then in vogue, Simon described it as 'jargon' and 'hocus-pocus', and added that 'to seek to establish the truths of physics, mathematics, astronomy . . . by certain passages of Scripture' was worthy neither of a theologian nor of a philosopher. Today all this is so well recognized, especially since the illuminating Encyclical *Divino afflante spiritu* of 1943, that it is hard to imagine the former Oratorian's audacity in setting out on such a road. But he was aware 'of being useful to the Church by strengthening her most sacred and divine possession'. He died a holy priest and a learned Catholic exegete. The *Encyclopedia Cattolica*, published at the Vatican, ranks him 'among the pioneers of biblical criticism'.

Such, however, was not the opinion of his contemporaries, to almost all of whom indeed the very word 'criticism' applied to the Bible was anathema. Bossuet, warned by the Abbé Renaudot, saw red[33] when he learned of the impious book which 'undermined the foundations of the Church'; he hur-

ried off at once to Chancellor Le Tellier and persuaded him
to order the burning of the two hundred copies held by the
bookseller. Condemnation by the Sorbonne and relegation to
the Index followed quickly upon this *auto-da-fé*. The Bishop
of Meaux never ceased until his death to pursue Richard
Simon with vigilant hatred, setting the police to take measures against the entry into France of such pernicious works,
and even suggesting to the chancellor that he should have the
author arrested. In this he was not alone. Numerous 'refuta-
tions' of Simon appeared, even in Protestant circles; he was
vilified notably by Vossius and Jurieu. No doubt there were
points in his work where he had gone too far. He made it
possible to believe, for example, that Revelation had altered
during the course of ages; he pretended to see in the biblical
text a host of interpolations; and his manner of solving the
difficult problem of the authorship of the Sacred Books was
most peremptory. These, however, were errors of detail, which
could easily have been rectified but for Richard Simon's in-
tolerant nature and for the fact that his adversaries did not
understand that he was opening up the only possible road for
Catholic exegesis. At the close of the seventeenth century
men were as yet unprepared to read that Moses was not sole
author of the Pentateuch, or that the story of Jonas, though it
had a moral content, was not historical. The philosophers of
the new century would be only too happy to claim kinship
with the great scholar whose work had no other aim than to
serve the Church. It was Richard Simon's misfortune to have
been born too soon.

10. PERILS OF THE EIGHTEENTH CENTURY

The eighteenth century marks one of the gravest turning-
points in the history of western thought. While the most
brilliant reign that France had ever known drew to its close in
an atmosphere of austere boredom, defeat, sorrow and latent
exasperation, the forces that had been silently at work undermining the edifice became more audacious. 'Heresy no longer
dwelt in secret solitude; it won adherents, became insolent
and boastful. Negation no longer wore disguise; it strutted

everywhere.'[34] The old king's death (1st September 1715) was welcomed with a 'thrill of joy', to use Saint-Simon's cruel phrase, but an explosion followed. Under the authority of a regent who was known to favour the new ideas, a moral if not an intellectual Libertine, it would be much less dangerous to be a nonconformist. The new age roared with laughter at the political, religious and social authorities riddled with the Persian arrows of Montesquieu;[35] it did not foresee that in its final years the lunette of the guillotine would lour against a blood-red horizon.

'The drama of the eighteenth century', wrote Pierre Gaxotte,[36] 'lies not in the wars and turmoil of the Revolution, but in the collapse and retreat of those ideas which had enlightened and dominated the seventeenth. The history of the eighteenth century, which many Frenchmen like to represent as graceful and carefree, is nothing but the history of that dissolution, of that retreat and of the increasingly grave consequences it entailed. The new subversive ideas became more and more popular. Books hostile to the established order, which hitherto could have been counted by the dozen, poured from the presses in hundreds. So much so that in France alone, between 1715 and 1789, the number of irreligious works and anti-clerical pamphlets exceeded two thousand. Pedlars went from door to door selling those that the booksellers dared not stock. Some—Voltaire's despicable La Pucelle, for instance— were copied over and over again by hand. Newspapers, of which there were still few in 1715, rapidly multiplied. Alongside the official Gazette de France, Mercure and the Journal de Savants there sprang up sixteen in Paris alone within a space of fifty years; others were founded in every province from the mid century onward. All served as vehicles of the new ideas, even those that were most hostile to them; the latter, by the very fact of opposing them, helped to give them importance and diffuse them.

The new ideas were spread abroad in several other ways too. Elegant circles were quickly won over and made them fashionable. 'Of all empires,' said Duclos, 'that of the intellectual world is the most powerful. . . . In the long run it moulds public opinion.' Now public opinion was moulded in the salons, which, though entirely social on the threshold of the century, became more and more literary, learned, 'philosophical'. Fontenelle was already holding forth at the Marquise de Lambert's, although she cherished pious memories of Fénelon. Very soon, however, battle was joined between the philosophical and anti-philosophical camps in that boudoir hung with buttercup-yellow moire, where Mme du Deffand received with exquisite grace. The most audacious subjects were discussed with restraint and elegance at Mme Geoffrin's, and far less peacefully in the drawing-room of Julie de Lespinasse. La Chevrette, near Montmorency, where Mme d'Épinay received, was the paradise of philosophers. Almost all who mattered were guests in those houses, where elegance and wit concealed many dangers.

On another level, and indeed on all sorts of levels, *cercles* or clubs, modelled on the English pattern, were also centres of discussion. The first to be opened (1730) was Le Club d'Entresol, on the Place Vendôme. Besides the clubs for noblemen, for magistrates and for middle-class folk, there were clubs for provincials visiting the capital, e.g. the Club Breton, all extremely liberal in their views and regarded by the police as 'haunts of the unruly'. In the cafés[37] the most heterodox ideas were debated, despite the presence of many police spies; an English traveller, Young, was astounded by the boldness of views that he heard put forward beneath the hundred chandeliers of the Café de la Régence. In the provinces numerous *sociétés de pensée*, ranging from mere lecture rooms to full-blown academies[38] were founded by a select few of the governing classes, nobles, magistrates and citizens; far from being shrines of conservatism, they gave an eager welcome to the prevailing ideas. Their mutual relations established throughout France, and even throughout Europe, a network of active though unconcerted influences. Even the illustrious platform of the Académie Française began to re-echo suspect beliefs when Mmes de Lambert, Geoffrin and Lespinasse assumed the role of 'Grand Electresses' and the energetic d'Alembert became its secretary.

Thus, as the century proceeded, it was possible to observe the break up of neo-classical ideas in every domain—political, social, literary and religious. The process became increasingly rapid and affords a striking example of the acceleration of history. Until about 1748 the ringleaders of this movement remained cautious, making use of allusion, insinuation and mockery rather than direct assault. Then, towards the middle of the century, they went over to a general offensive against all that the past had loved, believed and respected. The enemies of Christianity in particular threw off their mask. By 1770, as the last bastions of resistance fell one after another, the attack reached such a pitch of violence that even the masters who had pioneered the way—Voltaire, Diderot, Rousseau and others—appeared weak and lukewarm. History found thought in the last stages of a mortal crisis when she summoned France to revolution.

Did the established order not defend itself against this assault? Did the responsible authorities do nothing to halt the spread of ideas that were destroying the political and religious principles upon which everything rested? Yes. During the arbitrary reign of Louis XIV a vigilant police force and judiciary had deterred nonconformity from expressing its views in too loud a voice, and there is no reason to suppose that that vigilance was abandoned under his successors. In the sphere of religion, at any rate, regulations prohibiting acts, propaganda and books directed against the Church and her faith remained theoretically in force until the eve of the Revolution. The unhappy affair of the young Chevalier de La Barre, who was sentenced to death for public blasphemy, shows clearly that such crimes were still punished as such by the secular arm.[39] Nor was this an isolated case: throughout the century there were examples of impious persons burnt alive or condemned to the galleys. A close watch was kept on the printing and sale of books, and there were numerous inspectors of the Press. Edicts, frequently re-enacted, imposed severe penalties on those responsible for unauthorized publications; that of 1757 ordered capital punishment in cases of recidivism. Authors of works deemed scandalous, among them a certain Abbé de Capmartin, were promptly sent to the galleys; so too with readers of bad books, such as an unfortunate apothecary who rowed for nine years because he had bought *Christianisme dévoilé*. Between 1775 and 1789 eighty volumes were condemned by the Sorbonne and the Parlement, and ten printing houses were closed. Similar methods were employed in other countries: in Spain, where nearly all the great French works of the age were publicly burned by the executioner; at Venice, where cargoes of books might not be unloaded except in presence of the police; and even in Prussia, where Frederick II showed himself so favourable to the philosophers, his successor signed a decree (1788) prohibiting impious books.

These coercive measures obtained results in Spain and a few Italian states, but they were singularly ineffective elsewhere. The main result of a condemnation was to send the price of the forbidden book soaring sky-high and augment its sales. The Abbé Raynal's *Histoire philosophique des Indes* was placed on the Index, condemned at Paris, and thrice torn up and burned; yet it ran through no fewer than twenty editions. When Toussaint's *Les Mœurs* was prohibited, the *Correspondance littéraire* printed an article ending with these words: 'By having this work burned the magistrate, as always happens, has increased the curiosity of potential readers.' And when *Émile* was burned at Madrid, Rousseau's friend François Grasset told him of the fact as a piece of good news. 'The Spanish nobility and the ambassadors of foreign courts are now busy trying to procure the book at any price.'

Indeed this suspect literature was an object of endless intrigue in many localities, particularly in France. It was quite in order to cut off the hand of a pedlar caught selling scandalous lampoons, or to send an obscure pamphleteer to the galleys for ten years; but the great were protected. Voltaire at Ferney used to sweat with fear at the slightest alarm; he was always ready at a moment's notice to cross the Genevese frontier, near which he lodged, but in fact he was never in any great danger. Malesherbes, Director of the Press under Louis XVI, tolerated the most venturesome writers, because he thought that freedom for men of letters would serve as a kind of safety valve for public discontent. Mme de Pompadour openly protected the Encyclopaedists. The most anti-religious works of Voltaire often circulated under official stamps affixed to the parcels by his friend Damilaville, First Commissioner of the Stamp Office. In 1749 the whole stock of La Mettrie's most impious book was discovered in the house of one of the King's preachers at Versailles; moreover all prohibited books were on sale at Blaizot's shop in the Grands Communs, and he was bookseller to the court. It often happened that an illustrious writer under police observation was courteously forewarned of an impending search by the very agents appointed to carry it out. Exactly the same, or very nearly the same, state of affairs prevailed elsewhere than in the distraught kingdom of France. The Venetian police, whose business it was to control the entry of books, allowed the agents of foreign ambassadors to arrange for the unpacking of those precious cargoes at Padua, for their carriage to Venice in diplomatic bags and for their sale at considerable profit—of which they no doubt received a share. It is not surprising in the circumstances that official measures against evil literature had as much effect as a scarecrow upon sparrows.

Moreover there was a sale for such literature.[40] We shall presently notice the success of the Encyclopaedia. Between 1759 and 1784 *Candide* was reprinted forty-three times, and *La Nouvelle Héloïse* fifty times between 1761 and the Revolution. The unreadable *Système de la nature* ran through seven editions in ten years. Only one Christian book rivalled those of the philosophical clique: Fénelon's *Télémaque*, because it was regarded as a criticism of the political and religious system.

These facts reveal a state of mind. If the kind of literature we have been discussing could count upon favouritism even in high places, that was because it already enjoyed even more widespread good fortune—the climate of its age. The intellectual crisis in the eighteenth century, far more than in the seventeenth, was associated not only with a crisis of conscience but also with a moral crisis; Libertinism of the mind and Libertinism of conduct went hand in hand. It was not that all philosophers led exceptionable lives. Some *salons*, notably Mme de Tencin's, were extremely loose; Diderot and Holbach, for instance, gladly sacrificed to Bacchus and Venus. But not all were like that. Much more was at stake. It was a common saying that 'atheism does not necessarily lead to moral corruption'; of course not, but the evidence goes to show that a certain degree of moral corruption is conducive to irreligion. If a man sins frequently he is inclined to support doctrines which deny outright the fact of sin. The licence of which society, and particularly high society, afforded many examples, favoured rebellion against all morality. It is no mere accident that Voltaire's *Pucelle* is, from the moral point of view, utterly vile, or that Diderot, another philosopher, wrote *La Religieuse* and *Bijoux indiscrets*. The century which produced Crébillon and even the Marquis de Sade, the century whose artists were so fond of elegant engravings and engaging nudes, would certainly feel a greater urge to defy all principles than did the seventeenth, during which, whatever else may be said of it, discipline and behaviour were rigid. The whole century, in fact, prepared the ground for the philosophical spirit and helped it to triumph.

11. THE PHILOSOPHICAL SPIRIT

The philosopher of the eighteenth century was not fundamentally much different from what had recently become known as a Libertine or Rationalist. Voltaire and the Encyclopaedists were in large part heirs of Bayle and Spinoza, of Montaigne and Rabelais, and even of Pomponazzi. Cartesianism, in that distorted form which troubled Bossuet, also exercised a good deal of influence, as is clear from the fact that until the eve of the Revolution the *Discourse on Method*, its advantages and its dangers, were the object of passionate debate. But the notions destined to serve as a foundation for the new attitude of mind were strengthened and rendered still more active by other means.

First, by the progress of science. Scientism, born in the sixteenth century and developed in the seventeenth, won very large numbers of recruits during the eighteenth because science appeared to lend it support. One cannot insist too strongly that the great scientific movement of the eighteenth century contributed in a decisive manner to the triumph of 'reason' and 'enlightenment'. There was at that time no scientific or technical discipline which did not achieve some notable success. Geometers and astronomers, confirming the theories of Newton, calculated the distance between Earth and Moon, discovered new planets through the genius of Herschel, and measured the terrestrial meridian. Physics and chemistry, which were all the rage, made important advances: Benjamin Franklin (1706–90) demonstrated the identity of lightning and electricity; Fahrenheit in England, Réaumur in France and Celsius in Sweden invented the thermometer; Lavoisier accomplished the synthesis of water, Scheele discovered chlorine and Lebon found means of lighting with gas. Properly scientific methods were introduced in the field of natural history by Linnaeus and Buffon (1707–88), who systematized the world of living beings. There was much progress in the practical sphere. The steam engine, used in the early eighteenth century for pumping water from mines and adapted by James Watt for other industrial purposes, was used by Cugnot and Jouffroy as a means of propulsion in carriages and ships. Montgolfier, a paper manufacturer of Annonay in Vivarais, sought to realize the ancient dream of Icarus by flying through the air, and succeeded in 1783. It was almost inevitable, in face of such achievements, that the human mind should believe itself endowed with unlimited powers. Philosophy was closely linked with science, for both were often practised by the same individuals. Men were looking more and more to science rather than to the intellect for true 'enlightenment'; what science could not explain must be rejected without discussion. Taine[41] rightly observes that science was the 'vital source whence prophets great and small derived the spirit of rebellion'.

Along with this main cause there were others. The eighteenth century was a cosmopolitan age, in which men travelled widely, anxious to discover the vast world and the manners of peoples hitherto unknown. Earlier authors of the neo-classical age were stay-at-homes, spending their lives in Paris or at Versailles; Voltaire, Rousseau and their like were frequently on the road. During the eighteenth century many of the most popular works were travel books, even (in fact principally) those written by missionaries. This probing and collation of knowledge helped to destroy the edifice of received ideas. Men discovered that there were systems of thought other than those of the Christian West. The legend of the 'noble savage', endowed for the occasion with all kinds of virtues, was universally accepted; Voltaire made liberal use of it. Debates among Catholics on the Chinese Rites helped to spread the idea that wisdom was far from being a Christian monopoly, and that the Celestial Empire had had saints of a kind long before Christ. Some were deeply concerned about the salvation of these 'infidel saints'.[42]

It may, however, be asked why the new ideas made such rapid progress. The most immediate cause was quite simply political. It is impossible to overstress the capital fact that man's way of thinking in the neo-classical age was indissolubly bound up with the system of government and the social order.[43] Since the end of the reign of Louis XIV the governmental machine had appeared to be functioning badly; and the situation was even worse during the eighteenth century, when France suffered from an almost continuous financial crisis, which she failed to surmount. Nor could she have surmounted it in a social system that granted so many privileges. Social inequality, accepted in the preceding era, was disputed with a vigour proportionate to the growing incapacity of a self-styled ruling class. In 1748 Montesquieu's *Esprit des lois* struck a fatal blow at the regime by showing that the noblest system was one that guaranteed a maximum of independence together with the fullest measure of equality. Comparison of this ideal with the prevailing situation was overwhelming. There was consequently an indestructible link between the collapse of a politico-social organization and that of mankind's intellectual values. Christianity, or at any rate the Church, who had thrown in her lot with that of the secular regime, and whose hierarchy and morality were an integral part of the established order, found herself an ever more frequent target for the arrows of men who wished to destroy that order. The altar stood back to back with the throne; and its fall was inevitable if the throne were overturned. Caesaropapism had a heavy price to pay.

In order to explain the rapid progress of nonconformist ideas we must add yet another fact of paramount importance: whereas the rebellious clique included a large number of highly talented men, there was very little talent among those who defended religion and the establishment. In the days of Pascal, Racine and Bossuet genius was on the side of faith. It was on the opposite side in the days of Rousseau and Voltaire. Was this mere chance? Most certainly not; it was the result of a gradual process whose beginnings we saw at the time of the Renaissance. By losing most of the leading intellectuals Christianity lost much of her influence; she was not to recover it until many of them returned to her fold during the nineteenth century.

It is therefore against the background of an extraordinary ferment compounded of enthusiasm for all that was new, of contempt for the past, of sullen wrath against the injustices and absurdities of the established order, of moral licence and sparkling irony that we must observe the growth of the 'philosophical' spirit, as the phenomenon was ordinarily described. It was 'philosophical' to conduct experiments in one's private laboratory as it was to censure the government; it was 'philosophical' to break the Friday abstinence as it was to quote the epigrams of Voltaire; it was 'philosophical' to be a physiocrat as it was to parade immoral habits. The 'philosophical' spirit was not so much a system of thought as a general attitude to life.

For when we try to analyse concrete facts we are quickly at a loss. We are not in presence of a coherent whole, let alone of an orthodoxy. Although Voltaire, Rousseau and Helvetius, for example, were all philosophers, they followed different lines and were occasionally in positive disagreement on essential points. What then were the most widely accepted beliefs? The primacy of man, regarded as the focus of the universe; the omnipotence of human reason, considered as the arbiter of all thought and of all conduct. Hence the cult of science on the one hand, and on the other a declaration that natural morality suffices, having no need of divine instruction or of rewards and punishments beyond the grave. Such were the foundations of a philosophy that has continued to our own day, carrying still further the application of those principles. Not every aspect of 'philosophy', however, is reprehensible. It is possible to detect among the philosophers and their followers a sincere wish to serve the progress of the mind; that at least is something of real value. We have them also to thank for the rise of tolerance in the religious field. It was they who condemned the use of coercive measures and who taught (at least in theory, though not always in practice) deference to the opinions of others. In that respect they were indeed servants of what Chesterton has called 'Christian truths become foolish', truths which Christians had failed to keep upon a straight road.

From the religious point of view the philosophers divide into two groups. The majority were Deists. Deism, born in England and spread abroad partly by the anglomania of that age, retained a God, but a God remote, pale and shadowy, never intervening in human affairs and demanding no act of faith. His existence was arrived at by a simple process of reasoning: no watch without a watchmaker. But this unknown God, who was beginning to be called 'the Supreme Being', was not credited with any attribute apart from existence. If he imposed a religion at all, it was natural religion, as old as the world, embracing all creeds without distinction and sufficiently vague to rouse the fervour of M. de Voltaire.

The Atheists were much less numerous than the Deists, at least until about 1760 when their number began to increase. Among them too there were many divergences. They included descendants of the Libertines, who confined themselves to overthrowing dogmas and received ideas, professed or secret adherents of philosophical materialism such as Holbach and Helvetius, according to whom mind does not differ specifically from matter, and is even its product; the Deist Voltaire provided them with a host of arguments. Lastly there were exponents of a scientific materialism whose prophets were d'Alembert and, above all, La Mettrie, author of *Homme machine*. Each of these groups made a great noise in the world, but their influence remained slight.

Deists and Atheists were fully agreed on one point: their hatred of religion, its dogmas, rites and hierarchy. There Toland and Holbach thought alike, as did Helvetius and Voltaire. The number of antireligious lampoons published during the eighteenth century is incredible. *Priestly Imposture, The Priests Unmasked, Cruelty of Religion, Hell Destroyed, History of Fanaticism, Discourse on Miracles*—the titles speak for themselves. Nor had the points of attack changed: on one side, as in somewhat earlier days, the enemies of Christianity directed their blows at the supernatural in all its forms—mysteries, miracles and prophecies, all of which were alike declared absurd. On another side the ecclesiastical organism was their target; it was accused of being despotic, brutalizing and morally debased. The satires of the ungodly cannot be said to have taken a new lease of life; even those from the pen of Voltaire often seem a little down at heel. But an entire literature strove to ruin or to tarnish what western man had held sacred for eighteen hundred years.

12. 'KING VOLTAIRE'

During the eighteenth century protagonists and popularizers of the 'philosophical' spirit were so numerous that the very idea of drawing up a complete list is enough to make one feel giddy. Alongside the great ringleaders, whose names are to be found in every school textbook, there was an army of followers, disciples and plagiarists who dispensed the thought of the masters but whose memory has not survived. At Paris in 1748 friends used to stop one another and ask: 'Have you read *Les Mœurs?* But which of us today could name the author of that once fashionable book, François-Vincent Toussaint? Who has ever heard of Pierre Cuppé, Dumarsais, Fréret, Meslier; of the little hunchbacked Abbé Méhégan, glory of the Café Procope; of the former diplomat Benoît de Maillet, who had so many ideas about the origin of the world and man; or again, a little later, of Boulanger, Charles-François Dupuis, Sylvain Maréchal, Jérôme Lalande, all fanatical anti-Christians; or, finally, of the learned Naigeon whose *Recueil philosophique* was intended as the 'breviary' of irreligion? They were third- or fourth-rate philosophers; and even those of them who reached the lofty heights of the Académie can hardly be said to have attained more than relative immortality.

We shall therefore confine ourselves to the great figures who towered above them all. The most illustrious was undoubtedly Voltaire. None will deny that during a life long both in years (1694–1778) and in works he dominated his age. The title King Voltaire had meaning not only in that dazzling hour when the actresses of the Comédie Française crowned his bust upon the stage after a performance of *Irène*, nor only during the last twenty years of his life, when he was truly the leader of European thought. His 'royalty' has deep foundations: it rests upon his ability to share the feelings of his age, to be always fully alive to contemporary currents of thought, to be their spokesman while appearing to be their guide. Therein lies the secret of his immediate success, in that harmony with others to which the very greatest do not always achieve and which is so often deceptive when there is question of a man's intrinsic worth.

Of course Voltaire lacked neither talent nor, to some extent, real genius. Though an indifferent orator, an outstandingly platitudinous poet, and a novelist whose imagination was often forced and systematical, he was none the less a genius at adaptation, able as no one else to grasp the facts of present interest, the idea that would find an echo in public opinion, and to make therefrom a book, a pamphlet or a play, about which all the world would soon be talking. Wonderfully supple, his art adapted itself to every mode of expression. He is an epic poet in the *Henriade* (1728); a philosopher in *Le Désastre de Lisbonne*; a dramatist of every kind in fifty-three plays that were actually performed; an excellent historian in *Le Siècle de Louis XIV*; a profound critic in the *Commentaires sur Corneille*; a satirical story-teller in *Micromégas*, *Zadig*, *Candide* and *L'Ingénu*; a prolific letter-writer and memorialist; and once again a philosopher in his *Essai sur les mœurs* (1756), his dictionaries and his treatises. No other polygraph has ever produced in such abundance or with equal success. He never failed to make the dullest topics interesting and amusing, to devise the most brilliant methods of exposition in the shape of a refined and compact style, perfect as sculptured bronze or arabesque. What gifts he placed at the service of ideas he intended to promote!

What were his ideas? In the first place one may ask whether they sprang from his own mind. His thought gives the impression of being a collection of ideas common to his age rather than a personal creation. It is neither original nor profound, nor even a connected system; indeed it is often a mass of contradiction—'a chaos of clear ideas', says Faguet. Voltaire was a Deist who yet provided arguments for the grossest materialism; an almost complete sceptic and a destroyer in every domain, but at the same time a social conservative of the worst kind; a bitter enemy of all religious faith, but a convinced Gallican, for whom the alliance of throne and altar was indispensable to good order; and an anti-Semite into the bargain. It is possible to discover in his work support for diametrically opposite theses, and even the material for a collection of spiritual meditations! But the axis remains firm: rationalism justifying and sustaining a radical and militant antichristianism.

Antichristianism in fact is the real driving force of his work, to which he remained faithful throughout his life. From the publication of *Œdipe* in his thirtieth year until his last days, the one-time disciple of Pierre Bayle, the Chérubin of Ninon de Lenclos, laboured with unflagging constancy to 'crush the infamous one', the words referring, perhaps, not so much to Christ as to the religion founded by Him. He employed all kinds of literary forms to repeat the same arguments, particularly those innumerable pamphlets, anonymous and pseudonymous, which he used to call 'my scraps and little hot pies'. His principal weapon was sarcasm, which he handled with cruelty and small respect for truth, justice or moderation. His lampoons disguised as sermons and his imaginary Life of St Cucufa, whose canonization he had secured, raised many a laugh; but his sarcasm too often overstepped the limits of propriety, lapsing into the foulest indecency, for example in *La Pucelle*, where the pure figure of Joan of Arc is treated with a degree of coarseness that does nothing but disgrace the author. 'I'm tired of being told', he used to say, 'that twelve men sufficed to establish Christianity, and I'm longing to prove that only one is needed to destroy it.'

Of what did he accuse Christianity? Of many crimes. He claimed it was a gigantic imposture harboured and sustained by cunning priests for their own benefit. He charged it with being a tissue of absurdities, of mythical tomfoolery, good enough for the masses—and useful, too, for keeping them quiet—but deserving no belief whatever on the part of intelligent men. He denounced it as guilty of countless atrocities, e.g. the *autos-da-fé* of the Inquisition and the crusades, 'which cost millions of Christian lives'.

Upon these three themes Voltaire rang endless changes. His hatred of religion increased with the passage of years. The attack, launched at first against clericalism and theocracy, ended in a furious assault upon Holy Scripture, the dogmas of the Church, and even upon the person of Jesus Christ Himself, who was depicted now as a degenerate Socrates, now as 'a low-born charlatan', and in so sacrilegious a manner that even Renan refers to it with indignation. Voltaire's detestation of Christ and of His Church became a frantic passion, of hideous grandeur, tinged occasionally with a sort of bitterness and something akin to regret.

For in that complex and often contradictory personality the streak of fanatical irreligion sometimes takes on the appearance of a savage reaction against secret anguish. It has been maintained[44] that Voltaire possessed a frustrated craving for the interior life, for religious outpouring, a kind of inhibited mysticism. There is evidence of this in his attacks on Pascal. Moreover there are some aspects of his life which a Christian cannot but admire: his courage in defending Calas and Lally de Tollendal, whom he considered to have been unjustly condemned—even though his attitude in these cases was inspired partly by the needs of his own propaganda —and the energy with which he protested against history's long tale of butchery.[45] Such facts help to offset the contempt that may be felt for his cowardice, his duplicity, his rancour, his baseness—all that caused his own niece to say: 'Judged by the heart you are the last of men.' But from the standpoint of history, especially of Christian history, his role was paramount. He infected an enormous public with scepticism and militant irreligion. The French Revolution saw him as one of its guides;[46] the nineteenth century owed to him that anti-clericalism which continues to usurp the place of thought among many politicians. It has been suggested that he died a Christian,[47] but that is of no significance except for his own soul. The Church may have been able to absolve him *in extremis*, but history looks upon him none the less as one of the worst enemies that Christianity ever had.

13. THE ENCYCLOPAEDIA

Voltaire by himself could never have sufficed to give the new ideas that vigour and expansive force we have seen them to possess. He was powerfully assisted by a collective work, *The Encyclopaedia*, which has been said to mark 'the triumph of the philosophers'. This gigantic enterprise in the domain of publishing was conceived by a man of extremely inquisitive and powerful intellect who was better equipped even than the patriarch of Ferney to familiarize himself with every subject. The fiery temperament of Denis Diderot (1713–84) was one of mysterious contrasts—rationalistic yet sensitive, a combination of Voltaire and Rousseau; he was also a master of thought and language.

The idea had been familiar since the publication of Pierre Bayle's *Dictionnaire*. That of Thomas Corneille, which had appeared twelve months earlier, was also successful; so were the *Table alphabétique des dictionnaires* and many others, which ranged from two to six volumes. In England, Chambers's *Encyclopaedia*, or *Dictionary of the Arts and Sciences*, had appeared in 1728, and the Parisian bookseller Lebreton thought of having it translated. In 1745 he discussed the plan with Diderot, who showed him that it was possible to produce something much better and undertook to do so. The first volume came from the presses in 1751.

The purpose was explained by Diderot himself in a prospectus resembling a manifesto. The encyclopaedia was to be 'a general picture of the human mind's endeavour in every field and every age'. At once philosophical and practical, it would exhibit as far as possible the order and connection of the several aspects of man's knowledge' and at the same time contain 'the general principles upon which each science and each art rests, together with the most essential details which form its body and substance'.

It need hardly be added that in order thus to cover the whole field of knowledge Diderot required numerous collaborators. He managed to find them. His immediate assistant was Jean d'Alembert (1717–83), a natural son of Mme de

Tencin, an able mathematician and a careful thinker. All the leading names in philosophy were invited to contribute articles: Voltaire, of course, Montesquieu, J. J. Rousseau, Buffon, the Abbé Condillac, the German Baron Holbach, Helvetius, the economists Turgot and Quesnay, and even such theologians as Prades, Raynal and Morellet, all three of whom were afterwards at loggerheads with the Sorbonne. The literary critic was Marmontel, whose taste and judgment were sound.

The result of their collaboration, and that of others about which little is known, was not uniformly brilliant. The best was submerged in a sea of platitudes. Repetition, contradiction and inaccuracy were the least outstanding faults. Voltaire described *The Encyclopaedia* as 'a Tower of Babel', and d'Alembert himself admitted it to be 'a harlequin's dress made from a few pieces of good stuff and a heap of rags'. Nevertheless, despite this incongruity, Diderot managed to endow the whole, if not with unity, at least with a certain flavour by giving pride of place throughout to the basic elements of the 'philosophical' spirit—the cult of reason and progress together with a right to complete freedom and universal criticism.

Contributors to *The Encyclopaedia* were not invited to preach revolutionary ideas at every turn. Those large and splendid volumes cost far too much to justify a calculated risk of seizure and destruction, which would have ruined the bookseller and put an end to the whole undertaking. On the contrary, 'anyone who peruses the articles on political or religious subjects will find nothing but what is neutral, cautious and even respectful'. Subjects directly concerned with dogma were handled by theologians who were perfectly orthodox (though carefully chosen for their unimportance), or at any rate submitted to ecclesiastical censorship. The purpose was not to make a frontal attack by way of lampoon; it was infinitely more subtle.

The editors of *The Encyclopaedia* were undoubtedly irreligious and even atheistic. In 1749 Diderot published his *Lettre sur les aveugles à l'usage de ceux qui voient*, which was denounced by the Ecclesiastical Court of Paris and led to his imprisonment at Vincennes. Combining materialism and epicureanism, in his life as in his thought, he believed in nothing but reason or nature, science and the sovereign test of experience. D'Alembert was animated by a hatred of Christianity so narrow and sectarian that his contemporaries spoke of him as a 'fanatic in reverse'. The great majority of Diderot's collaborators, whether atheists or deists, practised irreligion stripped of all disguise.

Thus *The Encyclopaedia*, without openly attacking faith, dogma or the Church, employed a hundred means to discredit them in the minds of its readers, sowing doubt, negation of accepted values, sarcasm or disgust. In the article 'Bible', for instance, it protested the purity of its intentions towards Holy Scripture; but with every appearance of good faith it laid bare the numerous problems raised by a study of the sacred text, in such a way that the reader could only conclude that no part of it was worthy of belief. Referring to death, it declared that 'the true Christian should rejoice in the death of his child, for death secures for the child eternal happiness. . . . Our religion is both terrible and consoling'. That was one way of rendering Christianity intolerable. Tucked away in seemingly inoffensive articles—'Aius Locutius', 'Agnus Scythicus', 'Eagle', 'Brahmins', 'Juno'—were ambushes to entrap 'fanaticism and superstition'; more was in view than Graeco-Roman paganism or Hindu polytheism. Over and over again, when there was question of morality, it was said: 'Morality is possible without religion, and religion sometimes goes hand in hand with immorality.' The whole business was carefully devised. D'Alembert spoke of 'the sort of veiled aggression, a kind of secret warfare, which is wisest when one inhabits the vast regions dominated by error'. The result was to create widespread hostility towards all things religious, an atmosphere of unbelief from which the supernatural was excluded and in which the social sense supplanted that of the divine, an intellectual landscape from which the Church, all churches, must inevitably vanish. In this respect *The Encyclopaedia* went farther than Voltaire, who agreed at least that the masses should have a religion.

Despite precautions taken to camouflage their disquieting views, the authors of *The Encyclopaedia* met with difficulties. In October 1751, just after the appearance of the second volume, the scandal created by a thesis of the Abbé Prades[48] led to a royal decree suspending publication, which was not resumed until eighteen months later. In 1757 there was another suspension, caused indirectly by an attempt upon the life of Louis XV and the defeat of Rosbach. Licence to publish was revoked; but influential friends of the philosophers, led by Mme de Pompadour, intervened. Work was resumed by Diderot alone, since d'Alembert had prudently decided to withdraw. It was completed in 1772: twelve volumes of text, four of supplements and eleven of remarkable engravings. An impressive achievement.

Its influence was considerable. Throughout Europe every open-minded person interested in the progress of thought wished to read, or at any rate to peruse, the sumptuous folios. They were to be found on the shelves of at least one out of every three contemporary libraries; they were even smuggled into Spain; and counterfeit editions were made in Italy, at Geneva and at Lausanne. Nor was the spread of *The Encyclopaedia* hindered by the denunciations of many Catholic publicists or by the Church's official condemnation. The 'philosophical' spirit proved to have no more efficient means of propaganda.

14. THE CASE OF JEAN-JACQUES ROUSSEAU

Jean-Jacques Rousseau (1712–78) was the only man of his age whose fame was comparable with that of Voltaire. He was, moreover, the only writer of that period whose work seems to be not a mere medley of fashionable ideas, or a demolition site, but an instrument for the construction of a complete and coherent system, capable of supplying an answer to the questions raised by his contemporaries. It may therefore be asked whether he is to be placed without further hesitation in the enemy's camp. We have to submit that Jean-Jacques, who reminds us of nothing so much as a hunted man beset with perpetual anxiety, his heart wounded and bleeding, inspires a great deal more sympathy than does the fox of Ferney with his smirking sarcasm, his readiness to make use of powerful relatives and his skill in financial speculation. Rousseau's smile, as it appears in the magnificent bust by Houdon, has nothing of the 'hideous' quality that Musset was horrified to see 'fluttering' on the thin lips of old Arouet; it is that of a man who has groped his way to what he considered truth, who has experienced much anxiety and whose heart-rending sincerity reminds us a little of St Augustine.

He was more than once condemned to a wandering life by his unstable temperament or by his often churlish want of manners, not to mention the hostility of numerous enemies; yet the work he produced during those periods seems wonderfully optimistic. He saw man as naturally good. Despite appearances, there dwelt in man untainted reserves of fairness, generosity and godliness; society alone was responsible for his violence, falsehood and cruelty. One had only to establish the primacy of freedom in every sphere, to restore men to their natural equality, and all would again be well; paradise on earth was within our reach—a paradise, that is to say, governed by conscience, the reign of the heart. Liberty and equality were more than dear to Rousseau's heart, and such were the themes which he expounded in various literary forms upon a wide range of subjects. He had a gift of being able to communicate 'that movement which proceeds from the warmness of a heart for ever in ferment' and to rouse the souls of men with his sonorous style. A sensitive novelist in *La Nouvelle Héloïse* (1761), a political theorist in *Le Contrat social* (1762) and an educationist in *Émile* (1762), he was a less prolific but more profound author than Voltaire.

Religion had its place in his system of the world and of man. He spoke of it at length in Book IV of *Émile*, in a passage that was to become famous under the title 'Profession de foi d'un vicaire savoyard'; but the problem haunted him so deeply that he returned to it on many occasions. His attitude was nothing like that of Voltaire and the 'philosophers'; it was in fact so radically different as to cause bitter antagonism. He entertained no basic hostility towards Christianity, no desire to 'crush the infamous one'. On the contrary, his pages are embellished with words that a Christian can still read with pleasure. 'The sanctity of the Gospel is an argument that appeals to my heart . . . ; just to think upon it is to be convinced of its author's love and to feel drawn to obey His precepts. . . . The life and death of Jesus are those of a god.'

Concerning revelation he said: 'My heart inclines me to it; it is altogether consoling.' In reply to Voltaire, who had seized upon the disaster resulting from the Lisbon earthquake (1755) as yet another argument against the 'good God' who allowed such things to happen, Rousseau extolled Providence and its inscrutable ways as the most perfect Christian might have done. Though suspicious of all authority, he generally refrained from attacking the Church and her hierarchy, shunning the anti-clericalism of Diderot, d'Alembert and Voltaire. So frequently, in fact, did he emphasize the importance of religion, the 'interior instinct' which urged man to believe, the 'song which lulls our sadness, our hopes and our dreams', that many of his contemporaries considered him as a sort of lay theologian; even certain priests looked upon him as in some sense an apologist whose voice might serve their cause, and in our own day he has been described as one of the 'upholders of Catholicism'.[49]

It was, moreover, as an advocate of Christian beliefs that Jean-Jacques was regarded by the philosophers. Voltaire, their leader, created for the benefit of this hated enemy a whole litany of epithets, among which 'gloomy fanatic, travelling ape, charlatan and uncivilized baboon' were the least uncomplimentary. Standing aside from that odious gang, and refusing further collaboration with the Encyclopaedists, for whom he had written a few harmless articles on music, Jean-Jacques appeared to them not only as a champion of God, which might have been excusable, but also as an ally of 'the infamous'; worse still, as a contemner of the idols (Reason and Progress) which the antichristian clique had determined to set up. It is beyond doubt that many of the grievous sufferings to which Rousseau was subjected in his old age originated in the watchful hatred of those nonconformists who, in order to destroy their adversary, went so far as to involve him with the police.[50] If friendship meant having the same enemies, Rousseau would certainly have to be placed in the Christian camp.

The facts, however, are not quite so simple. Torn between the Calvinism of his birthplace, Geneva, and a superficial Catholicism grafted on to him by a too hasty conversion, Jean-Jacques reached maturity with an altogether personal attitude towards religion. His views show marked traces of Protestantism—belief in the right to free examination and in the infallible recourse to conscience; but they are characterized no less by a quietistic brand of Catholicism, in which self-surrender to God and total reliance upon feeling rendered moral effort useless. His attitude at all events was far removed from the true faith. The famous opening of the *Confessions*, where he calls on the 'Eternal Being' to compare him with other men no less in his misery than on those occasions when he was 'good, generous and sublime', is sufficient evidence of Jean-Jacques's pride. He believed himself the prophet of a new religion, the only pure and true religion, which alone fulfilled the purposes of Christ.

As for that religion itself, or, more generally, the system of thought in which it was contained, one is obliged to recognize it as substantially and fundamentally antichristian. If the cornerstone of Christianity is indeed the Redemption, what becomes of it in a setting where original sin is unacceptable and absurd since Nature is perfectly good in itself? What is left of Revelation in an edifice whose only builder is Conscience, 'infallible judge of good and evil, which renders man like unto God'? What remains of truth itself, which is of course among the attributes of God, once it is admitted that religion may be 'an illusion perhaps, but a consoling illusion'? Though in a manner different from Voltaire and the atheists of the Encyclopaedia, Rousseau placed man at the centre of the world, substituted the sensible for the supernatural, and made grace yield pride of place to feeling, and was abused as a champion of the true faith by the philosophers, his former friends. In a manner likewise different from theirs he was equally harmful.

His influence penetrated deeply; even during his lifetime he had fanatical admirers. After his death he became the object of a veritable cult, and pilgrimages were made to his tomb at Ermenonville. *La Nouvelle Héloïse* was the breviary of sensitive hearts. *Le Contrat social*, as yet unfamiliar to the general public, was read eagerly by a few ardent spirits who before long would hew from it the foundations of a new regime. The ideas of liberty and equality spread in proportion to the increasing numbers of his readers throughout Europe. The Revolution made him one of its gods and laid his ashes in the Panthéon, side by side with those of his enemy Voltaire; but it hardly supported the theories of Jean-Jacques on the natural goodness of man. As for his religious doctrines, they had their hour of glory in the spring of 1794, when Maximilien de Robespierre ordered the celebration of a festival in honour of the Supreme Being. They were destined thereafter, through the medium of romanticism, to nourish a stream of naturalism, of sensualism and even of modernism, whose traces are still visible in our own society.

15. DEISM IN ENGLAND

There are striking differences between such leaders of the 'philosophical' school as Voltaire, the Encyclopaedists and Rousseau. But that diversity is still more marked if we leave France and consider other lands where the movement had representatives.

England did not experience the fierce ideological conflicts of which the clash between the philosophers and Jean-Jacques is one example. Advanced thinkers all stood within the framework of Deism, of which indeed the United Kingdom has been regarded as the cradle. The religious climate of the country in the seventeenth century is sufficient explanation of that birth. Authoritarian measures had been employed without effect in an endeavour to stop the violent discord between Anglicanism and the Protestant sects. The Thirty-nine Articles had failed to impose a single orthodoxy, and the Puritan dictatorship of Cromwell had earned detestation. In fact, the English reformers were agreed upon one point only—hatred of Catholicism. Might not a natural religion, without creed or dogmas, find universal favour? Even some bishops of the Established Church thought so. A sort of latent latitudinarianism gradually took root in many minds,[51] and Deism was the result.

It arose early in the seventeenth century, when Francis Bacon was preaching his sensualist rationalism which left little or no room for theology. Lord Herbert of Cherbury (1583–1648), British ambassador at Paris and an amateur theologian, gave it fresh impetus in 1626 by explaining in his trea-

tise *De Veritate* that the supernatural was an absurdity and
that religion should be based on reason. He was an avid reader
of Sozzini. The pace was accelerated by Thomas Hobbes
(1588–1679), whose *Leviathan* (1654), in order to
strengthen the extremist doctrine of the Church's absolute
submission to the State, used powerful arguments to demonstrate that so-called revealed religion was nothing but a
priestly imposture and the Bible a collection of fables. That
book was a great favourite of Charles II. John Locke (1632–
1704) devoted himself less to the work of demolition than to
a constructive effort in his *Reasonable Christianity* (1695),
the first attempt to systematize Deism.

Meanwhile, however, other elements had become blended
with the idea of religion without dogma. In England, as in
France, men were infatuated with the progress of science; no
less a person than the Duke of Buckingham practised chemistry and physics. Cartesianism arrived from France, and from
Holland (with King William) the books and notions of Pierre
Bayle. All these streams flowed into the river of Deism; there
remained the vague belief in a God utterly remote from men,
demanding no worship and imposing no dogmas, but within
that framework each thought and expressed himself according to his temperament.

There were thus several forms of Deism, as numerous and
varied as there were individuals. There was the aggressive Deism of John Toland (1670–1722), a wild Irishman who passed
from Catholicism to Presbyterianism and thence to natural
religion; he was a zealous hunter of priests, a sworn enemy
of the Bible (especially of Moses, his *bête noire*) and a tireless discoverer of natural causes to explain away miracles.
There was the legalistic Deism of Collins, to whom the terms
'freethinking' and 'freethinkers', invented by Toland, owed
their long and widespread survival. There was the aristocratic
and highly sceptical Deism first of Lord Shaftesbury, who riddled with the arrows of his good humour the pious French
Calvinist refugees in London, and secondly of the contemptuous Lord Bolingbroke, who confided to his friends that in
his view religion was merely 'an instrument of government, a
politic means of keeping the masses in order', and who did
not hesitate on some occasions to ridicule natural religion like

the rest. Finally there was the pulpit Deism of Matthew Tyndale (1657–1733), who demonstrated with great learning that Christianity is as old as the world, that it is simply one expression among others of the clear, intelligible and perfect law given by God to man.

As the eighteenth century proceeded, English philosophers tended to draw nearer to their French colleagues, with whom they were in frequent correspondence. Mutual influence resulted, not all of which was favourable to natural religion or even to the Supreme Being. David Hume (1711–76), though claiming to be a Deist, caused much astonishment by maintaining, against the older Deists, that polytheism had preceded monotheism, that the Jewish Jehovah was not the one and only God, but a national deity, and that in any case the oneness of God was no more than a theory born of reason. Scepticism was gaining ground; it appeared without disguise in the scholarly but icy volumes of Gibbon (1737–94), in the philosophy of progress taught by Priestley (1733–1804) and his disciple Price. In 1765 Diderot wrote to Sophie Voland: 'The Christian religion is almost extinct in England. The Deists there are almost innumerable. There are almost no atheists; those who are so conceal the fact.' That last statement would be much less true twenty years later.

16. GERMANY: FROM THE 'ENLIGHTENMENT' TO KANT

In Germany the trend of ideas was somewhat different from its counterparts in France and England. Keen translators as they were of Locke and Tyndale, Voltaire and Rousseau, German thinkers, with the sole exception of Leibniz, often give an impression of being mere followers of foreign teachers. But the emphasis was so different that one can almost speak of an original school. To the French and English elements there were added others specifically German: the biblical tradition of Luther's homeland, a characteristically Germanic sense of nature, an equally Germanic love of the solid and practical; in short, what Dufourq calls 'that kind of residue of ideas and feelings which, like corpses on a battlefield, litter the soil of churches from which faith has fled'. Moreover the intellectual movement in Germany took place first and foremost among the professional class; the pompous Herr Doktor played the part filled elsewhere by writers, journalists and sceptical aristocrats. No German in the eighteenth century employed the sarcasm, or introduced into debate the flippant mockery of Voltaire, Diderot and Bolingbroke; everything proceeded with the utmost doctoral gravity.

The origin of the movement was clearly Cartesian. In the land of free inquiry Descartes was applauded by many when he declared that faith and reason rule in two different domains, but are both gifts of God and so cannot conflict. His disciple Leibniz (1646–1716), a profound thinker and a believer too, dreamed of giving religion a leading place in the organization of the world; in his *Meditations on Knowledge* and *New System of Nature* he sought to build a philosophy in which, 'starting with clear definitions, sure conclusions were derived from sure principles'. He came up against the apparent opposition of certain Christian dogmas to reason, and in order to get rid of it he maintained that 'if the objections of reason to any article of faith are insoluble one must conclude that the alleged article of faith is false and not revealed'. That was an easy way of jettisoning the theology of revelation, the mysteries and the whole supernatural order; it opened the door to rationalism.

Thus began the movement known as *Aufklärung*, the movement which 'enlightens'.[52] Enlightens what? The human intellect. *Was ist Aufklärung?* asked Kant, and he found it to be a process whereby the mind and conscience are liberated, an effort on the part of man to dare at last to make use of his reason. In every domain, even that of religion, he declared (though St Thomas Aquinas would not have agreed), reason is proscribed by theology. The self-appointed task of the *Aufklärung* was to place religion beneath the powerful ray of reason and dispel the shadows. The end was *Eine Vernünftige Erkentniss Gottes*, a rational knowledge of God.

In the land of the Wartburg, the principal battlefield was naturally the Bible. The *Aufklärung* quickly turned to biblical rationalism; its precursors were Hermann von der Hardt, professor of exegesis at Helmstadt, and Christian Thomasius of Leipzig University. The former explained the Old Testament by the tendency of Orientals to invent myths. Cain and Abel, he said, were two symbolic persons representing two hostile armies, the Deluge a symbolic account of a Scythian invasion. Thomasius undertook to demonstrate the inanity of all traditions concerning the sacred books. Spinoza was not far away.

The movement hardened with Christian Wolff (1679–1754), rector of the University of Halle. None could have been more solemn than this pedagogue with his impressive wig and high cravat. A scientist and philosopher of vast ambition, who dreamed of embodying the whole of thought in a triparite system, he set out to demonstrate religious truths (including mysteries and miracles) like so many theorems, a task which he began in 1728 with the publication of his ponderous *Philosophical Thoughts on God, the World, and the Human Soul.* It must not, he said, be thought that the intellect and conscience lack a 'sufficient reason' for assent; natural religion alone is logical and demonstrable, and from it therefore one must derive revelation. His book caused a great sensation, so much so that the Lutheran pastors took fright and explained to Frederick William I of Prussia that Wolffian rationalism carried to its extreme would persuade his grenadiers to desert on the battlefield, since the instinct of self-preservation was a 'sufficient reason' for flight; upon which the sergeant-king had the professor driven from his dominions.

This, however, did not prevent others from following in Wolff's footsteps. Baumgarten applied his method to speculative theology and ecclesiastical history, Eberhard to a demonstration of the superiority of Socrates over the Bible, Weltstein and Semler to a critical study of the canons of Scripture. Old beliefs were cast aside one by one until about 1790 the *Aufklärung* left very little substance in Christianity; a natural religion, a purely human doctrine, a form of rationalism that dared not avow itself irreligious, were all that remained.

The reign of Frederick II of Prussia (1740–86) marked the triumph of the *Aufklärung*. He was friendly towards the philosophers, and one of the first things he did after ascending the throne was to restore Christian Wolff to his chair at Halle. He felt it his duty as an 'enlightened despot' to help those whose task it was to enlighten the minds of men plunged in

the darkness of superstition; and so the party of enlightenment was encouraged in every possible way. A subsidy was
conferred on Lorenz Schmidt, who had just produced an edition of the Bible with rationalistic commentary. Cristof Nico-
lai, the German Diderot, deluged educated circles with the
106 volumes of his *Deutsche Allgemeine Bibliothek*. The
Saxon Edelmann, author of a ponderous treatise on 'the divinity of reason', issued a series of pamphlets which were professedly frivolous and bore such titles as *Simple Truths,
Moses Unveiled, Christ and Belial*. More serious exegetes
joined in the fun: Ernesti, a professor at Leipzig who resurrected the ideas of Richard Simon and gave them a rationalistic turn; Michaelis, professor of oriental languages at Göt-
tingen, who set out with determination to prove that Moses,
so far from being a man inspired by God, was simply an able
and cunning statesman. Reimarus (1694–1768), another professor of oriental languages, went further than them all; he
taught his pupils at Hamburg that Moses and Christ were a
couple of impostors, and that the kingdom of God conceived
by Jesus would have been established on earth by a revolution
during the Paschal feast, had not the Sanhedrin, alerted by
loyal Judas, intervened in the nick of time. Nevertheless Herr
Doktor Reimarus was careful to publish nothing in his lifetime.

The apogee of the *Aufklärung* was reached with the editor
of Reimarus's posthumous works, his friend Gotthold Efraim
Lessing (1729–81), son of a pastor and a man of truly ecclesiastical solemnity. A declared enemy of Voltaire, whose
secretary he had been for some while at Berlin, he proposed
to defend Christianity—an important matter if ever there
was one—against all the jesters and horrible atheists who were
assailing her from within and from without. More generally,
his purpose was none other than the *Education of Humanity*,
as he entitled a work published in 1780. A good writer, a poet
and dramatist as well as a philosopher and theologian, he
posed as the torch-bearer of the school of enlightenment, skilfully popularizing its ideas but adding masonic theories which
he had received from England, together with some notions of
his own that were destined to a glorious future. Among these
latter was the absolute equality of three great religions—Juda-

ism, Christianity and Islam—which should respect and support one another; the existence of an 'eternal Gospel'[53] wherein all could find harmony; the identity of revelation with 'the progressive education of mankind under God's direction';[54] and lastly the reduction of the Christian religion to an interior and moral activity which heralded the liberal Protestantism of the nineteenth century. Lessing's influence was considerable; it can be observed in the great historical writings of Herder no less than in the works of Goethe and Schiller, the two most illustrious German poets. One may, nevertheless, doubt whether it profited Christianity.

For indeed the *Aufklärung*, despite all it had to say about religion, ended by destroying the very foundations thereof. Once the rays of enlightenment had scoured humanity, what was left of revelation, of belief in a personal God, in the infallibility of Scripture or in the authority of Holy Church? German Protestantism was more seriously undermined by Lessing than was French Catholicism by the philosophers or Anglicanism by the Deists.[55]

A reaction, however, took place in the very camp of free-thinking. It was not unlike that of Rousseau, although it employed altogether different means. Moreover the genius who began it was an avid reader of Jean-Jacques, who, he used to say, had opened his eyes to truth. This was Immanuel Kant (1724–1804), professor at Königsberg. Being a rationalist and wishing to build his philosophy on the firmest possible foundation, he wrote two books, *The Critique of Pure Reason* (1781) and *The Critique of Practical Reason* (1787), which together formed an important study of the instrument he would use to establish the truth. He concluded that all our knowledge is subjective, that it has no reality except in the idea which we fashion from it for ourselves. Kantian idealism tended to base all human activity on the 'categorical imperative' of conscience, which bids us do good. But since that imperative itself must be securely based, the great philosopher had recourse to truths transcending human reason, the existence of God and the immortality of the soul; in every man, he says, the notion of duty is the expression of the divine will, the promise of eternity. Kant did not refuse to give Christianity a place in his system, regarding it indeed as one of the most beautiful forms ever assumed by natural religion; but Christianity, so far as he was concerned, was a purely moral affair, without churches or dogmas. 'There are two things I cannot contemplate without emotion,' he said, 'the starry sky above me and the moral law within me'—which was hardly strong enough to support a body of dogma. Though Kant was unaffected by the *Aufklärung*, and even opposed its over-simplified rationalism with rational scepticism, his work tended none the less to destroy faith in general and transcendent truths, since those truths were true only for those who fashioned them. His subjectivism lost the religious experience in a haze of good intentions and of beliefs that were, after all, irrational. The facts were summed up by Péguy in one of his astonishing and characteristic formulas: 'Kantianism has clean hands, but it has no hands.'

17. THE ROLE OF FREEMASONRY

The philosophers followed different paths that diverged at many points. Nevertheless they formed a kind of friendly society within which they maintained constant intercourse, exchanging visits and carrying on a vast correspondence that was sometimes acrimonious, as in the case of Rousseau's with Voltaire and Hume. There was thus a plentiful and fruitful encounter of ideas. Europe was the home of great minds determined to be 'free'; its customary language was French, whose universality was extolled by Rivard, and it witnessed the emergence of a common attitude of mind, resolutely 'modern' and expressing the 'philosophical' spirit. All are agreed that this mode of thought was mainly responsible for the revolutionary crisis, and that its influence is discernible in the political and religious demeanour of those who were later its protagonists; Mirabeau, Roland, Danton, Saint-Just, Robespierre and their like were unquestionably disciples of the philosophers. Time can show few such examples of the part played by the intellect in the march of history.

It may be asked whether one should go further and concede that all the destructive labour accomplished by the philosophers followed a concerted plan; whether there was a single director inspiring and co-ordinating, whether in fact they were employed by secret forces whose purpose was to overthrow the altar and the throne. At first sight this view seems highly improbable; the logical evolution of ideas since the Renaissance suffices to explain Voltaire, Diderot and the rest. But the hypothesis of a grand conspiracy is as old as the eighteenth century itself. Returning in 1782 from a congress at Wilhelmsbart, where the 'enlightened' freemasons had scored a victory over those of the 'strict observance', Henry de Virieu replied to a friend who asked him what secrets he had brought back: 'The whole business is more serious than you think. The plot has been so carefully hatched that it is practically impossible for the Church and the Monarchy to escape.' In 1827, after the turmoil was over, a similar conviction was expressed by Schlegel, professor of history at Vienna: 'One wonders whether those events were not prepared beforehand and in secret.' Meanwhile, in 1797, Father Barruel, S.J., a refugee in London and one of the most experienced anti-philosophical apologists, had published his *Mémoires pour servir à l'histoire du Jacobinisme,* in which he named freemasonry as ringleader of the infernal game, as the power that had 'foreseen, planned, organized, decided and decreed' it all, even the most terrible crimes.[56]

Freemasonry. There is perhaps no chapter of history that has been the subject of so much controversy, a controversy in which desire to establish the truth has often been less prominent than emotion. Too many writers are prejudiced for or against freemasons, and have argued accordingly. More unfortunately, they endow their concept of freemasonry in the eighteenth century with characteristics that belong rather to the attack it launched against the Church during the nineteenth and twentieth. Finally, in the dispute as to whether it was freemasonry that secretly directed the great rebellion against God and the Church, four attitudes have been adopted. Some say yes, freemasonry was at the centre of the conspiracy. No, say others, because there was never any such conspiracy. A third group answers in the affirmative, holding that while there was no actual masonic conspiracy freemasonry was cleverly used by those who sought to overthrow Christian society. The fourth and last group think that freemasonry was but one agent among many, and not the ring-leader at that; they maintain that it helped, sometimes un-wittingly, to prepare the way for the antichristian revolution.

Now as to the origin of freemasonry. Some of its legendary traditions trace it back to King Hiram's workmen who built Solomon's Temple at Jerusalem; even to Noah, shipwright of the ark of salvation; even again to Adam, the first of archi-tects if ever there was! In fact it derives from the journeymen builders who in the eleventh and twelfth centuries travelled from city to city, from site to site, in return for which popes and princes granted them certain privileges. At that period and until the sixteenth century it was a religious corporation whose members bound themselves to be 'faithful to God and the Church'. Virtually inactive everywhere, it took a new lease of life in England after the Great Fire of London in 1666, when the city had to be rebuilt. At that juncture the struggle between Protestants and Catholics reached its culmi-nation; a majority of the powerful corporation of freemasons sided with William of Orange while the minority upheld Stuart claims. Then it was that a number of peers and wealthy merchants joined the group as honorary members, and the character of freemasonry was rapidly transformed. Corpora-tive organization in the shape of 'lodges' remained; so did the various categories of apprentices, companions and mas-ters, not to mention the insignia of set-square, level, trowel and apron. But the lodges became more or less 'philosophical' bodies of initiates. In 1721 Anderson, a former Presbyterian, drew up a rule, and the lodges, though not without difficulty, were together formed into the Grand Lodge, under the presi-dency of such great noblemen as the Dukes of Montagu and Richmond. Freemasonry spread very quickly to the Conti-nent, and by about 1730 there were lodges at Ghent, Madrid, Florence, Hamburg and elsewhere.

The first lodge in France was one called Au Louis d'Argent, founded at Paris in 1732 by associates of English freema-sonry. It was followed before long by that of Saint Thomas, established by some officers with Stuart sympathies, and there-fore attached to Scottish freemasonry. Since the rules of ad-mission and conduct were as yet indeterminate, the two movements developed side by side, with a clearly marked tendency to erect lodges that were nothing more than groups of men who enjoyed good living. Michael Ramsay, a Scot who had once been converted by Fénelon but had subsequently embraced Deism, set about their reorganization. In 1773, after much effort on the part of such high dignitaries as d'Antin, Choiseul and Montmorency, some unity of discipline was attained (theoretically at any rate) with the formation of a national Grand Lodge independent of its English counterpart. It was controlled by a Venerable Assembly known as the Grand Orient, and its Grand Master was Louis-Philippe d'Orléans, Duc de Chartres, a cousin of Louis XVI.

The success of the movement was remarkable, as is shown by the presence of such personages at its head. The number of French freemasons was not above thirty thousand at the most, recruited from among the rich, the ruling classes and 'enlightened' circles. But in spite of their relatively small aggregate they exercised an undeniable attraction. The secrecy with which they surrounded their recruitment and the symbolism of their rites was partly responsible; but there was also the lure of a certain philosophical ideal, a certain spiritual aspiration and even a degree of mysticism. These features were not peculiar to freemasonry. Other movements which later joined forces with it claimed to offer refuge to souls who desired contact with the world of mystery and could no longer find it in religion. Among these were the Rosicrucians, who originated in the seventeenth century with the novels of Andreae; John Toland's 'Socratics'; and Weishaupt's 'Illuminati' at Ingolstadt in Germany, who dreamed of 'liberating the world' by founding an Order no less strict than the Society of Jesus.[57]

Freemasonry became the rallying point of all sorts of muddled tendencies (good and bad), Utopias and intrigues. Was it at that time antichristian? The question has been debated for more than two hundred years. One fact is inescapable: the lodges contained a large number of ecclesiastics who, moreover, enjoyed the privilege of admission without inquiry as to their respectability, since 'their profession guaranteed their character'. At Caudebec fifteen out of eighty members of the lodge were priests; at Sens, twenty out of fifty. Canons and parish priests sat in the Venerable Assembly, while the

Cistercians of Clairvaux had a lodge within the very walls of their monastery! Saurine, a future bishop of Strasbourg under Napoleon, was among the governing members of the Grand Orient. We cannot be far from the truth in suggesting that towards the year 1789 a quarter of French freemasons were churchmen; and there is no reason to think that all were, or considered themselves to be, bad Catholics. On the contrary, there must have been a great many of them who saw no incompatibility between their faith and their masonic membership, and who even regarded freemasonry as a weapon to be employed in the service of religion. One of these, in Savoy, was Joseph de Maistre, orator of his lodge at Chambéry; he dreamed of creating within the bosom of masonry a secret staff which would have made the movement a papal army at the service of universal theocracy.

It was not long, however, before the Church took the offensive against freemasonry. The Jesuits were the first to feel uneasy about this secret society, over which the Church had no control, and to forbid their members to join it. Prompted by them, the secular authority itself became hostile from time to time. Some bishops gave public approval to the action of parish priests who refused the sacrament or burial in consecrated ground to notorious freemasons, though it is true that others scorned such measures, regarding the freemasons as quite harmless. In 1738 freemasonry was condemned outright by Clement XII's Bull *In eminenti*, and thirteen years later the Bull *Providas Romanorum* of Benedict XIV renewed the interdictions of his predecessor. As things turned out, this condemnation proved almost ineffective. The French Gallicans took steps to prevent publication of the Bulls in France; there has not been found in the archives of the lodges a single letter of resignation from a priest consequent upon the attitude adopted by Rome. Repressive measures were confined to Ireland, the Sovereign Order of the Knights of Malta and some parts of Italy. But in Rome the masons continued to meet 'almost without concealment', as one of them said; which goes to show not only that the Sovereign Pontiff's authority had been greatly reduced, but also that public opinion and that of the masons themselves did not regard the movement as antichristian.

Was it, in fact, inimical to Christianity? Strictly speaking, no—at any rate not to any great extent. It is very rare that one finds in masonic documents of the eighteenth century, apart from those of German Illuminism, a violent attack upon the priesthood or dogmas of Holy Church. On the contrary, one comes across many pious declarations which reveal a strong attachment to the Mass as well as to Our Lady and the saints. It has even been held[58] that 'so far from being opposed to religion, freemasonry in the eighteenth century was crypto-religious; that it resurrected supposedly dead beliefs in God, in life after death and in prayer; and that it prepared the ground for a revival of faith'. But to talk like that is simply to play with words, for a closer look at masonic 'religion' shows that it had nothing whatever to do with dogma or with an established order. The rules drawn up by Anderson in the early days are quite explicit on this point: 'Each mason may retain his personal beliefs, provided always he observes the precepts of that religion upon which all men are agreed and which enjoin him to be good, sincere, modest and honourable, no matter to what religious denomination he may belong.'

Masonic 'religion', then, is clearly *natural* religion, purged of the dogmas, rites and symbols of Christianity. Based on a form of Deism which recognizes the existence of a 'Great Architect', it allows Him no right of intervention in the spiritual and moral life, and identifies His activity with that of reason. It is therefore fundamentally the doctrine of the philosophers. Consequently the Church, in condemning freemasonry, was not only within her rights but was also fulfilling a duty.

All this, however, is scarcely proof that freemasonry led the antichristian movement. The presence of so many faithful Catholics in its fold prevents us from believing that it could have played such a part. We cannot, on the other hand, deny that the most active elements of the philosophical party found their way into the lodges. The Nine Sisters at Paris was a meeting place of the most distinguished and advanced intellectuals. These included Condorcet, Lacépède, Parny, Greuze, Houdon and Voltaire, the last of whom made his entry, arm in arm with Franklin and amid loud acclamation, on 7th August 1778. It is difficult to say how far these philosopher-masons inclined the whole movement towards irreligion. Most freemasons were probably unaware of the real aims of their most active brothers, either in religion or, of course, in the field of politics where the great majority never dreamed of fostering a revolution. One thing is quite certain: being a centralized organization with branches throughout France, and indeed throughout Europe, freemasonry did a great deal to propagate the new ideas. History provides little or no evidence of a conspiracy; if such there was, it can have counted for very little in comparison with the demiurgic forces that came into play with the French Revolution. The 'masonic conspiracy' must be ranked with the 'Jesuit conspiracy', whose spectre is raised from time to time. There is, however, no denying that freemasonry, notwithstanding some of its tendencies and some of its members, was among the agents of the antichristian crisis, one of the actors in the great rebellion.[59]

18. THE CHRISTIAN COUNTER-ATTACK

The anti-religious offensive, whose principal aspects we have been studying, was both incessant and formidable during the eighteenth century. But while there is every reason to believe that it gained ground, it must not be supposed that the Church was indifferent and did nothing to oppose the insidious undermining of her walls. Though literary and historical textbooks have much less to say about them than about their adversaries, there were throughout the eighteenth century many writers, thinkers and theologians who directed counter-attacks against the swelling hosts of irreligion. An attempt has been made[60] to compile, with reference to France alone, a list of these works written in defence of Christianity. Including those of Protestant as well as of Catholic authorship, they numbered almost a thousand between 1700 and the Revolution. It has even been possible[61] to draw a graph of their publication and thereby to show that whenever a major work of the philosophers appeared in the shops it was followed by a host of books and pamphlets in-

tended to neutralize its effects. 'Never', says Hazard, 'were
so many works published against religion, but never were so
many published in its defence.' One might take each of the
great names among the philosophers and draw up a list of
adversaries devoted to refuting him. Thus Voltaire, Rousseau, Helvetius and the Encyclopaedists had watchful enemies who did not fail to score points against them. But those
brave spirits would be now almost forgotten but for the epigrams with which Voltaire overwhelmed them; e.g. Lefranc de
Pompignan, whose memory survives in the celebrated qua-
train:

> *'Savez-vous pourquoi Jérémie*
> *A tant pleuré durant sa vie?*
> *C'est qu'en prophète il prévoyait*
> *Que Pompignan le traduirait.'*

> ['*Do you know why Jeremiah*
> *Wept so much during his life?*
> *It was because, as a prophet, he foresaw*
> *that Pompignan would interpret him.'*]

The defensive literature of Christianity varied a great deal
in style. Much of it belonged to the domain of polemics,
positive or negative. Against Bayle and Rousseau, for example, Mgr de Partz de Pussy, Bishop of Boulogne, erected
ramparts of quarto; against the patriarch of Ferney, Father
Nonotte fired a broadside of five fat volumes entitled *Les
Erreurs de Voltaire*. Episcopal letters also played a part in
the battle, among them the famous document in which Mgr
de Beaumont, Archbishop of Paris, drew an uncomplimentary though not inaccurate portrait of Jean-Jacques. Father
Berthier, writing in the Jesuit *Journal de Trévoux*, conducted
so lively a campaign that Voltaire was obliged to attempt
his discomfiture by means of a lampoon. The Abbé Guéné,
serene and meticulous, delighted the public by showing up
the ignorance and incompetence of those who disparaged the
Bible. Among preachers who came to grips with the philosophers were the Abbé Maury, a future cardinal; Father Beaure-
gard, whom Voltaire described as a 'monster'; the Abbé Clément, whom he nicknamed 'the Inclement'. Others were
unfortunately inclined to mingle insult with argument. In the

Académie Française itself an attack was launched upon the philosophers by Lefranc de Pompignan, who had been elected in 1759.

The Christian counter-attack, however, seems to have lacked drive. As the Abbé Clément admitted: 'We don't know how to answer this subtle raillery and clever satire.' Nevertheless there were a number of Catholic laymen who undertook to fight the philosophers with their own weapons, particularly that of irony, and they achieved no inconsiderable measure of success. The first was Nicolas Moreau, a barrister of the Parlement de Paris; drawing inspiration from Swift and Voltaire, he wrote in satirical vein about an imaginary people whom he called Cacouacs. Who were these folk? Redskins, cannibals? Indeed no. 'The Cacouacs are not savages; they are highly intelligent, extremely polite, immensely learned, and skilled above all else in the art of magic. According to themselves they are descended from the Titans, who wished to scale the heavens. But, as children know better than their fathers, the Cacouacs now maintain that their ancestors were visionaries guilty of the utmost folly, not in desiring to fight against the gods but in believing that there was such things as gods.' It was not a bad idea, and the word was soon on everybody's lips. One after another there were published *Mémoires pour servir à l'histoire des Cacouacs Catéchisme à l'usage des Cacouacs, Discours du patriarche des Cacouacs pour la réception d'un nouveau disciple*, and many other booklets in which, it must be confessed, wit did not always shine. Next the Cacouacs were actually brought upon the stage of the Théâtre Français by Charles Palissot, whose comedy, *Les Philosophes*, delighted the groundlings. Its pseudonyms were transparent and its dialogue amusing. The highlight of the play was the entry of a character (obviously Jean-Jacques) walking on all fours and munching a lettuce as a sign that man must return to nature. The most virulent adversary of all Cacouacs and all *cacouacerie* was Fréron, a dour Breton, quietly spoken but a man of ferocious sarcasm. His *Année littéraire* flayed the whole tribe of philosophers, especially Voltaire, who took revenge by representing his critic on the stage as Frelon, a man of shameful habits, and

by causing the government to have the offending document
seized by the police.

But none of these engagements was really effective; such
parries achieved very little against the repeated thrusts of
Voltaire's biting sarcasm. The best way of replying to the
philosophers, as some people realized, would have been to
expound the essentials of Christianity—dogma and tradition
—ignoring whatever laid itself open to attack. Thus in 1750
Mgr FitzJames wrote: 'One must think seriously of reviving
theological studies and of training priests who will be able
to defend religion. The Christian religion is so beautiful that
I do not think it possible to know it without loving it; those
who blaspheme it do so merely because they do not understand it. If we could produce men like Bossuet, Pascal, Nicole
and Fénelon, the mere consideration of their teaching and
their characters would do more good than a thousand answers.' That was a sound idea and very well expressed.

How far were these wise counsels put into practice? Christianity had no lack of apologists, some of whom, e.g. Father
Lombard and the Abbé Pluche, obtained a hearing;[62] but
their methods are questionable, to say the least. Was it right
to base the truth of Christianity entirely on miracles, as was
done by Father Buffior in 1732 and by Father Merlin ten
years later? What validity can one assign to the reasoning of
Saint-Réal, the learned historian of the court of Savoy in
the seventeenth century, whose theological works were published forty years after his death? Who was likely to be convinced by the arguments of Father Touron, according to
whom the very least historical event was the direct result of
divine intervention? Father Guéné's *Méthode courte pour
discerner la véritable religion* and the nine large volumes of
Pluche's *Spectacle de la nature* avoided many of these ec-
centricities, but are none the less monstrous and irksome,
while Bergier's *Certitudes des preuves de la religion chrétienne*, though more readable, is doctrinally unsound.

That, however, was by no means the end of the story. The
constructive effort begun during the seventeenth century was
not abandoned. Biblical studies, impeded by the outcry that
greeted Richard Simon's works, petered out in the waste

lands of Dom Calmet's mediocre commentaries. But the Bollandists and Maurists continued their own useful labours; and the *Dictionnaire universel des sciences ecclésiastiques* by Louis Richard, a Dominican who employed the methods of the Encyclopaedia in a Christian setting, did much good.

Study of these numerous publications shows that many men were wide awake to the necessity of adapting the truths of religion to the needs of the age. They were to be found even in the most traditionalist circles. Among them was Dupréaux, author of *Chrétien parfait honnête homme*; and Mgr Lefranc de Pompignan, Bishop of Vienne, brother of the writer and himself the author of *Dévotion réconcilié avec l'Esprit*, which also contains some intelligent observations on the theatre.

In all Catholic countries and even, as we shall see, in Protestant areas, a serious, deeply interesting but little known effort was made to improve the orthodox methods of defence by expressing contemporary problems in Christian terms. Paul Hazard has even detected an 'enlightened Christianity', a movement in progress throughout Europe, which tended to strip religion of all superfluities and to present a system so liberal in its doctrine that none would be able to charge it with obscurantism, so pure in its morality that none would be able to deny its practical worth. 'Not a compromise, but a firm assurance that the same values upon which European civilization had rested for eighteen hundred years were still and would always remain in force.' The principal representatives of this outlook were Feijoo y Montenegro (1676–1764), a sturdy and outspoken Spanish Benedictine who insisted that theology should not concern itself with matters belonging exclusively to the domain of science; the Portuguese Franciscan Luis Antonio Verney, a disciple of Bacon and Newton; the Neapolitan priest Genovesi, a true lover of Salerno wine and good living, who taught his students such adventurous theories that the Inquisition intervened; and the Polish Piarist Konarski, who prescribed for his pupils the works of Descartes, Gassendi, Malebranche, Locke and Genovesi. The movement was thus highly significant. In Germany there was even talk of a Catholic *Aufklärung* led by Wiest, Brandmeyer, Franz Berg, a distinguished patrologist, and

Rosshirt, one of the few who understood the message of Pascal.

Two men deserve special notice as having seen more clearly than others the road that apologetics would have to follow. One was the Savoyard Gerdil (1718–1802), a native of Samoëns and later cardinal. Fluent in several languages and a writer on many subjects, he was also a scholar of vast erudition; while showing up the weak points of contemporary philosophy he looked back to Malebranche and attempted, in his *Essai d'introduction théologique*, to expound a system that would not clash with science. The other was Jacques Emery (1732–1811), Superior-General of Saint-Sulpice. We shall find him on the eve of the Revolution working for the reform of the priesthood and the revival of mysticism, as we shall find him subsequently resisting the persecution during the Terror and helping to restore the Church under the Empire. He is in fact one of the richest and most attractive personalities of his age. Realizing that it was futile to cross swords with Voltaire, Diderot, D'Alembert and their like, he conceived the idea of opposing the negative sneers of the philosophers with the thought and example of other thinkers—other men of science whose authority was indisputable but who had declared themselves believers. An initial move in this direction was made by Emery in 1772 with *L'Esprit de Leibniz*. Leibniz, 'the German Plato', the man whose thoughts laid bare the world and its mysteries and who believed in God. The book proved so successful that it was followed by the same author's *Christianisme de Bacon* and *Pensées de Descartes*. Later still, Emery thought of publishing selections from Chateaubriand; and the evidence suggests that Chateaubriand himself entered the field of apologetics as a result of reading the learned Sulpician's anthologies.

These efforts to range science and philosophy on the side of faith were certainly interesting and pointed in the right direction. Not all of them, however, were free from danger, and it is easy to understand why the authorities expressed concern on more than one occasion. We have seen this happen in the case of Genovesi. Franz Berg's audacity was more disturbing; he taught that Our Lord's contemporaries, even after the Resurrection, did not believe that He was God. No less suspect were the Abbé Gabriel Gauchat's views on the problems of revelation, on the origins of man, on evolution and on the authority of Scripture. As for those of the Jesuit Berruyer—who asserted that Christ taught no dogmatic truths until after His Resurrection—they were quite simply erroneous.

Equally dangerous perhaps, though in a different way, was a tendency which made its appearance towards the middle of the century and was much akin to that deriving from Rousseau; it led to a form of apologetics that was based upon mere feeling when it was not downright sentimental. Father André's *Traité sur le beau*, which inspired Chateaubriand's *Génie du Christianisme*, is unexceptionable. But the same cannot be said of Father Fidèle's *Religion sensible au cœur*, of Lamourette's *Délices de la religion*, of the Abbé Gérard's *Égarements de la raison*, or of La Baume-Dedossat's sickening *Christiade*. On the eve of the Revolution Catholic apologetics had sunk to the ponderous ecclesiastical wit of Barruel, who pretended to refute Buffon, and to the banality of *La Nouvelle Philosophie à vau l'eau*, a dialogue in popular style between M. Bonsens, a citizen of Paris, the philosopher Toupet whose villainy was leading him to prison, and worthy Jérôme, a boatman of the Gros Caillou. That sort of thing led nowhere.

19. HOW FAR DID THE NEW IDEAS PENETRATE SOCIETY?

Catholic apologetics stood in sore need of first-rate men such as Mgr FitzJames had envisaged with admirable judgment and foresight. The fact that Holy Church had no one like Pascal, Bossuet or Fénelon to defend her against Voltaire, Diderot and Rousseau was undoubtedly her most serious defect in the Age of Enlightenment, and the principal cause of her eclipse. But that eclipse was not total. There remains one question of capital importance: What degree of influence was exerted by the new ideas and how deeply did they penetrate society and determine public opinion? It is advisable to mistrust the effect created by distance and the light of subsequent events, which together tend to enlarge the philosophers and enhance their importance. No one doubts their considerable achievement; but it would be a serious exaggeration to represent that achievement as infecting the whole of Europe and penetrating alike to every level of the population.

On the threshold of the eighteenth century, as we have already seen, advanced ideas, Libertinism and Rationalism were virtually confined to a few hundred (at the most to a few thousand) writers, nobles and prosperous commoners who prided themselves upon their superior intelligence. The situation was, of course, very different in 1789, when the teaching of the philosophers had a much larger audience; but this does not imply that such doctrine had become a universal creed. However widespread its diffusion may have been, it had limits. Books and news sheets were dear, costing by contemporary standards as much as from four to eight times as much as they do today. Nonconformist propaganda met with official prohibition and police intervention. The latter was often muddled and absurd; but, though scorned in high places, it managed to intimidate the rank and file. Above all, in order correctly to estimate the progress of irreligion, we must remember that despite so many crises, so many upheavals and so many shortcomings, Christianity, and particularly Catholicism in those regions where it still prevailed, rested upon foundations of faith, practice and tradition so ancient, so solid, that they could not be destroyed in so short a time.

In countries such as Spain and Italy, which had hardly been touched by the Protestant heresy, philosophism seems to have done very little damage; it was for the most part simply a reflection of the French and English movements. There were occasions when events might be taken to contradict that statement; but the decisions from which they proceeded were due to motives of policy. The Spanish prime minister Aranda, for example, introduced freemasonry into Spain simply as a buttress against the Jesuits and the secular clergy. The Inquisition continued with unrelenting zeal to burn heretical books. Philosophers in the Latin countries sometimes considered that their French teachers went too far. Thus Alessandro Verri, while resident at Paris in 1766, wrote to his brother that close acquaintance with the French philosophers was 'just too much' for him, and while passing through Geneva he refrained from going out of his way to pay his respects to Voltaire at Ferney. It is surprising to find how seldom the bishops of Italy, Spain and Portugal refer to the new ideas in their pastoral letters; that they felt no need to refute them is sufficient evidence that such ideas were not widespread among the majority of their people. It was only among the upper classes that irreligion made some progress; St Alphonsus Liguori observed it at Naples. As for the German *Aufklärung*, it was almost exclusively a movement of university professors and of a few princelings who patronized them; its influence on popular Catholicism was insignificant.

The spread and penetration of 'philosophical' ideas[63] in France show two clearly defined characteristics: they were progressive and they varied a good deal from one social stratum to another. Their progress was exactly parallel with that of the books which helped to spread them. Until about 1750 it was rather slow and cautious. After that date and the appearance of Voltaire's *Essai sur les mœurs*, Condillac's *Traité des sensations*, La Mettrie's *L'Homme machine* and the first volume of the Encyclopaedia there are increasing signs that the new ideas had begun to reach a larger audience: the writings of the philosophers find their way into many libraries; more and more prominence is given to reviews of them in the newspapers; private diaries and notebooks make frequent reference to them. From 1760 onwards the movement made rapid strides; it became, as the lawyer Barbier said, 'the consuming mania of the day', and the philosophical tide appeared to meet no opposition. The question remains, who shared that mania and how far did that tide reach?

Apart from literary circles, where, as we have seen, it varied in many respects, irreligion gained ground first and foremost among the higher nobility. Of that there is abundant evidence in the large number of debauched, sceptical and elegant aristocrats, as well as in a host of duchesses and marchionesses whose impiety served to excuse their immoral lives. These undesirables were so numerous that they justified

Argenson's famous and terrible words: 'The nobility is to the people of France what putrefaction is to fruit.' 'One took care', said one of them, 'not to be ridiculed as a believer in God.' When it was learned in the *salons* that the poet Grosset had just 'been converted', i.e. that he had returned to the practice of his religion, there were roars of laughter. 'Philosophy has no more generous patrons than the nobility,' wrote the Vicomtesse de Noailles. That, however, was not true of them all; many a great aristocrat is known to have preserved intact his loyalty to the faith.[64] The lesser nobility as a whole were even less tainted. But the leaders of society flaunted their loathing of religion; and their example was followed by the Bar, the Bench and the higher grades of the civil service, though here again not without exceptions. The farmers-general of the revenue were all, or nearly all, won over: Bergeret, Claude Dupin, Silhouette—the aristocracy of money. The lower middle classes were less deeply infected; Barbier's memoirs indeed give one the impression that they realized and were alarmed by the consequences of philosophism. Although anticlerical, hostile towards the Jesuits, scornful of devotion to the Sacred Heart and highly critical of the papacy, they were not entirely irreligious. If the middle classes read and enjoyed Voltaire it was because he despised the mob no less than the priesthood. The penetration of genuine irreligion, let alone of atheism, into the middle-class circles did not begin until after 1770; and even then sentimental Deism found more favour with gentler spirits. It was during the last third of the century that the new mentality became widespread and vociferous, young people in particular creating uproar during Mass and publicly insulting priests. The leaders of the Revolution, many of them educated in Jesuit colleges, belonged to the category of middle-class youth or to that of the lesser nobility who had embraced irreligion.

Much more serious was the fact that some elements of the clergy succumbed to dangerous doctrine. One could name many priests who behaved as disciples and allies of the philosophical sect. Among them were the Abbé Prades, whose *Jérusalem terrestre* (1751) created a tremendous sensation, and the Abbé de Raynal, whose *Histoire philosophique des*

Indes was nothing less than an arsenal of unbelief. There were also the Abbé Millot of Besançon, who considered Thomism a mere 'conjurer's manual'; the Abbé Mably, secretary to Cardinal de Tencin, who regarded Greek ethics as far superior to Christian morality; the Abbé Viet, whose licentious remarks used to cause great mirth among the ladies at the Duc de Penthièvre's table. Finally, there were the Abbés Beauvais, Torné and Fauchet, all of whom were deputies to the Legislative Assembly or the Convention. It is important, however, not to overrate the importance of such cassocked mountebanks. These priests who held 'advanced' ideas received a good deal of attention because ecclesiastical courtiers talked so much about them; but they counted for very little among the clergy as a whole. The case of Mestier, parish priest of Étrepigny in the Ardennes, whose Will (a monument of atheism) was published by Voltaire, is exceptional. Careful research has shown that on the eve of the Revolution there were only seven atheists and three deists out of one hundred and thirty-five French bishops. Among the lower clergy there must have been a far smaller proportion of unbelievers. Though hostile for the most part to the holders of rich benefices and other well-fed dignitaries, the majority of parish priests and curates did not question the Church's authority, let alone her faith. Their resistance to the antichristian measures of the revolutionaries suffice to show their true feelings.

As for the common people—craftsmen in the towns and peasants in the countryside—it seems beyond doubt that they were virtually unaffected. There were a few blasphemers or hotheads in their ranks: Nivelet, for example, a cobbler who interrupted the parish priest of Saint-Benoît in the middle of a sermon and challenged him with the arguments of the Encyclopaedists; or that impromptu orator who used to gather crowds of ragged folk to hear him talk philosophy, and whose name was Marat. But there were not many such. When we find Father Sennemand declaring in 1756 that 'the chimney sweepers are beginning to talk of weighty things, and the shoeblacks to discourse about humanity', we are not obliged to take him literally; nor need we believe Barruel's story of a plan to flood the deep countryside with the works of Rousseau and Voltaire, bound as prayer books and at ten *sous* a volume. 'The wind of contagion is already blowing around the poor man's cottage and the craftsman's workshop.' Those words were written in 1786 by Mgr de la Luzerne, Bishop of Langres, but even at that date one can find little evidence to support them. No doubt faith languished and morality was at a low ebb, but there was no trace of genuine irreligion.

Daniel Mornet's conclusion is a fair summary of the facts. The books of the philosophers did not dechristianize France. 'But it is certain that they saturated most of the aristocracy with unbelief or at any rate with indifference, that such indifference was fairly widespread among the clergy, and that it made rapid progress among the upper middle classes, young people and students. A large part of France, though not exactly godless or hostile to religion, was cut off from the Church and her priests.' But that part by no means represented the whole or even a majority of the nation. 'The spread of unbelief seems less important than a more general and more certain evolution of opinion.' The great rebellion was directed not so much against Christianity, or even the Church, as against the political order with which they appeared to be associated.

One fact is significant and deserves to be understood. The twenty years preceding the Revolution were marked by an almost unimaginable increase of violence in the campaign against religion. 'It's raining bombs in the house of the Lord,' sneered Diderot in 1768; and Voltaire wrote to d'Alembert: 'The rain of books against the priests continues to pour down.' It continued, in fact, until the eve of the Revolution: four hundred books within a period of twenty years. Judging therefore by this vast flow of impiety, one might well conclude that the whole of France had been won over to irreligion and that the revolutionary explosion would at once sweep away Christianity. No such thing happened. The first stages of the Revolution were by no means antichristian, and still less anti-religious; they were not even anticlerical.[65] The fact that priests were treated with respect in the States-General and the Constituent Assembly proves that in 1789 public opinion was not fundamentally hostile to Christianity and that religion still had deep roots among the people.

When the old regime drew to its close the spirit of rebellion had not yet gained the masses, but it had achieved much by establishing itself in the minds of so many men whose task was to lead society. In the bloody storm that was about to break, and which the preachers of irreligion had done so much to generate, Christianity was challenged together with many other values. Would victory go to ungodliness or to those ancient loyalties that were still alive? The debate started amid the thunder of cannon at the Bastille; it remains to this day undecided.

CHAPTER II

SUCCESS AND FAILURE IN THE MISSION FIELD

1. DE PROPAGANDA FIDE

We must now leave Europe. Quitting the western world of the baptized and its suicidal tendencies, we must ask ourselves whether the world at large, all those people to whom Christ's word was promised, those continents where the Cross must needs be planted, offer a more consoling spectacle.

At the beginning of the seventeenth century the state of the missions had been most encouraging. The Church had just passed through the most brilliant phase of expansion in all her history,[1] and in 1585 an obscure apologist had written these optimistic words: 'While our beggarly mutineers and rebellious Huguenots set out to wage war against God, the Church, the Catholic religion and the See of St Peter, God overthrows idolatry in the Indies and brings beneath His yoke new men, men unknown to our ancestors. . . . The profit He derives in the mission field is greater than the loss in our aged, doting world.' Resolutely associated with the hazards and daring of the empire-builders, Catholicism had conquered so many lands and so many peoples during the past hundred years that the idea of supernatural compensation, as it might be called, does not seem far-fetched. Many of the great Orders, among them the Franciscans, Dominicans and Carmelites, had played a part in that enterprise; and the Society of Jesus, almost immediately after its foundation, gave to the Church St Francis Xavier, the greatest missionary genius of modern times. During those hundred years a spirit of holy rivalry had never ceased to drive men forth, one after another, upon the seaways that might lead to martyrdom.

About 1622 the map of Catholic expansion presents two markedly different features. In the West Indies the Spaniards

had established the Church wherever their *conquistadores*
set foot, from Mexico to the most southerly point of Chile,
including the Antilles and those remote Pacific islands which
they had occupied in defiance of the Treaty of Tordesillas[2]
and named the Philippines. In those vast areas millions of
natives had been converted, voluntarily or by force. The Portuguese had followed a different line in the territories reserved to them, i.e. in Brazil and the East Indies; they had
erected their *padroes* (columns bearing the arms of Portugal) on a narrow strip of coast, without penetrating far into
the interior. But that Catholic fringe was enormous; it followed the entire Brazilian littoral, encircled almost the whole
of Africa and India; was considerable, though more irregular,
in Indo-China, the Indian islands and China; and extended
even to Japan. Goa, city of eighty belfries, was from 1534
onwards the capital of Christian Asia, while Macao, gateway
to the Celestial Empire and a bishopric since 1570, was an
outpost of the Catholic faith and the starting point of future
penetration.[3]

Splendid therefore was the scene represented by those
huge maps painted by order of the popes on the walls of
passages in the Vatican; a magnificent work accomplished
by the toil and sacrifices of innumerable Spanish and Portuguese missionaries, from whom it is impossible to withhold
our admiration without monstrous injustice. Nevertheless
those gigantic achievements were not entirely free from im-
perfection. In 1625, 1628 and 1644 Mgr Ingoli, a Roman
prelate, made three strongly critical reports on the state of
the missions. He listed no fewer than twelve causes of disorder and abuse. Some were attributable to human weakness—neglect, egoism, avarice, inefficiency; but others were
inherent in the system. The partition of missionary zones
between Spain and Portugal led to some bitter rivalry which
was not terminated by Philip II's annexation of Portugal in
1580. Wherever the two nations met, as for example in the
Far East, there was open hostility between the Spanish
patronato and the Portuguese *padroado*. The missions were,
in fact, tied to the government of kings who claimed rights
and privileges that encroached upon the spiritual domain.
Spanish and Portuguese missionaries were often regarded by

the natives as mere agents of white penetration rather than as harbingers of Christ, so much so that in the Indies conversion was called 'turning prangui', i.e. Portuguese; nor had St Francis Xavier himself been able to overcome such abuses. Then, too, there was rivalry between the missionary orders, a rivalry which, though doubtless inspired by apostolic zeal, was none the less disastrous in its results. The Papacy was well aware of the situation, and indeed the most important event of the early seventeenth century was its decision to assume overall control of the missions. This idea originated with the Belgian Jean de Vondeville; it was taken over and developed by the Spanish Carmelite Thomas of Jesus. Submitted to the Holy See by another Carmelite, Dominic of Jesus and Mary (later general of his Order), and by the Capuchin preacher Jerome of Narni, it eventually reached fulfilment on 6th January 1622, during the brief but fruitful pontificate of Gregory XV. On that day there came into being the Congregation of Propaganda. Composed of thirteen cardinals and organized on the lines of a modern ministry, its business was to promote and control the spread of Catholic faith in all countries where it was unknown or under attack, i.e. in heretical and schismatic no less than in pagan lands.

Thenceforward the Church possessed an effective implement for sowing the faith. Under the direction of its secretary, who was almost always a man of outstanding gifts,[4] the Congregation *De Propaganda Fide* endeavoured to put an end to the often anarchical empiricism of the missions. It asked nuncios, bishops and missionary priests for reports, which it registered and preserved among its archives. It made a detailed study (sometimes with a little too much abstract and theoretical detail) of the problems, and proposed means for their solution. Besides giving financial help to the missions, it also sent them catechisms and liturgical books, for which purpose it established its own printing press at Rome. Like the German, English, Scots and Maronite Colleges, which prepared their students for the recovery of countries that had lost or abandoned the faith, it persuaded Pope Urban VIII in 1627 to found the Collegio Urbano for the training of future missionaries and also of young natives who might wish to become priests. At the same time it opened a polyglot press.

From 1622 onwards the task of carrying the Good News to all nations, a task bequeathed by Christ to his followers, was carried out by the Holy See. Throughout the seventeenth and eighteenth centuries there was scarcely a pope who failed to grasp its importance and collaborate in its fulfilment. Some of them took a direct hand in the work. Thus Alexander VII instituted vicars-apostolic and gave financial assistance from his own revenues to the Levantine, Armenian and Chinese missions; Innocent XI supported Propaganda against Portuguese claims; Clement XI laboured with representatives of the great Orders to found missionary seminaries. Several popes also tackled the thorny problems of the Chinese and Malabar rites with the manifest desire to serve the cause of truth, even though the result of their efforts was unfortunate.

The missionary enterprise, which had proved so successful in the sixteenth century, received a fresh impulse. In a period of twenty-five years the Congregation enlarged its horizons, clarified its plans and strengthened its resources. By 1640 it had won recognition of its right to control the entire missionary field and to approve the elections of superiors. Its universal activity produced a revival of fervour and some measure of reform among the old missions in Spanish and Portuguese territory.

We may safely say that missionary work continued to progress until the early years of the eighteenth century. Nevertheless it met with serious obstacles, of which the material difficulties were by no means the worst, despite their formidable nature. As in the previous epoch, it was still necessary to face interminable, exhausting and dangerous voyages, shipwreck and sickness, unspeakable discomfort; nor was it until the eighteenth century that technical improvements made the venture a little less hazardous. Between 1580 and 1640 seventy vessels out of three hundred and twenty-three fitted out at Lisbon disappeared without trace; and it is related that one ship, sailing to Goa with two hundred and seventy-five men on board, lost sixty-three through accident or epidemic on the voyage. On reaching India most missionaries had to spend some time (often a very long time) in hospital.

It is estimated that nearly five hundred Jesuits died of sickness or fell victim to persecution between 1650 and 1700. But those terrible conditions never dismayed the heralds of Christ or hindered the apostolate.

The real obstacles to missionary progress, which ended by bringing it almost to a standstill, were of a very different order. Some of them were internal. Notwithstanding the determination of its members and the backing of the popes, the new Congregation of Propaganda was frequently obstructed by an overlap of jurisdiction. In Canada, for example, we find the Dataria creating parishes subject to the archdiocese of Rouen at the very moment when Propaganda was establishing a vicariate-apostolic and preparing to give Quebec diocesan status. Rivalry between the missionary orders, so far from yielding to the efforts of Propaganda, was increasing, often to a degree that can only be described as sordid: Dominicans against Jesuits, Franciscans against Capuchins, Sulpicians and Priests of the Foreign Missions against older institutions—absurd antagonisms unlikely to edify the pagans. Even the controversies that were disturbing Catholicism in the West—Jansenism, Gallicanism, Quietism —had repercussions in the farthest missionary lands; the Jesuits, for example, were frequently censured by critics who borrowed arguments from the Jansenist arsenal. The wretched Quarrel of Rites was embittered by these divisions.

Other obstacles stood in the way, and were no less harmful. The Congregation of Propaganda was never able completely to eliminate secular interference in the affairs of the missions. Until the end of the eighteenth century the Spanish and Portuguese monarchs—often assisted in their opposition to Propaganda by the missionaries themselves—insisted upon their ancient right as protectors of the missions; and even when that function had ceased to be anything more than a mere name they continued to claim the right and to impede the activity of Rome. Even France, whose wonderful missionary achievements under Louis XIV we shall presently see, did not always understand that it was necessary for the Church to exercise undivided control in this particular field, and the absolutism of *le roi soleil* was felt here as everywhere else. The Catholic apostolate was also exposed to the hostility of other European colonizers; English, Dutch or Danish Protestants were frequently[5] behind the most savage persecutions of Roman missionaries, even when they did not themselves destroy the missions, as happened in Acadia[6] and Canada. Finally, in various places but particularly in Asia, there were outbreaks of xenophobia. These were too often provoked by the greed and brutality of the whites, and they led to the proscription of the Church in countries where she had appeared to be most firmly established, as in Japan.

All these causes explain why the missionary current, so swift and deep at the beginning of the seventeenth century, gradually dwindled to a mere trickle where it did not dry up altogether. The dismemberment of the Portuguese empire by the English and Dutch, the decadence of Spain and the ruin of France's colonial empire in the eighteenth century all contributed to this result; the suppression of the Society of Jesus created a terrible void in the missionary ranks; and, finally, the age of Voltaire was hardly favourable to the growth of heroic vocations.

2. THE APPEAL TO FRANCE

The Congregation of Propaganda was faced from the start with a difficult problem of personnel. To whom might it look to carry out its orders? Compulsory registration of all missionaries in its books would remain an empty measure if men could not be found to command in its name. It was impossible to make use of Spanish or Portuguese missionaries, because the *patronato* made them subject to their respective governments. Even the Jesuits, whose vocation placed them at the disposal of the Holy See, sometimes found themselves caught between instructions from Rome and orders from the viceroys at Goa. To whom then could Propaganda turn? To the Italians? Several of them had done excellent work; Father Matteo Ricci, for instance, who had brought Christ to China, or Fathers Ruggieri and Valignano.[7] Italy, however, was no more than a swarm of principalities without much prestige, and there was obvious need for a great missionary endeavour supported (and financed) by a first class power.

Quite naturally, though not without hesitation, Propaganda was led to think of France, a Catholic country which at that time possessed the hegemony of Europe.

France, indeed, having emerged from the anarchy created by the Wars of Religion, had been for half a century awakening to the call of colonization, which was likewise a summons to the mission fields. Henri IV had fiercely disputed the claims of Spain and Portugal to divide the new world between themselves, and in 1598 a secret clause of the Treaty of Vervins had given France the opportunity of overseas expansion. Jacques Cartier had already set foot in North America, and, being a good Catholic, had not failed to plant the cross of Christ alongside the armorial bearings of his king. The French Jesuits had already sent two of their members to Acadia, while the Recollects, invited by Samuel Champlain, had settled on the banks of the St Lawrence in 1615.

The missionary achievement of France during the next hundred years or so was truly prodigious. All the noblest, most generous and most active elements of French Catholicism devoted themselves to the task of evangelization with no less ardour than to the reform of morals and the improvement of the clergy. The same fervour which drove some to join the newly founded institutes and congregations impelled others to carry the Gospel into distant lands, where martyrdom might await them; and that impulse was so strong that its effects were felt throughout the reign of Louis XIV. Enthusiasm for the mission was destined to a long life from top to bottom of the social scale.

Kings and ministers preached by example. Father Cotton, the Jesuit confessor of Henri IV, was a devotee of the missionary cause. Under Louis XIII and Richelieu, Father Joseph, the Cardinal's 'Grey Eminence', himself organized the Capuchin missions to the Levant, and had himself appointed prefect. Louis XIV took a keen personal interest in the missions by granting them subsidies, encouraging their efforts and ordering his governors to assist them. Following their example, the great nobles and their wives gave financial aid to the apostles of far-off lands; the Duchesse de Chevreuse, for instance, the Duchesse d'Aiguillon and Mme de Miramion spent millions on their behalf. The Company of the Blessed

Sacrament included the evangelization of the pagans in its apostolic undertakings; it financed the Lazarist missions and informed Propaganda of its readiness to support the Congregation, while one of its members, Bishop Godeau, explained to the Assembly of the Clergy the need of missionary endeavour. This need was understood by all the spiritual leaders of Catholicism in France. Monsieur Vincent, as we have seen,[8] dispatched his sons to North Africa and Madagascar; M. Olier, before turning to the work of training future priests, had thought of becoming a missionary, and shortly before his death he told his friend Mgr Pallu that 'he would consider himself fortunate if he could spend the remainder of his life serving the mission at Tonking'. All the great figures of that classical age raised their voices to declare that the truths of faith must be carried to the pagans. This was a subject to which Godeau frequently returned; it was Fénelon's theme in his famous sermon on 'The Calling of the Gentiles'; Bossuet made it his own on many occasions and saw in the missionary apostolate 'the Redemption continued with its full scope'. Such also was the mind of St Grignion de Montfort, whose 'flaming prayer' exalted the sufferings of the missionary martyrs as the prolongation and consequence of the sacrifice of Christ.

It is still more surprising to discover that the *élite* were not alone in their enthusiasm for missionary enterprise. The masses were equally dedicated. Marie de l'Incarnation, Jeanne Mancé and Marguerite Bourgeoys, who were ready to face the hardships of Canada in order to serve the Church, all came from ordinary middle-class families. Nothing illustrates better the trend of opinion which sustained the missionaries than the number and success of books recounting their adventures. One best seller was Father Trigault's *Expédition chrétienne en Chine*, which ran to 1,117 pages. The *Relations des Jésuites de la Nouvelle France* was published by the fashionable house of Charmoisy. Between 1600 and 1661 there appeared in France alone no fewer than four hundred and fifty such works, some of them full of prodigies and miracles. They were read by all and sundry, from court to cottage, while *Mémoires et instructions sur le sujet des mis-*

sions étrangères[9] provided the more learned circles with the
first textbook of missionary theology.

The soil of France was therefore ready to produce a generation of men who would venture life itself on behalf of God.
Propaganda's appeal to the French arose from a journey to
Europe made in 1649 by Father Alexandre de Rhodes
(1591–1660). Born in the papal territory of Avignon, he
entered the Society of Jesus resolved to follow in the footsteps
of St Francis Xavier; and twenty years of apostolate proved
him to be one of the most successful missionaries of his age.
He was a quiet, shrewd man, and there was something Asiatic
about his thin face with its long beard, prominent cheek-
bones and rather narrow-lidded eyes. Appointed to the Japanese mission, he was obliged to halt at Macao on receipt of
news that all Catholics had recently been expelled from the
Land of the Rising Sun. He was then ordered to Cochin
China, and later to Tonking, where some Christian communities were already flourishing. There he was eminently successful: the king had a church built for him, and eighteen
members of the royal family, together with many government
officials, asked for baptism. A true disciple of Father Ricci
and a rival of Father de Nobili, Rhodes did his best to live
'as a Tonkingese among the Tonkingese', speaking their language and following their customs. Unlike the Portuguese
missionaries, many of whom were engaged in trade, he would
accept no gifts that did not contribute directly to the upkeep
of his schools and other foundations, and he astonished
Tonkingese society by his absolute detachment. His very virtues led to his banishment as the result of intrigue among
the royal concubines, the 'second wives' and the worst elements of the regime. Returning alone to Cochin China he
undertook the same apostolic task with the same success,
helped by a 'congregation of catechists' which he founded
among the natives. In 1650 there were estimated to be 30,000
Christians in Indo-China. Once again, however, Father de
Rhodes was obliged to depart, leaving to his beloved catechists the work of defending and continuing his work. His
superiors then sent him to Europe,[10] in order to make known
the needs of the Annamite missions and his ideas for their
future.

He believed that if the European priests were driven out by persecution, the missions in the Far East had no chance of success, or even of survival, unless a large body of native clergy was built up among the converted peoples. But that could not be achieved without bishops, and hitherto the number of bishops sent to Asia had been determined by the crowns of Spain and Portugal, which had appointed only men of their own choice. The Holy See, thought Rhodes, should exercise its right of universal jurisdiction; the Congregation of Propaganda should choose bishops from among its own subjects and send them out to ordain a native priesthood. He reached the Eternal City after a five-year journey. But no one was in a hurry to follow his advice; Rome is never in a hurry. Portugal had regained her independence in 1640, and still clung to her ancient privileges; Father de Rhodes was simply encouraged to recruit volunteers for Asia. Finding none in Italy or Switzerland, he proceeded to France, where twenty Jesuits offered to follow him. But he wanted secular priests also, who would place themselves unreservedly at the disposal of Propaganda. He found them, and as a result there came into being one of the noblest foundations of missionary France, the Society of the Foreign Missions, which would carry out his intentions though he was not its superior.

Inspired by the idea of serving as missionaries in the Far East, some members of the Apostolic Association[11] and of the Congregation of the Blessed Virgin had gathered around Father Bagot to form a small group known as 'Good Friends'. This band of young priests included Pierre Lambert de la Motte, François de Montigny-Laval,[12] Bernard Picques, Vincent de Meur and François Pallu, a canon from Touraine who was regarded as their leader. Before long Father de Rhodes was able to ask the nuncio Bagni to inform the Holy See that he had found 'some secular priests of outstanding worth, combining holiness and zeal, prudence and learning', whose one thought was to start for Asia. The Company of the Blessed Sacrament took a great interest in this project and let it be known that they would supply funds. It was likewise encouraged by the Assembly of the French Clergy. Thus was born 'the oldest of societies devoted exclusively to the missions . . . and also the most completely missionary, since all its members without exception were sent to the mission field', as it was later described by its superior, Mgr de Guébriant. The society was actually founded in 1659, when Pallu and Lambert de la Motte were leaving for Asia in circumstances which we shall presently describe, though it did not receive its final statutes until 1700. Subject directly to Rome, its members did not take religious vows, but undertook to devote their lives to the evangelization of the Far East, and it was approved both by Alexander VII and by Louis XIV. Before leaving France, Pallu and Lambert de la Motte asked de Meur, who had been elected superior, to undertake another task—the foundation of a seminary for the training of future missionaries. The idea had already occurred to the Duc de Ventadour as well as to Father Pacifique de Provins, the Capuchin apostle of the Levant. An attempt to give it effect had been made by the society of priests founded at Avignon by Authier de Sisgaud,[13] and also by the Carmelite Bernard de Sainte-Thérèse, who, as Jean Duval, had borne the title Bishop of Babylon. None of them had succeeded. Bernard, however, owned a fine property in the Rue du Bac at Paris. Seeing no hope of filling it with candidates for the mission in Persia, he agreed to sell it to the new Society of the Foreign Missions (1663), who made it their seminary and mother house.[14]

Thenceforward France was the home of a first-rate missionary enterprise. There was another. In 1702 Claude Poullard des Places founded his Seminary of the Holy Spirit[15] for the reception of penniless young men whom he would invite 'to serve in the poorest parishes'. But he also intended that they should man the most difficult and abandoned outposts of the mission field; and in fact they were destined to keep alive the mission in Guiana under the most trying conditions. The Sisters of St Paul, founded at Chartres towards the end of the seventeenth century by Father Chauvet, a native of Beauce, were originally devoted to the evangelization of the surrounding countryside; but they soon discovered another kind of missionary vocation, settling in the Antilles and the Île de Bourbon (now Réunion). Among other female orders and congregations that answered the call were the Sisters of Notre-Dame de Troyes, the Hospitallers of La

Flèche, the Franciscans and the Ursulines. Hitherto absent
from the missionary scene, Catholic France was now permanently in the forefront.

3. VICARS-APOSTOLIC

France was now directly associated with what Mgr Marella
has rightly described as 'the most radical, the most peaceful
and the most unexpected revolution' in the history of the
missions.[16] He was referring to the institution of vicars-
apostolic. Several of the most distinguished authorities on
missionary problems, among them Sarmiento de Mendoza
and Father de Rhodes, had maintained that the establishment in missionary lands of bishops with power to ordain
native priests was the only means of returning to the authentic
apostolic methods of early days, by causing the Church to
grow from the converted peoples themselves instead of imposing upon them her rigid framework and a hierarchy linked
with that of the colonialist kingdoms. Now, as Mgr Ingoli
clearly stated in his report of 1644, the bishops in the East
Indies had been unwilling to ordain a single native priest,
and had done nothing to establish missionary seminaries. It
was therefore necessary to send out bishops dependent upon
none but the Holy See, i.e. chosen by Propaganda for the
express purpose of carrying out that most delicate task, the
building of a native priesthood. It was also desirable that
such bishops should be drawn from the secular clergy, in
order to avoid jealousy between the great religious orders.
Mgr Cerri of Propaganda was expressing the opinion of
Rome when he stated that only the appointment of a Latin
bishop to Aleppo would end the interminable monastic
squabbles in the Near East.

In the Indies the Portuguese patronate remained the most
serious obstacle. Viceroys, government officials and archbishops, all emissaries of Lisbon, clung determinedly to the privileges allowed by the sixteenth-century popes to the King of
Portugal and to themselves as acting in his name. Ecclesiastical jurisdiction belonged to the Militia of Christ,[17] of which
the King of Portugal was grand master. Nevertheless 'Asia

Portuguesa' was in full decline: the empire of Albuquerque was being torn piecemeal by foreign rivals. The Dutch took Malacca in 1639, Ceylon in 1658, the Moluccas in 1666; the English established themselves at Madras in 1640 and Bombay in 1661, and the French at Pondicherry in 1674. Nothing now remained of the geographical foundations upon which the papal Bulls had erected the Portuguese patronate, and therefore Rome was free to take whatever steps she might think fit. As usual, she moved with extreme caution, seeking to avoid a clash with the young house of Braganza, careful also not to allow too much rope to certain Frenchmen whose Gallicanism was a source of anxiety.

The first attempt to create a vicariate-apostolic in India had been made by Mgr Ingoli, whose procedure was remarkably audacious at that period. Having chosen a young Brahmin convert, who had taken the European name Matteo de Castro and had had a brilliant career as a student in Rome, he sent him first to his own country with the title protonotary apostolic. The Portuguese authorities placed so many obstacles in Castro's way that he returned to Rome. Mgr Ingoli, undaunted, had him consecrated bishop and appointed him vicar-apostolic of Idalkan, a territory independent of Portugal. Again, however, the Patriarch of Goa thwarted his mission, accusing him of being a treacherous Brahmin, a dubious character and, moreover, an enemy of the patronate. The poor vicar departed for Rome, where Propaganda, refusing to admit defeat, moved him to the kingdom of Golconda, from which the Great Mogul had recently expelled the Portuguese. But the authorities at Goa continued to hound his steps; the unfortunate Castro was obliged to leave India once for all, and returned to die in the Eternal City. But his effort had not been fruitless; he had obtained a number of conversions, laid the foundations of a native clergy and established an Oratory of St Philip Neri among the Brahmins. Two other vicars-apostolic of Hindu origin continued his work in a small way, always exposed to the hostility of Portuguese authorities both civil and ecclesiastical. It was high time Propaganda revised its methods.

During his sojourn in Rome, Father de Rhodes had repeatedly urged the Congregation to increase the number of

vicars-apostolic, a measure that appeared to him absolutely
vital. If it were necessary to avoid offending Portuguese sus-
ceptibilities, he argued, all Propaganda need do was refrain
from appointing titular bishops, at any rate for the time
being, and give the vicars-apostolic titles of dioceses *in partibus infidelium*. After his meeting with Bagot's young priests
at Paris, he insisted that the vicars-apostolic should be
chosen from among them. In 1655 the Assembly of the
French Clergy voted an address to the Holy See begging for
the immediate creation of vicars-apostolic. Rome delayed;
some members of the Congregation would have preferred
Italians as the future guides of Asia, and even St Vincent de
Paul's exhortations were in vain. The matter was still under
consideration when things were brought to a head by the arrival of the young and enthusiastic 'Good Friends' François
Pallu and Vincent de Meur. They were soon afterwards
joined by Pierre Lambert de la Motte, who had come to beg
the Holy Father himself to authorize their departure for the
Far East. Mgr Alberici, secretary of Propaganda, was in no
hurry to receive them, but when at length he decided to do
so they made so deep an impression upon him that his attitude completely changed. Lambert de la Motte left the
offices of the Congregation not only with formal permission
for himself and his friends to go as missionaries to Asia, but
also with the promise that episcopal consecration would be
conferred upon him and two others. The future Society of
the Foreign Missions found itself, at the very moment of its
birth, entrusted with the first apostolic vicariates in the Far
East.

Accordingly, on 29th July 1658, the Holy See appointed
Pierre Lambert de la Motte bishop of Berytus (Beirut), and
François Pallu bishop of Heliopolis (Baalbek). The former's
jurisdiction extended over Cochin China, Chekiang, Fukien,
Kiengsi and Hainan; Pallu was to govern Tonking, Laos,
Yunnan, Hukuang and Szechwan. The rest of China, including Peking, was soon afterwards entrusted to Cotolendi, a
native of Provence and friend of Pallu. Thus all Far Eastern
territories, not officially subject to the patronate, came under
direct control of the Holy See. Propaganda had no illusions
as to how Portugal would react to this innovation. The vicars

were forbidden to travel by the Portuguese maritime route; they were advised to depart secretly and to conceal their titles until they had reached their destinations, and they were ordered to maintain unbroken contact with Rome by means of a code which had been specially devised for the purpose.

The experiences of these first French vicars-apostolic—especially of Pallu and Lambert—for Cotolendi died soon after his arrival in Asia—must be read in Mgr Henri Chappoulie's great work.[18] Their amazing adventures are at the same time a living example of the grandeur to which the missionary vocation can attain. For these two energetic and brave young men—Pallu was thirty-two, Lambert de la Motte thirty-four—devoted themselves to their task with a zeal that no difficulty was able to discourage. When on the point of leaving Europe they received from Propaganda detailed instructions which included, among much other sound advice, a warning to carry out their task in a spirit of contempt for worldly affairs, modesty, simplicity of life, patience and prayer—'all virtues of apostolic men'. In short, they were asked to strive towards sanctity and to give their apostolate 'a savour of eternity'. The marvel is that neither fell short of the demands made by such an ideal; they may not have been saints, but they were unquestionably men of God.

It is not easy to imagine the obstacles that awaited them. Misunderstanding and distrust on the part of the natives were nothing in comparison with the intrigues and even the violence of European Catholics. The Portuguese crown did not confine itself to vehement protests against these appointments, which it regarded as prejudicial to its own rights. It allowed its representatives on the spot to wage against the vicars-apostolic a regular war in which they stopped at nothing. Two incidents will suffice to show what fury inspired the supporters of the patronate. The chapter at Goa pronounced sentence of excommunication upon Mgr Lambert de la Motte; and when Mgr Pallu was shipwrecked on a stretch of coast held by the Spaniards, these latter (for once in full accord with Lisbon) threw him into prison, where he remained for two years awaiting the outcome of some hard bargaining. The natives themselves more than once helped the vicars-apostolic to defy Portuguese threats. In addition to these obstacles raised by the patronate there were others, caused by the clergy of older-established missions—Dominicans, Franciscans and even Jesuits—whose conduct was frowned upon by the ascetical Lambert and Pallu. The latter was particularly distressed by the shortcomings of the Jesuits, for two of his brothers belonged to the Society. In order to persevere in the fulfilment of their task the two vicars-apostolic were obliged on several occasions to appeal to Rome, sending representatives or travelling to the Eternal City in person. Annoyed by such hostility, they sometimes gave vent to rage and recrimination, which, though understandable, were hardly justified. We should much prefer to say nothing about these conflicts, but for our belief that they were the price of an intense religious vitality among men inevitably imperfect, no matter how lofty their ideal.

Meanwhile the Congregation of Propaganda displayed remarkable firmness. Alexander VII, Clement IX, Clement X and Innocent XI, each in turn, refused to entertain Portuguese protests. A series of Roman decisions increased the authority of the vicars-apostolic and enlarged their field of action. A Brief of Innocent XI in 1678 required all missionaries, secular and regular, working in territory subject to the jurisdiction of the vicars-apostolic to take an oath of obedience to them; and the Society of Jesus, whose novitiate Rome actually threatened to close, submitted to this ordinance.[19] In 1680 the Far Eastern missions were reorganized: six apostolic vicariates were created, with Pallu and Lambert de la Motte at their head. Only one Pope, Alexander VIII, deviated from this line; he established at Peking and Nanking two 'traditional' bishoprics dependent upon the religious authorities at Macao, that is to say, upon the patronate. But all his successors confirmed the policy of Propaganda. By the end of the seventeenth century the appointment of vicars-apostolic had become a permanent factor of ecclesiastical government and was no longer seriously disputed. In 1698 Innocent XII created several new vicariates in China. In order to end rivalry between the various missionary institutes, he decided to entrust them to Jesuits, Dominicans, Franciscans and Augustinians as well as to the Society of the

Foreign Missions; and that arrangement has lasted until our own day. Thanks to the initiative of Propaganda, then, the Church now possessed an instrument which she has never ceased to employ in the fulfilment of her missionary task.

The French vicars-apostolic achieved a considerable measure of success. Both died relatively young—Lambert de la Motte at fifty-five, Pallu at fifty-eight—but both had done good work for Christ. When they arrived in Indo-China that country was in the state foreseen by Father de Rhodes: the Christian communities, deprived of European missionaries as a result of persecution, had no leaders, and it was necessary to create a native clergy without delay. Taking as their starting point Siam, where Christianity was well established, the two vicars endeavoured to penetrate the hostile kingdoms of Cochin China and Tonking, relying on de Rhodes's body of catechists which had continued to flourish. The Breton Chevreuil was ordered by Lambert de la Motte to Cochin China, where, despite a persecution which claimed forty-seven martyrs, he managed to survive, moving from one hiding place to another. He sent two catechists, Trang and Ben, to his superior, who ordained them as the first Cochin-Chinese priests. Father Deydier, a native of Toulon, risked his life to enter Tonking disguised 'as a poor bongu'. He reorganized the catechists and sent two of their number to Siam for ordination; not long afterwards a French vessel called with Lambert de la Motte on board, and seven more were ordained. At about the same time a female association was formed on lines similar to those of what we now call Catholic Action; its members were known as Lovers of the Cross. The foundations of a native Church were thus laid in Indo-China. In order to train the priests of whom that Church would stand in ever growing need, a seminary was opened at Ajuthia in 1665. Its members soon included young men speaking no fewer than ten different languages; from it developed the famous Collège Général on the island of Penang. Lambert de la Motte breathed his last in Siam; Pallu died while preparing to enter southern China. At that date both Tonking and Cochin China probably numbered about 60,000 Christians. The road into the future lay wide open.

4. THE INSTRUCTIONS OF 1659

That road into the future can be even more clearly discerned in the instructions sent by Propaganda to the vicars-apostolic in 1659 and intended to serve as a body of rules for the working of missions subject to their control. The document contained advice and regulations for the personal conduct of missionaries, but it also laid down a method based upon firm theological and traditional principles, a veritable charter of missionary enterprise, which remains fundamentally applicable today. We do not know exactly who drafted these instructions; they doubtless represented a collective effort, as is often the case with documents from Rome. Mgr Alberici, secretary of the Congregation, employed a whole team of officials, among the most notable of whom was a Scotsman, Father Leslie, the most faithful and most useful friend of the vicars-apostolic. Father de Rhodes's influence, direct or indirect, is apparent in the text. Propaganda's aim, in brief, was not merely to sever the link binding missions to secular states, nor just to build up a native clergy; it also provided a genuine apostolical technique upon which it realized that all else depended.

Two opposite notions of the apostolate existed at that time. Some considered that since every aspect of pagan culture—manners and social organization, religious beliefs and rites—was intrinsically bad, it was necessary to destroy them all and to build the Church upon completely new foundations. Others thought it better to recognize the existence of native societies with their faith and usages, and to graft Christianity upon them just as the Church had done in the sixth century when St Gregory the Great directed her emissaries not to raze the temples and abolish the customs of the pagan Anglo-Saxons, but to christianize them. Generally speaking, the first of these notions had been applied (with a few notable exceptions) by the old Spanish and Portuguese missions. It still had many adherents. The other and more subtle method had been tried with great success in China by Father Matteo Ricci (died 1610), who had lived as a scholar of the

Celestial Empire and had made a close study of the manners and thought of China, in order to learn how they might be christianized; and Father de Nobili (died 1607) had acted in much the same way among the Brahmins in India.[20] Their method may be said to have been that of St Paul, who was a Jew among the Jews, a Greek among the Greeks, a Gentile among the Gentiles.

In his letters, his reports to Propaganda and his widely read *Divers Voyages*, Father de Rhodes had repeatedly emphasized the necessity of adapting the methods of the apostolate to local customs. He had sternly criticized the custom then prevalent in the Indies of making new converts lay aside their native dress. 'For my own part,' he said, 'when I was in China I stoutly resisted those who tried to make new Christians cut off their pigtails. . . . I used to tell them that the Gospel obliged a neophyte to cut out error from his mind, but not to cut off his pigtail.' There indeed was wisdom.

The instructions of 1659 were strictly relevant to this dispute. In 1623, a year after its foundation, Propaganda *advised* all missionaries to learn the native language. In 1659 it *ordered* them to do so and forbade the catechizing of future Christians in any but their native idiom. It went even further and told them: 'You must refrain from doing or saying anything with a view to making those peoples change their rites, their customs or their manners, provided they are not too blatantly opposed to religion and morality. What more absurd than to introduce France, Spain or any other part of Europe into China? That is not what you have to introduce, but the faith, which, so far from rejecting or insulting rites and customs that are not in themselves evil, desires their preservation.'

Those words reveal a profound understanding of the human soul. Having warned missionaries against comparing native customs with those of Europe to the detriment of the former, the instructions recommended them to practise the same virtues of reserve and patience as they would find among the Chinese, and to model their way of life as far as possible upon that of the peoples they were seeking to convert. The Congregation was, of course, well aware that many features of pagan conduct might be reprehensible, but it advised against any attempt to alter them at one stroke; better, it urged, 'to proceed step by step in eliminating whatever was considered undesirable'.

This admirable document called for no addition or alteration. If it had continued to serve as the Church's missionary charter during the next three hundred years many a tragedy might have been avoided and many a conquest assured. But failure to recognize hard facts, a spirit of aggressive vanity characteristic of Europeans and a certain narrowness of view, not to mention an undercurrent of sordid jealousy, prevented the instructions from producing the results which might have been expected. Forty years earlier Father Valignano, Jesuit Visitor of the Far East, had foreseen that conflict between the two systems was inevitable, a conflict which in the event did grave damage to the Christian cause.

5. THE CHINESE RITES

The first indication of trouble appeared early in the seventeenth century in Japan, where the Church had been preeminently successful. Following in the footsteps of St Francis Xavier, a number of Jesuit missionaries had lately done such good work that the Empire of the Rising Sun had deserved to be called 'the flourishing garden of God'. In 1600 it possessed no fewer than 300,000 Christians, and conversions among the upper classes seemed to forecast new harvests. But three years earlier a persecution had begun with the crucifixion of twenty-seven Christians, and that persecution continued relentlessly until Christianity was completely suppressed. It had complex origins: religious hostility to a doctrine that was opposed to various local cults, dislike of all that came from the conquering West, fear on the part of Japanese rulers on seeing the emergence of a Christian group led by nobles and capable of wrecking their own power. Other factors leading to its outbreak and continuance were the tactlessness of western Catholics (notably Franciscans and Dominicans from Manila) and the intrigues of Protestant English and Dutch traders.

A decree of 1614, seven times repeated, declared the Christian faith 'evil and contrary to doctrine'. The missionaries were expelled, and those who tried to re-enter the country were put to death; churches were destroyed and the faithful ordered to apostatize. The number of executions increased: sixty-eight in 1618, eighty-eight in 1619. At Nagasaki in 1622 there took place the 'great burning', which claimed thirty victims, among them nine Jesuits, ten Dominicans and three Franciscans, who walked to the stake with sublime serenity, led by the heroic Italian Jesuit Carlo Spinola. The 'great martyrdom' at Tokyo occurred in 1623, and from that date persecution became systematic under the Shogun Yemitsu. Suspects were rounded up by the police and ordered to trample on the cross. More and more hideous forms of torture were introduced and subtle methods of execution were devised; the condemned were suspended for days, head downwards, over a pit full of filth, or dipped in sulphurous water which corroded their flesh. A peasant rising in 1639, due to causes in no way religious, envenomed the hatred of Christianity. Fury knew no bounds, and an entire Portuguese embassy was massacred as soon as their ship touched the Japanese coast. There were a certain number of apostasies, but thousands of Christians perished in torment. The number has been given as 3,617, but one Japanese author speaks of 300,000 victims; more than two hundred of them have been beatified. Attempts to regain a foothold in Japan were made by the Franciscan Sotelo in the north, by Jesuits under Father Rubrio and by the French Dominican Courtet (1657), but all were doomed to failure. A final effort was made in 1707 by the Abbé Sirotti, who died shut up in a sort of hole scarcely larger than his body. The 'flourishing garden of God' was closed to Christianity for more than two hundred years, and a regular antichristian Inquisition was organized to prevent its return. Nevertheless small Christian nuclei continued to exist almost everywhere, though without priests, until the nineteenth century, even among the ancient race of the Ainus in the extreme north of the archipelago; they were discovered by Mgr Petitjean in 1865.

It was the memory of what had happened in Japan that moved Mgr Pallu to write in a report to Propaganda (1673) that only the creation of a native Church with its own priests and bishops would remove 'the suspicion princes may have that beneath the veil of religion the missionaries seek to make themselves masters of their states'. Sixty years earlier Father Sotelo had asked and obtained from Rome the promise to consecrate a Japanese bishop; and Propaganda, from its very start, had studied the possibility of modifying the rules laid down by the Council of Trent relative to the training of native priests and to the liturgy. Father Valignano too had recommended some adaptation. But as things turned out nothing of the kind was done. The Spanish patronate looked with a jaundiced eye upon all such proposals, and even caused Father Sotelo to be arrested. A bishop was nominated for Japan; but he was a European, not a Japanese, and only thirteen Japanese priests were ordained.[21] Signature of the decrees of adaptation was so long delayed that when they arrived the persecution was in full swing. Despite the far-sightedness of a few men, the Church was unable to strike roots in Japan sufficiently deep to make Catholicism Japanese and thereby strong enough for permanent survival.

In China the situation was different. Christianity, driven from the Empire at the end of the fourteenth century after the collapse of the Mongol dynasty, was not reinstated until the end of the sixteenth, thanks to the missionary genius of Father Matteo Ricci. Clothed in the silken robe of a scholar and bearing the name Li Ma-tzu, this able Jesuit had even managed to obtain audience of the emperor, whom he astonished with his knowledge of astronomy and whose favour made possible the spread of Christianity not only among scholars in the capital, but also in a few towns and country districts. Nevertheless, when Ricci died in 1610 the three hundred Chinese churches possessed no more than between two thousand five hundred and six thousand members—nothing comparable with the Japanese achievement. The Chinese authorities, however, had no cause for serious disquiet. During the next twenty years there were a few instances of persecution in various provinces. But these were local and sporadic; they did not hinder the development of Christianity.

The method employed was Father Ricci's. The Jesuits sent to China were selected from the most learned priests of the Society, in order that their prestige as scientists might impress the Chinese authorities. Map-making, cannon-founding and picture-painting became instruments of their apostolate, and Jesuit influence at court enabled other missionaries to work in the Celestial Empire. They were so successful that some of them received the title and insignia, though not the functions, of mandarins. The most famous of these learned Jesuits were the German Adam Schall, the Belgian Fernand Verbiest and, later, Fathers de Fontaney, Gerbillon and Bouvet of the French mathematical mission. Such was their ability that when the Ming dynasty was overthrown and replaced by the Manchu, after the civil war of 1644–63,[22] the Jesuits remained at the side of their new masters. There were certainly a few alarms, notably in 1665 when an edict of proscription threatened the young Chinese Church with ruin; but the Jesuits rode out the storm, and Kang Hsi, whose reign was to last until 1722, soon made them his familiar friends as well as inviting them to instruct him in science and philosophy.

By and large then, the whole seventeenth century was a period of continual progress for the Chinese Church, which is said to have numbered 150,000 faithful in 1650; the most flourishing communities were at Peking, in Shensi and at Nanking in the district of Shanghai. Learning of the success achieved by the Jesuits, other congregations asked to be allowed to send missionaries to China. Starting from Manila and travelling by Formosa, the Dominicans landed in 1631, the Franciscans in 1633; later came the Augustinians and the Society of the Foreign Missions in 1680 and 1688 respectively. It was clear that some apostolic emulation would result, but there was also reason to fear a certain amount of jealous rivalry. Not all the newcomers understood the Jesuits' method, their prudence and their skill in finding favour with the rulers of China; as early as 1638 some tactlessness on the part of the Franciscans had moved certain provincial authorities to take savage reprisals. In 1615, at the request of the Jesuits, Pope Paul V had granted the native clergy the privilege of reciting the Office, saying Mass and administering the sacraments in Chinese; and in 1658 indults of Alexander VII confirmed a number of similar canonical privileges, much

to the displeasure of the Spanish Franciscans and Dominicans.

China was on the way to becoming a battleground between
partisans of the two methods—adaptation and *tabula rasa*; but
this did not halt the progress of the Chinese Church. In
1692 the Jesuits obtained from Kang Hsi a general edict of
tolerance. About 1700 the number of Christians was estimated
to be 300,000. Penetration of the scholar class was still very
slow, but conversions were becoming more and more frequent
among the masses. A native clergy was in process of formation, some of whom were men of eminent sanctity. One of
these, Lo Win Tsao, known to the Europeans as Gregorio
Lopez, was at that time the only Chinese priest; he had
ministered to the seventy-five Christian communities in
Fukien during the persecution of 1665, and had made no
fewer than five thousand conversions. On the administrative
partition in 1678, for which Mgr Pallu had asked, he was
consecrated bishop and entrusted with the six northern provinces of the Empire. A systematic plan for the establishment
of an episcopal hierarchy in China had long before occurred to
Father Ricci; it was decided upon by Propaganda after the
institution of vicars-apostolic, and was given effect in 1696.
A whole network of vicariates, covering the Empire and its
appendages, was to be added to the ancient though decrepit
archdiocese of Macao and the more recent dioceses of Peking
and Nanking. The future of the Chinese Church seemed
bright, but that Church was doomed to darkness by a crisis
that had been maturing over a period of fifty years.

The trouble began in 1648, when Father Morales, a Spanish Dominican who had come to China after a long spell in
the Philippines, protested[23] against certain methods employed by the Jesuits in their apostolate. His attitude was one
adopted by all newcomers to the Chinese mission, whether
Franciscan or Dominican. Ever since the lifetime of Father
Ricci the Jesuits had done all they could to adapt Christianity
to Chinese manners and traditions, a move which appeared to
their rivals as an attack upon the purity of Christian doctrine
and an acceptance of abominable superstitions. The arrogance
and intransigence of Father Morales led to his expulsion by
the Chinese authorities. He went to Rome, informed the In-

quisition of what he had seen, and obtained a formal condemnation of Jesuit practices subject to their being such as he had described. The Jesuits immediately sent Father Martini to Rome; he presented the Society's methods in a very different light, and secured the Holy See's express approval in 1656. The truth was that the Jesuits and their adversaries were looking at the facts from opposite standpoints. The freedom allowed to scholars and the form of devotion practised by intellectuals were no doubt liable to do harm among an ignorant populace, just as the cult of Our Lady and the saints during the Middle Ages in Europe had led to the most ridiculous superstitions among the masses, notwithstanding the piety of such men as St Bernard. In 1669 Clement IX widely declared that the two decrees, of 1645 and 1656, though apparently contradictory, remained in force according to circumstances.

What exactly was the matter at issue? The phrase 'Chinese rites' is too narrow, it does not cover the whole field of dispute. The question was ostensibly one of usages, but these involved theological principles and a fundamental difference of apostolic methods. With a view to adapting Christianity to the ancient Chinese civilization the Jesuits had made a profound study of the classics; they had also inquired into the historical origin and interpretation of Chinese ceremonies, noting carefully whatever appeared to have been added by popular superstition. They had concluded that the honours paid to the great Confucius were not, properly speaking, a cult, and that Confucian temples were not built for the purpose of prayer to a deity, but as meeting places of the learned; moreover an imperial edict had made it illegal to pay divine honours to Confucius in any shape or form. Again, the Chinese ceremonies in honour of the dead were considered by Father Ricci's successors not as acts of worship, but simply as legitimate manifestations of filial piety and gratitude. None of these things, therefore, had been thought to deserve proscription. Furthermore their study of Confucius had led the Jesuits to believe that his teaching on the attributes of God was not essentially different from the Christian view. *Tien* (Heaven) or *Chang-ti* (the Sovereign Lord), in whom Confucius placed all his trust, was recognized by them as the true God.

A great majority of the Jesuits looked upon these conclusions as acceptable, although one of them, Father Visdelou, a leading authority on Chinese antiquities, unhesitatingly declared that some of his colleagues went too far. Other missionaries, however, saw things in a very different light. Not having moved in educated circles, and unacquainted with Chinese religion except in its popular manifestations, they were quick to observe therein all the marks of superstition. Confucius, they said, was looked upon by the masses as a god. The Chinese burnt joss-sticks before tablets on which were inscribed the names of their ancestors, to whom they offered meats and fruits—clear indication of idolatry! As for the terms 'Heaven' and 'Sovereign Lord', they were ambiguous and could denote some pagan Jupiter as well as the true God. Indeed the Franciscans, Dominicans and all non-Jesuit missionaries claimed that the word 'God' should be translated as *Tien-chou*, 'Master of heaven', a phrase manifestly inspired by contemporary western theology but seldom used in China; only so, they maintained, could all ambiguity be avoided.

The conflict thus begun was likely to develop into a dialogue as it were between deaf men, and it was envenomed by a variety of circumstances. Spanish Dominicans and Franciscans from the Philippines had little sympathy with the Italian, German, Belgian and French Jesuits who were achieving such brilliant results at Peking. Moreover the Jansenist affair, which was raging in Europe, afforded the enemies of the Society a splendid opportunity to declare that the Fathers showed the same laxity towards Chinese superstitions as they did towards the sins of their penitents. Such was the opinion of Arnauld and of Bossuet himself. In France alone, between 1657 and 1700, there appeared more than two hundred books on the controversial subject. The instructions of 1659 had desired 'progressive elimination of whatever might seem undesirable'; but the grave problem of choice between two methods of apostolate which should have been raised quietly with the sole object of dispelling error and uncertainty, became absorbed into an atmosphere of prejudice and endless intrigue. This fact explains why even the vicars-apostolic, whom Rome had sent to the Far East in order to found a native Church, were led, partly by distrust of the Jesuits and partly by sincere conviction of the presence of real danger, to adopt an attitude of implacable hostility towards the only method which, despite a few shortcomings, had proved capable of founding that Church. As soon as he had been appointed to succeed Mgr Pallu in 1684, Mgr Maigrot embarked on a pitiless campaign against the Chinese rites.

It is useless to go into the details of that wretched quarrel. It assumed a violent character in 1693 (the year after the Jesuits had obtained the edict of toleration from Kang Hsi), when Mgr Maigrot, supported by Propaganda, issued a pastoral letter condemning the Chinese rites. In vain the Jesuits asked the emperor himself to explain the exact significance of the Confucian ceremonies and of the current theological vocabulary. The report of the Great Council was not even studied at Rome.[24] In 1704 Clement XI officially decided against the rites, and in the following year sent out a legate, Thomas de Tournon, to impose his will. This young Savoyard prelate, a privy chamberlain, proved so incompetent that Kang Hsi had him placed under house arrest at Macao. There the unfortunate man died, befriended only by Father Visdelou and consoled in some small measure by the cardinal's hat conferred upon him by the Pope. Those missionaries who favoured the Chinese rites were brought to heel by the Constitution *Ex illa die* (1715), which obliged them all to take an oath of obedience to the decisions of the Holy See. The Jesuits submitted with the rest, though not without anguish and a bitter sense of frustration. In 1717 the Emperor Kang Hsi, furious at learning that his report had been treated with contempt and Li Ma-tzu's practices suppressed, retorted with an edict forbidding the preaching of Christianity. In 1724 his successor expelled all missionaries, excepting only the Jesuit scientists working at Peking. Meanwhile a second legate, Mgr de Mezzabarbe, was sent to deal with the situation. More intelligent than Tournon, he realized that in some respects Rome had gone too far, and on his own authority he granted 'eight permissions' concerning the christianization of certain Chinese rites. Benedict XIV, ill-informed, annulled them by the Bull *Ex quo singulari* (1742). That was the end; the quarrel which had lasted for almost a hundred years was finished. Rome had decided against the view of Father Matteo Ricci.[25]

The results of this unhappy dispute were deplorable. Most obvious was the fact that Christianity could no longer make the least headway in educated circles. 'Scholars and government officials', wrote a Jesuit in 1726, 'have been leaving us since we published the decrees by order of the Holy Father.' Twenty years later another informed his readers that 'Christianity in China is confined to the poor'.

If only those Christian communities had continued to grow; but they were doomed to decrease. In 1700 they included about 200,000 members in all provinces. From 1707 the authorities showed themselves ill disposed, though there seems no reason to attribute their change of attitude to the affair of the rites. Preaching was forbidden. A decree of 1717 expelled the missionaries, leaving only forty-seven for the whole Empire. Persecution began in 1723; though sporadic and varying in intensity from one province to another, it claimed many victims, among them the Dominican Mgr Sanz, who was beheaded in 1757, and four priests of his mission, who were strangled. The Jesuit scientists who had been allowed to remain in Peking tried in vain to oppose the current of hostility. The Chinese Church vanished into obscurity, from which it did not emerge until the nineteenth century, when European warships used the threat of gunfire to reopen the ports of the Celestial Empire. It survived because heroic teams of missionaries—Jesuits, Dominicans, Lazarists and others—were ready to risk their lives in order to perpetuate the Gospel there, and also because a handful of Chinese priests remained loyal to their faith regardless of difficulties. Among these latter were Andrew Ly, apostle of Szechwan, who for seventeen years ministered alone to a province as large as France, and Joseph Kio, who laboured untiringly in Kansu and Shensi. Yet in spite of all their courage and hard work Christianity in China never ceased to wane. The three dioceses of Macao, Peking and Nanking, still subject to the jurisdiction of Goa, dwindled to mere shadows, as did the three vicariates. When the Society of Jesus was suppressed there were no more than forty-nine white missionaries and forty-four native priests in China, while the vast Empire certainly contained no more than 125,000 faithful souls; and that little flock was to be further decimated by a terrible persecution which broke out in 1784.

A similar decline is observable in Indo-China. The affair of the rites had never reached an equal pitch of animosity in that part of the world, for the teachings of Confucius were scarcely known there; but the work so well begun by de Rhodes, Lambert de la Motte and Pallu was halted by a variety of circumstances, some of them internal (particularly, as always, rivalry between the religious orders[26]), and others external. Nationalist feelings were exasperated on several occasions, even in such countries as Siam where they appeared not to exist; and there was actually a sort of Buddhist counter-offensive, launched by the influential clergy of the 'Little Vehicle' and involving outbreaks of xenophobia which sometimes led to bloodshed.[27]

The most serious factor was a sudden manifestation of hostility on the part of Siam, which had been the starting point of the Indo-Chinese missions. Whereas in the lifetime of Lambert de la Motte and during the vicariate of his disciple Laneau ostentatious diplomatic relations had been established between Siam and France, to the great advantage of Christianity, a strong reaction began in 1687, leading to the arrest of the bishop and some missionaries as well as to the sack of churches. Animosity later subsided and the Church was able to regain her foothold, but the situation remained precarious. In 1730 she was the victim of yet another persecution; then, from 1754 onwards the terrible Burmese invasions razed the seminary of Ajuthia (which was rebuilt at Pondicherry) and many churches, dispersed the Christian communities and reduced them almost to nothing.

At the end of the seventeenth and during the eighteenth century the situation deteriorated throughout the Indo-Chinese peninsula. An attempt to penetrate Burma in 1693 ended in the martyrdom of two missionaries, Genond and Joret, who were sewn up in sacks and thrown into the river. The Italian Barnabites were not able to re-establish themselves there until 1727. At Tonking there were five outbreaks of persecution, in 1696, 1713, 1721, 1736 and 1773. In Cochin China it was almost continuous, with periods of special ferocity, as in 1750 and again in 1766, when the vicar-apostolic himself was obliged to flee. At the latter date there were only six missionaries in Cochin China and the number of faithful had been halved. The overall picture of the Indo-Chinese missions was thus far from encouraging. The only Christian communities that retained some measure of vitality were those of Tonking, those in the west directed by the Society of the Foreign Missions, and those in the east controlled by Spanish Dominicans. All were assisted in the work by forty-eight zealous native priests. About 1789 the number of Indo-Chinese Christians hardly exceeded 50,000. It was a small achievement after so many hopes and so much endeavour.

6. INDIA IN THE DAYS OF DE NOBILI AND
JOHN DE BRITTO

The problems confronted in China were even more acute in India. The Portuguese patronate exercised its authority with more suspicion and intransigence. Wherever missionaries settled, Portuguese monks and priests and the Knights of Christ saw to it that none trespassed upon their domain, as the French Capuchin Ephrem de Nevers learned to his cost. Invited to Madras by the local ruler in 1649, he managed to build a church and a hospital; but he was kidnapped by the Portuguese and thrown into the dungeons of the Inquisition, whence the Pope himself was unable to deliver him. His release was eventually secured by the Hindu king of Golconda, who threatened to go and burn Meliapur unless his protégé were set free.

This imperious domination of the Portuguese, however, had its advantages. Their missions accomplished a work that must not be underestimated, establishing settlements at almost every suitable point along the coast. Goa, spiritual and administrative capital as well as the starting point of all voyages in the Far East, was the headquarters of the missions. But Christian penetration of the Orient, begun so successfully by St Francis Xavier, took no account of native feelings.

Pranguism, that is to say, the imposition of Portuguese customs on all who sought baptism, remained the sole method recognized by the white clergy. Converts were given Portuguese names and were compelled to eat beef, to wear leather shoes and to fraternize with untouchables, all of which practices discredited them in the eyes of their compatriots who remained faithful to the ancient ways. But the Portuguese method was inspired not by lust for power, but by a genuine anxiety to maintain Christian equality and a determined rejection of racialism in any shape or form, which do honour to the history of Portuguese colonization.

This policy, however, was misunderstood, and it led in 1620 to the rebellion of the Christians of St Thomas. They had been reunited with Rome in 1599, but were angered by the decision to forbid them their ancient Syro-Chaldaic rite and their prayers in Malabar dialect. Accordingly they prepared to secede; their schism, rendered inevitable by the stupidity of a few Europeans, was consummated in 1663, depriving the Roman Church of 150,000 members, only some of whom were destined to return in 1930. The warning went unheeded in the comfortable presbyteries and wealthy religious houses of Goa.

At the beginning of the seventeenth century, however, the old methods were abandoned in an important region of India. Father Roberto de Nobili (1577–1656), an Italian of high birth, great intelligence and unbounded charity, was sent in 1606 to an outpost in the territory of Madura, where he discovered that his predecessors had achieved no results whatever. Understanding the true reasons of their failure, he donned the robe of yellow linen worn by the *sannyasi*, lived after the manner of Indian ascetics and studied their languages and sacred books; in short, he did his best to become a 'Brahmin among Brahmins', and was rewarded with increasingly numerous conversions. He allowed these new Christians to continue wearing the sandalwood *silak* on their brows, to retain the Brahmin girdle and tuft of hair on the head, and also to celebrate certain traditional festivals. He was destined to spend the remainder of his life at Madura, and when he died he left behind him a flourishing Christian community, with its own churches and catechetical school, ready to overflow into neighbouring districts. His method had been proved right.[28]

De Nobili's innovations, however, aroused great indignation, for they clashed with too many prejudices and too many interests. In 1610 one of his colleagues, Father Fernandez, denounced him to the Inquisition at Goa, which condemned him for having allowed the ritual baths of Hinduism, sandalwood incensation and 'all sorts of superstitious customs'; worse still, he had systematically confused the sacred truths of Christianity with the horrors of Hindu theology. Reported to Rome, criticized by the General of the Society and by his saintly cousin Cardinal Bellarmine, de Nobili defended himself with no less ability than energy. Judgment went against the Patriarch of Goa, who had accused him of having gone over to paganism as well as of having sought to drive the Portuguese from India. In 1623, after thirteen years of dispute, Gregory XV and the newly founded Congregation of Propaganda approved the methods of de Nobili, who, as one report said, 'had enlightened India'.

The controversy was unfortunately resumed eighty years later as a result of the affair of the Chinese rites. The Madura mission had continued to prosper. In order not to flout the rules of caste, the missionaries had wisely adopted a method of specialization: two of them lived as Brahmins, so as to be able to carry on their apostolate among the upper classes, while seven lived as *pandaram*, i.e. poor ascetics, among the labourers and even the pariahs. This innovation was held against the Jesuits as a breach of Christian charity. Once again use was made of the objections long since urged against de Nobili by Fernandez: the Fathers were said to tolerate pagan customs, and also superstitious rites, which were lumped together under the general term 'Malabar rites'.[29] One of the worst complaints against the Jesuits was their omission of two sacramentals from the ceremony of baptism, out of respect for the Hindu's instinctive abhorrence of saliva and human breath. In 1704 the matter was referred to the Papal Legate, Tournon, on his way through Pondicherry to China. He held a very brief inquiry and published a decree in terms suggested by the authorities at Goa. The missionaries protested and appealed to Rome; in 1739 Clement XII confirmed most of Tournon's decisions, and the missionaries received orders to take a written oath that they would no longer tolerate Malabar rites. But the question of the pariahs was left open, and the Jesuits were allowed to continue enlisting missionaries for service among the lower classes. In 1744 Benedict XIV himself warmly commended this arrangement. So while the number of Brahmin missionaries decreased, and Christian penetration of the upper classes was brought to a halt as in China, the *pandaram swami* (those who ministered to the rank and file) continued to make progress.

One of them, St John de Britto (1647–93), achieved great renown. A Portuguese Jesuit belonging to one of the leading families of the realm and a personal friend of King Pedro, he had the good sense to rise above the interests and routine of the patronate, and to follow resolutely in the footsteps of de Nobili. This cultured gentleman, whose health was never robust, did not hesitate to adopt the hard life of the *pandaram*, abstaining from meat, fish and eggs, being satisfied with a handful of rice, and sleeping on bare boards. Appointed head of the Madura mission in 1685, his influence was such that the number of conversions exceeded an average of one thousand each year. Nothing could hinder him; resistance on the part of local rulers, imprisonment and torture, obstacles placed in his way by other missionaries such as the Carmelite Pedro Paolo, denunciation to Rome and Lisbon—all were alike in vain. Setting out from Madura, he evangelized the plateaux of Marava, where the rajah's hostility rendered his task extremely difficult. There he perished beneath the executioner's sword, while six of his flock were subjected to torture. His rank and the manner of his life helped in no small degree to the success of a mission which continued to flourish until the suppression of the Society (1773) delivered it a mortal blow, at which date it numbered 200,000 souls.

Madura with its appendages was the only example of Christian penetration into the interior of India until the policy of Dupleix obtained for the missionaries limited access to the native kingdoms. Attempts by the Jesuits in the northern and central territories to win the favour of the Great Mogul, Aurungzeb, failed to convert him, and the ruin of the empire of Delhi after his death in 1707 made further activity impossible. Christianity was thenceforward confined to a narrow coastal strip, whence it made no progress in any direction. The rise of French power in India was accompanied by the arrival of French missionaries. Capuchins landed at Surat in 1639, and in 1642 at Madras, whither they had been invited by François Martin. French Jesuits, supported by John de Britto, settled in the Carnatic, where Fathers Bouchet and Martin were sometimes called upon to baptize so many people that they could no longer raise their arms; Pondicherry and Chandernagor also became busy centres of missionary work. But further progress was halted by a change in the policies of France.

The history of the Church in India at this time is hard to follow; its theatre of operations was extended all along the coasts, and the period was marked by frequent intestine strife as well as by repeated conflict between the French, English and Dutch. Nevertheless one fact must be emphasized—the growth of a native priesthood, which contributed to the future not one whit less than the achievements of de Nobili and de Britto. Recruited in many cases from among half-castes, and so utterly despised by the Europeans that it was necessary to promulgate a decree reminding Portuguese clerics of the right of native priests to enter the churches, that priesthood expanded during the seventeenth century under the auspices of vicars-apostolic many of whom were themselves drawn from the ranks of natives and half-castes. By about 1750, between the mouths of the Indus and Cape Cormorin, and thence to the delta of the Ganges, there were innumerable churches governed by native bishops. Several religious orders, realizing how much was at stake, founded establishments for the training of Indian priests, among them the Oratorians, led by Matteo de Castro, the Theatines and the Carmelites. One of these Oratorian institutes produced Father Joseph Vaz, the apostle of Ceylon, a half-caste priest of outstanding holiness who may perhaps eventually be canonized. For more than fifteen years, defying the Dutch who were at that time masters of the island, he preached Catholicism everywhere, reorganized the mission which the Portuguese had had to abandon, and left behind him at his death a Christian community with four hundred churches and nearly 100,000 souls.

7. MILESTONES ON THE INTERIOR ROUTE

The Gospel had reached Asia not only through the seaports of China, Japan and the southern peninsulas, but also by way of the interior. As early as the sixteenth century attempts had been made to explore an overland route to the Far East along which missionaries would be able to erect stations that would serve at once as posting houses and apostolic bases. The search continued for at least a hundred and thirty or a hundred and forty years; it became a matter of increased urgency when Propaganda, anxious to escape from the tutelage of the patronate, advised its envoys not to use the maritime route. It was through the interior that Father de Rhodes returned from Indo-China, that Mgr Pallu travelled thither, and that the messengers sent by the first vicars-apostolic made their journey to Rome. The whole story is full of strange happenings and adventures; it has never been written in full,[30] though it well deserves to be.

The overland route was opened up from three directions. The route from the east was developed mainly by Jesuit scientists from Peking, who at the request of several emperors (notably of Kang Hsi) explored and began to map the area beyond the Great Wall. About 1730, when persecution of the Chinese Church had already commenced, a French Jesuit, Father Gaubil, undertook to study the old caravan route from China to Turkestan; his work was continued until after 1760 by two of his brethren. The Jesuits, of course, never lost sight of their apostolic aims, and attempts were made to form Christian nuclei in Mongolia and on the borders of Tibet.

Tibet itself was approached simultaneously from the north, east and south. Father Ricci had long ago drawn attention to that country in the centre of Asia, the turntable, as he claimed, of roads leading from Europe to India and China. The journey (1602–7) made by Brother Bento de Goes had proved him right; and Father Trigault's famous book *De l'expédition chrétienne en Chine,* which narrated Bento's adventure, revealed to the West the importance of the 'roof of the world'. A series of attempts was afterwards made to penetrate the country and establish Christian settlements. Father de Andrade, a Portuguese Jesuit, came from Agra in 1624, followed a little later by Fathers Cacella and Azevedo. Next, about 1680, some French and Italian Franciscans arrived from the west. In 1704 Propaganda raised Tibet to the status of an apostolic vicariate, sending out a number of Capuchins and Carmelites. About 1725 a bold and exciting expedition under the Italian Jesuit Desideri started from India by order of the Patriarch of Goa, who wished to uphold his rights. Desideri made a long stay in Lhasa, discussed theology with the lamas, and brought back scientific notes whose accuracy has been admired by such modern explorers of Tibet as Sven Hedin. From the Christian point of view these undertakings were not outstandingly successful; from 1740 onward the lamas, warned by messengers from China, India and elsewhere, regarded missionaries as mere quartermasters sent to prepare the way for an invading army and would allow no European to enter their country.

Meanwhile, however, other lines of exploration had been followed. About 1689 Father Avril, S.J., whose countless adventures had led him from the prisons of the Czar to those of the Grand Turk, suggested that missionaries from Germany and Poland might use the Siberian route. A tenacious young Italian Jesuit, Father Grimaldi, attacked the barrier of Turkestan. But it all proved fruitless; gone were the days of the 'Mongol writ', when fourteenth-century Franciscans had been able to journey along the caravan trail across the steppes without the slightest inconvenience. Moslem fanaticism and the subjection of the Turkish peoples to Islam raised one obstacle after another.

Nevertheless there were a few exceptions, and Christianity was firmly based at several points, mainly in Persia, where the mission had been founded early in the seventeenth century by a team of Discalced Carmelites.[31] Its success was due partly to the fact that Shah Abbas was threatened by the Turks and hoped to obtain assistance from the West. Since

1612 there had even been a bishop in Persia, Antonio de Gouvea, and Catholicism was beginning to take root in the Iranian Empire, particularly among heretical and schismatic Christians. Soon afterwards Father Joseph du Tremblay assumed control of French missions to the Levant[32] and a second party was sent out, this time by the Capuchins. Persia was entrusted to Father Pacifique de Provins, who arrived in 1628, obtained permission to found several houses of his order and started to work in earnest among the Nestorians. As for the Jesuits, they were looking anxiously for the most convenient route across Asia, and could not ignore the splendid facilities offered by Persia. In 1652 Father Chézaud was sent to Ispahan from Syria, where he had achieved great things; and proof of the importance attached to the Persian mission is the appointment of Father de Rhodes, who joined it after concluding those negotiations at Paris and Rome which ended in the consecration of vicars-apostolic for Indo-China. Despite a number of crises, some rivalry between the orders and a few brief persecutions, the mission in Persia continued to flourish until 1757, when it was driven out in consequence of a palace revolution; nor did Catholicism disappear even after its removal. To it also was due in large measure the spread of Catholicism among the Armenians, not only within the boundaries of Persia, where Father Chézaud laboured with unflagging devotion, but also in Greater Armenia, whose population was subject to the Turks. Erzerum was reached in 1688 by Father Roche; he was followed by a party of French Jesuits who succeeded beyond all expectations. Catholic communities, though persecuted by the Turks, survived the departure of the missionaries, who were driven out in the middle of the eighteenth century; the atrocious massacres of 1915 finally destroyed them along with every other group professing allegiance to Christ.

8. FRENCH MISSIONS: THE LEVANT

Along the interior routes of Asia, even in Persia, Catholicism had really done no more than set up a few landmarks. A very different situation prevailed in the Levant, where, thanks to France, the Church was much more firmly established.

The history of French missions in the Levant inspires nothing but admiration. Barrès, in his famous inquiry, paid just homage to the participants and to the loyalty which marked their work. All that we know today as the Middle East was included then in the Turkish Empire. The Ottoman government was not officially hostile; it even allowed the continuance of patriarchates at Constantinople, Antioch, Beirut and elsewhere, together with numerous bodies of clergy. But the Sublime Porte, and still more its civil service, looked with scorn upon the Christians, whom they described as 'worse than dogs', and loaded them with ever-mounting taxation. The majority of those Christians belonged to the so-called Greek Orthodox Church or to various heretical sects (e.g. the Maronites) deriving from Eutyches and Nestorius. The Melchites, who remained faithful to Rome, had decreased considerably. All those Christian bodies, who continued to struggle heroically after so many centuries against the formidable pressure of Islam, were ravaged by apostasy, enervated by routine and torn by internal dissension; at Aleppo, for example, there were no fewer than fourteen varieties of Christians. The task before the missions, then, on arrival in the Levant, was to labour among the ancient decrepit Churches rather than to convert the Moslems, especially as all such converts were liable to the penalty of death.

Until the closing years of the sixteenth century there were no true missionaries in the Turkish Empire. The only religious body of the least importance was a small group of Franciscans at Jerusalem, usually Italians, to whom custody of the Holy Places had been confided in 1342, and who had managed to hold their own there notwithstanding all the vicissitudes of history. They welcomed pilgrims and provided chaplains for the French and Venetian consuls; but they were generally ignorant of the country's language and carried on no apostolate. The only Christian authority that counted in the Levant was the political power of France, and even that must not be exaggerated. The system of capitulations —the treaties between the Sublime Porte and the French monarchy[33]—was initiated in 1535 by François I, in order to outflank the Hapsburg Empire. It was retained by his successors, and its scope was boldly enlarged by every ambassador sent from Paris to Constantinople. Thus in 1604 Savary de Brèves, the envoy of Henri IV, renewed the capitulations, taking care that the treaty specified once again the right of France to protect all Christian subjects of the Ottoman Empire, all pilgrims to the Holy Land and all missionaries to the Levant. In point of fact, however, the right was merely theoretical; as Mgr Homsy has shown, it was subject to the goodwill of the sultans and dependent on their general policies. But the protective role of France was so well recognized by the people at large that all Christians came to be called 'Franks'.

When the call of the missions was heard in France it was natural that the Levant should benefit by the enthusiasm it aroused. All those who directed French policy in the seventeenth and eighteenth centuries were protectors of the missions. They included Louis XIII, who in 1639 reaffirmed his rights as protector of the Christians and thought of creating a Jesuit university in the East; Father Joseph, whose work we shall presently describe; the Regent, who financed the Syrian mission from his own purse; and Louis XV, who was careful to retain the religious clauses in the capitulations of 1740. It may be that the Most Christian Kings looked upon such acts as a means of excusing themselves for their alliance with the impious Turk. The generosity of the rich and powerful in favour of the missions was particularly great towards those of the Levant, as, for example, in the foundation of the bishopric of Babylon.[34] The result was what might be called 'Levantine France', Christian in faith and missionary in purpose. Its growth was frowned upon by the enemies of Paris, especially by the Venetians; but its radiance continued to increase, and its prestige has lasted till today.

The earliest French missionary ventures in the Near East were not altogether successful. A party of Jesuits sent to Constantinople in 1583 had succumbed to the plague, and a similar fate had overtaken a Capuchin expedition four years later. Encouraged by Father Cotton, confessor to Henri IV, the Society made another attempt, and in 1609 Father de Canillac managed to settle on the Bosporus. From there the

Jesuits gradually made their way towards Syria, Armenia, Persia, Greece and the Archipelago. But in 1615 or thereabouts they were still making very little progress, hampered by the intrigues of Venice and by the serious machinations of the Orthodox Patriarch, Cyril Lukaris, who had embraced Calvinism and dreamed of uniting the Oriental Church with the Protestant Churches.[35]

A decisive impulse was needed before the French mission to the Levant could really begin to flourish. It was given by a man whose position endowed him with the necessary strength —Father Joseph du Tremblay, Richelieu's friend and 'Grey Eminence'. Among the grand designs of that mighty brain was a crusade against the Turks. When he had seen his project to be unrealizable and had shed his warlike complex through the medium of his long-winded *Turciade*, the Capuchin turned his thoughts to missionary endeavour as another means of repelling Islam. To this enterprise he devoted his great strategical talents. First he sent two of his brethren, Fathers Pacifique de Provins and Hippolyte de Paris, to make a preliminary investigation. Their reports were encouraging. That was in 1622; the Congregation of Propaganda had just been created and was looking for assistants. Father Joseph suggested sending Capuchins to reinforce the Jesuits in the East and even, if need be, to replace them wherever their position had become untenable. He won the day and was appointed, together with his friend Father Léonard de Paris, Prefect of Oriental Missions. Louis XIII obtained permission from the Sultan to install the Capuchins in the Turkish Empire, and Richelieu granted them a substantial income from the salt tax. Father Joseph was a born organizer; he kept himself fully informed of conditions that might favour the apostolate in any region, and eventually partitioned the Near East into three areas. Greece and Asia Minor were entrusted to the Capuchin province of Paris; the northern half of Syria with Mesopotamia, Persia and Egypt to the Capuchins of Touraine under Father Pacifique de Provins; southern Syria, the Lebanon and Palestine to the Capuchins of Brittany. Notwithstanding the extreme unfriendliness shown by the Italian Franciscans at Jerusalem, the Capuchins made headway throughout the Near East, and when Mgr Pallu travelled through northern Syria in 1662 the district was occupied by no fewer than two hundred and fifty-eight Capuchins. Until the day of his death Father Joseph never ceased to take an active interest in this work. He helped the Maronites to feel at home in the Roman Church, to whose fold they had lately returned; he made plans for the establishment of a printing house that was to issue books in Arabic, Turkish, Persian and Syriac; and he drew up a scheme for the foundation of seminaries in eastern lands. The French missions in the Levant owed much to the mysterious friar who was Richelieu's right arm.

The impetus thus given long endured. The Jesuits felt its benefit, and their missions multiplied. Their most outstanding member at that time was Father Aimé Chézaud, who spent some time in charge of the mission at Aleppo before being sent to Persia; he had an extensive knowledge of native languages, great zeal as a preacher and boundless charity in caring for the sick and all unfortunates. The Carmelites settled on Mount Carmel itself and in many other places; they were favoured by the Moslems because of the respect in which the Koran held El Khader (the Verdant), the prophet Elias. Among them was Father Bernard de Saint-Thérèse, who, as Jean Duval, had been the principal figure of a curious episode. Mme de Ricouart (*née* Elisabeth le Peultre), a wealthy widow, admired Duval on account of his zeal and his knowledge of foreign languages. Resolved therefore to have the bishopric of Babylon restored,[36] not as a title *in partibus* but as a residential see of the Latin rite, she worried Propaganda to such good effect (and incidentally promised an endowment of six thousand Spanish doubloons[37]) that she eventually achieved her purpose. The diocese of Babylon was created in 1638; Jean Duval was its first titular, and it was understood that all his successors should be of French nationality. Other religious orders—Theatines, Dominicans, Barnabites—continued to send missionaries to the Levant; even those who were not French declared themselves 'Franks' as soon as they reached their posts, and spoke the language of Versailles. By about 1660 there was a whole network of French missionary stations reaching from Constantinople to Palestine and as far as Mesopotamia.

The full history of those missions is inevitably complicated. Local authorities, according as they felt inclined, treated the missionaries sometimes with oriental politeness, sometimes brutally, but most often with stern severity, forbidding all ritual pomp and the building of large churches, and even penalizing oriental converts. There were no martyrs in the strict sense, except Father Kumurdjian, who was beheaded for his faith at Constantinople in 1707; being an Armenian, he did not benefit much from French protection. But there were a number of persecutions. One broke out in Syria on the death of Louis XIV, when the Christian communities annoyed the Turkish officials with their display of grief; it resulted in a decree (1722) hostile to all Christians. Generally speaking, however, the Levantine missions were able to make slow progress until the end of the eighteenth century.

Looking back over that thrilling story, it is pleasant to revive the memory of one great man who is too little known. François Picquet (1626–85), French consul at Aleppo, was a model Christian worthy to be ranked with his friends Bernières, Renty and other members of the Company of the Blessed Sacrament. He was sent to Syria at the age of twenty-two and remained there for thirty years, carrying out his duties with exemplary intelligence and firmness. He gave proof of wonderful charity on all occasions and laboured unceasingly to protect the missions; he defended the Maronites,[38] whose submission to Rome had made them particularly suspect to the Turks; and he even managed to form a Catholic hierarchy among the Melchites.[39] Thanks to him, also, Christianity spread in all directions from Aleppo, which at that time was the chief commercial centre of the Near East. Ordained priest on his return to France, he was immediately appointed by Propaganda bishop and vicar-apostolic of Babylon, but he died on the way to his episcopal city. His name remains inseparable from the history of France in the Levant.

French missionary work in the Near East lasted until the Revolution. True, another French consul at Aleppo, an unworthy successor to Picquet, declared that there were too many missionaries in that part of the world; but almost all the representatives of France upheld their rights of protection

over Christians in the East, and continued to favour the
missions. During the eighteenth century, however, Russia
under Peter the Great began to play the part of protector of
Orthodox Christians, while Spain and Venice financed Spanish and Italian missions; the emperor too occasionally laid
claim to some measure of authority in oriental affairs. Among
the French people at large there was a progressive lessening
of interest in the missions, due to 'philosophical' influence;
but the government at Versailles had the wisdom to stand by
its policy of protection and encouragement. In 1740, when
the Marquis de Villeneuve negotiated a renewal of the capitulations, the rights of France as first protectress of Christians
in the Levant was expressly reaffirmed in the first and six
later articles of the treaty. Rome recognized the value of
French achievement in this field, and decided to record its
gratitude in official form: in 1742 a decree of Propaganda
ordained that whenever a representative of France attended
religious services he should receive special liturgical honours.

9. FRENCH MISSIONS: 'NEW FRANCE'

North America was another part of the world in which the
work of French missionaries proved of capital importance. In
the middle of the sixteenth century Jacques Cartier had
planted the fleurs-de-lis on territory which was described in
Ramusio's *Navigations and Voyages* (1556) as New France.[40]
In the early years of the seventeenth century French missionaries had established two houses on the banks of a great
river which was beginning to be known as the St Lawrence. An
eccentric layman, Lescarbot, had founded some modest settlements in Acadia (modern Nova Scotia), among them Port-
Royal and Saint-Sauveur, from which the neighbourhood was
first evangelized. Henri IV and Marie de' Medici both took
an interest in the undertaking, and the Society of Jesus sent
out two of its Fathers, who obtained good results. The situation was still more encouraging inland and farther north,
where the name of Samuel Champlain (1567–1635) was associated with French Catholic penetration. Author of the
grand design to people Canada with Frenchmen, he worked

for thirty-two years to settle colonists and at the same time to place the Church upon firm foundations in these new lands. At his request four Recollects landed in 1614; their labours were well rewarded, and it was even possible to consider the foundation of a seminary at Quebec, the capital of New France.

But the two French colonies were soon in difficulty. Acadia succumbed to an attack by Protestants from Virginia in 1613 when a Welsh adventurer named Argall swept down upon the little settlements, razed them to the ground and carried off the missionaries. In Canada the trouble was at first of a different sort. The Compagnie des Associés, founded by Champlain to support his work and recruited from the wealthy merchants of Normandy and Brittany, did not understand the policy of colonization, which was costly and for the time being showed no returns. Dissolved in 1619 by order of the viceroy, Prince de Condé, it was replaced by another society in which two Protestant shipowners, Guillaume and Emery de Caen of Dieppe, held a majority of shares. How was it possible in such circumstances to hope for effective support for the twin requirements of colonization and the apostolate, which in Champlain's view were inseparable? In 1627 Cardinal Richelieu, realizing the situation and calculating the benefits which France might expect from such an enterprise, suppressed all the trading companies and founded the Compagnie des Cent Associés, which was to follow the policy suggested by the aged pioneer.

Those vexations, however, did not halt the missionary task. The Company of the Blessed Sacrament, whose founder, Henri de Levis, Duc de Ventadour, was for some time Viceroy of Canada, interested himself in the work. The Recollects, under Father Sagard, began to make headway among the Hurons. Next a party of Jesuits—Fathers Jean de Brebeuf, Charles Lallemand[41] and Massé—set sail for the banks of the St Lawrence. Despite the hostility of the brothers de Caen, who went so far as to prevent the loading of cargoes destined for the missions, they did good work and made many more contacts with the natives, to whom Champlain promised all the rights of French citizenship in the event of their conversion—even if they wished to go to France. This promise,

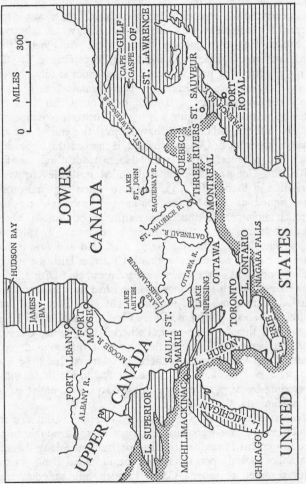

French Missions in Canada

contained in an instruction addressed to the missionaries, was far in advance of its time. But all this work was ruined, as in Acadia, by British Protestants. During the summer of 1628 a ship carrying four colonists and a party of Jesuits was intercepted by Scottish corsairs, the brothers Kirk, whose pilot was a French Huguenot, Jacques Michel. Next year Quebec was attacked by the same gang and forced to capitulate, for the Thirty Years War had prevented France from sending either a garrison or ships to defend it. There remained at Quebec only one French family, Hébert, to whom Champlain entrusted his adopted daughters, three little convert redskins.

The fall of Quebec might have seemed the end of French missionary work in Canada. Instead, it marked the beginning of a new advance. The attack had been made three months after the Congress of Suse had ended hostilities between Britain and France. In 1632, therefore, when the final peace was signed at Saint-Germain-en-Laye, it was easy for the French diplomats to obtain the restitution of Canada. Once again colonists set out accompanied, of course, by missionaries. The Jesuits now shouldered a twofold and formidable task: their aim was to cement with Christian faith the newly laid foundations of the colony and to spread that faith among the natives, which latter they accomplished by way of numerous adventures and terrifying risks. The aged Father Massé, Fathers Brebeuf, Le Jeune, Charles Lallemand, Gabriel Lalemant and then, a little later, Fathers Isaac Jogues, Garnier and Chabanel, were among the heroes of that glorious episode which would soon produce its martyrs. In 1635 the Jesuits opened a college at Quebec, the first in North America, preceding by six or seven years John Harvard's foundation at Massachusetts.

These events took place on the flood-tide of an age in which, as we have seen, missionary zeal was inseparable from the movement towards spiritual reconstruction. Many French Catholics looked upon Canada as the Promised Land, where they dreamed of serving Christ through toil, suffering and perhaps even the sacrifice of their lives. There was frequent talk of Canada in all Jesuit colleges, e.g. that of La Flèche. A number of successful books on the subject began to appear: *Grand voyage au pays des Hurons*, the Recollect Sagard's

Histoire du Canada and, above all, the *Relations* of the Jesuit Fathers (1632 onwards), which circulated widely in cheap editions.[42] These *Relations* were not mere narratives but appeals for support. The champions of Christ sought help from court, mansion and counting house, and also from cottage and monastery. Peasants from Normandy, Perche, Maine and Anjou set out to till those distant lands; sometimes they took with them their parish priest, and the rector of Thury was the first secular to land in Canada. Hence, no doubt, the many families named Gagnon, Beaulieu, Richer or Léger which one meets today in French Canada. There was the same enthusiasm in high society. The ambassador Brûlart de Sillery, renowned for his luxurious habits, became a priest and gave his entire fortune for Canada, while the Duchesse d'Aiguillon emptied her treasury to provide worthy buildings for the seminary at Quebec and to build a hospital. Fashion itself took a hand in the movement: to keep a Huron girl in one's house or to be godmother to a little Iroquois was considered the very height of style.

On the spiritual plane Canada would scarcely have been what it is today but for the presence on its soil of many women vowed to God's service. Two of them have since been beatified. Blessed Marie de l'Incarnation, an Ursuline of solid Touraine stock, was called by God to the highest mystical experiences,[43] but she never lost her gifts as a busy and resourceful woman; not content with having founded the first Canadian school for girls in 1639, she was, until her death in 1672, the living conscience, as well as on many occasions the spiritual *and* temporal adviser, of Canada at large. Her companion Madeleine de Chauvigny, widow of M. de Peltrie, though perhaps a little eccentric in her ways, embarked for Canada after numerous romantic adventures and used all her goods to finance the various foundations. The gentle Mère Guenet, a Sister of Charity from Caen, defied the objurgations of her family and left with two companions to establish the first hospital at Quebec. There was also Jeanne Mancé, the 'lay religious', whose calm courage and inexhaustible devotion to the sick and wounded were associated with the difficult beginnings of Montreal. Somewhat later, Blessed

Marguerite Bourgeoys, after founding in Champagne a community in honour of Our Lady's travels, discovered her true vocation and departed for New France, where her small institute, now known as the Congregation of Notre-Dame, took up the work of education with rapid and considerable success.

In due time all that effort and devotion bore its fruit. The French settlements, which were both guard posts and missionary stations, quickly multiplied: Quebec, Sainte-Croix de Tadoussac, Three Rivers and Sillery, all on or near the banks of the St Lawrence. Sillery was unique—a fine model village, where natives received Christian education and technical training. The most venturesome, Sault Sainte-Marie, was implanted far away, in the region of the Great Lakes; but the most remarkable and most rich in promise of all these foundations was Montreal. Remarkable, because of the many hazards and exchanges that had to be survived before the project was fulfilled. Jérôme de Dauversière, a tax collector and alderman of La Flèche, learned while engaged in mystical prayer that he was to found a mission on the upper St Lawrence. Next, Marie Rousseau, wife of a rich Parisian vintner, who had played some part in M. Olier's vocation, put him in touch with the Company of the Blessed Sacrament. Then six (later thirty-five) well-to-do persons became interested in the project, and formed the Société de Notre Dame to give it reality. It was then necessary to persuade the Compagnie des Cent Associés to hand over the land. Finally, Paul de Maisonneuve, a brilliant soldier, decided to take military command of an enterprise which would call for at least as much fighting as husbandry and prayer. Thus one day in May 1632, on an island in the St Lawrence and to the strains of 'Veni Creator', there was born a modest outpost surrounded with a simple palisade. Named Ville-Marie, it afterwards spread to the hill overlooking the river and was called, as it is called today, Montreal.

Nothing in that great adventure is separable from its fundamentally Christian and apostolic purpose. For many years —at least until about 1650—the sole aim of all those men and women, most of whom daily risked their lives and in any case accepted an existence full of hardships, was to serve Christ and His Church by erecting a new branch of Christendom on

Canadian soil. The future would witness the arrival of un-
scrupulous fur traders and vendors of alcohol; but at the
beginning, and in many places for long afterwards, young
Canada afforded an example of what Christianity can be
when lived in accordance with its day-to-day exigencies and in
obedience to all its principles.

Life in these settlements was on a military footing: every
man was required 'to have his arms in readiness and to take
his turn of guard duty'. But there was also an element of
monastic life: the church bell marked the course of the day
and announced the curfew. Sins were punished by law, notably
those of violence and adultery; and soldiers who failed to live
as good Christians were shipped back to France. 'It has become almost a proverb among the French', wrote Father
Buteux to the General of the Society, 'that anyone who wishes
to improve himself should cross the sea to New France.' Nor
were his words inappropriate. Canada was from the outset
what Calvin's city had intended to be, but without (or very
nearly so) the dictatorial, inquisitorial elements of Geneva;
it was the work of prayer no less than of material endeavour.

This pleasant aspect, however, must not blind us to the
more terrible side of the undertaking; for those small Christian communities grew up amid native peoples, some of
whom, e.g. the Iroquois, were systematically hostile,[44] while
others, though normally less ferocious, were capable of sudden
change under the influence of some superstitious commotion
or of a few witch-doctors. The Jesuit missions, with courage that often outstripped the sublime, tried hard to penetrate the redskin tribes, sharing their life, their hardships,
their sufferings, and even taking part in their hunts. Sometimes they revisited those who had tortured them, happy in
the thought that if martyrdom awaited, their blood would
fertilize a corner of Huron or Iroquois territory. A Protestant
historian of Boston[45] has paid this glowing tribute to these
and to their fatherland: 'Their weapons of conquest were
wholly peaceful, benign and beneficial. France never dreamed
of destroying the peoples whom she sought to conquer; her
missionaries desired only to convert them, to civilize them, to
embrace them as their children. Their methods may be compared with those employed a little later by the Protestant

United States towards the Indian tribes in their territories, with results that are known to all.'

It is impossible here to follow the details of those exemplary lives, but a few great names must be mentioned. St Isaac Jogues, a native of Orleans, who planted the cross near Lake Superior, was captured a first time by the Iroquois and subjected to hideous torture, his fingertips being gnawed off by the redskins. He went back to France, but asked to return to Canada, where he visited the same group of Iroquois and was murdered. St John de Brebeuf, a Norman from Vire, went among the Hurons, shared their fate when they were crushed in a terrible raid by the Iroquois, and was martyred, after unspeakable tortures, together with St Gabriel Lalemant. St Noel Chabanel of Toulouse, the youngest member of the mission, suffered martyrdom after tortures so cruel in their refinement that they cannot be so much as named. Finally, St Charles Garnier, a Parisian, was clubbed to death by a Huron traitor. To what purpose all this sacrifice? Apparently to very little—a few hundred missions, whose permanence was never certain. But the missionaries were sure that their labours were not futile so long as the faith was sown and began to germinate among their beloved savages. Tekakwitha, a girl belonging to the Mohave Iroquois, was baptized as 'Kateri' and died at the age of twenty-four, dreaming of the day when she might take religious vows; later another Iroquois girl, Gannansagonas, baptized as Marie-Thérèse, was admitted to the Congregation of Notre-Dame. Both put forth flowers of exquisite sanctity from a harsh land that had been drenched in blood. In Canada, as everywhere, the blood of martyrs was the seed of Christianity.

About 1650 Canada was still confronted with many dangers and many problems, but she struck roots sufficiently strong and healthy to ensure her continuance. The flow of immigrants, though not large, was regular; at that date there were some three thousand colonists, and a steady influx of missionaries to replace or reinforce earlier arrivals. In 1657, just before his death, Jean-Jacques Olier, who himself had dreamed of becoming a missionary, decided to send four Sulpician priests of the Society of Saint-Sulpice to New France. MM. de Queylus, Souart, Galinier and d'Allet took up residence at Montreal, where M. de Queylus, as Vicar-General of the Archbishop of Rouen, took canonical charge of the colony. This was the beginning of a new and important stage of religious expansion in Canada. Leaving to the Jesuits the strictly missionary tasks (an arrangement which later on did not prevent two of them from suffering death at the hands of the Iroquois), the Sulpicians devoted themselves mainly to the spiritual needs of the colonists, officiated in the parish church of Notre-Dame, whose twin towers still dominate the lower city, and founded a seminary which quickly filled and exerted an influence which has never ceased. It is to Saint-Sulpice that the Canadian clergy of today owe their characteristics of gravity, solid faith and contemplative piety. The reputation of the Sulpicians was such that in 1663, when the Société des Messieurs de Montréal, which had created the city, resolved to disband, it transmitted to them its rights and prerogatives. M. Olier's sons were destined to continue as 'Squires of Montreal' until the coming of the British regime.

The point of development reached by the Canadian missions seemed to necessitate the appointment of a bishop to direct them. That thought had been uppermost in men's minds for a long while; but whereas the Cent Associés wanted a Jesuit bishop residing at Quebec, the Sulpicians demanded one of their own society with his see at Montreal. In 1658, after many exchanges between Paris and Rome, Propaganda appointed François de Montigny-Laval as Vicar-Apostolic. A friend of Pallu and Lambert de la Motte, adopted like them by the small but devoted circle directed by Father Bagot, he also belonged to the powerful family of Montmorency as well as to the Company of the Blessed Sacrament. He was moreover a saintly priest, trained to a life of renunciation by Jean de Bernières in the Hermitage of Caen. His appointment was a critical step; for while the Gallican Church demanded that the new vicar-apostolic should be a suffragan of Rouen, Propaganda wanted him dependent upon itself. So heated was the dispute that Mgr Harlay de Champvallon decreed that no French bishop might take part in the consecration of M. Montigny-Laval, which was eventually performed by the nuncio. On his arrival in Canada, the vicar-apostolic suffered the effects of this crisis. M. de Queylus, who had hoped to be appointed, obtained from the papal Dataria confirmation of his own title as Ordinary in Montreal and of his dependence upon none but the Archbishop of Rouen; and so flagrantly did he oppose the 'intruder' that it was necessary to remove him for a time from Canada. The vicar-apostolic had then to deal with the traders who were becoming more numerous in the colony; he strongly condemned those who sold 'death water' to the natives, a step which involved him in trouble with various officials and even with Colbert. But in spite of all these difficulties Mgr de Laval led his flock in the ways of perfection, setting them the example of a blameless life— poor among the poor, utterly devoted to their service and austere towards himself. In 1674 his seminary (ancestor of the famous Laval University) was flourishing, and Rome considered his work to be now so fully accomplished that the title of vicar-apostolic was no longer appropriate. Quebec became the seat of a diocese dependent directly upon the Holy See, its titular, like all French bishops, being nominated by the king.

Officially Canada ceased to be a missionary land, and entered into the regular hierarchy; but she remained in fact a missionary land by virtue of the fact that her Christian inhabitants continued to spread their faith. Interrupted for a time by the terrible Iroquois offensives, missionary activity was resumed about 1660, since when it has never ceased. The sixteen Jesuits who at that time were the only representatives of the Society in North America were joined by twenty-three of their brethren from Europe, and soon began to make headway in all directions: eastward towards the maritime provinces and Acadia (once again French), where a whole tribe, the Abenaquis, was converted; northward, where the entire Saguenay valley and the shores of Hudson Bay were reached within a period of ten years; westward towards the Great Lakes in the footsteps of Isaac Jogues, where the foundation of Detroit in 1701 marked a decisive stage in the penetration of the interior. The most celebrated of these discoverers of territory and conquerors of souls was Father Marquette, who in 1673, together with his companion Louis Jolliet, a fur trader, set out in birchbark canoes, 'joyfully plying their paddles', along the course of unknown rivers. He covered more than 2,000 miles in search of lands and of peoples to baptize, left his mark at many places (notably Chicago) that have since become famous, and showed that the Mississippi, the great and mysterious river of the prairie, empties into the Gulf of Mexico and not in the region of California as was then believed. It must be admitted that these efforts as a whole accomplished little. Conversions among the redskins were few and far between, because of the strict demands of Christian morality; nor were the Fathers able to shelter them from contact with white traders, who too often led the tribes to alcoholism and venereal disease, those dreadful agents of depopulation.

The future of Canada lay not among the natives, but in those small groups of French colonists, whose vigour and tenacity were to prove extraordinary. Increase of population was fairly rapid: from 3,000 in 1660 to 6,700 in 1670 and 80,000 a hundred years later. The numbers, of course, were still insufficient, and it was regrettable that from the beginning of the eighteenth century France almost abandoned her systematic policy of peopling New France. However, the descendants of the first colonists did their best to keep alive and increase their small communities. Among them the Church too became more active and vigorous. Even when, as sometimes unfortunately happened, the see of Quebec was occupied by an unenthusiastic bishop, Christian life still had such powerful roots in New France that it never ceased to grow. The troubles which beset the Church in France had few if any repercussions there; Jansenism, Quietism, Gallicanism were seldom if ever topics of debate. The pernicious influences that poisoned the minds of men in Europe scarcely affected the solid peasantry of the St Lawrence, who were impervious to the irony of Voltaire. Nor were there courtier-abbés or prelates monopolizing wealthy benefices. The clergy, whose members came with greater frequency from among the Canadian people than from metropolitan France, controlled education, directed the consciences of their flock in a spirit of somewhat boisterous good fellowship, and formed the permanent backbone as it were of French Canada.

The solid virtues with which the Church endowed an entire population explains how the Canadian branch of the

French tree, when cut off from its parent stock, was able not only to survive but to become itself a wonderfully vigorous growth. From 1756 onwards the little French colony, face to face with British colonies which numbered almost a million souls, had to engage in mortal combat without receiving the least assistance from home. Despite the courage and genius of Montcalm and the heroic resistance of a whole people, the scales were unequally weighted; the struggle was lost in 1759, after the opposing generals had fallen on the Plains of Abraham near Quebec. The disastrous Treaty of Paris (1763) sealed the doom of Canadian France. It did provide, in principle, for freedom of worship 'so far as the laws of England allow'. In fact an attempt, led by the British governors, was made to introduce Protestantism; but it met with invincible resistance. Few if any Canadians embraced Anglicanism or the doctrines of other Protestant sects. Standing fast around her clergy, and employing the French language to assert her right to remain herself, French Canada was destined to continue until today faithful to the past which had given her birth. The 80,000 colonists of 1763 have now increased to 3,000,000 and continue to multiply. France's missionary achievement in the Great Century has no more substantial witness upon earth.

The same will to survive and to remain Catholic and French is found in two dependencies of Canada: Acadia and Louisiana. After the tragedy of 1615 life had been resumed on those earliest sites of French settlement. Catholic organization had been re-established in a small way by a few Jesuits, and later (after 1632) by Capuchins. In 1670 Acadia included only six parishes, which were subject to Quebec. In 1713 the Treaty of Utrecht handed over to Britain that handful of Frenchmen, who were soon judged undesirable by the British authorities. The objectives of their policy were to get rid of the priests and to settle a Protestant population in the country; Halifax was founded in 1749 as a centre of religious penetration no less than as a mercantile port. That policy led to an act of barbarism worthy of our time. In 1755, when the decisive war for Canada was at its height, the British, uncertain of what attitude the Acadians might adopt, resolved on mass deportation. Regular man-hunts were organized, and those caught, to the number of about fifteen thousand, were distributed among the various British possessions in America. But neither cunning persecution nor the policy of deportation was a match for the tenacity of the Acadians. Exalting the memory of bygone struggles, taking as their heroes Fathers Le Loutre and Maillard of the Congregation of the Holy Spirit, together with other brave missionaries who had encouraged them to hope, they remained, as their descendants have remained to this day, resolutely Catholic by faith and French at heart, either in Acadia, whither some returned, or on the coast of the United States as far north as Boston.

As for Louisiana, an immense area theoretically occupied by France under Louis XIV but hardly colonized at all, missionary work was carried on in very difficult circumstances due to unfriendly rivalry between Jesuits, priests of the Foreign Missions and Capuchins, as well as to numerous wrangles with the Archbishop of Quebec, upon whom it was dependent. Moreover the missionary stations were widely scattered. It was only in the region of the lower Mississippi that a French Catholic population grew up, a population, however, which became more and more intermingled with Negro elements because of the increasing number of black slaves on the sugar plantations. The result was a way of life very different from the austere morality of Canada, but the people were none the less loyal at heart. In 1763, when the bungling diplomacy of Versailles ceded Louisiana to Spain, the French population resisted with almost the same determination as those of Acadia and Canada. Even today New Orleans remains the centre of French Catholicism in that part of the United States.[46]

10. THE CHURCH IN FRANCE AND THE PROBLEM OF BLACK SLAVES

In the south of Louisiana and away to the southernmost point of America stretched the Spanish domains and Portuguese Brazil. A few areas of these enormous territories, however, had never been occupied by colonists from Madrid; such were the Antilles, excepting San Domingo, Porto Rico and Jamaica. At the end of the sixteenth and beginning of the seventeenth century, therefore, other states took advantage of these openings to send out settlers of their own. Britain, for example, occupied several islands, notably Barbadoes and Trinidad—to which Jamaica was added in 1655 after it had been taken from Spain. Two Normans, Emambuc and Rois-sey, set out for these parts and persuaded Richelieu to en-courage French settlement there. By 1635 France held Mar-tinique, Guadeloupe and Saint-Christophe, to which was added in 1697, by the Treaty of Ryswick, the western half of San Domingo (modern Haiti). All the Antilles islands were very soon centres of a flourishing trade; huge fortunes were made either by smuggling contraband into the Spanish Em-pire or by importing 'ebony wood', i.e. black slaves, in ex-change for sugar, tobacco and indigo, which were exported to Europe and Africa.

Colonists and merchants had been accompanied from the start by missionaries—two Capuchins in 1635, followed soon afterwards by four Dominicans; the Jesuits landed five years later. Whether or not the climate of the Antilles was of such a kind as to excite men's passions, it is a fact that rivalry be-tween the religious orders reached a higher pitch there than anywhere else. Even the celebrated Capuchin, Pacifique de Provins, a veteran of the Levantine and Persian missions, who had been appointed Prefect-Apostolic by Propaganda, failed to impose his authority. It was not long before the strange affair of Governor Poincy, who had revolted against the metropolitan authority, led to the expulsion of both Capuchins and Dominicans; the Jesuits alone remained, and they only for a while. In 1663 the king became sole owner of the islands, and he managed to establish some sort of control over the clerical as well as over the civil administration; but that control amounted to very little, and bickering contin-ued between the various orders, each of which intended to have its own distinct Christian group. The affair of Father La Valette, which ultimately brought about the suppression of the Society of Jesus,[47] is sufficient evidence that to preach the Gospel was not the sole concern of Christ's missionaries in those parts. Rome herself did not succeed in creating an apostolic vicariate. In 1781 Versailles was again compelled to issue an edict for the reorganization of the Church in the subject islands.

It is not surprising in these circumstances that Christianity did not take firm and vigorous root in the islands as it did in Canada. True, nearly all the original colonists and their descendants, the creoles, were Catholics; some of them, especially the women, were most fervent. But the vast majority yielded to the sweets of pleasure afforded by their black concubines and led far from Christian lives. Even a number of priests were ready to follow their example. Attempts to evangelize the Caribs were fruitless, despite the courage of the Jesuits, two of whom were killed in 1654; elsewhere, the last of the natives quickly disappeared. The missionaries found the true reward of their thankless task among the blacks from Africa. Their devotion, said one missionary, was proportionate to their lack of intelligence, but they were found to possess that precious simplicity exalted by the Gospel. Negro children of both sexes brought up in the faith were the joy of the good Fathers, though once they had reached puberty their catechists often led them astray.

In Guiana a first but unsuccessful attempt was made by the missionaries of Christophe d'Authier de Sisgaud. The Jesuits followed them and remained until the suppression of the Society (1773), when they were replaced by the Congregation of the Holy Spirit. The situation was akin to that of Louisiana, except that Louisiana had a much more extensive trade and was consequently far wealthier. About 1725, however, Father Lombard tried to make headway among the natives by employing the famous method of Reductions practised by the Jesuits in Paraguay. But among the colonists Christianity became a mere matter of form, incapable of exercising any moral control. Furthermore in Guiana, as in the Antilles and even Louisiana, the presence of black slaves, whose number was continually increasing, confronted the Christian conscience with a serious problem.

The trade in blacks had begun very soon after the conquest of South America by Spain and Portugal; it assumed enormous proportions when exploitation of the colonial empires called for the replacement of manpower which had been

reduced almost to nothing by disease, ill-treatment and massacre. Traders organized a systematic round-up of Negroes in
Africa, stretching their nets far into the interior of the continent. Captives were transported across the Atlantic in conditions so appalling that not infrequently a third of the human
cargo had to be thrown to the sharks. After landing at American ports the slaves (men, women and children together)
were herded into enclosures similar to cattle pens to await the
arrival of prospective buyers. Having become the property
of some wealthy landlord or mining company, they were subjected to forced labour, which had no limit but their powers
of physical endurance. The younger women, more fortunate,
were made to share their master's bed. It was an exact repetition of ancient slavery, notwithstanding the repeated enactments by the sovereigns of Lisbon and Madrid, who sought
to kindle a spark of humanity into the trade and, above all,
to safeguard the spiritual right of those unhappy people, most
of whom were baptized.

The problem did not appear even to the eighteenth century
in the same light as it does to us. Jurists readily admitted
that slavery was permissible in the case of prisoners of war
and children sold by their parents. In Book XV of his *Esprit
des lois*, Montesquieu let fly the cruel shafts of his irony at
those who considered slavery quite natural. What could the
Church do in face of such a situation? It was impossible for
her to put an end to abuses upon which the whole economic
system was founded, or to join battle with all the colonial
authorities. Besides, even Bartholomew de Las Casas, apostle
and courageous champion of the Indians, had allowed the
trade in blacks. The Church therefore tried to work on two
levels: she proclaimed and did her best to safeguard the
rights of the slaves not only to be Christians but also to
practise their religion, and at the same time she sought
through charity to relieve their sufferings. Most missionaries
believed it impossible to do more than that. Very few dared
follow Mgr Pallu. Having seen with his own eyes what was
going on in America, he denounced the whites who seized the
goods and persons of the natives, and, while claiming to be
better Christians and more faithful Catholics, lived in a world
of injustice.

Freedom of faith for the slaves, which had been demanded by all the missionaries, was solemnly recognized, so far as French possessions were concerned, by Colbert's famous *Code Noir*.[48] In the preamble the king stated that his purpose was to enforce the discipline of the Church. One article decreed that all slaves must receive religious instruction and baptism; others insisted that the Sunday rest must be observed by slaves, condemned concubinage of masters with slaves and threatened offenders with heavy fines and even enfranchisement of their slaves. The *Code Noir* also contained some provisions which we today can only regard as outrageous, notably in respect of fugitive slaves, who, after a third escape, were condemned to death. But although imperfect and, alas, often flouted, the code marked a definite stage of progress; by recognizing slaves as possessed of legal existence it made France under Louis XIV the sole exception to contemporary principles and conduct in the matter of slavery. One cannot but see in that document the forerunner of Christian influence.

Missionaries were more active, however, in the field of charity than in the purely legal domain. Here, by and large, no matter to what order they belonged, they proved worthy of their vocation. They did their level best to behave as the spiritual fathers of their faithful blacks, welcoming them on landing, trying to muster families so that they might be sold to one landowner, taking charge of orphans and abandoned children. I say they did their level best; but the sugar plantations were remote and vast; masters sent their slaves more willingly to labour than to church. Difficulties notwithstanding, communities of black Catholics sprang up in the French islands, separate from the white communities, having their own parish priests; and despite some moral laxity and the influence of Voodoo, a pagan cult imported from Africa, they produced a touching manifestation of Christianity.

The most striking representative of that apostolate among the black slaves in the first half of the seventeenth century was St Peter Claver, S.J. (1580–1654), a native of Catalonia. Settling at Cartagena in Colombia, he spent thirty-nine years, to use his own words, as 'the slave for ever of the Negroes'. He washed and nursed the sick on arrival, even if they were suffering from leprosy or the plague; he defended his beloved blacks against the brutality of their masters, visiting mines and plantations, a living embodiment of the charity of Christ. Later a Frenchman, Father Boutin, continued St Peter Claver's work. But many others, whose names history has not recorded, were in no way unworthy of such a model. About 1725 a picturesque Dominican, Father Labat, felt the urge to travel, and the narrative of his journeys still makes pleasant reading. Appointed parish priest of Macouba in Martinique, he became an almost legendary figure among the black slaves on the plantations, among the freebooters, and also among the Carib natives, who one day offered him as a mark of respect a tasty cut of well roasted human flesh! Proof of the missionaries' influence became evident during the French Revolution, when the blacks of Haiti under Dessalines rose against the colonists and massacred nine-tenths of the white population. The surviving tenth owed their lives to the missionaries, whose houses served as places of refuge and were spared.

11. IN THE PATRONATES OF LATIN AMERICA

Important from every point of view as was the task undertaken by French missions in America, it bore no comparison, as to numbers and extent, with that of the Spaniards and Portuguese. Both these peoples had to do with enormous empires already more than a century old and extending the whole length of a continent, where European colonization, though far from having reached all the territories shown on maps, continued, as it was to continue for another two hundred years, to make steady progress, bringing in its wake the missions. For that was the most significant aspect of the story: since the beginning of the great adventure evangelization had been part and parcel of discovery and conquest; missionaries followed in the footsteps of *conquistadores*, and very often travelled with them. Thanks to those men of God, among whom were many saints, the cross had been planted wherever soldiers and colonists had gone. On the threshold of the seventeenth century, therefore, there were Hispano-American and Lusitano-American areas of Christendom (theoretically combined until 1640) numbering more than ten million souls, among whom were Europeans, creole descendants of the early conquerors and converts both native and of mixed blood. Thanks to the work of the missions, it was considered normal in those territories to associate religion with all the activities of life, even with politics and economics. That tendency, moreover, was noticeable in both Spain and Portugal. It was further accentuated by the fact that they had carried the religious hierarchy and institutions from Europe to the New World.

Latin America was, as it continued more or less to be until the end of the eighteenth century, the domain if not the favourite home of the patronates. The Portuguese patronate was challenged in Asia, but in America the principle was hardly called in question. That principle had been laid down in 1609 by John Solorzano Pereira (1575–1654), a professor at Salamanca, in his great treatise *De Indiarum iure*, which recognized the sovereign as possessing discretionary authority in the matter of ecclesiastical administration, the right within his own dominions to bar missionaries and religious superiors, to establish missionary stations without reference to the bishops (even though the latter had been appointed by himself), and to allow or forbid the publication of Bulls and other papal documents. This theory was maintained by the Spanish monarchy until the end; the Bourbons being no less strict than the Hapsburgs in upholding their rights, it was revived and emphasized by Joaquim de Rivadavia in 1755. Portugal, after regaining her independence in 1640, reaffirmed the same pretentions—though not quite so successfully, because she was less feared at Rome. Once Propaganda had decided to assume control of all missionary work, Rome endeavoured to resist the patronate, in America as elsewhere, and Solorzano's treatise was condemned by the Inquisition. But it was very difficult for the Holy See to oppose the court of Madrid on this point, for Naples and Palermo were in the hands of Spain; the condemnation of Solorzano was not published in America, and his theories continued to have the force of law. The Council of the Indies at Madrid remained the real master of Christendom in America. Moreover local bishops behaved with extreme docility towards the authorities of the patronate, and the viceroys presided over the closing sessions of provincial councils. On the other hand, since the Church was the sole instrument of education and trade, and provided the social and administrative grades, there was an understanding between the two powers, and fusion between the spiritual and temporal reached its highest development.

Such was the Church in America, and fairness requires that it should not be judged by the standards of present-day Catholicism. Many of its features are disconcerting. Extreme piety, fruitful in devotion to Our Lady, to the Blessed Sacrament and to the saints, was coupled with a manifest leaning towards superstition, which was not confined to native Christians. Outward austerity, imposed by public regulations, produced a swarm of penitential brotherhoods and even of flagellants; but it did not preclude a degree of sexual licence incompatible with the morality of Christ. Religious art was almost unbelievably ostentatious. One Chilean monstrance, for example, was adorned with more than 3,000 precious stones, including 417 diamonds and 425 emeralds; nor was it rare to find the interior of a church or chapel covered in gold leaf. Features of that kind may shock a twentieth-century European Catholic, but they were quite in keeping with the character of the country, its tropical passions, its *gana*, its violence. We must not forget that while that brand of Catholicism had its faults, it left an abiding mark upon the whole of Latin America, one of the pillars of the Church, and that while it erected so many ornate baroque buildings it also produced holy men and women who were models of self-renunciation: St Francis Solano, St Rose of Lima, St Turibe, Archbishop of Lima, and the Bethlemites of Guatemala who identified themselves completely with the poor. It has often been said that the Inquisition was responsible for the authoritarian character of Latin-American Christianity with its permanent 'roasters' set up in the city squares. But Salvador de Madariaga, an historian by no means prejudiced in favour of Christianity,[49] has shown the falsity of that picture.

Soundly organized into half a dozen provinces and thirty-eight dioceses (including the Philippines), the Spanish Empire swarmed with priests, of whom there were perhaps too many. The number in the province of Puebla alone has been placed at six thousand. There were marked differences, too, between them. The bishops all belonged to the aristocracy, and six out of seven were Spaniards. Parish priests and curates, many of whom were recruited from among the creoles, had received little or no training; for seminaries were few, and those few were often badly run. The better elements were provided by the religious orders. The Jesuits were leaders in this respect, and showed a remarkable vitality; but all the main orders were represented, all enjoyed numerous privileges and all possessed enormous riches that were constantly increasing. Less wealthy than the male congregations, the various institutes of women were occupied mainly with the education of girls. The most striking fact, indicative of a state of mind, was the almost total non-existence of a native Indian clergy. An early attempt to found an Indian seminary at Tlateleco in Mexico had failed, and had never been repeated; in the whole of Spain's enormous empire there were never more than two dozen native priests. Papal appeals, scoldings from Propaganda, nothing could overcome a tenacious opposition whose effects are still with us.

It might be easy to exclude the natives from the priesthood, but two other problems remained: that of their relations with white Christians, and that of the attitude which the Church should adopt towards them. These problems became increasingly grave towards the end of the sixteenth century. Under the influence of ideas which dictated measures against the Jews and Moors in Spain, the gulf became wider between the conquerors and the conquered peoples; Indians, who in the sixteenth century had produced a veritable *élite*, were barred from Spanish society and reduced to an inferior status. The missionaries alone, let it be said to their honour, dared to take a different position; the lessons of Bartholomew de Las Casas were not forgotten. In their eyes an Indian was the equal of a Spaniard on the supernatural plane, and they continued to regard the apostolate as the true end and justification of conquest. Many of them, however, realizing that the whites too often set their converts bad examples, tried to prevent contact. Thus, even in places where the two populations were geographically intermingled, some Indian parishes (the *doctrinas*) were created quite separately from their Spanish counterparts. An experiment in a more complete form of isolation, known as Reductions, was long practised with remarkable success by the Jesuits.

It was a strange experiment,[50] destined to set in motion a mighty flow of ink and to call forth paeans of praise from the 'philosophers' themselves. Beginning in the early years of the seventeenth century it attained its full development between 1650 and 1720, then ran into difficulties and ended with the suppression of the Society. A Reduction was a large village, containing in some cases as many as five thousand souls, where Indians lived by themselves under the direction of two or three Jesuits. The ground-plan was everywhere the same— square, with the houses grouped around the church and presbytery. The Fathers were spiritual guides, temporal rulers, administrators and, if need required, military leaders. The system of government was authoritarian, paternalist and communal. Each family had its cottage and garden; but cultivation of the arable land was collective, the Fathers providing seed, directing the work and storing the harvests, but distributing to each family its daily provisions. The life of each person, too, was carefully regulated, with obligatory attendance at Mass, confession, communion and other services. On Sundays there was choral singing with violin accompaniment provided by the Jesuits. Such for more than a century and a half was the existence of about sixty Christian villages totalling 100,000 souls; they were strung out between the district of Tucuman and a point south of Buenos Aires, Paraguay with its Guarani population being the main centre. Established in areas at that time unoccupied by whites, the Reductions at first enjoyed *de facto* independence of the Spanish authorities; the bishop and governor called as a matter of etiquette, but the Jesuits took good care that no other white man entered those fortunate regions. Several things led to the ultimate failure of the Reductions: the ambition of civil and ecclesiastical authorities; avarice on the part of traders and officials, who believed that the Jesuits were hoarding gold; rivalry between Spaniards and Portuguese, settled by boundary agreements which cut across the territory of the Christian republics; and, in the eighteenth century, growing hostility to the Society of Jesus. The idea of trying to make people live in a kind of City of God on earth was perhaps chimerical; it was rendered possible only by the apathy of the Indians. But there can be no doubt that the Guaranis were happy under the wise governance of the Fathers, or that they lived Christian lives as far as they were able.

The situation in Brazil was, on the whole, similar to that of the neighbouring Spanish dominions: the Portuguese patronate (independent of Madrid after 1640) subjected it to the immediate influence of Lisbon. The Portuguese quickly exploited the country, and soon reached so far into the interior as to alarm Spain. The Church kept pace with this expansion, sent her missionaries to evangelize the occupied territories and created new bishoprics. Religion in Brazil had many of the characteristics familiar in Portugal—numerous confraternities, ostentatious ceremonies. Black slavery, however, was more important there than in the Spanish territories because of the manpower required for the sugar plantations. The result was a rapid increase in half-castes, due partly to the wisdom of the Portuguese in the matter of race relations and partly to certain patriarchal customs similar to those prevailing in the Antilles. Owing, however, to indifference rather than to policy nothing was done to form a native clergy. In Brazil as elsewhere the best of the missionaries protected the natives and slaves. One name remains associated with this work—that of the famous preacher Antonio Vieira (1608–97), a former ambassador who had been moved by charity to become a Jesuit. He protested to Lisbon about the iniquities committed by high officials and traders, and denounced the treatment accorded to the blacks, with such courage that the colonists later reported him to the Inquisition, arrested him and shipped him to Lisbon, whence he returned armed with new powers on behalf of those whom he called his *almazinhas*, 'little souls'.

It would therefore be unjust to imagine that Catholicism under the patronate was a lifeless thing, an affair of outward show and rigid conformity. The Latin-American Church may have been open to criticism, but it also had vigorous and congenial features. The task originally undertaken by the missionaries was not abandoned; as colonization expanded so did the mission. In Florida three attempts, costing several lives, were necessary before Catholic communities could defy the menace of the Apaches, who perpetrated a terrible massacre in 1697. After some vain endeavours by Franciscans and Carmelites a party of Jesuits led by Father Juan de Ugarte managed to obtain a foothold in California; they received powerful financial assistance from Europe, created three Reductions modelled roughly upon those of Paraguay, and were so successful that by the time of the Society's suppression there was a whole chain of Christian settlements extending from Lower California to the extreme south of Sinaloa. The Franciscans held their ground in New Mexico and Texas, despite opposition from the Apaches, who on one occasion murdered sixteen thousand Christians, of whom twenty-four were missionaries. As for South America, missionary posts were with difficulty established by Jesuits on the Marañon in Upper Peru, and by Franciscans in the Llanos, the Chiloe islands and Patagonia. On the eve of the French Revolution there appeared an adventurer of Christ who seemed to embody once again all the courage and saintliness of the great missionaries who had made Latin America Catholic. He was Father Junipero Serra (1713–84), a native of Majorca. Though lame and far from robust, he joined the Franciscans, became professor of theology at Palma, and then, in 1749, left for America. He set about evangelizing the redskins of the Sierra Gorda, revived the missions which the Jesuits had had to abandon in Lower California, and ultimately reached northern California. Here, in spite of formidable obstacles, he founded a sort of Reduction, which earned the name New Arcadia. This was the beginning of the now flourishing member of the United States. In 1927 President Coolidge had Serra's statue erected in the Capitol at Washington among those of the 'fathers and founders of the American homeland'.

To the Spanish empire of South America there officially belonged the Philippines, whose importance in the history of Asiatic missions we have already seen. There, ever since Magellan planted the cross in 1521, a Catholic community had developed with extraordinary rapidity and peculiar characteristics of its own. Manila, where in about 1600 there were no more than two thousand Spaniards, now had four hundred missionaries, among whom all the great orders were represented—Augustinians, Dominicans, Franciscans, Jesuits—and the archipelago was a starting point for China and Japan. Conversions were numerous among the gentle people of the islands. It was a triumph for the method of *tabula rasa*: the Church had absorbed almost the entire population. Moreover, Catholicism as practised in the Philippines had found favour with the Filipinos, being opulent, completely free from puritanical narrowness, and offering plenty of ceremonial display; the churches, too, built in a supple and sumptuous variety of baroque, were calculated to rouse their enthusiasm. A great effort had also been made to provide educational facilities, chief among which was the University of St Thomas at Manila, founded by Dominicans and still a leading institution. In 1751 there were 904,110 Catholics in the Philippines.

That flourishing Church, however, experienced some grave crises. Relations were almost always strained between the missionaries, who were regulars, and the secular ecclesiastical authorities. The former had obtained from Rome a number of rights and privileges which made them virtually independent of the bishops. Even the intervention of Urban VIII did not succeed in bringing them to heel, and all efforts to create a native clergy foundered upon the jealously guarded monopoly of the orders. Meanwhile relations between the native masses and the Spanish clergy gradually deteriorated. In 1768 it became necessary to supersede the Jesuits. Mgr Santa Justa, Archbishop of Manila, seized his opportunity and hurriedly recruited a body of Philippine priests, giving them a summary course of training until he was able to open a seminary. Thus there came into being a clergy drawn from the ranks of the people, more or less hostile to the typically Spanish hauteur of the religious, and destined to lead the nationalist revolutions of the nineteenth century.

Events in the Philippines were indicative of what was happening, though less openly, throughout the Latin-America patronates. Despite her mistrust of the creoles, half-castes and natives, whom she had almost everywhere excluded from the priesthood, the Church had given those people unity, a strong sense of their destiny and the principles of justice and fraternity. Those principles were involved later on, during the age of revolutions. Indeed the regime of the patronates received its ultimate fulfilment in rebellion.

12. SETBACKS AND DISAPPOINTMENTS IN AFRICA

Africa holds a very modest place in the work accomplished by the missions during the neo-classical era. To tell the truth, whether we consider the whites and Moslems of North Africa or the blacks in other parts of the continent, it is hardly possible to speak even of setbacks and disappointments; the picture had not been altogether promising at the end of the preceding era. Despite such high hopes as had been aroused, for example, by the consecration of the first black bishop, son of a local princeling, in 1518, the African missions had taken a noticeably downward turn. They had, it is true, been partially reinvigorated by the Jesuits, but most of them were merely vegetating. San Salvador and even St Paul de Loanda, which had supplanted it as the Catholic capital of Africa, were visibly decaying. Ethiopia, where victory might have seemed assured, had been lost by about 1622. In the Mahgreb and other Moslem regions individual efforts, e.g. that of the Belgian Father Clénard, bore witness to a great deal of courage but obtained few results; and that situation lasted during the seventeenth and eighteenth centuries.

Africa was the only part of the globe in which the missionary impulse of that glorious age proved fruitless; it was likewise the only region where the decline of fervour in the eighteenth century had serious repercussions. The failure can be explained by a variety of causes. In North Africa the period coincided with a sort of reawakening such as Islam has experienced from time to time, bringing with it an increase of xenophobia. Again, the Portuguese patronate, of which Africa was a dependency, was more interested in the wealth of India and the Indies, East and West, than in the poor fringe of paltry trading stations bordering the Dark Continent. Indeed its hold upon Africa was so feeble that rebellions were not infrequent, and the revolt of San Salvador in 1627 was supported by Britain and Holland. The missions could not flourish in such circumstances. Above all, one of the main reasons for the decline of Christianity in black Africa was the slave trade, a monstrous though profitable traffic which did untold harm and in which all the great Christian countries took a hand. Portugal imported so many Negroes that in 1750 or thereabouts they constituted one-fifth of the population of Lisbon. The Spanish crown held a monopoly of that sinister line of commerce. Holland was deeply involved and earned millions of florins. The Royal African Society, patronized by His Britannic Majesty, sought to oust the Dutch; its rival was the Compagnie Française de Guinée, formed in 1685 and deriving no less immoral gains.[51] One clause in the Treaty of Utrecht (1713) gave victorious Britain an exclusive right for thirty years to provide the Spanish dominions with slaves . . . ! The trade reached its zenith about 1770, when the official number of slave ships was estimated at 500, carrying an annual cargo of 28,500 slaves. It is not difficult to imagine the ravages effected in Africa by this inhuman practice: whole districts were completely denuded of their inhabitants. From the religious point of view Europeans were looked upon with hatred as mere traffickers in human flesh, and all the charity of the missionaries was powerless to alter that opinion.

Not that the missionaries lacked courage and tenacity. It is wonderful to see with what energy and perseverance small teams of men laboured to restore ruined stations and plant the cross once again in those unfruitful territories. From 1622 onwards Spaniards and Frenchmen, in agreement with Propaganda, took over from the Portuguese on the west coast. In 1634 two Norman Capuchins arrived at Rufrique, decided after a rapid inquiry that evangelization was possible, and returned with five companions; but they were obliged to re-embark five years later, exhausted and discouraged. At Cape Verde, on the site of what is now Dakar, disappointment assumed another form. Little Prince Anabia, who had been sent to Versailles and baptized by Bossuet, with Louis XIV as his godfather, went back to fetishism as soon as he returned to Africa. A party of Capuchins from Brittany, including Father Colombin de Nantes, settled in Guinea, founded a dozen stations and obtained a foothold in Dahomey; but they were obliged to flee from the hostility of Negro sorcerers, who burned all their convents. The Spaniards held on somewhat longer in the same area, but they fell foul of the Portuguese authorities and had to leave. Attempts to regain a foothold in the Congo were no more successful. Spanish Capuchins, led by Father Francesco de Pampeluna, did good work for a time in Angola, converting Queen N'Zinga of Matombe; but they succumbed to the climate, to Portuguese exactions and to the machinations of slave traders. Jesuits, Dominicans and even secular priests followed, and the Congo became an apostolic prefecture. But about 1700 a dispute between the seculars and regulars proved the last straw, and the missionaries departed. While St Paul de Loanda was nothing but a vast slave market, Lower Congo and Kwango were utterly depopulated by the trade. It was not until 1776 that fresh teams of missionaries set out, consisting of French secular priests under the leadership of Mgr Bellegard, Prefect Apostolic; most of them, however, fell victim to the deadly climate. Meanwhile two priests belonging to the Congregation of the Holy Spirit, having been shipwrecked on their way to Guiana, installed themselves at St Louis in Senegal, one with the title of Prefect Apostolic; they succeeded in forming a small Christian community which managed to rub along until it was broken up by the Revolution.

Things were no better in East Africa. In Mozambique, which had been an apostolic vicariate independent of Goa since 1622, the missions fell victim to Moslem fanaticism, particularly that of the Ismaili. The Jesuits who tried to settle at Quilimani, Chinde and Sena were either martyred or forced to leave. Capuchins, Dominicans and Augustinians tried to penetrate inland, but with little success. Moreover, the small Portuguese colony was steadily declining. None of the successive plans for reorganization of the missions achieved anything whatever. At the end of the eighteenth century the bishopric of Mozambique numbered only three parishes and two convents. This setback may perhaps be explained by the missionaries' desire to 'portugalize' the natives and by their lack of firmness in opposing the slave trade.

It is not so easy to account for the failure in Madagascar; the causes just mentioned were certainly not responsible. The island had been entrusted to the Lazarists, chief of whom were Fathers Nacquart and Gondrée, who were ready with a detailed plan of evangelization. We have already seen them at work, selfless and brave until overwhelmed by climate and fatigue.[52] This initial failure did not discourage the sons of Monsieur Vincent, and others left home for Madagascar—seventeen priests and ten lay brothers in twenty-six years, not to mention five or six secular priests and ten Recollects. One of the most resolute was Father Estienne. After being shipwrecked he made a fresh start, restored the mission, tried to mediate between the French colonists and the Malagasies, and died by poison at a meal given by a native chief. His death was the signal for a general uprising in which French families were slaughtered and which marked the end of that first missionary enterprise in the great island (1764). Evangelization was not resumed until 1830. Abandonment of Madagascar, however, had one good result, for it enabled first the Capuchins and then the Lazarists to foster a zealous Christian community in the Île de Bourbon, a colony which had no natives and which lasted until 1775. The same work was undertaken in 1721 on the Île de France (modern Mauritius), where there were about three thousand Christians at the beginning of the French Revolution.

Ethiopia was no less disappointing. In the sixteenth century it might well have been believed that the Monophysite 'Realm of Prester John'[53] would embrace the Catholic faith and that the Negus Seltan Sagad would prove himself another Theodosius or Clovis. Rome had actually created a patriarchate of Abyssinia. Unfortunately the Patriarch, Father Alfonso Mendez, S.J., was extremely incompetent—a rare phenomenon in the ranks of the Society. Not content with combating polygamy, which was tolerated by the Monophysite clergy, he went so far as to forbid the Ethiopian Church to practise circumcision or to keep the sabbath as it had done from time immemorial. It was another 'quarrel of rites' in miniature, and the result was disastrous. On the death of Seltan Sagad, his son Facilidas (Basilides) turned persecutor; the missionaries were expelled, and the leading Catholics disappeared. The Sultans of Suakim and Massouah, warned by the Negus, massacred all missionaries on whom they were able to lay hands. A mere handful of Catholic priests was left in

Ethiopia, and their numbers quickly dwindled. In vain the Jesuits sent out Fathers disguised as merchants, e.g. Father Parisiani who resided at Mocha in hopes of being able to re-enter the kingdom of the Negus. In vain two courageous Capuchins, Fathers Cassien de Nantes and Agathange de Vendôme, abandoned work in Egypt and made their way into Abyssinia; denounced by a Lutheran trader, they suffered martyrdom at Gondar in 1638. The dream of Catholic Ethiopia vanished. No more than a dream, either, was the ambitious project outlined to Louis XIV about 1675 by 'Père Tranquille' (celebrated for his *baume tranquille*[54]), who sought to obtain from the king diplomatic intervention with a view to converting the Negus. And the same is true of a heroic but futile attempt by the autochthonous Bishop Ghebre Exaner in 1784. The Realm of Prester John was thenceforward closed to the Catholic faith until 1848.

As for the Moslem areas of North Africa, they too were resolutely opposed to Christian infiltration. In earlier epochs there had been little more than isolated ventures, ranging from the designs of St Francis of Assisi upon the Egyptian Sudan and the efforts of Raymund Lull to Jesuit enterprise in the Christian prisons. A number of these undertakings had ended in martyrdom. Exactly the same situation prevailed throughout the seventeenth and eighteenth centuries. Profiting as best they could by political circumstances, the missionaries occasionally succeeded in entering Moslem territory, helped by the French consuls and sometimes acting as consuls themselves. But as soon as the pashas and beys underwent a change of heart they were driven out or put to death. In Egypt the Capuchin Fathers Agathange and Cassien, by order of du Tremblay, laboured from 1633 without much success among the Coptic and Jacobite communities of Cairo. They made their way into the Thebaid and thence into Ethiopia, where, as we have seen, they suffered martyrdom. Sixty years later, by order of Louis XIV and with the support of the French consul, the Jesuits made a new attempt. Their leader was Father Sicard, who managed to remain in Egypt until his death (1726), trying in vain to convert the Coptic priests, but sending valuable reports to the Academy of Sciences at Paris.

In Barbary, as it was then called, the situation was more complex. France, which had taken over from Portugal, established diplomatic relations with the Turkish authorities who governed Morocco, Algeria and Tunisia, theoretically in the name of the Sultan at Constantinople, but in fact with almost complete independence. The French Government had had consuls at Algiers, Fez, Marrakesh and Tunis since 1564 and 1582. But these diplomats exerted very little influence, and, worse still, were powerless to stamp out piracy, which was one of the main resources of Barbary. The European fleets paid a heavy annual tribute to the Moslem corsairs. About 1620 it was known that there were three thousand French slaves at Algiers and thirty thousand in North Africa as a whole.[55] The principal aim of the missionaries was naturally to succour these unfortunates and prevent them from apostatizing. Many were ransomed by the Mercedarians and Trinitarians, who sent out missions at regular intervals for that purpose.

At the beginning of the seventeenth century something more was done, in the shape of Christian settlement. Recollects and Discalced Augustinians, but chiefly Capuchins, entered Morocco, with whose government Richelieu prided himself upon enjoying diplomatic relations. As things turned out, the undertaking was fraught with danger and vicissitude for the luckless Capuchins; they were sometimes flung into prison and held to ransom, sometimes authorized to visit the slave jails, but in a period of fifteen years they converted no more than thirty Moslems and a Jewish rabbi. At length, about 1640, the French Capuchins gave up the struggle. Work was resumed some fifty years later by the Andalusian Capuchins, who succeeded in maintaining ten of their brethren in a few Moroccan outposts, always more concerned with relieving the miseries of European slaves than with missionary labours in the strict sense.

At that juncture there came upon the scene St Vincent de Paul and his Lazarists. They had a house at Marseilles, financed by the Duchesse d'Aiguillon, whose generosity was truly inexhaustible; it had been founded expressly for missions to convicts in the galleys and for the relief of captives in Barbary. In 1645 Father Guérin left for Tunis, where he made such a favourable impression on the Bey that he was able to ask permission for himself and one other missionary to reside there. 'Certainly,' replied the Bey, 'two or three if you like. I will protect them as I will protect you . . . for I know that, so far from doing harm to any man, you do good to all.' So another Lazarist, Jacques Le Vacher, was sent to Tunis, where he arrived on the very day that Father Guérin and the French consul died of plague. Le Vacher therefore took over as consul at the express wish of the Bey, and in 1650 Rome appointed him vicar-apostolic for Barbary. First at Tunis, then at Algiers, the good Lazarist fulfilled both duties with apostolic charity and zeal. He opened six chapels at Tunis and five at Algiers, which were often served by slave priests; he also went frequently among the captives, whom he helped to endure their lot, and even obtained the release of a few. That splendid missionary life had a worthy end. In 1683 Louis XIV resolved to destroy Algiers, which was a nest of piracy. The Pasha had recently been assassinated, and the place was governed by a pirate chief, one Mezzomorto, known as Kara Mustapha. When Duquesne's fleet appeared before the city Mustapha met Le Vacher on the mole and bade him ask the French admiral to depart, otherwise he and other Christians would be put to death. The Lazarist would not yield to blackmail, and sent word to Duquesne that he should continue the attack. He was immediately tied to the mouth of a cannon and his body flew in shreds into the sea. Five years afterwards another Lazarist, Michel Montmasson, with a lay brother named Francillon, suffered martyrdom in Barbary. One hundred and fifty years were to pass before the cross was again planted in Algiers and Tunis.

Thus throughout the seventeenth and eighteenth centuries the whole of Africa proved singularly resistant to Christianity. The collapse of the missions consequent upon the revolutionary crisis helped still further to diminish the opportunities of Holy Church in the Dark Continent. Who could have foreseen in 1800 that during the nineteenth century Africa would be the principal missionary land, a territory where the most rapid progress would be achieved? Fifty years later the great African venture began with Father Liebermann and the Holy

Ghost Fathers, Mgr de Marion-Brésillac and his Fathers of the African Missions, Cardinal Lavigerie and his White Fathers.

13. JESUITS IN RUSSIA

No history of the missions at this period would be complete without some mention of those in Russia, which form a unique and most remarkable episode. No Catholic, it need hardly be said, would consider the empire of the czars as a missionary country in the ordinary sense of that phrase, or regard the Russians as pagans. But a long and persevering effort was made throughout the neo-classical period to establish brotherly relations with the world of Russian Orthodoxy, in the hope of being able one day to effect a reconciliation.

At the beginning of the seventeenth century Catholicism was practically non-existent in Russia; it was represented by a mere handful of adventurers and traders—notably those of the Sloboda at Moscow—whom it would have been difficult to describe as models of Catholic faith. Moreover the Orthodox Church, which was then on the flood tide of revival,[56] made their situation more and more precarious, and conversions to the schismatic creed were steadily increasing.

The idea of sending missionaries to Russia was suggested to the Congregation of Propaganda by a Croat priest, George Krijanich, who made the undertaking his life's work. Having learned Russian and obtained permission to celebrate Mass in Slavonic, he set out first to make reconnaissance with a Polish mission, and returned with such enthusiastic reports that Propaganda looked upon him as scatterbrained. He started on his next journey quite alone, in 1659, and had many adventures in Russia, now in correspondence with the court, and now as an exile at Tobolsk in the heart of Siberia. He finally left the empire of the czars in 1676, and was killed by the Turks in 1683 while serving as chaplain to the Austrian forces before Vienna.

A second attempt to reach an understanding was made in 1672, but in the opposite direction. Czar Alexis, who had been educated by an apostate Catholic and a russianized Pole, was at that time threatened by the Turks and decided to seek support from the West. His ambassador was Menzies of Pitfodels, a Scottish Catholic much preoccupied with reunion of the Churches; but neither Rome nor the Christian courts of the West would listen to his appeal, and although he had some oecumenical talks in Paris nothing came of his mission.

Work began in earnest about 1685, when the Jesuits took a hand in the affair. Helped by influential Catholics of the Sloboda, notably Fathers Gordon and Menzies, and supported by Prince Galitzin, the Society managed to obtain permission to establish a house in Moscow. A few converts were received (e.g. Father Artemiev), and the news caused a minor sensation in the West. But the *coup d'état* of 1689, which brought Peter the Great to power[57] by ousting his half-sister Sophia, put an end to the undertaking. Those westerners who had assisted the young prince were mainly Protestants; the Jesuits were driven out while their more distinguished converts were exiled to remote convents, Artemiev being sent to Archangel.

The Jesuits, however, had not abandoned hope. When Peter the Great embarked upon his policy of westernization and made his famous journeys to London and elsewhere, the Society obtained permission to install two Fathers at Moscow;[58] but their situation was precarious. If the Czar was prepared to tolerate the presence of Catholics in his dominions it was only because he was obliged to humour the western powers. Half through conviction, no doubt, but half also through cunning, he gave his approval to an attempt at reconciliation which roused the enthusiasm of Leibniz and found favour with Pope Clement XI. Peter Tolstoy, Russian ambassador at The Hague, even made contact with the Nuncio. But all this did not prevent the Czar from butchering some Uniate Basilians. True, during his second journey to the west he had talks with a number of Catholic personalities, notably with Mgr Bentivoglio, the nuncio at Paris, who asked him to grant Catholics freedom of worship; but nothing came of their exchanges. On the death of Peter the Great there were only a few semi-clandestine missionaries in Russia—Franciscans at St Petersburg, Capuchins at Moscow—and there was little or nothing they could do. The Jesuits had been forbidden access to the country in 1719.

The situation was more or less the same about 1740. Negotiations conducted by Princess Dolgoruky, who had embraced Catholicism during a journey to France, met with no success; her French tutor, Jacques Jubé, former parish priest of Asnières, was a Jansenist, hostile to the Jesuits and extremely cunning. A Spanish Dominican in the Dolgorukys' suite did make a few converts by adopting the Slavonic liturgy, but that was all. In 1740, however, profiting by the tolerance of the Czarina Anne, the Jesuits returned to Russia. Twenty-three years later, when Catherine II assumed power, they considered that the door was open and made a great effort. The first partition of Poland had considerably increased the number of Uniates, and Moscow treated them outrageously; nevertheless the Society of Jesus decided that circumstances favoured an advance into Russia.

Their decision marked the beginning of a paradoxical story. Catherine II, anxious to found schools in her dominions, was easily persuaded to make use of these experienced teachers. The Society, though officially banned in Russia itself, was free to come and go in her adjacent dependencies. The two hundred Jesuits who had become Russian subjects were accordingly permitted to stay on as teachers and preachers, and the Society's property was even exempted from taxation. In the following year Rome suppressed the Society of Jesus, which thereupon found itself in the extraordinary situation of having legal existence nowhere but in imperial Russia. The Czarina forbade publication in her states of the Bull suppressing the Society, and warned the Holy See that if it tried to interfere with *her* Jesuits she would compel all her Catholic subjects to embrace the Orthodox faith. We even find a bishop ordaining two Jesuits and another opening a novitiate for the dissolved Society, to the great indignation of the Dominicans and Franciscans in Russian Poland. Thus did the 'enlightened despotism' of Catherine, a disciple of the philosophers, enable the sons of St Ignatius to survive and expand in Russia; their missions extended as far as Odessa, Saratov and the Caucasus.

14. A DISAPPOINTING BALANCE SHEET.
REASONS FOR HOPE

If we pause on the eve of the French Revolution and try to determine the credit balance of work accomplished by the missions during the neo-classical period, we have to admit that it is disappointing. The high hopes of the sixteenth century, strengthened by some splendid achievements at the beginning of the seventeenth, had not been fulfilled. The Congregation of Propaganda, whose purpose was to rouse enthusiasm in the Catholic world for the missionary vocation, had sought to 'denationalize' the missions and establish native churches; but its success had been far from complete, owing to lack of personnel, of funds and of accurate information. Delicate problems raised by the contact of Christianity with non-European civilizations had been considered from a narrow and formal viewpoint which rendered any solution almost impossible. Furthermore, many men whom the Church desired to enlighten had rejected Christian truth. These included Chinese scholars, Buddhists of the Little Vehicle, natives of North America and, above all, adherents of Islam.

It seems that the missions were everywhere at a standstill, if not in full retreat; and the impression is confirmed by a report made to Propaganda in 1765 by Mgr Stephen Borgia. Those missionaries who remained at work were appealing for help in their distress. 'We sorely need that God should look down upon us with pity and send us reinforcements,' exclaimed Father Dallières, one of the few Jesuits then in China; 'the mission cannot possibly survive in the circumstances to which our troubles have reduced it.' Many others throughout the world were saying likewise. But the flow of reinforcements steadily decreased; from the beginning of the eighteenth century onwards all missionary orders and congregations experienced a grave lack of vocations.

The urge which had driven so many men to leave home and evangelize the world was now exhausted. There was no longer a sale for books dealing with the missions; the Jesuits had even ceased to publish their *Relations*; no longer were the nobility and gentry of either sex pouring out wealth to found missionary stations and seminaries. During the seventeenth century apostles, explorers, scholars and statesmen had worked hand in hand; in the Age of Enlightenment such interest as they took in the outer world was not directed to evangelization. The influence of the philosophers had effected a complete change of outlook. Voltaire, the leading mischief-maker in this as in most other fields, had discredited the spiritual aims of the missions; twisting the Jesuit accounts of their work in China to suit his ends, he represented the missionaries as preoccupied with their own advancement in the mandarinate and even in business circles, squabbling meanwhile among themselves. Alas, the affair of the Chinese rites provided him with a mass of evidence. Montesquieu, d'Alembert and Diderot joined in the chorus. Buffon alone among savants paid homage to the civilizing influence of the missionaries, to their gentleness, charity and fervour; but a single advocate counted for little in such a case. The majority of Catholics had become so indifferent to that great work that they stood by and watched it founder, applauding the cruel blows to which it was subjected, rejoicing even in the suppression of the Society of Jesus,[59] which did such grave harm to the missions.

Day by day the Jesuits found themselves disowned, expelled and sometimes imprisoned. Portugal, which had struck the first blow, distinguished herself by the shameful manner in which she treated the Fathers. Arrested as criminals, the missionaries of Macao and the Indies (one hundred and twenty-four of them in all), followed by twenty from Brazil, were deported to Lisbon in appalling conditions and imprisoned for fifteen years in the fortress of St Julian. The attitude of governments, of their officials and even of some bishops towards these men, who could be charged with nothing but their religious vows, was so disgraceful that the Chinese pagans of Canton actually hid the Fathers for whom the bishop and Governor-General were searching, while in India their arrest was forcibly opposed by some Dutch merchants and British administrators. At Constantinople the French ambassador, Saint-Priest, honourably refused to carry out instructions from Paris and retained the secularized Jesuits as managers of their houses and schools. It is estimated that three thousand five hundred missionaries were obliged to leave their posts. Priests of the Foreign Missions, Lazarists and Fathers of the Holy Ghost had to be sent to take their place. These men did their best, often with great courage; but a great void had been created.

Towards the end of the eighteenth century it might have been asked whether the Church was any longer capable of performing her age-long task of kindling Christ's fire upon earth, a task which she always tried with invincible constancy to fulfil. At that period mankind was witnessing a new widening of world horizons. As in the great age of discovery, explorers were setting out upon hitherto unknown sea routes. Wallis, Vancouver, the illustrious Captain Cook, Bougainville, Surville, Marion, La Pérouse, Levaillant[60] and D'Entrecasteaux were undertaking voyages that stirred the minds of men, revealing to them strange peoples and strange lands. It seemed as if Christianity was renouncing her right to baptize them.

The answer to that question was apparently decided by the outbreak of the Revolution, which struck a final and seemingly mortal blow at the French missions. Persecuted along with all the clergy, with their sources of recruitment dried up and their seminaries closed, the missionary bodies found themselves quite unable to send out those reinforcements for which their distant brethren were clamouring. Between 1792 and 1815 the Society of the Foreign Missions managed to send only nine priests; nor were the Lazarists and Holy Ghost Fathers in any better case. Rome was occupied by the French in 1798; Spain and Portugal were equally powerless to help. The missions were not reorganized until around 1830. Who then in the year 1800 would have dared to predict that the nineteenth century was going to be the greatest missionary age in Christian history?

All seemed lost; but recovery was assured—for two reasons. (1) Difficulties notwithstanding, the impulse given by Propaganda to the creation of native Churches continued to be felt. Even those who had been hostile to such a policy realized at the end of the eighteenth century that it represented the Church's one chance of survival in missionary lands. The most striking example was that of the Spanish Dominicans in eastern Tonking, who laboured systematically under the vicariate of Mgr Hernandes to build up a native clergy, giving the habit of their Order to thirty-eight Vietnamese in twenty-eight years. The courage of the native clergy in China as in Ceylon, in Annam as in the Indies, and its resolute defence of the faith in circumstances that were often extremely difficult, provided the Church with one of her future opportunities.

(2) Although the missionary vocation had become less frequent, those who received it were as firm, as heroic, as their predecessors. It is also highly significant that during this period of decline we meet some of the most attractive missionaries there have ever been, though it is impossible here to name them all. In North America we have already seen the amazing work of Father Junipero, 'last of the Conquistadores', as his latest biographer has called him. In China we find Father von Laimbeckhoven, the last Jesuit bishop, who, after being spurned by the Church, remained at the head of his flock at Nanking for no fewer than ten years and was regarded by them as a saint. In China again there were Father Raux, a Lazarist, and two of his brethren; using the same methods employed by the early Jesuits, they managed to regain a footing in Peking (1785), thanks to their skill as mathematicians, astronomers, geographers and even as metallurgists. Nor indeed must we forget the founder of the Korean Church, Seng houn-i, a layman who had been baptized while serving as a young diplomat at Peking. Returning to his country in 1784, all alone and without priestly assistance, he straightway formed a number of Christian communities whose heroism was later proved by persecution.

Among all missionaries of those unhappy years the most remarkable was undoubtedly Mgr Pigneau de Béhaine (1741–99) of the Society of the Foreign Missions, Bishop of Adran and Vicar-Apostolic of Cochin China. His life reads like some wonderful adventure story. Arriving in Indo-China in 1767, he found it a prey to fire and sword. A rebellious civil servant at the head of a ferocious rabble was overrunning the countryside, attacking the cities, butchering the ruling princes of Cochin China and driving out the monarch of Ton-

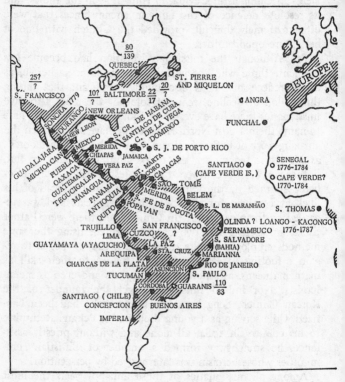

Catholic Missions at the End

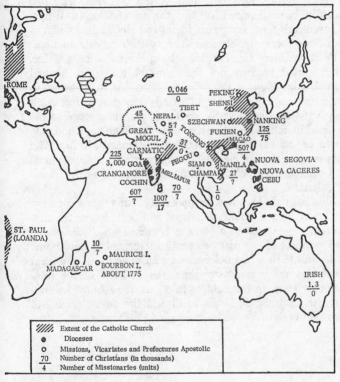

ROME

ST. PAUL
(LOANDA)

0.046
0

PEKING
SHENSI

45
0
NEPAL

GREAT
MOGUL

5?
0

TIBET

SZECHWAN

TONKING

FUKIEN

NANKING

125
75

225
3,000
GOA

CARNATIC

3?
0

PEGOU

MACAO

50?
4

CRANGANORE
COCHIN

MELIAPUR

SIAM

CHAMPA

MANILA

NUOVA SEGOVIA

NUOVA CACERES

CEBU

60?
?

100?
17

70?
?

2?
?

1
0

MADAGASCAR

10
?

MAURICE I.

BOURBON I.
ABOUT 1775

IRISH

1.3
0

/////	Extent of the Catholic Church
●	Dioceses
○	Missions, Vicariates and Prefectures Apostolic
70	Number of Christians (in thousands)
4	Number of Missionaries (units)

of the Eighteenth Century

king. The Christian communities had fled before this whirl-wind, churches were sacked and the missionaries expelled. The vicar-apostolic showed both firmness and ability. He managed to rescue his seminarists and reorganize the scattered communities. Above all, he boldly supported the claims of Nguyen-Anh, legitimate heir of the Nguyens, who had recently been deprived of the throne of Cochin China. Nguyen-Anh thus became his friend and ally, and sent him to Paris, together with his son Kanh, with a request to Louis XIV for military aid. Let down by the French India Office, who refused to carry out the terms of the treaty he had signed, Mgr Pigneau de Béhaine succeeded nevertheless in mounting an expedition, and exactly ten days before 14th July 1789 he landed at Saigon to restore his protégé to the throne. In return the Nguyen, now the Emperor Gia-Long, could do no less than protect the missionaries. When Mgr Pigneau de Béhaine died, Gia-Long gave him a state funeral and erected a mausoleum which is still known as the Tomb of Adran.[61]

The balance sheet was disappointing, but there was reason for hope. After a period of collapse and degradation, the missions were destined to a glorious future. Though the efforts and sacrifices of the past two centuries seemed to have borne little fruit,[62] they had not been in vain. The dawn of a great missionary era would soon dispel the darkness of the revolutionary years. In this field, as in others, the Church had not lost the fight; she had only to discard the errors which had sterilized her activity, and victory would be hers.

CHAPTER III

CHURCHES OUTSIDE THE CHURCH

In the year 1686 a Calvinist pastor named Jurieu, being then a refugee in Holland following the revocation of the Edict of Nantes, searched the Apocalypse for signs of hope. He found so many that he forthwith made them known in an impassioned work, *L'Accomplissement de prophéties*, which roused enthusiasm among the *émigrés* at Rotterdam, Berlin and London, as well as among the Huguenots who had been driven from the Alps and the Cevennes. Deliverance was at hand: Holy Scripture proved as much. The Beast—Louis XIV or Rome?—would soon be stricken unto death. A union of Protestant princes would erect an invincible coalition against the persecuting powers. The Church would conquer innumerable souls—by the Church, of course, he meant all those sects which had sprung from Luther, Calvin and others; all those sects which he treated as a whole, despite their manifold differences and dissensions. He saw the triumph of the Reformation rising over Europe like a dawn.

Our learned pastor, it need hardly be said, was wrong in placing too literal an interpretation on the sacred text; for example, by calculating the time at which those famous 1,260 years would end, he concluded that the exile of the *émigrés* would last for no more than four years. Such precision is rarely confirmed by events. He was not mistaken, however, when he foretold the increase of Protestant power, the growing importance of the part to be played in Europe by the reformed states, and even the defeat of the impious king who had injured the 'Church'. Events soon proved him right.

There is one particularly striking feature in the history of Protestantism between the Treaties of Westphalia and the French Revolution. Unable to become a Church in the full sense of that word, and ever more obedient to the spirit which, because of its fundamental principle of free judgment, drove it to unending self-division, Protestantism foresaw that in order to survive it would have to form a party. It would have to rally against the Catholic Church, which had been strengthened by its own reform, all those whose traditions linked them with the great religious revolt of the sixteenth century. Between Lutherans, Calvinists and Anglicans there was little understanding and still less mutual love; but their adversaries were identical. Gone were the days when Richelieu's genius inveigled the Protestant princes of Germany to serve the interests of Catholic France. The reformed states were now united and would henceforth be strong. The arrival in England of William of Orange (1688), together with the accession of Frederick I as first King of Prussia in the same year, marks the beginning of a policy that was to last for more than a century.

In the purely territorial domain the situation did not alter much during the hundred and fifty years that followed the Treaties of Westphalia. In 1648 the non-Catholic West included two-thirds of Germany and three-quarters of Switzerland, the northern countries of Scandinavia and the Baltic, England and a part of Scotland, a few small areas of France and the whole Danube basin. That distribution remained constant. The revocation of the Edict of Nantes struck a severe blow at French Protestantism, but was far from destroying it.

Nor was the balance seriously disturbed by a fair number of individual conversions in Germany,[1] which were offset by several instances of apostasy. Moreover, as we have seen,[2] the second half of the seventeenth century was marked by a hardening of the Protestant attitude, which revealed itself in increased severity towards the Catholics.

The territorial partition of the West among the churches, such as had been effected at Münster and Osnabrück, endured until the twentieth century; but the ratio of forces changed, because two of the countries where Protestantism in one form or another was most firmly established assumed first-rate importance. First, Britain. The end of the seventeenth century and the whole of the eighteenth witnessed the attainment of world-power status by the little kingdom of the Stuarts, then by diminutive Prussia. The sea and industry (the latter assisted by the Industrial Revolution) altered the bases of Britain's economy, and thereby facilitated her expansion. The British Navy embarked upon the conquest of the ocean; outstripping the French fleet and that of her Dutch friends, it rose within a period of fifty years from 260,000 to nearly a million tons. The replacement of wood by coal, 9,000,000 tons of which were mined in 1789, afforded British machines an apparently inexhaustible supply of energy. The population of the realm, too, made gigantic strides, almost doubling in a period of fifty years and reaching a figure of 9,000,000 at the end of the eighteenth century. As for the growth of cities, London contained something like a million souls; Manchester, which in 1701 was a small town of 6,000 souls, numbered 100,000 a century later. The Earl of Chatham and his son, William Pitt the Younger, would one day make political use of these material advantages.

Europe had been subject in turn to Spanish and French hegemony. Now Protestant Britain assumed leadership. It was because of their confirmed anti-Catholic sympathies that William of Orange, a Calvinist, and his wife Mary were called to the throne; and they had been obliged to pledge support for the unyielding bigotry of their subjects. Even the small group of non-jurors, led by Archbishop Sancroft, who refused to recognize them and held James II to be the sole legitimate king, did not return to the Catholic Church, but affiliated themselves with that of Scotland. Later, it was because of her marriage to the Protestant George of Denmark and her submission to the Anglican doctrines that the second daughter of James II was chosen to succeed William III. In 1707, when Scotland was united to England, the Act of Union guaranteed the Presbyterians the right to practise their religion, but made no reference to the Catholics; and the favour shown by the Schism Act (1714) to all nonconformists in the realm was carefully withheld from papists. Moreover the Act of Establishment (1701), which regulated the order of succession to the throne, expressly declared that no one who was not of the reformed faith might wear the crown. It was in accordance with this Act that the last of the Stuarts were set aside, and a descendant of Sophia of Hanover, Calvinist grand-daughter of James I, brought to London the Hanoverian dynasty, which, though German and alien to English ways, was firmly Protestant. All attempts made on behalf of the Jacobites (not all of whom were Catholics) ended in defeat and bloodshed; the disaster of Culloden (1746) was final. George I (1714–27), George II (1727–60) and George III (1760–1820)—the first two insignificant, the last ambitious and more energetic—all followed the anti-Catholic line willed by their people. And when George III thought of taking a different course his audacity was answered with rioting in the streets of London. Britain had been a bastion of Protestantism since the day she expelled her king in order to defend her beliefs together with her liberties; and a bastion of Protestantism she was determined to remain now that she was on the way to becoming the most powerful state in Europe.

Another Protestant bastion had appeared in northern Germany—Prussia. Her emergence is one of the most astonishing factors in the history of that period, one of the finest examples of what the human will can do when exercised in the continuity of a reigning house. Entering history at the time of the Westphalian treaties, thanks to the painstaking and resolute genius of the Grand Elector Frederick William (1640–88), first creator of the Prussian Army, the Hohenzollern dynasty did for its country very much the same as the Capetians had done for France. The victory of Fehrbellin revealed to the world the valour of the Prussian soldier. The Grand Elector's son, Frederick I (1688–1713), making skilful use of the emperor's difficulties, 'set Prussia on the throne of kings' by assuming the royal title. Next, the 'Sergeant-King', Frederick William I (1713–40), methodically and with fierce determination forged an unrivalled instrument of war, created a centralized and highly organized civil service such as existed nowhere else in Europe at that time, and finally, by means of systematic colonization, raised the population of Prussia itself from 400,000 to 600,000 souls. The seal was set upon all this work by Frederick II (1740–86), a man of genius, an enlightened despot, a subtle diplomat and a brilliant soldier, under whom the Prussian state was increased from 75,000 to

124,000 square miles and her population from 2,300,000 to 6,000,000. His army became the best in Europe, his treasury the wealthiest and his country's economy one of the most flourishing. Within a period of one hundred and fifty years the Hohenzollern family, once a mere nestful of rapacious squireens ready to snatch territory in all four quarters of Germany, rose to equality with the leading houses of Europe.

That astonishing ascent was closely linked with the Protestant cause. No Prussian Hohenzollern ever forgot that his family had been first enriched by the secularization of the Teutonic Order's property at the time of the Reformation. In no other family were the principles of Erastianism[3] regarded with such respect. 'Princes', declared the Sergeant-King, 'should be considered as popes in their dominions,' and he appealed to the *summum jus circum sacra*. None of the Prussian monarchs failed to exercise that right; they controlled their Church through the privy council and the *Geistliches Departement*, a ministry of spiritual affairs, and they supervised the three general consistories—Lutheran, Prussian Calvinist and French Calvinist—of Berlin. On the other hand the attitude of the Hohenzollerns towards Catholicism varied, and was not characterized by the continuous, systematic anti-papal feeling of the English. It was tolerant under the Grand Elector; bigoted under Frederick I; distrustful and interfering under the Sergeant-King, who behaved courteously towards the Catholics only when their money seemed likely to be useful; more easy-going under Frederick II, who nevertheless exacted an oath of obedience from his Catholic subjects, notably from the priests of Silesia, which territory he had annexed. The fact remains, however, that Protestantism was the basis of the Prussian State, gave it its distinctive features and dictated its policies. The King of Prussia was very soon posing as champion of the reformed faith. In 1732 he gave asylum to some Protestants who had been expelled from Salzburg by the archbishop, just as his ancestor had done for the victims of the Revocation. In 1735 he accorded a similar welcome to twelve hundred Czech dissenters who had been driven from Bohemia. He intervened at various dates to defend his co-religionists in Hungary and Switzerland. He obliged Joseph I to restore some chapels he had confiscated and harboured many Lutheran pedlars who sold heretical pamphlets in Catholic territory. He even aspired (though without success) to the presidency of the German Evangelical Fellowship. And finally, in 1774, when the Protestants of Bohemia agitated for and obtained the right to build new chapels, Frederick II was busy at every stage of the proceedings.

The twofold rise of Britain and Prussia, then, marks a considerable strengthening of the Protestant position in Europe. It compensated in large measure for the slow but steady decline of another Protestant country, the United Provinces of Holland, whose maritime strength now disappeared, and even for the eclipse of Sweden, another bright star of the Reformation, which was overshadowed by the increasing significance of Russia. The collapse of Catholic Poland, too, was yet another source of compensation. More important still, the two powers in whom the spirit of the Reformation henceforth reposed its trust did not go separate ways; they allied to form a regular Protestant party, which was joined by other countries, e.g. Holland. That politico-religious alliance was to dominate Europe until 1789 and even beyond.

It was Louis XIV who, by revoking the Edict of Nantes, sealed the Protestant union which had not existed until then. Stirred by Jurieu, Claude and other French refugees at Amsterdam, men began to dream of a veritable Protestant crusade against the Sun-King. He became the *bête noire* of the Protestants, a sort of werewolf, whose cruelty and injustice were proclaimed in a thousand pamphlets. Franklin tells us in his memoirs that when he was a young man he used to hear tell of the King of France as the ogre in the fairy-tale, partial to human flesh. William of Orange, now master of Britain, thought it prudent to acknowledge Jurieu's *Soupirs de la France esclave*, which was published in 1689. Henceforward the alliance of Great Britain, Prussia and the United Provinces was one of the bases of European diplomacy, and the Protestants of all countries were convinced, as Wesley later said, that they were 'fighting proud France and vanquishing the powers of Hell'. In 1692 the French Navy sustained a disaster at La Hogue; that date and many a one thereafter marked the ascendancy of the Protestant party over France, who, without always knowing as much, somehow embodied the Catholic cause and in any case appeared as leader of the Catholic *bloc*. Utrecht and Radstadt in 1714, Paris and Hubertsburg in 1763, were the two principal stages of a process which ended by making Protestant Britain mistress of the seas and Protestant Prussia predominant in Germany. Meanwhile the three Catholic powers—France, Spain and Austria—steadily declined.

2. RENASCENCE OF FRENCH PROTESTANTISM

With the ascendancy of the Protestant powers we may link another and equally significant phenomenon—the renascence of French Protestantism. When Louis XIV died, soon after signing the edict of March 1715, whereby he resumed the policy of constraint against the Huguenots, he was firmly convinced that his victory over heresy had been finally established by his suppression of the Camisard revolt. Next year the regent confirmed this legislation, but in point of fact Protestantism was far from being crushed. Ten days before the king's death Antoine Court (1695–1760), a preacher full of audacity, convoked a synod in a quarry near Nîmes. Summoned by secret messengers, the faithful met henceforward in what were known as Assemblies in the Desert; and there, standing at the foot of a T-shaped scaffold, an itinerant pastor would preach, preside over the Lord's supper, baptize and perform marriages. The number of these assemblies grew year by year; the reformed churches were reorganized in the Cevennes, in Poitou, in Saintonge and in Paris itself. In 1724 the government, alerted by the bishops, published a stern edict providing the death penalty for all such preachers and consigning to the galleys those who took part in their assemblies; but it soon became clear that the law was unworkable. Two pastors were indeed executed at Montpellier, and Court was obliged to take refuge in Switzerland; but in many places governors and other officials adopted a more lenient attitude on the strength of their own authority. Cardinal de Fleury, the Marquis de Gudane and the Maréchal de Mirepoix counselled clemency. Some parish priests married Calvinists without inquiry. There were still cases of repression, violence and the hanging of preachers[4] continued, but the climate slowly changed.

A final revolt took place in 1752, following an ordinance which forbade Assemblies in the Desert; and when the Seven Years War broke out (1756) a number of pastors stirred up their flocks and rejoiced in the French defeats. More prudent and more able was Paul Rabaut (1718–94), a noble and truly evangelical figure, a minister for many years 'in the Desert'. He advised loyalty, maintaining that French Protestants must not betray France. Meanwhile the government realized that it would be absurd to risk a revolt of the Camisards. Some mitigations were obtained through the good offices of Comte de Gébelin, a Huguenot whose intelligence and talents had found favour at Versailles: men condemned to the galleys for religious offences were released, confessional schools were tolerated and tacit permission was given to hold 'Assemblies in the Desert'.

In 1767, on the proposal of Gilbert de Voisins and Peinau, parish priest of Tonneins, the difficult question was at length raised concerning the registration of births and marriages. This was the function of the Catholic clergy, who took no cognizance of heretical unions. In order not to leave so many honest spouses in a state of legal concubinage, it was necessary to distinguish the sacrament from the juridical bond of marriage, and to allow the latter right to Protestants. No fewer than twenty years of discussion preceded the famous edict of 1788, which gave French non-Catholics a legal status independent of the parish priests. Thus, for example, in order to marry, it was sufficient for adherents of the reformed religion to have their banns published by a law officer and to take the conjugal oath before four witnesses, one of whom might be the pastor. This wise measure was principally the work of Turgot, Malesherbes and the latter's nephew Mgr de la Luzerne, Bishop of Langres; the Protestant negotiator was Paul Rabaut's son, Rabaut Saint-Étienne, afterwards a member of the Convention. Must we attribute this undeniable success of the Protestant cause to the progress of a spirit of tolerance during the eighteenth century? Partly, no doubt;

but it was also due in large measure to the power of contemporary Protestants. There was no longer a question of pretending to get rid of them.

3. 'NO POPERY!'

The tie which bound the Germanic Lutherans and Calvinists to the Anglicans of Great Britain, and formed them into a single *bloc* with the Huguenots of the Cevennes 'Desert', was undoubtedly their common hatred of Catholicism. That elemental feeling, born amid the violent conflicts of the sixteenth century and aggravated by the Wars of Religion or the revocation of the Edict of Nantes, remained extraordinarily virulent in the eighteenth century. Even in such countries as the United Provinces of Holland, where the government slowly adopted a regime of tolerance, and still more so in England and the small German Protestant states, Rome, the hierarchy and the Jesuits were still objects of a detestation which manifested itself in almost unbelievable ways. The man in the street was quite convinced that the Pope was Antichrist or the incarnation of Satan, and that the Roman Mass was nothing else but sorcery. In German almanacs of that period we find impossible stories of children kidnapped by priests to provide recruits for their own ranks or to satisfy the unnatural lust of monks; and fables of this kind were repeated in some of the worst pages of the infamous Marquis de Sade. During the eighteenth century this current of popular anti-Catholicism joined forces with the irreligious tendencies of the intellectuals; Voltaire and Diderot were the successors of Luther and his disciples. The libellous *Monita Secreta* on the Society of Jesus were widely read and believed.

It would be idle and tedious to enumerate all the many instances of anti-Catholicism in action at that time. In Germany there were popular riots, which in Württemberg led to large-scale expulsions of Catholics; there were also violent episodes in the Palatinate, while Frederick II himself wrote the *Letters of a Chinese* and *Phihuhu's Narrative*, two lampoons in which the Papacy was caricatured with exceptional virulence. In England antipapism was characterized by a degree of passion that is nothing less than astonishing when we consider the insignificance of those small scattered Catholic groups which dragged out a miserable existence, quite incapable of reviving the Gunpowder Plot whose memory inspired such terror. There had grown up in the British Isles a whole body of anti-Catholic folklore, which the last Camisard refugees undertook to enrich with a new selection of horror stories. Many incidents occurred to illustrate that inexpiable loathing.

In 1728, for example, an unfortunate Irish Catholic, who had somehow managed to enlist in an English regiment, refused to attend the Anglican services; he was flogged uninterruptedly on two successive days, and in so horrible a fashion that he craved for mercy in the shape of death. Even Wesley, an upright man and one so deeply imbued, as we shall see, with Catholic spirituality, could not forbear on one occasion from invective against 'the nefarious company which, from the days of St Cyprian, has obtained the government of the Church'. His *Public Advertiser* was one long cry of terror in face of the papist peril. Towards the end of the century, when it might have been supposed that people had become a little more intelligent, there were some indications of fanaticism. In 1767 a priest was condemned for having ministered to a dying man; and in 1779 when Saville, an intelligent and courageous statesman, introduced a Bill into the Lords for the enfranchisement of Catholics there was an explosion of popular wrath. Up went the cry 'No Popery!' and the 'Protestant League' ran riot for the next ten years. Petitions against the Relief Act were signed by thousands; and from Scotland came Lord George Gordon at the head of puritanical gangs wearing blue cockades, to prevent the peers passing so iniquitous an Act. Noble lords were manhandled in their carriages; embassies of foreign states were sacked, together with the London houses of a few aristocrats suspected of papist sympathies and some warehouses belonging to Catholics. Such was Black Wednesday, 7th June 1780, which claimed no fewer than 285 dead. Anti-Catholicism had evidently lost none of its vigour.

It need hardly be said that all attempts to effect a reconciliation between Catholics and their separated brethren proved fruitless. Spinola, Leibniz and Bossuet[5] had failed in this respect; but a handful of men had the courage not to despair of reunion and to continue discussions. In south-eastern France, for example, the brothers Andry and Mgr Cattelan, Bishop of Valence, were answered by Benoît Pictet, a Genevan Calvinist. At Paris Count Zinzendorf (of whom more presently) saw Cardinal de Noailles. Later, Rouvière, a lawyer of the Parlement de Paris, addressed to the dissenters his praiseworthy *Essai de réunion avec les Catholiques romains;* and in 1788 Martinowick published his *Plan de réunion,* in which he called upon Lutherans, Calvinists and Orthodox Greeks to become reconciled with the Catholics. Conversations were even held between Catholics and Anglicans, notably by Eusèbe Renaudot, grandson of the founder of *La Gazette;* by the learned Ellies Dupin with the Anglican Bishop Wake, both of whom were alive to the intermediary role Anglicanism might play; then by Father Le Courayer, and later still, on the eve of the French Revolution, by Dutens, a Calvinist from Touraine, who subsequently became an Anglican. As things turned out, those generous souls had little influence and achieved nothing. Some of them were actually condemned by their Churches, e.g. Le Courayer, who fled to England; all were heavily criticized—even Wake, bishop though he was. Catholics remained intransigent on matters of dogma, but non-Catholics of every sort continued slaves to the traditional feelings of their co-religionists. Not until the middle of the nineteenth century were contacts renewed in a less stormy atmosphere.

4. THE IMPOSSIBILITY OF PROTESTANT UNITY

Anti-Catholicism was able to forge emotional links between the various elements of Protestantism, and above all to seal political alliances; but would it suffice to establish a real unity? The Protestant Reformation had been bedevilled from the outset by internal forces of strain and rupture. It had originated in personalities and purposes that differed widely from one another. Luther had nothing in common with Calvin; and Henry VIII, who merely drifted accidentally into schism and heresy, had nothing in common with either of them. The historical evolution of the non-Catholic Churches had helped to drive them still further apart. By the end of the sixteenth century, notes the Protestant historian Courvoisier, 'the Lutherans had adopted an attitude of unalterable hostility to the Calvinist reform—more papist, one might almost say, than Calvinist'. And those who professed loyalty to the doctrines of Geneva assumed a more stubborn attitude, though in a lesser degree. In England, for example, the Puritans entertained nothing but contempt for the High Church Episcopalians; Cromwell's Roundheads never forgave their leader for having compromised with the Anglicans; and in 1662, when Charles II attempted to impose a common prayer book by the Act of Uniformity, two thousand pastors refused to comply.

Besides the foregoing reasons for mutual antagonism there were others deriving from the very essence of Protestantism. 'Each and every one of the faithful is a priest,' declared Luther; it was precisely the interference of authority in matters of faith against which he and his competitors rebelled. The mere notion of orthodoxy was therefore irreconcilable with any form of Protestantism true to its principle of free judgment. To describe an opinion on a religious subject as a dogma was to betray the spirit of the Reformation; it was a still worse act of treason to ask the state to deny a believer freedom to express his views as and when he chose. Nevertheless, as soon as the various branches of Protestantism had set themselves up as Churches, they had been compelled, with a view to their own survival, to admit the principle of orthodoxy. In Germany, Luther tried to escape the necessity; but in order to avoid anarchy he allowed the princes an overriding authority, and they forthwith imposed a creed. At Geneva it was forbidden to believe differently from Calvin, as Servetus learned to his cost. After the disappearance of the founders, the situation inevitably hardened, for the continuation of their work remained an extremely difficult task. The Protestant Churches, in fact, were victims of a tragic inconsistency: in order to preserve the living heritage of the masters, they had to sacrifice the very thing they had been taught to consider as its vital factor.

By what right then was one to prevent a man, a group or a sect from laying claim to the sacred rights of conscience against a Church which called itself reformed but was unfaithful to the spirit of the Reformation? By what right did Calvin burn Michael Servetus? By what right did the Council of Berne in 1623 dismiss Faber, a pastor and professor at Lausanne, driving him into exile at Grenoble because of his opinions on the soul? By what right did the reformed Church of France in 1669 oppose the Socinian views of another pastor, Isaac Husseau? Worse still, by what right were the inoffensive Quakers persecuted in England and hanged in America? The Catholic Church is entitled to foster and seek to impose orthodoxy, because her authority is founded upon the principles of tradition, the Power of the Keys and Apostolic descent; but as soon as those principles are abandoned any pretensions to impose a creed are vain.

All coercive measures too were futile. No Protestant Church, even when armed with the secular sword, managed to prevent the birth within herself of groups that opposed her with the challenge of imprescriptible rights belonging to the conscience enlightened by God. The phenomenon of sects, which is of the very essence of the Reformation, began during the lifetime of the great reformers; it was destined to endure and grow into the vast swarm we see today, particularly in North America.[6] The history of Protestantism is largely one of progressive dismemberment, of a ceaseless multiplication of prophets more or less inspired, who put forward an original interpretation of the Christian message and are followed by more or less numerous disciples.

The Protestant Churches attempted in various ways to halt this process. One method was to formulate and impose a doctrinal scheme. An effort was made in Switzerland by Turrettini of Geneva and Heidegger of Zürich; Calvinists and Zwinglians agreed on the terms of a *Consensus Helveticus* which stated the faith in such a way that Courvoisier was able to declare: 'The confessional document, the elaborated formula, takes the place once occupied by Holy Scripture.' In

Holland the attitude of 'the soft', i.e. of the evangelical Arminians[7] who were more sensible of the divine mercy, provoked a vigorous reaction among 'the hard' under the leadership of Gomar. In 1618–19 the Synod of Dordrecht officially
promulgated the most severe theses of Calvinism—the total
impotence of man without God's grace, redemption by the
merits of Christ alone, rigorous predestination. The result of
these quasi-conciliar decisions was very small; though persecuted for some time, the disciples of Arminius soon obtained
the right to believe as they thought fit. Again, all Jurieu's
passionate efforts to uphold and defend a Calvinist orthodoxy
were in vain. The Synod of Charenton (1631), though more
moderate than that of Dordrecht, made a similar attempt
in France. Later still, once more at Dordrecht in 1686 and at
Amsterdam in 1690, 'orthodox' Calvinism began solemnly to
reassert its principles—a proof, if one were needed, that they
were not unanimously accepted.

If strictness failed, was some other method likely to succeed? It might perhaps consist in abstracting the great general
principles common to all the reformed Churches and interpreting them so broadly that all could accept them. The man
who best conceived this project was Georges Calixte, whom
we have already met[8] as one of the protagonists of reconciliation between Catholics and Protestants. Seeing clearly that
Evangelicalism was drifting toward the rocks of self-destruc-
tion, he suggested to the Lutherans, the Calvinists and others
that they should agree on the principles accepted by the
Church until the fifth century, and allow freedom of belief
to everyone within that framework. Such was the central point
of the *Consensus Quinquesecularis*, which he taught for
many years at Helmstedt and expounded in such written
works as his Latin treatise on the *Desire for Concord in the
Church* (1656). Souls as generous as himself were won over
to these ideas. Such were Hornejus, Joachim Hildebrandt,
Jean Daillé in France, John Dury in Scotland; and the Polish
Prince Radziwill actually assembled a congress at Orla to discuss them. Vain hopes! Stern theologians of the great reformed Churches were on the watch and soon launched a
vigorous counter-offensive. It was all too easy to accuse Calixte
of popery; no fewer than eighty-eight errors and heresies were

discovered in his doctrine. Lastly, while Lutherans were driving Calvinists from the territory of Anhalt-Zerbst and Calvinists were driving Lutherans from the universities of Hesse, in Sweden, Ussadius, a partisan of agreement, was condemned to death for having publicly admitted that works are useful for salvation, and only just managed to obtain a reprieve.

The same difficulties were experienced in England, where the government attempted on several occasions to establish interconfessional agreement—always excluding Catholics, of course. But while their measures were able to effect a *modus vivendi*, they could not create a unity. Failure awaited the efforts of William Laud, of Cromwell, of Charles II with his Act of Uniformity (1662), and of William III, who immediately after his accession set up a Committee of Reform and Union, in the hope of reconciling Calvinism with the Anglican High Church. None of these efforts succeeded; English Protestants were no more capable than their brethren in Germany of uniting to form a single evangelical and reformed Church. Indeed an admission of their failure may be seen in the very documents in which union was proclaimed. Together with Catholics and Jews, Unitarians were excluded from the 'Indulgence' because they did not believe in the Holy Trinity; and the Quakers were frequently in trouble with the law.

The dissolution of Protestantism into Churches, tendencies, groups, movements and sects continued; it would be a well-nigh impossible task to trace and enumerate them all. Those which appeared at the end of the sixteenth century[9] survived in more or less modified forms. Others evolved, their origin being in many cases determined by a faint difference of interpretation, some trifling point of discipline or the ambition of an individual. The Anabaptists, whose insolence and radical theories had struck terror into Lutheran Germany, had become more discreet under Menno Simons, and the Mennonites flourished in Holland. The Moravian Brethren, heirs of the Hussites, professed a joyous asceticism and recognized no authority but that of Holy Scripture. There were still a number of Waldenses in the alpine regions of France and Savoy; others had fled to Bavaria and Austria. They were more or less loosely attached to the reformed Churches, but lived closely confined within the framework of their peculiar traditions. We have already noticed the Arminians; they were not peculiar to the United Provinces, but had adherents in France, among whom was Pastor Amyraut. In Holland too, which rejected all the established Churches, the French *émigré* Jean Labadie formed a number of small communities, which were the forerunners of Pietism. At the other extreme of Protestantism, the Socinians[10] stood for religion in a form so rationalistic that it seemed hardly to deserve the name 'faith'. Not far from them were the Unitarians. Their first prophet was John Biddle, who lived in the time of Cromwell. John Lindsey (1723–1808) subsequently and somewhat paradoxically organized them into a Church with a definite creed and a kind of hierarchy.

The land *par excellence* of Protestant variations was Britain. In Scotland the heavy hand of John Knox had forged unity among Presbyterians; but Presbyterianism contained within itself two tendencies, one accepting the hierarchy imposed by the civil authority, and the other clinging to absolute religious democracy. The multiplication of sects in Britain was altogether amazing. 'There are as many creeds as heads,' declared the Venetian Sagredo in 1655; he knew a family in which the father and six children each belonged to a different one. Puget's *Heresiography* enumerated two hundred and sixty-four obediences, some of which had only a few hundred members.

Adherents of the Churches properly so called fall into two main groups: those who accepted the official religious system established by Henry VIII, and those who did not. Overriding that classification there was the puritan mentality, which adopted a solemn, austere and moralistic attitude in matters of religion—'aridly inebriated', says Albert-Marie Schmidt, 'with the co-ordinated multiplicity of its virtues'. There were puritans on every religious front. Practically speaking it is possible to distinguish three groups: (1) The Anglican Church, accepted a hierarchy of bishops and monarchy holding office by divine institution, but included (*a*) the High Church, which had retained many usages of the Roman Church and whose creed was based on the Thirty-nine Articles, and (*b*) the Low Church, Calvinist by conviction, temperament and behaviour. (2) The Calvinist and puritan Presbyterians, modelled on the pattern of Geneva and Scotland, admitted an established Church but entrusted its government to councils of Elders elected by the parishes and meeting in synods. (3) The Independents, founded in the reign of Elizabeth I by Robert Brown, were likewise puritan in outlook; they recognized no intermediary between themselves and God, and placed a literal interpretation on the words of St Paul: 'Go out from the midst of them, be separate and touch no unclean thing.' In their eyes both the Anglican and the Presbyterian Churches were unclean; it is among these radical separatists that we find the strongest tendency towards subdivision. But there were also the Congregationalists, some of whom accepted a synodal organization while others rejected it. The left-wing Gentlemen Independents contrasted with the left-wing Levellers, who lapsed into pure rationalism during the eighteenth century. Still further left stood the Mechanic Preachers, a truly revolutionary movement against which the Government took stern measures; they were quickly followed by Winstanley's Diggers, who looked back to the integral communism of early Christian times. With the Levellers and Diggers we are no longer in the realm of Churches, but in that of sects, whose numbers increased with amazing rapidity: Brownists, Barrowists, non-dissenting Puritans, Burtonists and so on. There were more than a hundred of them, and we have still to mention the various Baptist movements, whose origins can be traced to the first Protestant revolutionaries, before the advent of Calvinism. They were passionately devoted to the principle of religious freedom, hostile to the theology of predestination, and still more resolutely opposed to all the established Churches, which appeared to them as nothing less than manifestations of Antichrist. John Smith, who had lived in Holland and consorted with the Anabaptists and Mennonites, did much to advance the Baptist cause in England, but he could not prevent his heirs from splitting up into General Baptists and Particular Baptists. In presence of such anarchy one cannot refrain from quoting Father Delteil's amusing observation: 'Catholicism is to religion what marriage is to love.' Outside the rules laid down by the authority of Rome and her tradition, extramarital fantasies were only too numerous.

5. GEORGE FOX AND THE QUAKERS

Among all those swarming sects one deserves particular notice, not only because of its romantic origins and customs, but also because of the attractive characteristics in the moral attitude of its members. It called itself, as it does today, the Society of Friends. Its adherents liked to refer to one another as 'Children of Light', but from the moment that their existence became public they were nicknamed 'Quakers'. One day when their founder was standing in the dock, as he was often obliged to do, he invited the magistrate to 'honour God and quake before His Word'. 'Quake?' exclaimed His Honour, 'quake yourself!' A rumour spread that at meetings of the sect those upon whom the spirit of God alighted began suddenly to tremble and grimace in the most extraordinary fashion. The word was intended as a joke, but it passed into current usage. And the 'Quakers', who were not lacking in humility, adopted it themselves, as if by way of challenge.

The founder's name was George Fox (1624–91). He was a tall, strongly built man with bright, piercing eyes and solemn countenance. Wearing a leather jacket and broad-brimmed hat, he went about over hill and dale, preaching to all sorts of people the message with which he believed himself to have been entrusted. His voice was powerful, capable of reaching thousands in the open air. Tireless, he could talk for three hours on end, and was described as convincing, uplifting, persuasive. 'To hear Fox speak in the forecourt of a church', said one of his followers, 'was to live for a moment in light and fire.'

Light, the interior light, the fire of God, was indeed the principal, nay, the sole foundation of the doctrine he taught. As a lad searching for truth in all sincerity, he conceived a strong dislike for the Anglican system as well as for the anarchy of the various dissenting puritan confessions. Associating with a small group of 'seekers', he concluded that all such obediences were futile. In 1646, being then twenty-two years of age, he was riding one day to Coventry when it occurred to him that 'all Christians are believers, be they Protestants or Papists'. The notion was rare at that date and shows an uncommon breadth of mind. As he meditated upon this idea, it was revealed to him that 'the only true believers were those who were born of God and had thus passed from death to life'. His task was immediately clear: he must draw men from the churches built by men and lead them to the Church of God, persuade them to lay aside human forms of worship and to worship in spirit and truth.

Now that position was as alien to Protestantism as it was to Catholicism. Fox despised Luther, Calvin, Henry VIII and Elizabeth no less than he despised the whole series of Roman pontiffs. The Church of which he dreamed, contemplating a return to that of early Christian times, would be an invisible Church, whose members would be united in the Spirit alone —a mystical Church gathering together all Christians and raising them above particular forms and creeds. His only dogma was to believe in the interior light which comes from God; to experience, in the depths of self, that heat which inflamed the hearts of the disciples at Emmaus when the risen Jesus spoke to them; to live by the 'divine seed' which is planted in every man. 'Remember there is something of God in you,' Fox often cried when preaching. Later, in 1676, his disciple Barclay spun out a whole theological system from those principles, denying original sin, declaring that the redemption was the eternal work of the divine 'Logos', and at the same time adopting the Catholic doctrines of justification, sanctification and good works.

Such, however, was not the original keystone of Quakerism. It consisted in the vehement and categorical rejection by Fox and his disciples of all external worship, of the sacraments (even baptism and the eucharist), of all ecclesiastical organization and of priesthood in any shape or form. The Quakers forgathered in what were known as 'silent meetings', at which the congregation meditated at length without uttering a word until the spirit of God, as they supposed, swept down upon one of them. The person thus privileged straightway rose and began to prophesy; women, of course, were far more subject to such visitations than their menfolk. Yet in

George Fox's view even those meetings and manifestations were of secondary importance; what really counted was the moral attitude. 'One must not commentate upon the word of God,' he used to say, 'but *live* it.' Indeed the Quakers gave evidence of their sincere endeavour to live in God and by God. They behaved in brotherly fashion towards one another, justifying the name of their Society as one of friends; and they displayed nothing but charity towards the poor and destitute, towards prisoners and exiles, as well as towards the black slaves in America. Their ordinary demeanour was austere; they eschewed all worldly pleasures, taking no part in games or hunting, and never attending the theatre or a dance. All adopted the same peculiar style of clothing: men wore sombre colours, without collar or buttons; women, dark grey, with green apron, white shawl and plain head-dress. In order to prove themselves completely obedient to the divine commands, they refused to take an oath, to carry arms or to pay tithes. They addressed everyone as 'thee' and 'thou'. Their tombstones bore no name. There was something anarchical about the Quaker system, but its adherents were none the less hard-working, thrifty, enterprising, practical and no less honest than capable in business. On the whole they were the most estimable and most harmless of heretics.

Harmless though they were, the authorities did not long consider them to be so. For indeed the liberty they claimed as 'Children of Light' led them to excesses which could not but arouse suspicion. Fox and his friends used to enter churches and chapels, interrupt the sermon and inveigh against the preachers, especially puritan pastors, whom they regarded as 'priests of Baal', 'hireling ministers'. Sometimes when a clergyman was telling his congregation that the Bible is the sole foundation of faith, they would cut him short and cry: 'That is not true, the sole foundation of faith is the Spirit.' As soon as the movement had begun to recruit disciples many an Anglican, Presbyterian or other service was halted by a powerful voice 'declaring the whole truth to priest and people'. The interrupter was often soundly thrashed; still more often the trouble makers were arrested by government agents and imprisoned. Between 1651 and 1656 more than two thousand Quakers were locked up; twelve thousand between 1661 and

1689. It was not until the reign of William III that the Toleration Act put an end to the persecution of the Children of Light.

The principle of interior illumination led the Quakers to some astonishing behaviour. Some 'silent meetings' at which the divine spirit was poured out more abundantly than usual ended with the whole congregation shouting and stamping their feet. At Whitehall, during a service attended by Cromwell, a Quakeress (doubtless to render her testimony more convincing) appeared in the simple attire attributed by mythology to Truth when she emerges from the well. Another of these women, less zealous, used to walk about the streets with her face covered in soot, thus signifying that according to Scripture beauty is deceptive. One day, too, a Quaker forced his way into the House of Commons wearing only a loin-cloth and carrying a chafing dish filled with burning sulphur, thereby warning members that even so they would ultimately burn in hell. The most sensational of all Quaker scandals occurred in 1656. James Naylor, a former noncommissioned officer, was visited by the Spirit and appointed prophet in the neighbourhood of Bristol, where he enjoyed considerable success. Imagining himself to be none other than Jesus Christ, he entered the city in a manner similar to Our Lord's entry into Jerusalem on Palm Sunday, riding on horseback and escorted by a mob of crazy females screaming 'Holy! Holy! Holy! the Lord God of Israel! Hosanna in the highest!' After repeating this contemptible performance on several occasions, Naylor the prophet was condemned to be flogged, pilloried and branded on the tongue with red-hot iron. And while he endured those sufferings with extraordinary fortitude, one of his followers raised a placard above the crowd. 'This man', it proclaimed, 'is king of the Jews.'

Such aberrations, however, did not discredit the Quaker movement, nor did persecution hinder its advance. Those pious people resisted their adversaries with the inexhaustible strength of inertia and smiling resignation. Imprisonment for their faith seemed to them the happiest of lots, and when every parent had been jailed the children continued with invincible tenacity to hold 'silent meetings' and even to preach. Thus the sect progressed. Though Fox had absolutely no intention of creating any Church, a simple form of organization was gradually evolved; it had no clergy, of course, but the authority of the group was accepted in order to enforce a minimum of discipline.

By 1700 the Society of Friends had about fifty thousand members in England, Scotland and Ireland; it had also obtained a firm foothold in America with William Penn. Nevertheless, when persecution ceased progress slackened, and before long there was a noticeable decrease in numbers. Was this because the noble founder left no heir? Or because it was impossible to make men live in the religion of the Spirit alone? Every nascent Church, if it is to become rooted in reality, needs someone like St Paul, and Quakerism produced no such figure. During the eighteenth century the Society of Friends continued to exist and hold its meetings, where prosperous citizens, leaning on their canes and with broad felt hats pulled down over their eyes, awaited inspiration from the Holy Ghost; but there were no more raids upon 'steeple-houses' nor public invectives against preachers of lies. In 1789 the Quakers numbered barely twenty thousand;[11] and it was a French journalist, Antoine Benézet, who did most to keep alive the flame of early days, trying to alleviate the misery of the slums, to obtain the liberation of black slaves, or defending his fellow countrymen driven from Acadia. The Quaker movement was a kind of spiritual outgrowth on the tree of the Reformation, an outgrowth, as someone has said, 'at the farthest frontier of Protestantism'. It was too lacking in solid doctrinal bases to enjoy permanent success.[12]

6. INTERNAL CRISES

Orthodoxy and unity were not the only problems with which Protestantism had to deal. The various Churches sprung from the Reformation had also to overcome the paramount difficulty facing all religions in their historical development: to maintain the original tension, to prevent the initial fire from sinking low and dying out. This well-known phenomenon, which we have observed time and time again within the Catholic Church itself, always dragging down the spirit's flight, weakening faith, transforming enthusiasm into routine, was equally familiar to the Protestant confessions. They experienced no such violent doctrinal crises as those of Jansenism and Quietism, but they fell victim to that principle of dissolution which permeates all human things. And they did so very quickly, as Protestant historians themselves inform us. At the beginning of the seventeenth century 'the Reformation was no longer what it had been during the first half of the sixteenth. The spirit which animated such men as Luther, Zwingli and Calvin had disappeared.'[13] What would the position be two hundred years later?

'The different Protestant Churches, especially the Anglican and Lutheran,' say Mousnier and Labrousse,[14] 'were afflicted with maladies similar to those of the Catholic Church: subjection to the State, unsatisfactory recruitment and training of the clergy, lukewarmness of faith, a general tendency to rationalism and deism as well as to natural religion which affected both morality and belief.'

State interference was the primary cause of that decline. In Lutheran Germany the founder himself had permitted it, for fear of mortal anarchy. Rulers, moreover, made extensive use of the rights allowed to them. Controlling ecclesiastical appointments, regulating behaviour and even faith itself, taking it upon themselves to reform the catechism (as happened several times in Prussia), and obliging pastors to cultivate their gardens and plant mulberry trees for silkworms, the German sovereigns, great and small, treated their Churches in a manner more brusque and authoritarian than was ever employed by Louis XIV. Among the Calvinists the situation was not quite the same, for there it was rather the Church that dominated the State; but confusion between the two powers, established at Geneva by Calvin and in Scotland by Knox, was none the less harmful to spiritual interests. The Anglican Church, being less subservient to royal authority than its Germanic sisters, was sometimes able to oppose the sovereign's will, as, for example, when the Calvinist William III attempted to give it a less 'episcopal' and more 'reformed' look; but, like (and even more than) the Catholic Church, it could not escape the danger resulting from the constant meddling of the secular power in the appointment of bishops and parochial clergy, which often seemed to be determined by intrigue, by political considerations and even by money, rather than by personal merit.

Since like causes produce like effects, a glance through the list of Protestant aberrations and defects is sufficient to remind one of the criticisms levelled against the Catholic Church. There was a serious lack of training among the Lutheran pastors, who were recruited mainly from the ranks of wealthy peasants and the sons of civil servants. The pulpit echoed theological discourses learned by heart, diatribes against Rome or denunciations of other reformed Churches and sects. Hampered by princes in its charitable, educational and judicial functions, the Lutheran clergy practised a routine form of Christianity, devoid of warmth and enthusiasm. Lutheranized convents and chapters were in effect reserved for the nobility, and worldly prelates had the same vices as worldly prelates everywhere. As for the people, they too often indulged their worst inclinations behind a mask of carefully regulated and superstitious devotion. The situation was as bad among the Anglicans, where moral decadence, drunkenness and debauchery attained their zenith under the first Hanoverians. Many of the clergy were arrogant, sure of themselves as sole depositories of true Christian faith. Religious duties meant very little to them; many thought it sufficient to take part in the Lord's Supper once a year. Societies for the propagation of the Gospel met with indifference and even sometimes with opposition; and it is significant that the Methodists, authors of a spiritual revival, were persecuted as spoil-sports.

The situation was better among the Calvinists, whose clergy were better trained. Calvin at Geneva and Knox in Scotland had founded theological colleges which continued throughout the seventeenth and eighteenth centuries to prepare men for the ministry. Moral conduct as a whole was stricter. The principal defect of the Calvinist Churches lay in a kind of fossilization which rendered faith mechanical and conduct mere conformity—a danger which threatens all religions which identify themselves with governmental systems. For examples of Calvinist faith at its most vigorous we must look to the French Churches, where fervour was sustained by persecution. They were more or less clandestine groups in which laymen took the place of their imprisoned pastors: Israel Lecourt near Le Havre, Claude Brousson in Languedoc, Lagardère in Rouergue, and prophetesses like Isabelle Vincent, 'the shepherdess of Crest', galvanized faith with their fiery sermons. Small bands of exiles who had been obliged to risk their lives in order to flee their hostile fatherland, preferring danger to betrayal of their faith, had settled in Prussia, Holland and England; and there they continued to derive courage and hope from their beliefs. Pierre Coste, an admirer of John Locke; Elie Benoist, author of the *Histoire de la Révocation de l'Edit*; Gédéon Flournois, who wrote a dramatic account of the sufferings of his co-religionists; Jurieu above all—combative, vehement, apocalyptic: all these bear witness, each in his own way, to the preservation of militant Calvinism among the 500,000 French Protestant refugees.

As years went by and the current of irreligion became stronger,[15] Protestantism experienced its effects. Because of the principle of free inquiry it offered a more propitious field than did Catholicism to those who sought to get rid of dogmas. In all the Protestant bodies, whether Churches or sects, the very notion of a Church tended to disappear; if the true Church were invisible, upon what should orthodoxy be based? The fundamental dogmas of the Trinity, Our Lord's divinity and the reality of redemption were all disputed. It was within the very bosom of Protestantism that the second half of the sixteenth century produced the movement initiated by the Sozzini, uncle and nephew,[16] which led to the astonishing phenomenon of 'Christian agnosticism'. After the death of its founders Socinianism continued to flourish; the Synod of Rakov in 1618, which met under the auspices of John Crell, Martin Ruais, the brothers Stegmann, Wolzogen and Sozzini's grandson Wiszowaty, laid further stress upon the radical aspect of their doctrine. It exerted a profound influence on a great number of Protestant circles; one might even say that it was one of the temptations of the Protestant conscience, to which it suggested a rationalistic religion without dogma as the ultimate goal of the Reformation. Persecuted almost everywhere, denounced with fury by such men as Jurieu, Socinianism spread in all directions; it appears in the

works of Isaac d'Husseau, a French pastor, in the lampoons
of Peterson, in Blount's commentary upon the *Life of Apol-
lonius of Tyana*, and in the writings of Pierre Bayle. During
the eighteenth century the Socinian current united quite naturally with that of the philosophers. Edelmann, for example,
author of *Die Gottlicheit der Vernunft* ('The Divinity of
Reason') was a Socinian who had read Spinoza.

The crisis of human intelligence in revolt against faith affected Protestantism no less, and perhaps more, than it injured Catholicism. Libertinism of the mind as well as of
morals was no monopoly of cultured Parisian circles. Protestant England witnessed the birth of Deism,[17] which led, as
we have seen, to the limits of agnosticism. Lord Shaftesbury,
one of its exponents, used to advise his friends to laugh up
their sleeves at the follies which the clerical crew imposed on
mankind. Anglicans also included such amiable and indulgent
sceptics as Falkland and Chillingworth, the founders of Latitudinarianism, in whose eyes all religions were equal, none
deserving to have its teaching followed in every detail. Again,
it was in Lutheran Germany that the *Aufklärung*[18] claimed
to enlighten men's minds, with the result that they denied the
supernatural. Protestant thought, buffeted by the tides of
Philosophy, often landed on the farthest shores of rationalism.

In 1690 the Walloon synod of Amsterdam had fulminated
against 'those ministers who are doing their level best to
overthrow Christianity'. What would it have said a hundred
years later? For while, as in Catholic France, the masses remained true to the faith of their fathers, there were many
signs of increasing agnosticism and rationalism even among
the higher ranks of the clergy. At Geneva, in 1694, the city
council resolved that the Elders of the Consistory, those
guardians of pure Calvinist faith, should no longer serve the
communion tables, so little respect they seemed to have for
the Lord's Supper. In 1720 there met in England two conferences of 'dissenters', i.e. of Puritans, Presbyterians and other
Protestants more solid than the High Church Anglicans. One
of them consisted of seventy-five pastors from Devonshire and
Cornwall, the other of one hundred and fifty from the London area. When the question of the Holy Trinity was raised,

nineteen pastors in the first assembly and fifty-seven in the second declared that they did not believe the doctrine. More revealing still was the abandonment of Calvin's catechism by the Genevan Church in 1780; from that date onwards there was no reference to Our Lord's divinity, either in courses at the Theological School or in the liturgy.

7. THE REACTION OF BELIEF

This effort to undermine the foundations of faith met with reaction, both in the intellectual field and in that of the spiritual life. Throughout the seventeenth and eighteenth centuries there existed a number of vigorous Protestant apologists whom Catholics are inclined to underestimate, eclipsed as they were by Pascal, Bossuet and others, but who were quite the contrary of negligible. On the threshold of that period stands Duplessis-Mornay, hero of earlier struggles; he led the way with his serious and all too bulky *Traité de l'Église* (1600). In 1636 the learned Grotius, whom we have seen associated with all the great contemporary intellectual movements, produced his *Treatise on the Truth of the Christian Religion*; it was written in Flemish verse to enable Dutch sailors to evangelize the infidel, and was translated into many languages—Latin, Chinese, French, Persian and Malay. This pleasant little book excelled in its popular demonstration of the necessity for a creator and of the sublimity of Christian morality. Between 1684 and 1689 Jacques Abbadie (1654–1727) published a treatise bearing the same title as that of Grotius, but very different in tone. Abbadie derived his inspiration from Pascal, or at any rate had objectives similar to those of Pascal; in his view the essential factors of apologetics were the *interior* proofs of religion, 'the light that enlightens us and the force that strengthens us' from the time of our adherence to Christ, the unique, undeniable and sublime message of Christ in which man achieves his complete fulfilment. Abbadie's was an 'apologetic of the heart' and Mme de Sévigné declared that nothing had ever moved her so deeply.[19] The Genevan pastor Benoît Pictet with his treatise *Contre l'indifférence des religions*, the exegete Basnage and the Arminian La Placette, author of a *Traité de la foi divine*, followed more or less in the footsteps of Jacques Abbadie, where we shall presently find Turrettini.

Very different from them all was Pierre Jurieu (1637–1713), the vehement exile of Rotterdam and pastor of the Walloon church in that city. Despite his numerous attacks upon Bossuet and Louis XIV, his determination to resist the impieties of Bayle (whose removal from office he managed to secure) led him to erect a monument of Calvinist orthodoxy, the masterpiece of which was his *Apologie pour la morale réformée*, a work widely publicized by his *Lettres pastorales*. Bossuet's own dogmatism was not more emphatic nor his faith more unshakable than the dogmatism and faith of Jurieu.

Later, between 1730 and 1788, the Italian Calvinist Alfonso Turrettini, a refugee at Geneva, assisted by his translator Vernet, published the ten volumes of a new *Traité de la vérité de la religion chrétienne*, in which he harmonized the internal and external proofs so effectively, and expressed himself with such broad-mindedness and moderation, that in 1753 a firm of Parisian publishers undertook a revised edition for the use of Catholics.

There were thus many Protestant champions of Christianity, of all kinds and in all countries. Another important venture into the domain of apologetics was Leibniz's *Essays on Theodicy*, which demonstrated the conformity of faith with reason and found Christian solutions to the great problems of evil and liberty. Newton, in his *Principia Mathematica Philosophiae Naturalis*, sought to recommend Christianity to those who professed unbelief. Other apologists arose within the Anglican Church. Among these were the idealist Bishop Berkeley; the theologian Bentley, author of a *Confutation of Atheism*; and the pious layman Boyle, founder of a chair of apologetics at St Paul's, whose occupants, the 'Boyle lecturers', were chosen from among the most learned clerics to refute the impious. There was also the Society for the Promotion of Christian Knowledge, founded in 1699, whose members, not content with publishing books, went out to fight irreligion among the poor. Distinguished clerics of the High Church made a similar effort during the eighteenth

century in enormous treatises such as Butler's *Analogy* and
Warburton's *Divine Legation of Moses*. Even more ambitious
was Canon Bampton of Salisbury, who instituted an annual
series of public lectures to 'strengthen faith and confute heretics'; while Bishop Horne of Norwich, a devotee of Pascal and
of Jansenism, waged bitter warfare against unbelief with his
sermons and pastoral letters.

These apologists, like their Catholic counterparts, were
divided into two groups. Some, like Butler, thought to defend
their position, often with more courage than skill, by relying
upon a literal interpretation of Scripture and proclaiming
an orthodoxy that escaped them. Others considered it necessary to borrow from profane thought whatever might be useful to the Christian cause; they believed it desirable to take
account of deistic and atheistic criticism, and that in any
case it was indispensable to express Christian dogma in terms
comprehensible by persons who were not theologians. Pastor
Amyraut created a scandal by supporting these ideas; so did
another pastor, Jaquelot, by defending Descartes somewhat
after the manner of Malebranche. Nevertheless it was the
second group that won the day. While dogmatic and authoritarian apologetics slipped into decline, more capable defenders of religion came upon the scene, men who were anxious
to do constructive work by giving their faith new foundations.
Students of primitive Christianity, led by Aubertin, Blondel,
Jean Daillé, Claude Basnage, Aubert de Versé and Jurieu
himself, sought to show that Protestantism 'retained the ancient doctrine', and thus give the lie to both papists and
unbelievers. The Bible, as cornerstone of the reformed faith,
was the object of much labour. Jean Leclerc studied the
problem of inspiration. Before him, Louis Capelle (1585–
1658), rector of Saumur, had embarked on the exegesis and
historical study of the sacred text along paths in which he was
afterwards outpaced by the Catholic Richard Simon, and in
which he was followed by the Anglican Walton and the Lutheran Albert Bengel. These bold spirits, moreover, like their
Catholic rivals, were victims of harsh criticism and supercilious contempt; the two Buxtorfs, for example, maintained that
every detail of the Bible was inspired, down to the last comma

and full stop, and that it was heretical to approach the sacred text from an historical standpoint.

At the end of the seventeenth century and throughout the eighteenth modernist tendencies (to speak anachronistically) prevailed. Protestant thought, while defending the principles of faith, tended to absorb many philosophical elements, to seek support for religion in human speculation. Werenfels at Basel, Osterwald at Neuchatel, Turrettini at Geneva, and in Germany Lessing and the champions of the *Aufklärung*, were the originators of this current, which was to be that of liberal Protestantism during the nineteenth century. It was doubtless a loyal and praiseworthy effort to stop the widening gap between modern culture and religion, a task of vital importance to the Church. But those who undertook that task were far from the position of the first reformers, who had believed whole-heartedly that the word of God alone sufficed to build the Church.

8. PIETISM

To remain completely faithful to the Word of God was the aim of other believers who were equally hostile to the petrified orthodoxy of the official Churches and to the scepticism of the 'Enlightened', equally disgusted with the moral degradation of many self-styled Christians and with the narrow, often pharisaical moralism of too many Puritans. And so in all the Protestant Churches there began another sort of reaction, parallel with the intellectual reaction but of far greater scope.

Some, especially in Germany, set out upon a path of mysticism that became increasingly unstable. Already in the sixteenth century Pastor Weigel had taught that God becomes incarnate in each one of us and that we deify ourselves by following with our interior gaze the grace He has deposited in our being. In 1624 died Jakob Böhme, the cobbler poet. He had been hounded by the Lutherans, but had sought refuge in his ecstasies and continued to pursue the *magnum mysterium*, 'the secret nature which lives, suffers, dies and is resurrected in each one of us, and is none other than Christ Himself'.

Later Schöffler, known as Angelus Silesius, another esoteric and profound poet, carried a stage further the substitution of personal intuition for dogmatism in all its forms. 'Nothing exists but God and myself,' he said. 'Neither of us can be above or below the other.' There must be no more theology, nothing but total identification of the interior man with God. Rather similar notions are to be found in the teaching of Jean Labadie, a Jesuit turned Protestant, who lived as a refugee first at Middelburg in Holland, then in the house of the Princess Palatine Elizabeth at Herford. His eloquence and charm won him many disciples among the fair sex, whose sole guide, he insisted, must be the Holy Ghost speaking in each one of them. This mystical current flowed unceasingly throughout the neo-classical age. In the eighteenth century it was represented by a man who did not lack prestige—Emmanual Swedenborg (1688–1772). Son of a Protestant bishop of Stockholm, he claimed to have discovered in frequent ecstasies the secret of the 'circles' of the Spirit and to have received instruction from Jesus Christ Himself. With a view to realizing the New Jerusalem, he published his *Vera Christiana Religio*, a monumental treatise in which all the Christian dogmas were reinterpreted 'spiritually', that is to say in the light of that complete harmony which governs all nature, of that mysterious correspondence between the human microcosm and the universal macrocosm. All that was necessary in order to attain perfection was to surrender oneself to the Father who is Love, to the Son who is Truth, to the Holy Ghost who is Beauty.

These radical mystics were never very numerous. In 1789 there were two thousand Swedenborgians in Sweden and some three thousand in Germany. More important were the movements included under the general name of Pietism. Their common ideal may be expressed as follows. In order to remedy the disorders afflicting Christianity it was necessary not to reaffirm her dogmas, which had no practical value, but to restore life to men's souls, i.e. to rekindle piety, to exalt the sentiments of faith and love. In short, it was a question of taking literally the words of the Lord's Prayer: 'Thy kingdom come.' The true and only duty of true Christians was to promote the reign of Christ in themselves and among mankind at large; hence the social, educational and charitable undertakings of many Pietist groups. Clearly such an outlook was far removed from that of arid Calvinism or of Lutheranism bogged down in its routine. 'Intense appreciation of the Saviour's sufferings, shame and gratitude before the mystery of the Incarnation, generous love of Christ and of one's neighbour—those are the Christian truths rediscovered by Pietism.' 'Thus a neo-Protestantism was constructed, indifferent to dogma, but passionately concerned with the potentialities of feeling, with personal or communal expressions of inspiration, with works of charity.'[20]

The origins of the Pietist movement are complex. They may be traced to some Anabaptist circles at the very beginning of the Reformation, whose members, unscathed by the excesses in which that sect indulged,[21] saw in the second baptism the true rebirth of the soul into the Spirit. They are found also among the Moravian Brethren, self-styled Brethren of the Law of Christ, a sort of monkish brotherhood descended from the remnants of the Hussites. Four hundred communities of the Brethren, established principally in Bohemia and Moravia, practised a form of Christianity at once ascetic and joyous, peace in the Holy Ghost taking the place of dogmatic belief; officially they accepted the Confession of Augsburg, but remained as far as it was possible to be from the Lutheran spirit. Finally, Pietism owed something to a large body of literature, works written by pious souls who wished to soar towards God beyond the barrier of creeds. Such were Bayly's *Praxis Pietatis*, the Lutheran pastor Grossgebauer's *Cry of Alarm from Ravaged Sion*, Heinrich Müller's *Mirror of the Heart according to the Gospel*, the meditations of Genesius, the essays of John Schmid, and above all the *Bouquet of Eden*, a collection of beautiful spiritual texts compiled by Abraham Freye in 1673. This last exerted an undeniable influence; it nourished the mind and heart of Spener, who initiated the first great Pietist movement.

James Spener (1635–1705) was an Alsatian, educated at the University of Strasbourg, a lofty and fervent soul filled with desire to serve God. Through his teachers, notably John Schmid, he made contact with the thought of John Arndt, author of *True Christianity*, who, disgusted with formalism

and dogmatism, had never ceased to repeat that the true urge
of faith and love of Christ must be rediscovered by reading
the great mystics, Tauler or the *Imitation of Christ*. Spener
was overwhelmed by Arndt's cry to the Crucified: 'O head
covered with blood and wounds!' His oratorical gifts and
powerful intelligence caused him to be appointed dean of the
pastors at Frankfurt at the age of thirty-one; and after his
conversion to a more interior and exacting form of religion
he invited his parishioners to tread the road he had marked
out for himself. Those who elected to follow him organized
themselves into small groups, *collegia pietatis*, which were
destined to become a spiritual leaven in the heavy lump.
They prayed, fasted, meditated the writings of the mystics,
instructed the youth and combated drunkenness and debauchery. Spener's book, *Pia Desideria*, explained the doctrine
of his movement, and at the same time sharply criticized official Lutheranism, its amorphous mass and its pastors devoid
of true faith. There were protests against the Pietists, and
the outcry grew louder when Spener dared publicly to criti-
cize the Elector of Saxony's immoral ways. The official theologians examined his writings and discovered no fewer than
two hundred and eighty errors. But the future king of Prussia,
Frederick I, summoned him to Berlin, appointed him to the
pulpit of St Nicholas and allowed him to continue his apostolate until his death. When Spener died his work had deeply
stirred the German Churches.

Pietism had by then spread to many districts and in various
forms. In some souls it was linked with the most exalted mysticism; there raged a veritable epidemic of ecstasy with Rosa-
mund d' Asseburg, Magdalen Erlich and Eva Jakob. But the
University of Tübingen had become the centre of a grave,
austere and donnish variety of Pietism. At Halle, August
Hermann Francke (1663–1727) directed the movement towards social and charitable activity, and he built a model
orphanage. At about the same time he founded at Leipzig
the Collegium Philobiblicum, whose popular courses, open
to all, provided a 'pious' commentary on Holy Scripture.
Youth movements, too, were organized among the students
at Halle, Jena and elsewhere—'The Order of the Grain of
Mustard Seed', 'The Slaves of Virtue', 'The Confessors of

Christ'. Though fiercely attacked by the theologians, notably by Loscher of Wittenberg, Pietism continued to spread, one circle of initiates within another, distributing Bibles to the common people and initiating large-scale charitable undertakings. It became still more vigorous after the foundation of Herrnhut.

The name Herrnhut ('the Lord's shelter') was that of a village hidden away in the forests of Lusatia on the Bohemian frontier, a village created entirely by the will of one man and destined to become a high place of the spirit. It was something between an abbey and a phalanstery. All its inhabitants, to whatever Church they might belong, lived there in fraternal unity, even celebrating divine service in common. In the streets, silent as cloisters, the 'brethren' on meeting would greet one another with such words as these: 'Is your soul an image of God?' 'Is all sin destroyed in you?' The community was divided into ten 'classes', themselves subdivided into companies; the members of each company practised mutual confession and common ownership of goods. Piety was strong at Herrnhut, fostered by frequent meditation, reading and instruction upon the sufferings of Christ crucified and His Passion which redeemed the world. Prayer was continuous, parties of adorers relieving one another every hour. At dead of night jubilant voices were heard far off in the pine forests singing those beautiful chorales, 'Spotless Lamb' and 'Side of Christ pierced with the lance'.

This extraordinary lay convent, inhabited by several hundred men, women and children, was governed by a venerated chief known as the Elder, Count Ludwig von Zinzendorf (1700–60), a bright-eyed giant with the smile of a child. As a student at Halle he had joined a small Pietist group and been thoroughly converted. At the age of twenty-two, having inherited a fortune, he purchased a large estate in Lusatia, meaning to live there according to his principles. Just then some Moravian Brethren, driven from Austria, arrived by way of the Bohemian passes; in various parts of Germany also Lutherans and Calvinists were being persecuted for their Pietist views. To all those people Zinzendorf offered the most generous asylum, requiring them to agree upon only one point of doctrine—faith in redemption by the blood of

Christ. From youth upwards the founder of Herrnhut had read Fénelon, Mme Guyon and the Quietists, and had pondered the new devotion to the Sacred Heart. His doctrine reflected his reading. It was, to tell the truth, a Protestant form of Quietism, full of confidence in God, ardour and tenderness. It gave not a fig for the gloomy faces of the puritans, or for the ratiocinations of university professors. The one thing necessary was to live in God, to love, to yield oneself to interior impulse. Could not all Christians adhere to that ideal? At Paris Zinzendorf met Cardinal de Noailles, through whom he was able to negotiate an understanding with Benedict XIII, and he invited Wesley to spend a fortnight at Herrnhut. The established Protestant Churches, of course, looked with a jaundiced eye upon these spiritual anarchists who despised them. Preachers inveighed against Herrnhut, and indeed Zinzendorf's behaviour was sufficiently odd to make him vulnerable. King Frederick II banned the propaganda of the Herrnhutists in his dominions, and even forbade his subjects to read their 'spiritual hours'. But the movement was too strong to be halted. It had groups almost everywhere, passing beyond the frontiers of Europe and sending missionaries to Greenland and the East Indies. The Lutheran Church thought it politic to recognize Herrnhutism as a sect, and Zinzendorf assumed the episcopal title, a gesture hardly consistent with his ideal. After him Spangenberg endeavoured to continue his work, though not without great difficulty. Herrnhut declined as a religious centre, but its spirit had penetrated far and wide. Traces of it appear in Lessing, but more particularly in Schleiermacher (1768–1834), who in the nineteenth century taught that the essence of religion lies in our dependence upon God. German Protestantism was certainly indebted to the Pietists of Herrnhut for having saved it from the mortal danger of fossilization.

9. WESLEY AND METHODISM

In England the revivalist who attempted to drag high churchmen from their routine and the puritans from their hypocrisy bore a famous name—John Wesley (1703–91). No

Catholic can speak of him without affection or remember his apostolate without admiration. True enough, he naturally detested popery, considered himself far removed from Catholic theology and often publicly denounced the ostentation and practices of Rome. The fact remains, however, that he was heir to a long line of truly devout souls, whose direct influence is apparent at many points of his thought. But we are impressed above all by his unceasing testimony to the word of God, by his Pascalian conscience in face of great problems and by his friendship for the poor, the lowly and the outcast. 'If a single soul falls into the abyss, whom I might have saved from the eternal flames, what excuse shall I make before God? That he did not belong to my parish? That is why I regard the whole world as my parish.' The man who spoke those words was indubitably made of the stuff from which the Catholic Church fashions her saints.

Wesley was a man of small stature, thin and pale, with steely eyes and an expression that was often supercilious; but he exuded a mysterious and pervasive charm. Disdaining the periwig he let his black hair grow long and fall in curls upon his shoulders. When speaking he would often raise his slender hands to heaven. Was that because, while preaching to the crowds, he was examining himself with fear and trembling? Be that as it may, all who heard him bore witness to the fact that he was disturbing, moving and persuasive.

It was a long time before he discovered his apostolic vocation; throughout his adolescent years he was buffeted by the blows and counter-blows of contending doctrines. Anglicanism, in which he had been brought up by his father, the austere vicar of Epworth, soon impressed him as inadequate. The rigid predestinationism of the Calvinists appalled him; it was 'very shocking'. Lutheranism seemed to exalt faith too far above love. 'What a labyrinth!' he exclaimed, feeling utterly lost. One tender and firm voice, however, had spoken to him from his earliest years, the voice of his mother, an admirable woman who had brought nineteen children into the world and had reared them successfully in spite of poverty. Every day she read *The Imitation of Christ* and applied its precepts in her own life. 'Keep the commandments, believe, hope, love.' What mattered individual creeds, theological interpretations and obediences? Nothing really mattered but God's call to the soul and the manner of the soul's response.

At the age of twenty-two, as a young deacon and fellow of Lincoln College, Oxford, John Wesley answered that call. His brother Charles, together with his friends Robert Kirkham and William Morgan, shared his religious interests and regarded him as their leader. He recommended to the little band a veritable rule of life: prayer, spiritual reading, fasting and mortification, frequent communion, visits to the poor and other works of charity—practices of which St Ignatius would not have disapproved. Their comrades made game of these 'sacramentarians', 'enthusiasts' and 'Bible punchers', and especially of the famous 'method' for the infallible attainment of heaven. 'Methodists!' Wesley adopted the nickname, just as the faithful at Antioch had adopted that of 'Christians' and the sons of St Ignatius that of 'Jesuits'. Fearless, he answered mockery with the declaration: 'We have set ourselves the task of persuading men to be true Christians.'

His purpose was henceforth clear; but how accomplish it? At the age of thirty-two he could still be described as something of an 'ecclesiastical Hamlet', and he wondered anxiously how he could manage to rechristianize the Oxford colleges, the poor urchins to whom he taught the catechism, the miners, the prisoners, and even the rich, whom concern for their own comfort had incarcerated more strictly than any old lag in the county jail. He had not yet found the means of his apostolate; he did not even known where to look for them. Various but convergent influences were at work upon him. He read Tauler, John of Avila, Molinos and, above all, *La Vie de Monsieur de Renty, Gentilhomme de France*, by Father Saint-Jure, S.J., which he had bought for three shillings in a London second-hand bookshop. Would he, like St Vincent de Paul's contemporary, found something similar to the Company of the Blessed Sacrament?[22] On board ship bound for America he met some Moravian Brethren, with whom he joined forces; their radiant piety and supernatural peace made a deep impression on his mind. Lastly, on his return from overseas he made the acquaintance of Count Zinzendorf, with whom he stayed and who revealed to him the beauties of German Pietism—a little too sentimental and quietistic for his liking. Had he still to discover a method and define his position? All his purely intellectual resolution was mysteriously transformed. On 24th May 1738, while listening to that passage in the Epistle to the Romans where St Paul speaks of the change engendered in the soul by faith, he experienced a sudden shock. Christ and Christ alone had saved him, John Wesley; He had taken away his sins and exempted him from the law of death; he had, in short, felt upon his brow the drop of blood of which Pascal speaks. Rising up, he there and then bore witness publicly to that overwhelming experience. Henceforward his whole message was substantially just this: we must love Christ, give ourselves to Him without reserve, and all things else will be added unto us.

His mind was now made up: he would go forward alone. He would seek to do nothing but proclaim the simple truth he had discovered in that moment of enlightenment. Assisted by his brother Charles, a talented hymn-writer, and by his friend George Whitefield, a popular orator of extraordinary power, he set out upon the great adventure of bringing back his lethargic contemporaries to some awareness of their spiritual duties. At first he tried, like a good and faithful clergyman, to speak in the churches; but he was soon asked to leave the pulpit and not to re-enter it. His ardour and frankness were not in good taste. Besides, he accepted invitations to services attended by the lowest classes—ragged miners and evil-smelling labourers. Bishop Butler, a learned apologist, was shocked by his peculiar exhibition of active (as distinct from written) apologetics. So Wesley and his companions, bypassing the churches, adopted another form of apostolate— the open-air sermon in a public square or, better still, in some quiet corner of the countryside. All and sundry were welcome, and there were no beadles or ushers to bar the way. The first of these 'field preachings' took place on 2nd April 1739 on a hillock near Bristol. Wesley was destined to give nearly fifty thousand.

What did he tell those huge audiences which listened to him long and eagerly? Even in Catholic Ireland he managed to obtain a hearing. What he had to say was very simple. 'A Methodist', he explained, 'is one who has the love of God in his heart. He does good to all men, to strangers as well as to neighbours, to his enemies as well as to his friends—and that in every possible way.' Methodism then did not pretend to be an original theological system; Wesley on many occasions affirmed his loyalty to the Thirty-nine Articles of the Anglican Church. His teaching was moral rather than metaphysical. Purity, modest attire, abstention from alcohol, charity and goodwill towards others, public confession and attendance at the Lord's Supper every Sunday—he asked for nothing more, and that would suffice to 'recover the divine resemblance by rebirth into the spirit of Christ'. Methodism, as we see, left the framework of Protestant theology when it proclaimed the value of good works. Indeed it broke the bounds set by the Churches of the Reformation, for it declared: 'Be Papist or Protestant as you like, provided you follow the true religion, that of Thomas à Kempis, Bossuet and Fénelon.' It was in fact an essentially practical doctrine, which could have become integrated with all religions.

That was its attraction for the very practical English. Before long Wesley's powerful voice and the more theatrical voice of Whitefield were heard in all parts of the realm—on the lonely moors of Northumberland, in the slums of London, in abominable prisons where the convicts died of frightful epidemics, and in the long galleries of the Cornish mines. Sometimes more than twenty thousand people massed to hear God's tribune, and when he finished speaking many a cheek was wet with tears. The great ones of this world occasionally confessed themselves moved and conquered—Franklin, for example, and the contemptuous Walpole. His brother Charles's touching though sometimes bizarre hymns began to be sung throughout the English-speaking world. Apostles came forward to work with the new prophet—Grimshaw, Howell, Harris, Fletcher, Romaine, Berridge. The Christian Library, edited by the Methodists, carried their opinions into men's homes, and many were those who treasured Wesley's rendering of the *Imitation*.

Success of that kind was not achieved without provoking violent resistance and reaction, just as Fox and his Quakers had done. The Methodist creed alarmed the stodgy puritans. 'Papists! Jesuits!' Such abuse was often heard at the field preachings. The established Churches, whom this current of clear air might have rejuvenated, hastened to close their doors; very few clergymen of the Establishment went over to Methodism. Anglican bishops formally opposed the innovators, making their pretext those rowdy scenes, hysterical fits and frenzied outbursts which sometimes occurred among the vast crowds. The civil authorities also took a hand, and zealous officials, using their right which empowered them to impress vagabonds for service in the army, rounded up Methodist preachers and forcibly enrolled them. One such unwilling soldier, Thomas Beard, died on service. Now and again more violent manifestations ended in bloodshed, as when the preacher William Seward, like St Stephen, was stoned to death. It was not until the reign of George III that the situation improved. 'The Methodists are honest folk,' said His Majesty, 'and I shall dismiss anyone who wrongs them.' From that moment their cause was triumphant, and public opinion underwent a rapid change. Towards the end of his life the aged reformer knew that he had won the fight.

By that time, however, Methodism was no longer what it had originally been, a mere impulse towards the revival of religion—of all religions—from within. Yielding to the necessity which obliges all spiritual undertakings (even those sprung from the freest outpouring of the soul) to organize themselves in order to endure, Methodism had been compelled little by little to construct for itself a framework of institutions. As its adherents became more numerous it grouped them into small societies or 'circuits', which combined to form 'districts'. The first 'general conference' of representatives from every circuit met in 1744, which is regarded as the official date of the movement's birth. In 1760 there were already 50 circuits with a total membership of 30,000; in 1791 more than 200 with 100,000. In principle, Methodism made use of the structural system so dear to the puritans, i.e. synodal, presbyterian, or congregationist; but in America it accepted a form of episcopal government. Since there were too few clergy, lay assistants were appointed and empowered to direct small prayer meetings.

All those factors set Methodism apart from the official Church of England, into which Wesley had been born and which he refused to leave as long as he lived. He always de-

clared himself 'a clergyman of the High Church, son of a
clergyman of the High Church, reared from his infancy in the
most complete obedience'. But events obliged him willy-nilly
to make a choice. What was the aged leader to do, for example, when the Methodists of America asked for ministers, and
the Anglican bishops refused to ordain Methodist candidates; or when Anglicanism foundered in the newly independent United States, and with it all legitimate religious
authority? Whatever he should have done, this is what he
did. Exceeding his own powers as a simple priest, he conferred
ordination upon a number of young preachers and sent them
across the Atlantic. Methodism thus ceased to be a great
religious family created for the regeneration of the Anglican
communion, and became itself a Church. The schism was
peacefully consummated soon after Wesley's death.

Both as a spiritual movement and as a Church, Methodism
exerted considerable influence within the reformed Churches
all over the world. Linking the several currents of Pietism,
reinvigorating the older Puritanism, and at the same time
breathing austerity and charity into Churches that were becoming either lax or fossilized, it was the principal agent of a
Protestant revival. And yet, like all Protestant bodies, it fell
victim to the law of dismemberment and broke up into sects.
Even in Wesley's lifetime, Whitefield more or less parted
company with him, moving further in the direction of Calvinism. After them the movement split into several groups,
which may be classified under the two main headings of
Episcopalian Methodists and Congregational Methodists, the
first with an episcopate, the second without. Today the
world's 30,000,000 Methodists are subdivided into more than
twenty sects, chief among which are Wesleyans, Primitive
Methodists, Bible Christians and Independent Methodists.
That fact shows that Methodism has failed to transcend the
bounds or to escape the doom of Protestantism. But it is
equally certain that the Methodist ideal was extremely fruitful in giving Protestantism a new lease of life. At the dawn of
the nineteenth century, which was heralded by the Industrial
Revolution, this practical religion seemed adapted to contemporary needs. Its claim to impose the Gospel precepts
upon all, together with a compulsive and meticulous moral

code, no less than its grave and somewhat naïve assurance of being the sole embodiment of true Christianity, may cause a Catholic to smile, just as its contempt for theology may seem to indicate serious defects. But the sincerity of the Methodists, their courage in defence of just causes,[23] their social broadmindedness and their apostolic fervour are worthy of a respect and admiration that no Catholic can dream of withholding. Towards the end of the eighteenth century there appeared within the Anglican Church (from which Methodism was becoming ever more estranged) a new revivalist movement, initiated in the University of Cambridge by Isaac Milner and Charles Simeon. It was developed by John Venn, vicar of Clapham, and Wilberforce, a member of Parliament. These men, like the Methodists, insisted more upon moral effort and charitable works than upon theological doctrine. The movement was called Evangelism, and it subsequently exercised a very real influence.

10. THE PROTESTANT ORIGINS OF THE UNITED STATES

The Pietist-Methodist awakening was not the only indication of unquestionable vitality within the various Protestant groups. We have also to note an expansion closely linked with that awakening, important in itself during the neo-classical period and still more important with reference to the future. It was brought about in two ways: while the reformed Churches entered the mission fields, a tide of emigration, due to complex causes, deposited on the east coast of North America successive waves of people almost all of whom were Protestant. Thus was formed the human conglomeration that would one day constitute the United States, a new transatlantic power deeply imbued with the spirit of Protestantism.

With one short-lived exception, the Thirteen Colonies, which became independent of Britain and joined together in a federal state towards the end of the eighteenth century, were all of Protestant origin. That does not mean that every one of them owed its existence to religious motives, for commercial interests also were at work; but a vast majority of the colonists themselves belonged to one or other of the Churches and sects, whether Anglican or Protestant. In several cases, too, they had emigrated in order to defend a faith threatened by Catholics or by some form of Protestantism. And so the Protestant factor was closely associated with the whole history of American origins.

Virginia, the first English colony in America and which later became known as the Old Dominion, was founded in the reign of Elizabeth I, the Virgin Queen, a determined anti-papist. When Sir Walter Ralegh reconnoitred the coast and landed a few colonists to face the fearful hazards of their situation, his only purpose, no doubt, was to exploit the privileges he had been granted; and subsequent arrivals from London and Plymouth, who established the first permanent settlements in 1607, thought exclusively in terms of trade. But the atmosphere of the young colony became extremely puritan under the governorship of Captain John Smith. Work, discipline and prayer were the order of the day; the capital, Jamestown, named after King James I, was more austere than London in that sovereign's time; and in 1619, when the miniature House of Commons which was to administer the colony held its first session, it met in the choir of the little church at Jamestown. The religious atmosphere of Virginia, in fact, is noticeable even today. In the reign of Charles I some Italian and French Capuchins tried to gain a footing there, but all in vain; the first citadel of Protestantism in America held firm.

Further north, religious motives pure and simple led to the establishment of yet more resolutely puritan bastions—those of New England, which were destined to play an important part in the moral formation of America. In England, about 1620, Anglicans and Presbyterians joined in bitter conflict with the Independents, those separatist puritans who would recognize neither the episcopal organization of the High Church nor the synodal assemblies and councils of elders. Persecution drove a number of Independents to flee the country. Thirty-five of them, living as exiles in Holland, dreamed of a transatlantic settlement; these Pilgrim Fathers, as they are called, embarked for Virginia, where the landlords had allotted them concessions. They were accompanied by other adventurers, not all of whom were puritan Independents, and the *Mayflower* carried one hundred and two 'pilgrims' to America, where they would be allowed to pray in their own fashion. The ship was caught in a storm, and after a frightful crossing made land near Cape Cod. Before disembarking, all the adult men signed a Covenant which laid down the principles of the biblical society they intended to found. Thus was born the little colony of Plymouth; in spite of difficulties that were often tragic, it lasted for seventy-one years before merging with the more powerful neighbouring colony of Massachusetts. Its political achievement therefore was small, but its religious and moral influence was considerable. Even today descent from one of the Pilgrim Fathers is a mark of something akin to aristocracy.

Massachusetts had a different origin. In 1629 some other dissenters, mostly landed gentry and prosperous merchants of the Anglican Low Church, obtained a royal charter and set sail better equipped than the Pilgrims. Led by John Endicott, they settled first at Salem, and then, in 1630, founded Boston. Their first governor, John Winthrop, managed to surmount all kinds of obstacles and to resist the Indian menace. The foundation grew quickly, and in 1634 Boston had four thousand inhabitants. The scheme was that of an authoritarian theocracy controlled by a powerful minority, comparable with the system then in force at Geneva. Winthrop, like Calvin, considered himself a viceroy of God, charged by the Lord to enforce the divine will. The great landowners, together with the ministers of religion, were to all intents and purposes the legislators. The 'Lord's Brethren', it was said, were no better than their lordships the bishops of the High Church, and tension became so acute that the colony was split.

First to depart was Roger Williams, one of the noblest characters in this story, 'a fool of God'. Condemned to exile for having criticized the all-powerful oligarchy in the name of biblical principles, he departed in 1636 with a few friends and went to found on Rhode Island a settlement which he named Providence. A generous Act of Toleration brought to the new foundation Protestants of many obediences, especially Anabaptists, and Rhode Island quickly expanded. Driven in her turn from Massachusetts, an excitable woman named Anne Hutchinson arrived and founded the colony of Ports-

CANADA
QUEBEC
ACADIA
LOUISBURG
THREE
RIVERS
MONTREAL
ST. LAWRENCE
LAKE
CHAMPLAIN
NEW
HAMP-
SHIRE
MASSACHUSETTS
PORT
ROYAL
HALIFAX
L. ONTARIO
NEW
YORK
BOSTON 1630
PLYMOUTH
LAKE ERIE
NEW HAVEN
RHODE IS.
PROVIDENCE
CONNECTICUT
LOUISIANA
PENNSYL-
VANIA
PHILADELPHIA
NEW
YORK
NEW JERSEY
1676 (FORMERLY
NEW AMSTERDAM)
BALTIMORE
DELAWARE
OHIO
WASHINGTON
MARYLAND
VIRGINIA
YORKTOWN
PORTSMOUTH
ATLANTIC
OCEAN
NORTH
CAROLINA
CHESAPEAKE
BAY
SOUTH
CAROLINA
GEORGIA
FLORIDA

THE ENGLISH COLONIES
IN AMERICA
0   MILES   500

mouth. Meanwhile, in 1639, the 'grave and judicious' pastor
Thomas Hooker, likewise rejecting Winthrop's oligarchical
theocracy, went off to establish yet another colony in the forests of Connecticut, where John Davenport built New Haven.
It need hardly be said that if the puritan system of these new
colonies was more democratic it remained no less rigid than
before, as is clear from the Blue Laws of Connecticut. There
the decrees of Moses were applied so thoroughly that any
breach of the sabbath rest meant imprisonment, and adulter-
ous couples were punished with death.

Meanwhile, in 1634, two years before Williams left for
Rhode Island, Lord Baltimore tried a most original experiment in Maryland. Sir George Calvert was a Catholic who
enjoyed the friendship of Charles I and Henrietta Maria. Unable to employ him because of his religion, the king raised
him to the peerage and gave him the freehold of a vast American estate between the Potomac and the fortieth parallel,
which the new peer, in gratitude to his sovereign, named

Maryland after the queen. Thither he invited all Catholics who wished to practise their faith in complete freedom; but this popish subject of an Anglican king, as wise as he was broad-minded, proclaimed an Act of Toleration inspired by that of Rhode Island, but more comprehensible since all Christian creeds were authorized, Jews and atheists being alone excluded. There followed an idyllic period of some forty years, during which Catholics, Episcopalians, Puritans and Baptists lived fraternally in a bond of friendship rare at that time.

It was too good to last; the neighbouring colonists viewed with stern disapproval this reprehensibly indulgent fief, when —abomination of desolation!—Jesuits were allowed to evangelize the Indians. Violent incidents occurred during the Cromwellian era. The revolution of 1688, which brought the Calvinist William of Orange to the throne of England, spelled disaster for Maryland; the Puritans seized power and showed themselves equally hostile to the dissenting sects as they were to the Catholics. Thus ended the one and only tolerant colony in America.

The Protestant solidarity which wrought the destruction of Maryland by no means restrained the virtuous Puritans from employing force to obtain possession of settlements belonging to their Huguenot co-religionists. In 1609 the Dutch had explored, and in 1618 occupied, some fair territory west of Virginia. One Hudson, a captain in their service, had landed on the bank of a river that was to bear his name, on a long, narrow peninsula called by the Indians 'Manhattan', i.e. 'the place of surfeit'; and quite close to the little French station of Nouvelle-Avesne a village was built and called New Amsterdam. This place had prospered rapidly, so much so that by about 1650 it was the leading port in North America. In 1664 Charles II intervened and claimed ownership, maintaining that the neighbourhood had been discovered by John Cabot as long ago as 1498. A strong military expedition gave credit to this paltry legal argument, and New Amsterdam passed to the English king. Charles made a present of it to his brother the Duke of York, whence the name New York adopted by the town and its environs (1676). Fifty years later Delaware, a former Swedish colony occupied in 1655 by the

Dutch and belonging theoretically to New Amsterdam, was claimed by New York, invaded by the English and, after various disputes, raised to the status of a colony (1702). At this latter date there extended from Chesapeake Bay to the extreme north of Massachusetts an unbroken chain of ten colonies, all Protestant; for the vacant space between Virginia, Maryland and New York had recently been occupied in extraordinary circumstances by the strongest of all Protestant sects, the Quakers.

Very soon after its foundation by George Fox, Quakerism had crossed the Atlantic and entered the young colonies, where there was no lack of souls athirst for a living faith. Quakers male and female began 'to deliver the message' in the streets and squares, without regard to the 'paid ministers' of the Established Church and the puritan 'false prophets'. The reaction was violent, particularly in Massachusetts. Men and women were flogged, imprisoned or expelled; some even had their tongues pierced with red-hot iron, like the unfortunate Mary Dyer who resumed her apostolate after having been forbidden to preach. But this official cruelty did not prevent the little band from continuing their pious offensive. Settling in the Barbadoes, the Quakers sent their missionaries, clad in grey fustian, to rouse the consciences of all and sundry, and they took advantage of the toleration prevailing at Rhode Island to establish a firm foothold there. At length, in 1681, they obtained abrogation throughout the colonies of the penal laws affecting them.

Their greatest and most remarkable success, however, was achieved in Pennsylvania. In the same year that they won the right to practise their religion unhindered the Quakers embarked upon an extraordinary undertaking, known among themselves as the Holy Experiment. Its leader, William Penn (1644–1718), was the son of an admiral who had left the Commonwealth camp and assisted in the restoration of Charles II to the throne. An earnest soul, disappointed with Anglican conformity no less than with puritan moralism, and trained to a more profound religious sense by Pastor Amyraut in France, he had heard Quakers preaching and had been won over to their simple, touching faith. His public declaration of their faith by word and deed cost him more than one sojourn in prison, during which he wrote such famous books as *No Cross, No Crown*. After many vicissitudes, in return for an unpaid debt of £16,000 which the Government owed his father at the Restoration, he was granted American territory as large as the whole of England and Wales, a magnificent forest region between Massachusetts and Maryland. He called it Sylvania, to which the king asked him to add his father's name, and thus was born Pennsylvania. To that enchanting region, where, it was said, one forgot 'the troubles and perplexities of unhappy Europe', he invited the Quakers to come and make the Holy Experiment of life according to God's heart. There love would reign, not violence. There would be no soldiers or policemen. They would fraternize with the Indians. The capital would be called Philadelphia, city of brotherly love.

When news of this splendid project reached England, there was a cry of 'Madman!' But contrary to all expectations the Holy Experiment did not fail. The redskins, in fact, treated the Quakers as friends. Waves of immigrants arrived, knowing they would find tolerance in Pennsylvania. Among them were Scotsmen, German Lutherans, Welshmen—and even some French Catholics, for the constitution granted Catholics the same rights as other Christians. Philadelphia became a neat little town with red-brick houses surrounded by gardens, with wide avenues intersecting at right angles and named after trees, where on summer nights the fire-flies traced their joyous arabesques. William Penn had not made a bad attempt to make his realm a sort of earthly paradise.

This beautiful harmony was disturbed when William of Orange's accession led the founder to support James II through loyalty to the Stuarts; there was trouble with the Scots and the Welsh. Returning to Europe, Penn was arrested, imprisoned for a time and deprived of his title of governor. He died grief-stricken and with a sense of failure. His son, a convert to Anglicanism, jeopardized the work. The Assembly rebelled against him, and war was declared against the Indians. The Holy Experiment thus fell victim to the lot of most human undertakings. Nevertheless Quaker influence remained strong in Pennsylvania until the War of Independence; though the Quakers were no longer a majority, magistrates and deputies were still chosen from their ranks because they were good, honest and fair-minded. Philadelphia, too, became one of the cultural centres of the New World, as it still is today.

South of Chesapeake Bay vast unoccupied territories stretched away to Spanish Florida. Charles II, doing as his father had done for Lord Baltimore, gave them to his faithful friends—Clarendon, Monk, Shaftesbury and Sir George Carteret, a former governor of Jersey. But times had changed; some of these great lords were imbued with the philosophical spirit, and Deism took root in the new colonies, which were called North and South Carolina in honour of the king. Soon afterwards Lord Berkeley and Sir George Carteret purchased from the Duke of York the territory situated between the Hudson and Delaware; it became New Jersey, in memory of Sir George's governorship, and numerous Puritans from Connecticut came and left their mark upon it. Only the extreme south was left. In 1732 General Oglethorpe, a philanthropist of Pietistic leanings who was moved by the fate of imprisoned debtors, persuaded King George II to give him this region as an asylum for those unfortunates. Such was the origin of Georgia, whose paternalistic climate was dominated by Methodist piety, teetotalism and good morals. The result, however, was not altogether satisfactory, for the colonists did not willingly submit to those constraints. Not until it became a royal province, much less austere and religious, did the colony prosper.

All thirteen colonies, then, had been founded before the middle of the eighteenth century; all, as we have seen, originated to some extent from Protestant intentions or Protestant enterprise. Their mosaic of peoples represented a complete cross-section of the Churches and other groups deriving from the Reformation: Anglicans, Presbyterians, Congregationalists, Quakers, Scottish Calvinists, Dutch Mennonites, Lutheran Germans, Baptists and Moravian Brethren—all were there, in a complex whole that no longer had a sense of ultimate unity. Moreover there were marked differences between groups within each colony, as well as between the several colonies themselves. The northern puritans, heirs of the Pilgrim Fathers and the settlers of Massachusetts, bore little resem-

blance to the wealthy colonists of the south, who were inclined to take life easily and among whom the advent of black
slaves had implanted some unpleasantly colonialist tendencies. All, however—officially at any rate—were bound together
by religious convictions, stern sexual morality, suspicion of
the theatre and a degree of conformity that was sometimes
carried to the point of fanaticism,[24] as well as by the profound sense that they, as descendants of men whose defence
of their faith had created a world, belonged to an *élite* destined to great achievements. 'God', said one of them, 'has
passed the nations through a sieve in order that He might
sow the finest grain in these virgin lands.' The definitive
seal was set upon American Protestantism by the Methodists.
Although the youthful Wesley had failed in his attempt to
improve the landlords of Georgia and, above all, to make
them more charitable towards their black slaves, the influence
of his thought was deep throughout America. To him the
colonies owed their discovery of a less formal faith, a stronger
sense of religious experience, and that characteristic which
was to be the best feature of the American soul—human brotherhood, philanthropy.

By the end of the first third of the eighteenth century history was about to make the colonies, despite their different
origins, conscious of their unity. The people whom the Indians
called 'Yankees' were emerging from the womb of time. As
soon as the decisive conflict began between France and England, the colonists combined against the Catholic kingdom
whose possessions encircled them. 'There will be no rest for
the thirteen colonies', exclaimed Benjamin Franklin, 'so long
as the French are in America.' The struggle for independence,
waged this time with the help of France, finally accomplished
the unity of America. On the religious plane it involved a definite weakening of the Churches connected with Anglicanism,
but it helped to strengthen the religious convictions of the
masses. On many a battlefield, before the charge, the insurgents recited prayers while the pastors roused their courage.
It was then that the most respectable type of virtuous and
liberal Protestant, whose whole authority is derived from
moral prestige, became embodied in the man in whom young
America recognized herself—George Washington.

11. THE MISSIONARY AWAKENING OF PROTESTANTISM

The expansive power of Protestantism was soon manifested in another field—that of the missionary apostolate. For two centuries none of the reformed Churches had given a thought to the distant lands where Christ was unknown; they had more immediate concerns. Luther concluded from the Gospel narrative where Jesus charges his Apostles to go 'to the uttermost bounds of the earth' that the latter had obeyed and had evangelized the world, but that modern pagans, descended from men who had refused the light, did not deserve a second offering of such a gift. Calvin's doctrine of predestination led him to think that pagans, Jews and Mohammedans could not be in their present spiritual condition except by the will of God, that it was therefore useless to importune Providence, and that the proper thing to do was 'not to devote oneself to the service of the Gospel until the door was opened by the hand of God'.

However, as early as the sixteenth century we find in the various Protestant bodies men who took a very different view. In 1590 Adrian Sanavia, a professor at Leyden, afterwards pastor at Antwerp, and finally Dean of Westminster, published a treatise on the duty of evangelizing the whole world. Not long afterwards, again at Leyden, Justus Heurnius declared that 'the colonies have not been given to the Dutch for the purpose of exploitation, but in order that they may be led to the Word of God'. A scheme of missionary theology was outlined in William Teelinck's *Ecce Homo* (1622), and Anthony Waelens laid plans for a Protestant seminary with the same end in view. Such ideas, however, woke few echoes among the masses, and the most distinguished theologians were resolutely hostile towards them. Sanavia, for instance, was taken to task by Theodore Beza, Johann Gerhard and the entire Faculty at Wittenberg. Evangelization of the world, said Beza, should be left to 'those locusts vomited forth by hell who hypocritically bear the name of Jesus'.

The first Protestant missionary endeavours were undertaken by Frenchmen in the mid sixteenth century. Thanks to the influence of Admiral Gaspard de Coligny an expedition was sent to Brazil in 1556. It was led by Villegagnon, who was joined in the Bay of Rio de Janeiro by some pastors from Honfleur; but the enterprise was ruined by feuds, due mainly to Villegagnon's abjuration. Six years later another settlement was established in Florida by Jean de Ribault of Dieppe. But the Spanish admiral Menendez appeared on the scene soon afterwards and massacred them, 'not as Frenchmen, but as heretics'. All that was not particularly encouraging.

And so, until the seventeenth century, Protestant penetration was limited to following the political advance of the reformed nations, without seeking to found missions in the true sense. In accordance with the principle *cujus regio, hujus religio*, when Dutchmen or Englishmen seized Catholic territory they drove out the papists and installed their own pastors. That is what happened in the Sunda Isles, which were occupied by Dutch sailors. Cromwell's *Western Project* (1654) made quite clear that in his eyes Protestant expansion and the weakening of the Catholic powers went cheek by jowl. Political and commercial considerations, therefore, remained more decisive than the apostolic spirit. Thus in 1627, when Richelieu forbade the Huguenots to belong to colonial companies, some of them, both in France and Canada, joined the Dutch East India Company; among them was Jesse de Forest, a Protestant of Avesne, who went to North America and founded a place which was called Nouvelle-Avesne until it was absorbed by New Amsterdam, which in turn became New York.

It was in France, despite the trials and tribulations that were soon to overwhelm the Protestants, that the latter first became aware of the need for missions to pagan lands. The pious pastor of Charenton, Charles Drelincourt, wrote in his *Visites charitables*: 'I am distressed by the fact that very few Christians have taken to heart the Lord's command, "Go ye and teach all nations." How does Jesus allow such a state of affairs? Did not Jesus Christ come on behalf of all men?' And he concluded in a noble surge of faith: 'The command of Jesus remains; the promise will be fulfilled.' The revocation of the Edict of Nantes, by depriving the French Protestants of any permanent starting point for their missions, prevented them from accomplishing that task, but a longing for it remained in their hearts.[25]

The first Protestant missionaries worthy of the name were John Eliot, an Englishman, and Hans Egede, a Dane. The former, who had studied Jesuit methods, tried to evangelize the American Indians by settling them in villages and teaching them how to farm. The first of these settlements was founded for the Mohicans near Boston, at a place which they called Nomenettum, i.e. 'Happiness'. A little later other villages were built among the Delaware tribe by David Braihaerd. The Bible was translated into Indian, and in 1649 there took shape an institution which in 1701 became the Society for the Propagation of the Gospel in Foreign Parts. As for Hans Egede, a sort of Lutheran Charles de Foucauld, he abandoned his ministry in the Lofoten Islands and set out to evangelize the Eskimos in Greenland, living among them for fifteen years without making a single conversion, but happy in the conviction that the grain he sowed would germinate after him, if God so willed.

Meanwhile the Protestant expansion was beginning, helped by political events. In 1655 the English occupied and 'reformed' Jamaica; in 1681 the Dutch did likewise with Portuguese Guiana, and soon afterwards an English expedition drove the Capuchins from Florida. But those were not true missionary undertakings. The real task was shouldered by the sects. We have already seen the Quakers at work in Pennsylvania, establishing friendly relations with the redskins, which enabled them to make a few conversions. Next on the scene were the Moravian Brethren with their friends the Herrnhutists. Some relieved the heroic pastor Egede in Greenland; others settled in Labrador; others again set out for the Antilles, Île Saint-Thomas and South Africa, and even visited the Kalmuks of the Mongolian plateaux. Then came the Methodists, whose founder had declared that the whole world was his parish. His followers in America took over the mission to the redskins and started a very successful one to the black slaves; they also sent preachers to India, Oceania and China. One of their number, Dr Coke, compels our admiration. He was the first 'superintendent' sent by Wesley to America, and has been called the Francis Xavier of Methodism. He laboured hard for many years to spread Christianity among the redskins and blacks; then, in his old age and like the Catholic saint who had been his inspiration, he embarked for Ceylon and died on the voyage.

At the end of the eighteenth century one of the great centres of Protestant missionary work was India. In Ceylon, with the fullest support of the Dutch authorities, groups belonging to several Churches and sects managed to convert about 300,000 natives. At Madras, then at Tranquebar and Tanjore, the Dane, Ziegenbalg, who belonged to a missionary society founded at Halle, won favour with the rajahs and made a few conversions. More notable, however, was William Carey, a Baptist shoemaker from Nottingham; a true 'pioneer of organized missions', he was eaten up with apostolic zeal. First at Calcutta, then at Serampore (where he died in 1834), he accomplished an enormous task, studying Indian dialects, writing grammars and dictionaries, training missionaries as well as preaching himself, and influencing native life to such an extent that he managed to secure the abandonment of that barbarous custom whereby widows were burned on their husbands' funeral pyres. Finally, with the devoted help of Mrs Wallis, he laid the foundations of the Baptist Missionary Society.

The impulse had been given. The achievements of the Protestant apostolate were as yet far from rivalling those of the Catholic missions, decadent as the latter had become by the end of the eighteenth century. The established Churches of the Reformation entered the field in 1795 with the London Missionary Society and in 1810 with the American Board of Commissioners for the Foreign Mission.

12. THE PROTESTANT WORLD

During the neo-classical period Protestantism, strengthened and enlarged, asserted itself more and more in face of Catholicism. The characteristic type of Protestant man had become clearly and rapidly defined in the sixteenth century.[26] Though rigid in morals, unyielding in matters of principle, hostile to luxury, debauchery and worldly amusements, he was disfigured by narrow-mindedness and sectarianism. Notwithstanding the differences imposed by locality and diverse loyalties, that type still harmonized with an ideal that was officially revered. Hence a certain appearance of similarity between individuals as different as a German Lutheran squire, a Dutch sailor, a Camisard of the Cevennes and a Scottish merchant; all were good Bible readers and confident of possessing the truth. That, of course, did not mean that all were faithful to the ideal. We have seen that decadence had already submerged large areas of the Protestant world, especially the Anglican and Lutheran Churches; even among the French refugees, who had given unequivocal proof of their faith, there were some (in London, for example) who seemed more preoccupied with commerce and the theatre than with psalms. Such deterioration is so much part and parcel of human affairs that it need not astonish us; Protestantism was no more immune than was the Roman Church.

It must also be remarked, however, that the Protestant ideal was often incarnate in persons of unimpeachable morals and lofty aspirations. Among them were Pastor Amyraut, so charitable and apostolic; the apologist Abbadie, whose soul, like that of Pascal, expressed itself in words that still have power to move us; the austere and pugnacious Jurieu, harder upon himself than towards others; the philosopher Leibniz, whose whole thought was permeated with God; Rembrandt and Bach, artists who derived their inspiration from the living springs of Holy Scripture. Surely a Catholic must look upon these men as truly brothers in spirit. Nor must we omit the names of many women, illustrious and obscure, who gave evidence of a faith to which no believer can remain indifferent: Elizabeth of Nassau and Marie Huber; Charlotte de Caumont La Force and Anne Rose Calas, the heroic English-born wife of the unfortunate victim of the Calas affair. A long list could be compiled of such women, whose interior life is revealed in their letters and diaries.[27]

To the psychological features of Protestant man the neoclassical age added another in the shape of philanthropy. The spirit of charity was certainly not the most prominent characteristic of the early reformers; one need only recall Luther's disdain of the peasantry, and the treatment of the Anabaptists. Puritan England long cherished an ill-concealed contempt for the poor and outcast, whose unhappy fate was attributed to their own sins; the state of the prisons and the view of vagabondage as a crime were both significant. The example of Calvin's charitable undertakings at Geneva had few followers. It was under the influence of the sects—Quakers first, but above all the Methodists—that Protestantism became more attentive to suffering and injustice. Improvement in the treatment of convicts, solution of the factory question and suppression of the slave trade were among their noblest ambitions during the eighteenth century. Later, the novels of Dickens and *Uncle Tom's Cabin* came from Protestant circles that had been revived by the Pietist and Methodist awakening, and nineteenth-century Protestantism was essentially humanitarian.

But Protestantism did more than produce a certain type of man; it played a considerable part in the evolution of society. Without accepting the opinion of some historians that it was the source of capitalism and democracy, or that of Karl Marx, who considered it the product of 'nascent capitalist economy', one must note that the Protestant stream quickly encountered those two great constitutive factors of the modern world. There was no immediate relationship of cause and effect, but there was certainly convergence at the end of a certain period. It is fair to say that Protestants were more alive than others to the fundamental forces of the age and adhered to them more closely. There is undeniably some sort of relationship between Protestantism, capitalism and democracy.

A Catholic, in principle, lays more stress on contempt of this world's goods, even when he is very far from practising it. Protestants can read in Calvin such words as these: 'Riches come to men as a blessing from God. . . . Riches in themselves are by no means to be condemned. . . . Abraham was a rich man, both in cattle and money.' If the possession of wealth proves one is blessed by God, why renounce it? There is a 'spirituality of success'. The *bourgeois* class, which was still a recent phenomenon in the sixteenth century, derived from it a justification which it could have done without but which gave it an easy conscience. It is significant that modern capitalism found its favourite climate in puritan England and the Protestant United States. When the great English commercial and industrial growth began, numerous books were devoted to its vindication. *Spiritual Agriculture, Spiritual Navigation* and, above all, Richard Skele's *Vocation of the Merchant* (1684) explained that the Christian duty of a landowner, a sailor or a merchant was to look after his affairs, and that he was bound to make use of the advantages offered to man by Providence. Economic progress, indeed, eventually became in itself a driving force, and money-making an object of worship. The self-denial of St Francis of Assisi, imitated in the eighteenth century by St Benedict Joseph Labre, was hardly conceivable in the Protestant climate, where even the Quakers had a keen eye to business.

While England prepared the triumph of the capitalist system through the Industrial Revolution, the psychological features of capitalism became more and more pronounced.[28] So did those of modern democracy, by which I do not mean to say that it was the offspring of Protestantism alone. E. Chenevière, in his *Pensée politique de Calvin*, has protested against this over-simplification; but he is wrong in saying that 'there is no relationship between the Reformation and modern democracy'. Many political and social sources united with other intellectual currents to produce democracy; nor should we forget that Erastus, the strictest upholder of the theory of royal authority, was a Protestant. But it remains no less certain that the psychology of Protestantism, its rejection of all authority not emanating from conscience alone, its inclination towards egalitarianism, and even in many cases its sacerdotal organization, coincided with the components of democracy. When Calvin wrote that 'civil liberty is an outstanding sign of God', and that 'voting is a sacred act', he was suggesting rules of conduct to future democratic regimes. It was not by chance that the modern parliamentary system developed first in Protestant England; nor that the first great modern democracy was born in Protestant America, based upon the *Declaration of the Rights of Man*, a curious mingling of biblical truths and philosophical precepts. Without in the strict sense giving birth to democracy, Protestantism *helped* in that birth and, to some extent, gave the child its qualities.

Protestant man and Protestant society expressed themselves

with ever increasing originality in art and letters. Biblical inspiration had long fed the literary stream whose principal representatives in France were Maurice Scève, Du Bartas, Clément Marot and, above all, Agrippa d'Aubigné, who died in 1630. The persecution to which French Protestantism was subjected in the seventeenth century denied it a voice among the classic masters; writers were more concerned to defend their harassed faith, to encourage their oppressed brethren or to fight their persecutors, though a handful of refugees in London and Berlin wrote biblical dramas (e.g. those of La Roche Guilhem) full of allusion to current events. But wherever Protestantism was able to spread its wings masterpieces were produced. Chief among these were Milton's *Paradise Lost*, *Paradise Regained* and *Samson Agonistes*. Later came William Blake, who thought himself a rebel against all religion but was in fact a Protestant from top to toe; he used the same themes, but satanized them, and his smouldering verses pretend to depict the marriage of heaven and hell. In Germany the great biblical writer and most eloquent literary interpreter of the Protestant soul was Klopstock (1724–1803), 'divine Klopstock' as Goethe called him, author of a *Messiad*, of religious tragedies such as *The Death of Adam, David* and *Solomon*, as well as of many odes which manifest his faith. He exerted a distinct influence upon others, on Wieland, for example, and even upon Schiller and Goethe, both apparently far removed from Christian inspiration, but who would not have been such as they were had they not inherited the traditions of many men for whom the Bible had constituted an inexhaustible well-spring. It was in the same Protestant climate, which the Pietist awakening sought to render at once more brotherly and spiritual, that we find on the one hand Oliver Goldsmith's *Vicar of Wakefield* and on the other hand the famous *Night Thoughts*, in which Edward Young (1683–1765) meditated the fragility of all things, the nothingness of man and the greatness of God. And in Germany we have those mysterious songs in which Novalis (1772–1801), having broken with all Churches, sought to lay hold upon the ineffable secrets of divinity.

Art too belied Chateaubriand's celebrated but unjust remark: 'The Reformation clipped the wings of genius and confined it to earth.' In one respect the opposite is true; for the Protestant artist, like all the predestined, was certain that he had been specially called by God and that his work was the fulfilment of a vocation. True, there is no architecture that can be described as Protestant in the strict sense, for chapels were either mere copies of Catholic churches or looked like anonymous assembly rooms; but other forms of art provide abundant evidence of the creative power to be found in Protestant spirituality. No work is more significant from this point of view than that of Rembrandt (1606–69), whose 'Presentation of the Child Jesus in the Temple', 'Raising of Lazarus', 'Descent from the Cross' and 'Supper at Emmaus' are bathed in supernatural light. Rembrandt, a constant and attentive reader of the Bible, was also one of its most brilliant illustrators. He was also the pupil and disciple of Jewish rabbis and Anabaptist pastors, from whom he sought instruction on the sacred text. In Germany the same biblical inspiration that animated Rembrandt, though not to the same point of genius, reappears in Rottenhammer's 'Holy Family' and in Sandrart's 'Dream of Jacob'. In England the moralizing piety of the puritans had something to do with the art of such men as Gainsborough and Reynolds.

It was chiefly in music, however, that the Protestant soul expressed itself. Music had been closely linked with the Reformation from its earliest days. Luther's was the bright idea of employing the language of sound to release in the German people obscure powers of being. All the Protestant Churches sought to give their members a feeling of solidarity; all therefore had recourse to singing, in which hearts are sensibly united, but excluded the instrumental accompaniment used by the Catholic Church. Lutheranism gave birth to the chorale, a thing of great emotional power, and linked to a very ancient Germanic tradition; Calvinism was responsible for setting the psalter to music; Goudimel, illustrious victim of St Bartholomew's Day at Lyons, composed the music for no fewer than one hundred and fifty psalms. In this field Germany led the whole Protestant world and even, it must be admitted, the whole Christian world. She gave to religious music a style whose influence it has never ceased to feel. The cantata and the oratorio entered into common use and afforded scope for the highest talent, and intransigent biblical faith is apparent in Gerhardt's *Canticles of the Passion* and in the sacred symphonies of Heinrich Schütz.

It expressed itself above all in the work of two geniuses who were exact contemporaries, Frederick Handel (1685–1759) and Johann Sebastian Bach (1685–1750). The former, an extrovert soul, as well as an artist of prodigious fecundity, who drew his text directly from the Bible in his immense oratorio *Israel in Egypt,* undertook to commemorate the Saviour's life in the still vaster *Messiah.* He also composed many psalms, odes and cantatas before becoming blind on the very day that he finished writing the final chorus of *Jephtha:* 'How dark, O Lord, are Thy designs!' Handel was an artist of sweeping movement, inexhaustible inspiration and exact construction; he has been compared to the cathedral builders. Bach, the descendant and ancestor of a long line of musicians, was very different from Handel. He was an introspective soul whose entire work speaks of concentrated meditation, an artist no less prolific and original than the other, a peerless master of the organ as of choral resources, the composer of so many cantatas, oratorios and 'Passions' in which his greatness has never been surpassed. Such was Bach, a Lutheran, who in obedience to his prince, the convert Elector of Saxony, was the author of sublime Masses. If Protestantism had produced none but those two mighty men, it would have falsified Chateaubriand's pessimistic words.

One may ask, nevertheless, whether Handel and Bach belonged exclusively to the world of the Reformation. *Messiah* and *The Passion according to St Matthew* are surely the common property of the Christian soul, irrespective of their authors' creeds.

On the eve of the French Revolution, Protestantism showed contradictory features. It proved itself, as never before, unable to achieve unity or to halt the process of dismemberment which had bedevilled it for nearly three centuries. Though torn like Catholicism by forces of decadence and rebellion, it was scarcely affected by the violent crisis of the Revolution; it was not compelled to make that radical revision of its values which persecution imposed upon the Catholic Church. One question, however, still remained: Did it not stand in need of that trial; would not the coming century, which witnessed a colossal increase of its territorial gains and of its power, prove to be also a period of slow decline?

13. THE SEPARATED CHURCHES OF THE EAST

Besides the two great Christian masses, Catholics and Protestants, there was a third, consisting of very ancient Churches which had been separated from Rome by the Schism of 1054 or by still older heresies. With the exception of Moscow, all those oriental Churches were submerged in decadence and obscurity during the seventeenth and eighteenth centuries. Prostrate for the most part beneath the Turkish yoke, they dragged out a more or less precarious existence, now tolerated and now persecuted, but always humiliated. It is to the credit of a few unknown men that they were able in such difficult circumstances to keep alive the flame of faith against the day of reawakening.

The most important of many was the Greek Church, heiress of Byzantium, who proudly proclaimed herself 'orthodox'. Her leader, the Patriarch of Constantinople, enjoyed not a primacy of jurisdiction like the Pope in the Catholic Church, but a primacy of honour. Having managed to reach an understanding with the Turks, the patriarchs laboured skilfully to maintain and strengthen their superiority. From the Phanaar quarter, where they had resided since the end of the sixteenth century, they gradually extended their authority from the Danube to Crete and from Dalmatia to the frontiers of Persia. From the eighteenth century onwards they obliged the three patriarchates of Antioch, Jerusalem and Alexandria, which had been separated from them a thousand years earlier, to receive titulars appointed by Constantinople. Not one Syrian occupied the see of Antioch after 1724. At Jerusalem, with the exception of Nectarius and Chrysanthus, two distinguished scholars and builders, the patriarchs were too often conspicuous by their absence, preferring the Golden Horn to the Holy City. In Egypt, where the Church had suffered much, the title Patriarch of Alexandria was little more than nominal; it was conferred on a prelate of Constantinople.

There was no longer a Byzantine emperor, but the Churches that had once been nicknamed 'imperialist' (*melkites* in Greek), because they had been loyal to him, remained attached to his shadow. The influence of the Patriarch of Alexandria was strong even in the Bulgarian and Serbian Churches which had been declared autocephalous, the former in the tenth and the latter in the thirteenth century. In Serbia the revolt of the Highlanders against this process of hellenization eventually subsided about 1650, after seventy-five years of strife. In Bulgaria, Rumania and even Georgia the liturgy was modelled upon that of the Greeks. In 1767 the Bulgarian patriarchate was actually abolished. Only the little archdiocese of Sinai, hidden away in the desert and huddled around the celebrated monastery of St Catherine, preserved its freedom.

Ruled thus by a single head, the Greek Church survived; but it made no great effort to rejuvenate its thought or to inflame its fervour. Violently hostile to the Latins and of all that in any way suggested Rome, it was more interested in fighting the Catholics tooth and nail over the Holy Places, to the cynical amusement of the Turkish soldiery, than in studying theological problems. Mount Athos, the wonderful monastic republic with its four hundred large monasteries and four hundred and fifty-six hermitages controlled entirely by Greeks, remained a centre of retreat and prayer; but its intellectual life was indifferent, and its spiritual life a matter of routine. So many of its houses were decadent that it was necessary to introduce reforms with which the name of Eugene Bulgaris, superior of Vatopedi from 1753 to 1759, is permanently associated.

There was, however, one point upon which an otherwise somnolent Church showed vigorous determination, and that was its resistance to Protestant doctrines. In 1621 the Cretan Cyril Lukaris succeeded to the patriarchate of Constantinople. Having studied at Padua and Venice, he had become imbued with Calvinism, and eight years later he published a *Confession of Faith* which was markedly Protestant; but the reaction was so violent that he was unable to hold his throne, despite Turkish support, and after many tragic adventures he died by strangulation. The heretical theories were condemned by a number of councils, e.g. that of Jerusalem in 1672. This did not mean, on the other hand, that the Reformation exercised no influence whatever on the Orthodox Church. The institution in 1639 of Holy Synods, whose business it was to elect the patriarchs, owed something to the Protestant consistories; while the subsequent abandonment of Indulgences, together with the exclusion from the Canon of Scripture of deuterocanonical elements admitted by the Latins, were indications of latent Protestantism.

As for other oriental Churches, separated from Rome and from Byzantium, they struggled on, exposed to persecution by the Turks (who treated them differently from the Greeks of Constantinople) and rent by frequent internal crises. The Jacobite Church of Syria and Mesopotamia, a Monophysite group—heir, that is to say, of Eutyches, who had asserted 'the one and only nature of the incarnate Word'—visibly decreased; it was divided between several obediences and lost a considerable number of its members, who returned to the Roman fold in 1662. The Nestorian Church, once triumphant in Asia, had been obliged by the whirlwind of Tamerlane to seek refuge in Chaldaea. Pestered at frequent intervals by the Ottoman authorities, it was hammered both by Islam, which deprived it of numerous adherents, and by Rome, which created a Chaldaean patriarchate in 1681. The Armenian Church, which had also long been Monophysite, remained so in spite of some attempts at reconciliation with the Holy See. Divided between Greater Armenia in the Caucasus and Lesser Armenia in the Taurus, it suffered from dissensions between its various 'Catholicates' as well as from persecution by the Turks; and in 1679 one of those internal disputes brought large numbers of the faithful into the Roman Church. The most decrepit of all the eastern Churches was that of the Copts in Egypt. Ill-treated by the Turks, who obliged them to wear a distinctive dress and took every opportunity to round them up for sale in the slave-markets, these unfortunate Christians declined to such an extent that the sacrament of penance disappeared from their midst and they accepted circumcision. It was not until the eighteenth century, under the influence of Catholicism, that a revival took place in Christian Egypt.

Lastly, the Monophysite Ethiopian Church, which had finally turned its back on Rome in consequence of some unfortunate events already described,[29] was the only one in the entire Orient to preserve a fairly active religious life within the framework of unfettered political freedom. Its powerful monasteries continued as houses of ecclesiastical culture, but also of impassioned theological debate—so impassioned indeed that it degenerated on several occasions into clan warfare and led to the killing of three *abunas*.

14. THE CHURCH IN CZARIST RUSSIA

There remained Moscow, the 'Third Rome', standing aloof from all other Christian bodies of the East. Away in the fastness of her snowy plains, her prestige was steadily increasing. The Russian Church had looked upon herself as sole heiress of Byzantium ever since the enslavement of her venerated mother by the Turks.[30] In the fifteenth century the Metropolitan Zozimus had declared: 'Two Romes have fallen; Moscow is the Third Rome, and there will never be a fourth.' The sacred deposit had been entrusted to her—the deposit of true faith, betrayed by the Latins and violated by the Infidel. With the growth of Russia's political power, due to the princes of Moscow and their work of territorial expansion, that idea had taken an ever firmer hold of the Russian mind. It had been exploited by those princes, who found it an instrument well adapted to their purpose. In the Byzantine tradition they discovered caesaropapism, a doctrine which identified religious with political authority and made the Autocrat God's viceroy on earth. After 1547, when they assumed the title 'Czar', i.e. Caesar, like the emperors of ancient Rome, they secured increasing mastery of the Church, making themselves the centre of a veritable liturgy similar to the Byzantine rite, and continually interfering in religious affairs. History would show how far that submission of the spiritual to the temporal could be carried.

Under Boris Godounov, a brilliant adventurer who had reached the throne by cunning and intrigue in 1598, the Russian Church cleared a decisive stage of her development. The

Patriarch Jerome of Constantinople came begging alms for his unhappy flock, and Boris persuaded him to make Moscow an independent patriarchate, a step which was ratified in the following year by the Synod of Constantinople. It was an act of capital importance. Independent of Byzantium, to which a mere thread of respect would thenceforth bind her, Moscow was the only free patriarchate of the Orthodox Church; and she came to be considered more and more as the spiritual capital of orthodoxy, the lighthouse whose distant lamp gave hope to all Christian subjects of the Turk. But who would in fact play this part of guide and protector of the Eastern Church—the Patriarch of Moscow or the Czar of All the Russias? The answer to that question was not long in doubt.

The beginning of the seventeenth century was marked by what Russian historians call 'the time of trouble'. Spurious emperors arose, and one of them, in order to secure the throne, delivered Moscow to the Catholics of Poland. For eight whole years the country was ravaged with fire and sword. Resistance hardened at the call of the Patriarch Hermogenes, and monasteries were transformed into fortresses. A counter-attack from Nijni Novgorod, supported by Prince Pojarsky, drove out the Poles and restored order. In March 1613 a national coalition conferred the throne upon a young nobleman, Michael Romanov, whose father was an eminent ecclesiastic related to the former sovereigns. Such was the beginning of a dynasty that would govern Russia for three hundred years.

During the reign of Michael Romanov, a sickly man afflicted with dropsy and too weak to hold the sceptre, relations between Church and State were excellent. His father Pharetos, first Metropolitan and then Patriarch, guaranteed him the support of the clergy, and even countersigned his decrees. His mother, 'Sister Martha', prayed for his glory. Hand in hand with the civil authority, the Church waged war upon the Poles and Swedes and helped the Czar to curtail the powers of the National Assembly, which he had been obliged to recognize on his accession. The theocratic regime was thus based upon the fullest accord of God and Caesar.

The situation deteriorated under Michael's son Alexis, a second-rate personality like his father, gentle and timid but given to sudden fits of rage. Profoundly pious and having ever in mind the memory of his grandfather, he too placed himself in the shadow of the patriarchate, hoping thereby to escape from the disorders that troubled the beginning of his reign. To the See of Moscow he appointed Nikon, son of a peasant and abbot of the great monastery of Solovki, with whose qualities he had been deeply impressed. Intelligent, broad-minded, resolute and sincere in his faith, the new patriarch foresaw that the growing might of the imperial crown was likely to place the Church in subjection, and he determined to hit back without fear or favour. Loaded with honours and high-sounding titles by Alexis, and virtually master of his sovereign, Nikon set himself to counteract all measures that could make the Church dependent on the State. He was quite right in doing so, but he made the mistake of proclaiming his intention from the house-tops. He declared in open Assembly: 'I am not here to do the will of the Czar.' And when Alexis sent him some magnificent presents he refused to thank him, on the ground that those contemptible earthly goods were intended merely to obtain for the Czar a few favours in heaven.

A coalition was formed against the patriarch, consisting of all those whom his abrupt and haughty manners had offended, from his former monastic brethren to the *entourage* of the Czar. He might have been able to withstand these assaults, had not one of his moves precipitated an immediate and overwhelming crisis. The proud peasant had a measure of genius; long before Peter the Great he saw that Russia stood on the edge of a precipice. He realized that she was still an oriental state receiving the new ideas from the West, and that she would have to be westernized in order to save her from her neighbours. The idea was sound, but when he attempted to give it effect within the Church he met with violent resistance; a revolution broke out, known as the *Raskol*, whose religious consequences we shall presently describe. Nikon was attacked on all sides. In vain he attempted to recover his prestige by announcing that henceforward the patriarchate of Moscow would be completely independent of Constantinople, no longer seeking investiture from her—which in any case had never been done. The innumerable enemies whom Nikon's character had provoked found it easy to denounce him as a heretic, a rotten Latin, a dangerous innovator, a trimmer and a cheat. Deposed by the Council of Moscow in 1666, he was sent to a remote convent, there to meditate on the uncertainty of human affairs. The game of underhand warfare between priesthood and empire had ended in victory for the secular power.

The trend was now accelerated. The Church found herself deprived of all her rights, one by one, and eclipsed by the unrestricted authority of the Czar. The troubles which marked the end of Alexis's reign—the rising of Stenka Razone—and those which followed his death did not interrupt the process. Victim of the discords engendered in her bosom by the *Raskol*, the Church was unable to profit by circumstances and regain her authority. When Alexis's daughter Sophia seized power, aided by the *streltsi* (musketeers of the imperial guard), she proved herself more caesaropapist than her father, leading her troops in person against the *raskolniki*, appointing one of her own creatures patriarch, and even interfering in abbatial elections. The way was now fully prepared for one who would complete the domestication of the Church—Peter the Great (1682–1725).

The terrible genius who created modern Russia within a period of forty-five years was from the religious as from every other point of view infinitely complex and contradictory. Throughout his life he wavered between superstitious devotion and the most flagrant manifestations of unbelief. Did he really seek the truth? It seemed that he did at the beginning of his reign, when he inquired into Catholic theology and Protestant theories, and had the liturgy of his own Church explained to him. Then, with a sudden change of attitude, he organized disgraceful entertainments, in which he took part with his 'Eaglets'; mock-processions included a 'prince-pope' mounted on a pig, and 'bacchanal masses' insulted the Eucharist, which was not dear to Catholics alone.

This strange protector of the Church could evidently not imagine her as an instrument of government. The new Russia was to be strictly organized: the State subject, with no question of appeal, to the Czar; the administration controlled by his representatives; all the nobility obliged to enter the im-

perial service and included with the civil service in the *tchine*,
a hierarchy of fourteen degrees. The 'secret chancellery', a
State police force with unlimited powers, would guarantee
the good behaviour of the whole and the submission of all.
The Church could not have been anything but a mere cog in
that huge autocratic machine.

Nevertheless Peter wisely refrained from too much haste.
He treated the last two patriarchs with respect, confining himself to stern silence when they timidly protested against flagrant interference by the civil authority. Adrian, the last of
them, died in 1700, and Peter forbade the election of his
successor; he entrusted the direction of religious affairs to an
Ecclesiastical Council presided over by the Metropolitan of
Riazan, Stephen Javorsky, with the title 'Patriarchal Exarch'.
It was a significant title, for at Byzantium the exarchs had
been delegates of the Czar. That situation lasted for twenty
years, the ghost of patriarchal government governing nothing
at all. Peter's confidential adviser during this time was The-
ophanes Prokopovich, a theologian of Kiev, who had aposta-
tized from Rome and rejoined the Orthodox Church, a man
more or less imbued with Protestant ideas and definitely
anticlerical. Following his advice, the Czar accomplished a
number of ecclesiastical reforms by means of imperial ukase:
he suppressed titles and dignities, taxed the property of bishops and monks, and set about reforming the monasteries on
quite reasonable lines.

In 1721 the final blow was struck. Summoned to the new
capital at St Petersburg, the bishops from all over Russia
were informed that the Czar had just signed an ecclesiastical
regulation to which they were invited to declare their submission. The patriarchate was abolished. Its place was taken by
an institution modelled on the Protestant consistories, the
Holy Synod, consisting of five bishops, four archimandrites,
a monk-priest, two archdeacons and two other clerics—a total
of sixteen members. The Holy Synod was forbidden to meet
except in presence of a lay official called the *Ober-procurer*,
who would prepare the subject-matter of its deliberations,
direct its debates and transmit its 'decisions' to the Czar. Any
act not approved by the Czar would be null and void; all
bishops would be nominated by him; canonizations would be

proclaimed by ukase, and he would even have the right to appoint fast days and grant dispensations by rescript. It is impossible to imagine a more complete subjection of the Church to the temporal power. The system remained in force until 1917.

There was little or no opposition to that overwhelming blow. Javorsky, exarch of the patriarchal see, attempted to parry it by attacking Propokovich's theology, which savoured of Protestantism. But his effort was mere shadow boxing; his great theological treatise never received the imperial *imprimatur*. And so the synodal Church imposed itself upon the whole of Russia, with its priestly civil servants exercising police duties, helping in the work of tax collecting, and bound under the pain of death to violate the seal of the confessional whenever the safety of the State was at issue.

All the great Czar's successors preserved his measures intact. Catherine II went still further by reducing the numbers of the Holy Synod to six, in order the better to control them, though she generously decided that priests should be exempted from the knout.

The Third Rome had done more than Byzantium to identify the spiritual with the temporal. Beneath his cloth-of-gold mantle lined with ermine and the dalmatic of red velvet, the Czar was more master of Church and State than ever the Basileus had been. On the day of his accession he placed the diadem upon his own head and crowned his wife. The Viceroy of God no longer had need of an intermediary between himself and heaven.

15. FROM OLD BELIEVERS TO EUNUCHS OF GOD

There was, however, some opposition to this official Church in bondage. Too often stupid and violent, it was led by men who did not always understand the essential matter in dispute, who lost themselves in petty details and who sometimes foundered in the worst aberrations; but these same men gave proof of a will to spiritual independence which it is possible to admire. The most determined resistance came from the *Raskol*.

At the end of the sixteenth century, when the great majority of Ruthenians in the kingdom of Poland and part of the Ukrainians in Russia returned to the Catholic Church,[31] the most intelligent among the Orthodox clergy sought to counteract that movement. Forty years later the Metropolitan of Kiev, Peter Mogila (1632–47), a religious figure of the very first order, thought that the best means of combating Uniatism was to reform the Orthodox Church itself, morally and above all intellectually. He founded in his episcopal city a theological academy, which studied not only the Greek Fathers, but also the Latins and the scholasticism of St Thomas Aquinas. He himself drew up the *Catechism of the Eastern Orthodox Church*, and set about revising the old Slavonic liturgical books in accordance with Greek editions from Venice.

Raised to the patriarchate in 1652, Nikon was already familiar with Mogila's ideas, and they coincided with his own. He studied the works produced at Kiev and decided to bring about the reform of the Russian Church, endeavouring at the same time to make it independent of the State. He sent to Greece for books—German and Venetian editions of liturgical texts and of the Fathers—and careful study soon revealed that the Slavonic liturgy used in Russia was hopelessly corrupt. He therefore set to work with his accustomed energy. In 1654 he summoned a council at Moscow, which agreed to revise the Slavonic translations of the Bible and liturgical books, as well as to end certain forms of devotion that were evidently superstitious. These measures did not lack wisdom, but the people failed to understand them. It was easy for a small party of hostile monks and parochial clergy, whose ringleader was a secular priest named Avvakum, to stir up the holy indignation of the masses. Nikon, they declared, was seeking to deliver the Holy Russian Church to the sorceries and iniquities of the West. He dared to suggest that priests might shave, whereas everyone knew that Christ and the Apostles wore beards and that the impious use of the razor was a Roman heresy! He said that processions need not necessarily move directly towards the sun, and that a blessing might be given with the open hand instead of with three fingers conjoined! It was all quite dreadful, and a torrent of indignation burst forth against such abominable errors. Those who claimed thus to defend venerable usages against monstrous innovations nicknamed themselves 'Old Believers'.

The fall of Nikon, which was due as much to this religious explosion as to the machinations of those who upheld caesaropapism, brought no peace of mind. The reforms envisaged by the patriarch, or at any rate the most fundamental of them, were still pursued; the movement gained ground and the whole of Russia was soon in a state of ferment. Old Believers and adherents of the official Church were everywhere at loggerheads, and a veritable schism (*Raskol*) developed. Within half a century it included nearly a quarter of the population.

Indeed the *Raskol* was supported not only by fanatical conservatives and nationalists hostile to the slightest degree of western influence, but also by some perfectly wholesome elements which aspired to a purer Christian life and looked to the old monastic ideal as their model and their guide. Again, there were those who objected to the total submission of Church to State and remained faithful to the ancient concept of two powers, allied but equal.

The original purpose of the *Raskol* was to withstand Nikon and his friends; but it very soon found itself opposed by the imperial Church and its formidable weapons of coercion. Headstrong and ferocious, quick to hurl anathema against the official Church ('the whore of Babylon'), cavillers and clever dialecticians who appeared to have inherited the methods of Byzantine theologians, the *raskolniki* struggled even to the point of martyrdom. Peter the Great was certainly not a man prepared to tolerate this kind of rebellion, and immediately he had secured the throne he took action against them. His successors did likewise, and the Russian people, used to regarding their monks as true witnesses of Christ, stood aghast at the spectacle of convents at open war with Moscow, the venerable monastery of Solovki besieged by imperial troops for ten years, communities of nuns put to the sword, and fire devouring Christians who, like the archpriest Avvakum, seemed to incarnate the ancient national religion. Nothing, however, could subdue the Old Believers, who met persecution with indomitable resistance. Rather than submit, tens of thousands of men, women and children, wearing white shirts, crowded together inside rings of faggots, logs and straw, to which they set fire with their own hands. During the eighteenth century only one czar took pity on these fanatics and tried to end the persecution—Peter III, husband of Catherine II and perhaps himself an Old Believer. But his dominating wife soon cut short his merciful endeavour. Persecution did not prevent the Old Believers from extending their influence; for the most part sober, hard-working and well disciplined, they rather paradoxically assumed leadership of the new Russian society just when the Empire had completed its westernization; many of them acquired wealth through commerce, industry or shipping on the great rivers, and became extremely influential. The *Raskol*, however, was not officially recognized until early in the twentieth century, when it numbered about 20,000,000 adherents.

The magnificent unity of the Russian Orthodox Church was at an end. A rupture had occurred, which, true to the process we have observed in the Protestant body, was a prelude to further dismemberment. Two main tendencies soon became apparent within the *Raskol* itself. When the first generation of bishops had vanished from the scene, it was natural to ask from the canonical standpoint who was to ordain priests. Some, known as the *popovtsy*, agreed that they should be elected and submitted for acceptance by the faithful, and that a single priest would suffice to confer valid ordination. More categorical and more logical were the *bepopovtsy*, who declared themselves ready to do without priests altogether. Then sects arose in the excitable atmosphere engendered by the *Raskol*. Some very curious doctrines and still more curious practices began to spread among small coteries. Several influences were at work in those tumultuous circles: Protestantism in various forms, e.g. Quakerism and Baptistry, introduced by foreigners whom Peter the Great and Catherine II had invited to Russia; Judaism, whose adherents were experts on the Bible and taught the Russians to read it; and, later, Freemasonry linked with German Illuminism and with the Rosicrucian movement. So numerous were these sects that no history of Russia can boast of having listed them all. Bordering the *Raskol*, but in some respects very far removed from it, swarmed a strange agglomeration which included many fanatics; eighteenth-century Russia already had its Rasputins. The Sabbatists, like the Jews, substituted Saturday for Sunday and held that the Messiah had yet to be born—in Russia. The Dukhobors, 'God's Wrestlers', had a moral kinship with the Mennonite Anabaptists; they denied a future life and believed in some sort of metempsychosis. The Molokarj, 'Milk-drinkers', practised long fasts, during which they took nothing but milk beverages. The Biegumy, 'Runners', refused any kind of permanent domicile, and were veritable wanderers on earth. The Dyrkovzj, 'Hole-borers', made a circular opening in the wall of their cells, and prayed before it as a sign of spiritual freedom. The Klysty, 'Whippers', imposed on themselves penances no less severe than those of the most zealous Spanish flagellants. The Skakouny, 'Jumpers', leaped, capered and twisted themselves into all kinds of outlandish positions during their ecstasies. There was absolutely no form of aberration but had its devotees in Russia. Morality was sometimes given short shrift; the 'Skoptsy', for example, mutilated themselves in order to avoid temptation of the flesh, and these 'Eunuchs of God' had no good reputation.

16. HOLY RUSSIA

That anthill of sects may perhaps express genuine, though incoherent, religious aspirations; it certainly does not reveal a healthy moral state. Russian Christianity, in fact, suffered from an even more serious form of those same diseases which had afflicted the Latin Church before the Council of Trent. And since no serious reform was undertaken from within, those diseases continued on their way throughout the neo-classical period. 'The eighteenth century', writes M. Dauzas, 'was an age of such complete degradation in the Russian Church that all hope of its recovery seemed lost.' The situation might have appeared desperate but for two remaining advantages: the solid faith of the people and the presence of a few great saints.

The most conspicuous fact was the mediocrity of the secular clergy. Recruited from among the peasantry, and transmitting their office from father to son or son-in-law, the parish priests formed a distinct and utterly despised caste. The *moujiks* saw them live very much like themselves; the landowners treated them as little better than serfs. Too many of them were lechers or drunkards, and had no theological training whatever. Some did not know the meaning of the Eucharist, others thought the prophets of Israel were disciples of Christ; they confined themselves to reciting by heart a few liturgical formulae which most of them did not understand. There were seminaries, of course, where pupils spent six or seven years in classical and theological studies; but they were not open to candidates for the secular priesthood, being reserved for monks destined to high office in the Church. The monks, who, since the eleventh or twelfth century, had formed a spiritual *élite* and produced so many saints, had long been in a state of decadence. Many religious houses, despite their splendid reliquaries, led lives of mere routine, following rigid observances and practising undesirable asceticism, but having little or no true spirituality. There too ignorance was the common lot. When the monastery of Solovki wanted a monk to write the founder's life, they had to bring one all the way from Serbia; and when they drew up a protest against Nikon's reforms, only twenty of them were able to sign it—the rest were illiterate. One would search in vain among the Russian regulars for anything corresponding to the Maurists and Bollandists. That lacklustre Church possessed no living, original theology; the one serious effort of the kind was undertaken at Kiev, but it led to the *Raskol* and petered out. Until the end of the eighteenth century Russian religious thought was torn between conflicting influences, some Protestant, others Catholic (and even Jesuit after the Society had established itself in the empire of the czars[82]), and others again, before long, philosophical and rationalist.

Nor was the situation improved by the attitude of the State. Even before the final suppression of the patriarchate, caesaropapism interfered without hesitation in the affairs of the Church, and still more so afterwards. Peter the Great's famous ecclesiastical regulation did not confine itself to creating the Holy Synod; it laid down the conditions required for ordination, limited the number of clerics attached to each church, and entrusted the appointment of bishops to the sole discretion of the State, entering into the smallest details with a view to ensuring the domestication of the clergy. The Autocrat's 'reform' was yet more categorical among the regular clergy. Peter loathed the monks, whom he described as 'profiting by the work of others, spreading heresy and superstition'. He actually tried to issue a ukase forbidding his subjects to take the monastic habit and turning the monasteries into houses for wounded soldiers, but had to give way before a storm of protest. He contented himself with closing a number of religious houses, fixing the age for profession at thirty in the case of men and fifty in that of women, as well as confiscating a great deal of monastic property. Later, Catherine II resumed the task so well begun; under pretext of adjusting the 'ecclesiastical lists' she suppressed some more monasteries and seized the revenues of many others.

Such measures did not achieve the hoped-for effects. Domestication of the secular clergy hastened its decline; the parish priest was now a police agent, and was despised accordingly. The faithful could hardly respect a cleric whom they saw administer a public whipping to some unfortunate who had bungled the imperial titles or, when reciting the official prayers, had confused certain august personages whom the incessant palace revolutions placed upon the throne. But the people continued to love and venerate their monks, who still seemed to embody the grand Christian ideal of the past; and as Russia became increasingly westernized an ever greater number of souls turned to the cloister, in order to escape from a world that was becoming less and less Christian. In Russia, having a vocation (*spasatsa*) was known as 'wishing for salvation', a phrase which assumed its full significance during the eighteenth century, especially in the second half, when a growing number of vocations heralded a revival. The czars had managed to reduce the secular clergy to the rank of civil servants, but with the monks they failed; the people would not allow it.

For the people remained profoundly religious. The governing classes allowed themselves to be won over by impiety, thanks to the influence of western ideas and, above all, to that of a moral crisis compared with which the laxity of

France under Louis XIV seemed nothing. The conduct of the Russian aristocracy is faintly reflected in that of the czarinas who succeeded Peter the Great, and that of their numerous *entourage*—'effeminate little gentlemen', as the Metropolitan Daniel described them. Moral and intellectual libertinism, as always, went hand in hand. But among the people things were very different, though they undoubtedly had serious faults. Their ignorance of religious matters was appalling, so too was their superstition; many had not risen above the magical and totemistic stage of religious life, regarding their monks and priests as sorcerers, their icons as talismans. Their morality too was often deplorable; the worst aberrations sought an excuse in some peculiar theories. It was held, for instance, that a man must sin in order to be forgiven, and that salvation was guaranteed provided one did not deny Christ. There was also the story of a drunkard who obtained admission to Paradise by confessing his weakness to St Peter, who had once denied his Lord.

The common people as a whole led lives very similar to those of the western peasantry in the early Middle Ages, but like them they believed. Every hovel had its little icon; the prayers said in front of it were hardly understood, but at least they were never omitted. Every family meal began with the sign of the cross, which indeed was used frequently on all occasions. Every father and mother hastened to have their children baptized within three days of birth, as the law prescribed. The whole life of the masses was framed and regulated by religion; a man's religious convictions were no more disputable than his loyalty to the Czar—indeed the two things were one and the same. Even the new class of artisans, merchants and small industrialists, which came into being under Peter the Great, remained docile and faithful. The Voltairean *bourgeois* was a species of humanity unknown in Russia.

Some curious and picturesque types were to be found among those pious folk. One met pilgrims, not only those who went in huge bands numbering tens of thousands to venerate the holy icons at some monastery, or travelled miles to kiss the relics of a saint, but also individuals, true vagabonds of God, belonging to all classes, who spent their whole lives wandering in search of truth and the heavenly kingdom. Then there were the *yourodstvo*, 'fools of Christ', who wished to take upon themselves all the insults and humiliations they believed Jesus to have suffered. Practising absolute detachment and flaunting all conventions, these hairy prophets were sometimes discovered walking about quite naked or wearing the oddest clothes, imitating the cries of beasts, uttering incoherent words, pretending to be deaf mutes and eating offal. Some of them played an active part in the public life of the Russian people, giving voice to what others thought, denouncing profiteers and exploiters, and even criticizing the czars; for none dared lay hands upon them. At Moscow the church of Vassili the Blessed, among the most famous in that city, was named after one of them.

The unquestionable improvement which began in the middle of the eighteenth century was due beyond all doubt to popular faith, to the moral and spiritual pressure it exerted in direct opposition to the official trend. There was no concerted reform such as the Catholic Church had experienced two centuries earlier. No council met to decide *ex cathedra* how to make the Church once more aware of her duties. There were only isolated personalities, each at work in some particular district or class; but their influence was so great that they stirred whole masses of the faithful, and their efforts led to a revival. During this wonderful period of its life the Russian Church gave impressive proof of a law governing Christianity throughout the world: the history of the Church is first and foremost that of her saints.

Russian Orthodox saints are not recognized by the Catholic Church. The criteria of sanctity in Russia were still at a primitive stage, akin to that of the Catholic Church in the Barbarian and early Middle Ages. Canonization among the Orthodox was generally a matter of popular opinion rather than the outcome of a long and careful process. It is therefore in a broad sense only that one can speak of Russian 'saints', though many are admirable from any Christian point of view.

It was in the monasteries that the flame was rekindled. Despite all their faults, they were still bastions of faith, attracting all who wished to lead lives dedicated to God, and providing the Russian hierarchy. The monks exercised considerable influence, whether they remained in their cloisters or went out to become bishops. The originator of the revivalist movement was St Dimitri, an emaciated and stooping little man, but with so firm and persuasive a voice that he was nicknamed the Russian Chrysostom. As superior of a convent he taught his subjects to work, and spent twenty-five years collecting the *Acta* of the Russian saints. Appointed Metropolitan of Rostov, he continued to lead the austere life of a monk, declaring that 'an archbishop was not born to glory in himself'. Patiently he began to fight against the ignorance of the clergy, against immorality and against the fetishism of the Old Believers. When he died, in 1709, the road was already marked out.

Dimitri was followed, fifty years later, by St Tykhon of Zadonsk. He too started as a monk in a community where learning was held in scant respect and where, all alone, he made a thorough study of the Fathers. Appointed bishop of Voronezh, in a region still largely barbarian, he was confronted with the ignorance of a parochial clergy among whom illiteracy itself was no rare phenomenon, and also with the indolence of uneducated monks. After four years of effort he resigned his see and went to live in the monastery of Zadonsk, where he spent his time in study and prayer, anxious only to bear witness and leaving God to render his work fruitful. His brethren and even his superiors, irritated rather than edified by his example, loaded him with insults; but he received them with a smile, convinced that the humiliations he endured were helping to restore the kingdom of God on earth. He died in 1783, and his mystical writings had a profound effect upon the whole of Russian spirituality.

The same gifts of benevolence, gentleness and mysterious spiritual radiance characterized St Seraphim of Sarov (died 1833), the solitary who dwelt in a forest and whose voice wild animals obeyed. At the same time he was a fierce ascetic. Thirty years in a hermit's cell, eight of them in absolute silence, and three years as a stylite on top of a pillar—such was his preparation. Then, when he felt able to go and speak of Christ, he left his seclusion and went from town to town, preaching the gospel of joy, the love of God's dear Mother, the spirit of peace and hope. He was found dead, a candle in his hand, before an icon of the Blessed Virgin.

It was in this monastic climate, improved by the example of saints, that there appeared (or rather evolved, for its origins were very ancient) the *staretz*, a new religious type exclusive to Russian spirituality, which has never since lost its importance. Etymologically the word signified 'old man'; in monasteries it was often applied to the master of novices. It was gradually extended to include those men, not necessarily priests or monks, and not invariably old, who exerted a moral and spiritual influence in various circles, rather like the Indian *guru*. The *staretz* then is the guide, the counsellor, the wise man who is consulted in the difficulties of life and speaks in the name of God. Dostoyevsky's Zosimus is a good example. Towards the end of the eighteenth century the institution of *startchestvo* was raised to a high degree of eminence by Païssy Velitchovsky, who, disgusted no less with routine theology than with pagan wisdom, went to live on Mount Athos. There for seventeen years he shone like a star. Young monks soon took him as their guide, and with them he founded a monastery of sixty cells, dedicated to the prophet Elias, which quickly became too small. Tormented by the Greeks, who controlled the monastic republic, he went to Moldavia and there built a monastery which housed seven hundred monks at the time of his death and which was visited by thousands of pilgrims from the farthest corners of Russia, wishing to see the man of God and to seek his advice. When he died in 1794 his reputation was such that he had disciples throughout Russia, and his spiritual doctrine of 'interior activity' had been embraced by countless souls. On the fringes of the gloomy forest of Brynsk, in the territory of Kalouga, there soon arose a monastery which followed the teaching of the great *staretz* and where the monks led lives of prayer and self-denial as taught by Païssy. That monastery, named Optina, a house of white walls and gilded domes, was destined to be the citadel of Russian spiritual life until the twentieth century. There the *staretz* Leonid, dressed in a blue blouse and weaving girdles for a living, welcomed such visitors as Tolstoy and Dostoyevsky.

Thus the late eighteenth-century religious awakening in

Russia, born of the faithful masses and kept alive in their midst by the *startsi*, had a deep influence on the contemporary Russian soul, in which it implanted certain fixed ideas that can be traced in the literature and even in the politics of nineteenth-century Russia. Henceforward the Russian people believe that they possess the sacred deposit of faith, and ought therefore to assume a kind of Messianic role. By taking upon itself the misery of the world they save all men and prepare them for a happy future. 'What matter', exclaims Dostoyevsky, 'if the czars believed themselves to have domesticated the Church, or if Peter thought to reshape his empire on the lines of the atheistic West? The State is transformed into a Church, returns to the Church, becomes the universal Church.' The State and the Church of Holy Russia, inseparably linked together, provide for the salvation of the whole world.[33] Those were indeed grandiose ideas, in which the most sincere Christian aspirations were mingled with the fumes of nationalism and its pride. 'Marxism', says Count Nicholas Berdyayev, 'has employed the moods of the Russian soul, its religiousness, its dynamism, its intransigence, its faith in the peculiar destiny of Russia, its craving for sacrifice, its quest for social justice and the kingdom of God on earth.'

CHAPTER IV

STORM AND STRESS

1. THE KING OF NAPLES PAYS TRIBUTE TO THE POPE

On 28th June 1776 the guns of the Castle of Sant' Angelo awakened Rome with the din of repeated salvoes. Above the ancient mausoleum of Hadrian a gentle wind, stealing from the Sabine hills, stirred the pennons of two standards—those of the reigning pontiff and the Church. Suddenly, though dawn had hardly broken, the narrow streets filled with a motley throng—uniforms and liveries, religious habits of all kinds and plain soutanes. Perched on cornerstones and fountains was an army of racketeers, occupying the best places for resale to wealthy men who wished for a good view of the procession. The splendid ceremony about to take place was the occasion of a joyous, popular holiday. The Neapolitan ambassador, on behalf of his king, was going to 'present the palfrey'.

The Apostolic throne had been occupied for about eighteen months by a pope in every respect after the Roman heart. Fifty-eight years of age, tall and thin, with kindly look and stately bearing, he had everything calculated to please—and knew it. When elected on 15th February 1775, after a conclave of two hundred and forty-one days and at the two hundred and sixty-fifth scrutiny, Giovanni Angelo Braschi da Cesena had chosen the regnal name Pius, that of the last pontiff to be canonized. But Pius VI had little in common with his saintly predecessor, the austere Dominican Pius V, apart from untiring energy, a jealous desire to do everything himself and a habit of requiring too much of others. There was no trace of austerity; he loved nothing so much as display, pomp and lavish expenditure, for which the Romans never dreamed of reproaching him. He built and adorned, purchased magnificent works of art for the Vatican collections, cleared the ancient Via Appia and even began drainage work in the Pontine Marshes. All this pleased the people, who were ready at the same time to pardon his voracious nephews, his dishonest officials and the whole shady tribe that formed his *entourage*. After so many lustreless pontificates they were enjoying themselves under a pope like those of the Renaissance, one who gave a strong impression of dominating the world, the age and life in general. When Pius VI moved through the city in one of those gleaming processions of which he was so fond, women would cry out delightedly: '*Come sei bello!*' ('How handsome you are!')

The ceremony of 28th June was one of those whereby the Holy See at that time loved to proclaim its power. As age-long overlord of the kingdom of Naples, the Roman Church received each year, on the vigil of SS. Peter and Paul, tribute of vassalage in a picturesque form dating from the fourteenth century. The king's ambassador used to bring the Holy Father a white mule richly caparisoned and bearing a small chest containing seven thousand crowns. The Pope received the offering in the porch of St Peter's, and restored the mule for another eight hundred crowns. This was the occasion of a sumptuous parade in which Prince Colonna, High Constable of Naples, was escorted through the city with drums and trumpets, lancers and cuirassiers, not to mention innumerable footmen and pages. The rest of the day was devoted by the rank and file to merry-making; then, late in the evening, cardinals, diplomats, pretty women and courtier-clerics applauded a concert of lutes and theorbos, followed by competitions of poetry and also of ballet danced by Berber girls, in the beautiful gardens of the Neapolitan ambassador. On the same day minor vassals came to pay tribute to the Cardinal Camerlengo. Some of the offerings were strange enough: a sparrow-hawk from Monte Capello, two live pheasants from San Ippolito, a dog and a hunting net from Rotella d'Ascoli, two thousand crowns and a chalice from Sardinia, a white racehorse from Terracina.

This age-old pomp, like that which attended many other ceremonies, was calculated to give the Romans an impression that the city of St Peter was still the capital of Christendom and the Apostle's successor an unchallenged ruler; and other circumstances helped to confirm this notion. In the Quirinal and Vatican palaces, and even in the summer residence at Castel Gandolfo, the Pope's life was regulated by an etiquette no less rigid than that of Versailles in the days of Louis XIV. It was now the rule that all visitors admitted to audience with the Pope must make a triple genuflection; some remained kneeling throughout the interview. Official terminology included such expressions as 'His Holiness', 'the Sacred Palace', 'the Sacred Decrees'. The machinery of the Curia was also elaborated. The various congregations were reorganized, while the Secretariat of State, executive agent of papal decisions, co-ordinated the work of all. The sight of pilgrims flocking to Rome in hundreds of thousands during Jubilee years—that of 1775 brought a million—might easily have suggested that the Sovereign Pontiff's prestige was in no danger of eclipse.

As a temporal sovereign the Pope reigned over the most splendid city in the world, a city wonderfully full of life, to which there was a constant flow of distinguished visitors from all parts of Europe: rulers, statesmen, diplomats, writers and artists. He reigned, too, over a patrimony that was still considerable, an irregular lozenge reaching from the Po to the Maremma, from the Tyrrhenian coast to the March of Ancona and Romagna. Finally, and above all, he enjoyed as spiritual sovereign a primacy of honour and of jurisdiction. The doctrine of infallibility, though not yet dogmatically defined, was making steady progress. The labours of the brothers Ballerini, following upon those of Golti, Billuart and Petitdidier; the systematic propaganda of most religious Orders; the heartfelt aspirations of ordinary Christian folk—all these factors helped to create an unforgettable image of the Pope as judge of faith and arbiter of doctrine, as a kind of reaction against the authoritarianism of state and secular governments. The figure of the Roman Pontiff loomed over the western world with unquestionable majesty.

But that picture contained many falsehoods and illusions. The splendours of the liturgy concealed the sores of a decaying faith; behind the Sistine choir and the illuminations of St Peter's a careful observer might have perceived less comforting realities. All was far from well in papal circles; there was even talk of downright scandal. The rulers of the Church wasted a good deal of time in place-hunting, in proceedings for beatification to satisfy religious institutes, in disputing matters of etiquette, and in diplomatic manœuvres to decide upon future *papabili*. The 'Pasquino'[1] found plenty of material for its epigrams. The Holy City of Christendom by no means afforded an edifying spectacle of regularity and good behaviour; indeed it surpassed all criminal records. Everything was for sale in the open market—sacred or so-called sacred objects, such as questionable relics and amulets. Immorality of the worst kind was blatant. The papal states, impressive on the map, were in fact an agglomeration of mediocre territories (excepting the districts of Bologna and Ferrara) managed by a backward administration, where, said the spiteful Président de Brosses, one man in every three was a priest, one worked very little and one did nothing at all.

As for the effective power of the Pope, it was likewise debatable. In the political field, surrounded though he was by fine words and genuflections, the Sovereign Pontiff often appeared as an Italian princeling of second-rate importance; the great powers never sought his advice in momentous international discussions, and it often happened that his more distant possessions were occupied by some unfriendly monarch—Avignon, for example, by the King of France, Benevento by the King of Naples. And yet he called himself the arbiter of Christian Europe!

Even at the strictly spiritual level his authority sometimes met with obstacles; the French Gallicans were not alone in their opposition to any direct interference on his part in the affairs of national Churches, and the Germans were even more hostile. In most Catholic countries the bishops refused appointment at his hands and obedience to him alone. The primacy of jurisdiction was admitted only in the narrowest sense; and many thought that infallibility should not be allowed to the Pope except jointly with the Church, expressing his will in a general Council. There were indeed many fissures in the awesome image of the Roman pontiff.

Furthermore, if Pius VI left for an instant the little closed world that separated him from reality, his heart must have been wrung by the spectacle of Christendom at the end of the eighteenth century. There were evil omens everywhere.

The Catholic world was in confusion: Poland was collapsing; Spain, Portugal and Austria appeared to have gone astray and France was evidently close to terrible events. The Protestant *bloc* had been making continual progress for a century. In Canada and in those English colonies that were soon to become the United States, the various Churches born of the Reformation were firmly established. The Christian soul had recently endured some violent crises in which loyalty to the Church was manifestly at stake; one of them, Jansenism, was far from ended. The marvellous worldwide expansion of the Mission had been halted; at many points ground had been lost which had lately been purchased with the blood of martyrs. One more crisis, too, was ravaging the minds and consciences of men: the intellect was in rebellion against Christ and His message; reason claimed to have supplanted faith. What remained of the Pope's authority in a world that was suffering the pangs of birth? Clear-sighted as ever, Président de Brosses declared: 'If the Pontiff's credit grows less day by day, that is because the intellectual attitude which produced it is likewise vanishing.' Was Rome then doomed to be no more the world's guide but simply the reminder of a glorious past?

When things began to go wrong for the ostentatious Pius VI the Romans entertained Pasquino by reviving an epigram that dated from the time of Alexander Borgia and attributed a malignant influence to the number VI:

'*Sextus Tarquinius, sextus Nero, sextus et iste;
Semper sub sextis perdita Roma fuit.*'[2]

Pius VI was in fact the last pope of the old regime, and he would drain the cup of bitterness which had been offered to his predecessors and which they had been unable to avoid.

2. THE PAPACY IN THE AGE OF ENLIGHTENMENT

Six popes had succeeded to the Apostolic See since the death in 1721 of that energetic pontiff Clement XI,[3] who reconstructed the League against the Turks and promulgated the Bull *Unigenitus*. How good or bad were they? The answer will depend in each case on one's point of view. What is certain is that none was without merit. The popes of the seventeenth century had all lived worthy and respectable lives, and had laboured with some success to enhance the prestige of the Papacy; those of the eighteenth yielded them nothing in respect of virtue, piety and faith, as well as having an exalted idea of the sacred duties they had assumed. It was deplorable, however, that the popes of the earlier period had never really understood the tragedy played out before their eyes, and had allowed the Church to suffer grave humiliation in the twin political and spiritual fields. Those of the eighteenth century must be blamed even more severely on the same grounds. Though extremely respectable and even energetic, as well as successful in the spiritual government of the Church, they were not such as one could have wished the Vicars of Christ to be in that 'Age of Enlightenment', when the walls of the ancient Christian citadel had been undermined at so many points. With about one exception the predecessors of Pius VI had been found wanting.

For that situation the secular powers were largely responsible. It is impossible to judge the popes fairly without recalling the circumstances of their election. The one and only serious mistake of the Council of Trent was, as we have seen, its failure to define with sufficient exactitude the relations between Church and State; as the system of absolutism developed, sovereigns were increasingly disposed to interfere not only in the appointment of their own bishops, but also in papal elections. The King of France, the King of Spain, the Emperor and other Catholic rulers all had agents, partisans and clients at Rome, even in the Sacred College. An ambassador, like Cardinal de Bernis, would make advance preparations for the Conclave with a masterly skill more suitably employed elsewhere. As soon as it opened there began the game of offensive and counter-offensive, of objections, bargaining and secret promises. Hence the frequently enormous length of those holy gatherings; hence too, above all, the outcome of the scrutinies. Whenever cliques and parties opposed one another in violent struggle for the choice of a pope, the successful candidate was always someone who would inconvenience nobody, either by his character or by his intellectual stature.

It is remarkable that the eighteenth-century popes, elected thus and almost invariably for political rather than for spiritual reasons, formed on the whole a creditable line. None of them can be censured in respect of his private life. Excepting Pius VI, whose regrettable aberrations we shall see presently, none of them practised nepotism. For six years Benedict XIII, a good but feeble man, allowed the Neapolitan Carmelite Coscia to enrich himself by every means; but his successor had the adventurer arrested and compelled him to disgorge. Generally speaking, the choice of new cardinals was not bad, although one must seek political motives for the conferment by Innocent XIII of the red hat upon Dubois and de Tencin. All these eighteenth-century popes wished sincerely to continue the great Tridentine work of reform; all encouraged the foundation of seminaries; all reminded the bishops of their pastoral duties. It is due to them that devotion to the Sacred Heart overcame all resistance and took a permanent place in Catholic life. To them likewise is due the reorganization of the Index upon lines which have never since been altered. To them, again, belongs the merit of having laid down the rules for beatification and canonization. As regards the canonizations promulgated during those three-quarters of a century, they manifest a solicitude to uphold the authority of the Church against the Powers, together with fidelity to the lessons taught by the saints of the Catholic Reformation. Among the men and women raised to the altars during those years were Gregory VII, John Nepomucene and Stanislaus Kostka—all frowned upon by the partisans of national Churches; Vincent de Paul, Jeanne de Chantal and Francis Régis—leaders of the age of spiritual grandeur; Joseph Calasanctius, one of the great Christian educationalists; and those heroic missionaries Francis Solano and Toribio Mogrobejo (Turibe). The choice was significant of a determination to maintain continuity.[4]

It was in a domain other than that of spiritual government that the popes of the eighteenth century proved deficient; they lacked character and breadth of understanding. Innocent XIII (1721–4), a well-meaning but sickly old man who allowed Parma and Piacenza to be taken from the Holy See, yielded to the manœuvres of the French clique, which sought the purple for Dubois, and finally involved the Church in the disastrous policy of completely rejecting the Chinese rites.[5] Benedict XIII (1724–30) was a humble Dominican who remained a monk beneath the tiara, happier in the convent of the Minerva than in the papal palaces. A holy and austere man, he spent nine hours a day before the altar; he heard confessions and ordained priests and consecrated bishops in person; he strove with all his might against immorality and the luxury of the cardinals. But when political questions were referred to him, he would invariably reply '*Fate voi*' ('Do it yourself'), leaving the egregious Coscia to act as he pleased. Clement XII (1730–40), a blind octogenarian and great-grandnephew of the saintly Florentine bishop Andrew Corsini, was pious and immensely charitable; in one year he gave 300,000 crowns to the poor. He was also zealous in asserting the rights of the Church, but incapable of defending them; and though far-sighted in face of the Jansenist revival and Freemasonry, he had no time to take serious measures. After the much more outstanding reign of Benedict XIV there were two more tame (indeed worse than tame) pontificates. Clement XIII (1758–69), a peaceful, gentle and good-hearted man, was more preoccupied with establishing devotion to the Sacred Heart than with vigorous intervention in the Polish crisis. His condemnation of Rousseau, Helvetius and the *Encyclopaedia* accomplished little or nothing; nor was he able to defend the Society of Jesus against calumny and open attack. Clement XIV (1769–74), a holy Franciscan and an admirer of such devout souls as Mme Louise de France, had no lack of intelligence nor even of courage; but his personality turned out to be hopelessly weak when it came to steering Peter's barque through the storm unleashed by the assault of the Powers upon the Jesuits.

Amid that gallery of undistinguished faces, however, one figure stands out; the features are striking and vigorous, vivid indeed and even truculent. Few modern Catholics are familiar with the name of Benedict XIV (1740–58); he is the subject of no recent full-length biography, while most of his enormous and interesting correspondence lies unpublished in the Vatican archives. Nevertheless, a study of the man and his work shows that he alone among the pontiffs of his age heralded the great popes of our own days—Leo XIII, Pius XI, Pius XII—who have set the prestige of the Church upon unshakable spiritual foundations and have supplied Christian answers to contemporary problems.

At the end of a troubled conclave Prosper Lambertini outstripped his rivals, thanks to a few well chosen words. 'If you want a saint,' he said, 'take Cotti; if you want a statesman, take Aldobrandini; but if you want an honest fellow, take me.' It was a timely piece of modesty; beneath the appearance of an 'honest fellow', a ready friend of punsters and wits, Benedict XIV concealed a clear intelligence, a good training in Canon Law but awake to every problem, extreme refinement in human relationships and far more energy than some have recognized. His character is particularly interesting because of the rare harmony it achieved between qualities that are seldom found together. A profound believer and a living exemplar of piety, he revived the ancient tradition of the Mandatum on Holy Thursday, visited the poor and sick in person, enjoyed conversing with such lofty souls as Brother Leonard of Port Maurice, and devoted a number of official documents to the proper use of the breviary, to the laws of fasting and to mental prayer. At the same time, however, no pope of that age showed himself so realistic or so capable a man of affairs. The phrase 'enlightened despotism' has been used in reference to his administration of the Papal States; and indeed the revival of the port of Ancona was due to him and his French collaborator Mareschal. Some have charged him with a lack of vigour in international politics, of having adopted a too conciliatory attitude; but a more equitable view shows, on the contrary, that Benedict XIV preferred at all times to take his stand on principles and declare the rights of the Church, rather than to involve himself in the game of intrigue from which the Holy See had nothing whatever to gain. Justice forbids us to blame his caution in this respect.

But what we admire in him above all else is his concern with the great contemporary problems raised by the manifold crisis of intellect and conscience. In face of Jansenism he remained firm but kindly, thereby facilitating reconciliation between men of goodwill. Confronted with a host of mutually hostile theological schools, he declared that unless and until the magisterium of the Church has given judgment on any point, complete freedom must be allowed, since charity obliges every man to respect his neighbour's opinion. Himself a scholar and an assiduous reader, he repeated time and again that the Catholic intellect should be as carefully trained and as fully enlightened as that of its adversaries. He founded societies for the study of Roman and Christian antiquity; he patronized the great scholar Muratori, and also Bottari, whose *Roma Sotteranea* (1754) opened up to archaeologists the virgin field of the Catacombs; he protected the Bollandists, enlarged the Vatican Library and founded the *Bibliotheca Orientalis*. He read, fathomed and refuted the philosophers whose names were at that time on the lips of all. Voltaire, with whom he corresponded, admired him even to the point of dedicating his tragedy *Mahomet*, 'a satire on the errors and cruelty of a false prophet, to the Vicar of a God of truth and meekness'; but that did not prevent Benedict XIV, once he had carefully studied the King of Ferney's works, from condemning them outright.

All these facts reveal a man sensitive to the intellectual needs of his age. But he was more than that. Alone of all the pontiffs in the neo-classical period, Benedict XIV realized that mere condemnation of errors is not enough, that Christian doctrine must be set against them not only in its principles but also in its concrete application. He too prepared the way for his successors by resuming the custom of publishing great doctrinal Encyclicals to grapple with the problems raised by modern thought. Such was the magnificent *Vix pervenit* of 1745, in which, dealing with the old theories of the Church on usury, he stated the problem of money in new terms adapted to the economic conditions of the age.

His contemporaries were not blind to Benedict's real greatness. Walpole described him as 'a sovereign without favourites, a pope without nephews, a censor without severity, a scholar without pride'; and one member of the House of Lords publicly declared: 'If he came to London we should all turn papist.' Count de Rivera said that at his death, marvellous to relate, the people spoke no ill of him and Pasquino was silent. Unfortunately the weakness of his successors did not allow the work he had begun to bear all its fruit. In face of the steadily mounting ambitions of the secular powers, of all those more or less enlightened despots who hated the very idea of having a spiritual ruler and judge set over them; in face also of the great intellectual rebellion which seemed to remove Christians farther and farther from the certitudes of their faith, more than a single Pope would have been needed to uphold the rights of the spiritual power and those of Catholic truth. Benedict XIV succumbed to the weight of a task which the times had rendered insupportable.

3. THE SUPPRESSION OF THE SOCIETY OF JESUS

During the two pontificates which followed that of Benedict XIV a single event, whose gravity escaped no one, showed how feeble the Papacy had become under pressure of the Powers and of the so-called philosophical spirit. The Society of Jesus, founded by St Ignatius to provide the head of the Church with a body of men dedicated to his service, was suppressed by the Pope himself at the bidding of secular governments. The whole history of the Papacy can show no other example of such craven cowardice.

The Jesuits had numerous implacable enemies in several quarters. Their extraordinary achievement had sufficed to incur jealousy; more than 23,000 members, 800 residences, 700 colleges and 300 missions were a source of irritation to less flourishing orders and institutes.[6] But their influence was even greater than those figures suggest. In France, Spain, Portugal, Poland and many small states in Germany and Italy they were confessors to the rulers, and in many cases, as at Versailles, controlled the profitable appointment of bishops and abbots. In their colleges they educated the sons of the nobility and of the wealthy middle classes—another means of exerting influence. All the same, they did not neglect the masses, and there were no better missioners. It is therefore not surprising that their enemies were legion. Oratorians, Doctrinarians, Piarists and other congregations objected to their dogmatic theories and to their discipline. The Priests of the Foreign Missions had been on bad terms with them since the affair of the Chinese rites. In Germany the secular clergy accused them, not without reason, of monopolizing the university chairs. At Rome itself some cardinals (e.g. Passionei) were vexed by the sight of them in every department of the Curia. Again, the Jansenists, whose vigilant and often successful enemies the Jesuits had been, awaited the hour of revenge; they more or less controlled the administration, and were supported in France by the Gallicans, as well as by all those who desired that the State should be completely independent of Rome.

Critics, official or otherwise, attacked them at all points; periodically they would rake up certain theories of a few among the more daring Jesuit theologians, according to whom tyrannicide was permissible, i.e. the killing of a sovereign who violated the divine law. More justifiable was the complaint that they engaged in big business through the medium of their *socii*, who were not priests. Above all, however, behind this carefully organized campaign were the atheist philosophers, clearheaded and resolute enemies of the Church, who objected to them merely as stout defenders of the Pope, 'advance guards of the court of Rome', as Frederick II described them. 'Once we have destroyed the Jesuits', wrote Voltaire, 'we shall have the game in our hands.' To which d'Alembert added: 'The rest are nothing but Cossacks and Pandours, who will never stand firm against our disciplined troops.'

The drama began in Portugal. Strangely enough, it began soon after Benedict XIV had conferred the style 'Most Faithful' upon the Portuguese monarch (1748). By no means faithful to religion, on the other hand, was Sebastian de Carvalho e Mello, Marquis of Pombal, the prime minister chosen by a weakling ruler, Joseph Emmanuel I (1750–73). Pombal, a remarkable man in many ways, had been trained at London, in the most advanced philosophical circles; and he had returned, if not an atheist, at least a Voltairean and resolutely anticlerical. One cannot find fault with his determination to reorganize the declining Portuguese kingdom by applying methods known elsewhere as 'enlightened despotism'. But he considered that nothing of the sort could be done until he had broken the power of the Church, domesticated the clergy and popularized the new ideas. No opportunity was lost to stir up trouble—the tax paid every fifteenth year by the universities to Rome, the activities of vicars-apostolic in the East, the Holy See's delay in conferring the red hat upon the Nuncio at Lisbon. The confessors of the king and his household were Jesuits, and they spoke about these matters to their penitents; Pombal came to hear of it and had them dismissed. The sons of St Ignatius were removed from the list of cathedral preachers. At that juncture a sort of peasants' revolt broke out among the vine-dressers who were paid starvation wages by the Society of the Upper Douro; five hundred people were arrested, of whom seventeen were condemned to death, and it was rumoured that certain Jesuits had publicly sided with the rioters.

Trouble came to a head with the so-called War of the Guaranis. In Uruguay and Paraguay, as we have seen,[7] the Jesuits had carried out their missionary task by settling Indian converts in those celebrated Reductions, which were nothing less than small republics administered by themselves and *de facto* independent of the secular authorities. Now a treaty of delimitation, signed by Spain and Portugal in 1754, provided for the transfer to Portuguese control of several Reductions containing about thirty thousand Indians. When the officials from Lisbon sought to take possession of these new districts they met with ferocious resistance. In many places the natives, rather than yield, practised a scorched-earth strategy. Pombal was furious. He had a manifesto drawn up by some professional pamphleteers, accusing the Society of having fomented rebellion in order to safeguard the enormous riches it was alleged to possess in America, and he asked Benedict XIV to hold an inquiry. Believing he could settle the affair, the Pope appointed as 'visitor' Cardinal Saldañha, Patriarch of Lisbon, who was in fact—like all his brothers, cousins, nephews and other relations—a creature of Pombal. In less than three weeks, and without even crossing the Atlantic, the strange inquisitor drew up a report hostile to the Jesuits, whom he accused of engaging in questionable transactions, scandalizing the virtuous colonists, and of numerous other misdeeds. Behind the charge of undesirable trafficking, it seems, stood English and Portuguese slavers, whose trade at that time was particularly flourishing and who regarded the Jesuits as too kind towards the 'ebony wood'.

Father Lorenzo Ricci, General of the Jesuits, had already protested against Saldañha's report, though in moderate terms for fear of unleashing a worse storm, when Clement XIII became Pope. Courage and energy were not Clement's outstanding gifts; he kept silence, fearing, as he said, that Pombal might profit by Portugal's close relations with England to imitate Henry VIII and bring about a Lusitanian schism. But on the night of 3rd September 1758, as the king was driving to the home of his mistress, he was fired upon, probably by the lady's husband and brothers. It was a splendid opportunity to accuse the Jesuits. After the earthquake of 1755, which they had had the effrontery to declare an act of divine chastisement, here were these abominable villains blaming it on the king himself. The Jesuit houses were immediately surrounded by the mob, and the Fathers thrown into prison. Some of them remained there for twenty years in horrible conditions; the more fortunate were put aboard ship and landed at Civitavecchia in the Papal States. The Pope, timid as ever, made a feeble protest, whereupon his Nuncio was conducted to the frontier. A few members of the Society, whose speech seemed too forthright, were summoned before a tribunal of the Inquisition, presided over by Pombal's own brother. The most deeply 'involved' of them all, an octogenarian missionary named Malagrida, was sentenced to death and burned alive (1761). Ten years later Clement XIV, urged, it was said, by the Powers who wished to overthrow the Jesuits, conferred the red hat upon the zealous inquisitor Paul Carvalho.

At the time of Father Malagrida's execution the anti-Jesuit storm was blowing just as hard in France; twenty-five theological treatises by members of the Society had been solemnly burned in another 'auto da fé' before the grand staircase of the Parlement de Paris. But in France the affair took a very different course from what it had done in Portugal; unaccompanied by personal violence, it assumed a legal and administrative character for which the French Government was not responsible. In France the whole business seemed to be engineered by Jansenists, especially by Jansenists *parlements*. Circumstances favoured them; suspicious as he was of the *parlements*, the king could not embroil himself with them at a time when the expenses of the Seven Years War were aggravating his financial difficulties month by month. The lawyers who befriended Port-Royal had long awaited the hour of their revenge.

In 1743 Father La Valette, an impetuous southerner with big ideas, went to the Antilles. Appointed procurator of the Jesuit Missions, which were in a very poor way, he managed to set them on their feet once more by organizing a vast undertaking for the sale of colonial products in Europe. Some of his competitors denounced him to Rome, whither he was summoned to explain how a religious, in violation of Canon Law, could indulge in such lucrative enterprises. A number of Parisian Jesuits had already voiced their disapproval, but his clever tongue had enabled him to escape from that dangerous predicament. As it happened Father La Valette and his prosperous dealings were ruined by an epidemic which decimated the Negroes on the plantations, as well as by the enforced surrender of many ships to English pirates. He left a deficit of 2,400,000 *livres*, and his bankruptcy involved that of the import company at Marseilles which sold his products in France. In order to obtain repayment of the million and a half *livres* due to it, the house of Lioney & Gauffre sued the Society of Jesus as collectively responsible. The Jesuits had recourse to the perfectly truthful plea that each of their houses was legally independent of the rest; but judgment went against them.

At that juncture they made a tactical error so appalling that one wonders how an institute renowned for its shrewdness could have been led to do so. Instead of paying up in order to save the reputation of one of its members, the Society appealed. Furthermore it appealed not to the king's Great Council, as it was entitled to do by virtue of the privilege of *committimus*, but to the Parlement de Paris. This was equivalent to walking straight into the lion's mouth; it was done because the Society mistakenly believed that Mme de Pompadour was working against it in revenge for the king's

Jesuit confessor having refused her absolution. At the beginning of May 1761 the Parlement gave judgment: the Society was ordered to pay one and a half million *livres* together with costs and damages.

But before the case was ended the Abbé de Chauvelin, a member of the Grand Chambre and a notorious Jansenist, aggravated the affair. In a violent sermon he denounced the Society's constitutions as contrary to the laws of France, since the members—and even the laymen subject to their influence—placed obedience to the Pope above loyalty to the king. This indictment, in which the orator referred to Ravaillac, the Gunpowder Plot and a recent attempt on the king's life by one Damien, was welcomed alike by Gallicans, Jansenists and philosophers, as well as by many religious orders equally hostile to the Society. The Parlement decided to have the constitutions and theology of the Jesuits examined, and ordered the Society to submit its constitutions for that purpose within three days. Thus a trumpery affair in the courts became overnight a trial of religious policy; it was then that the twenty-five books were condemned to be burned. A judgment was given which would have virtually compelled the Fathers to close all their schools.[8]

It must be said, to his honour, that Louis XV took no hand in the business, and that Mme de Pompadour herself appears to have done nothing against the Jesuits. Choiseul even temporized, refused to order execution of the judgment and appealed to the Assembly of the French Clergy for a considered opinion. Out of fifty-one bishops only one, Mgr Fitzjames of Soissons, a friend of the Jansenists, demanded the suppression of the Society of Jesus. The royal government did even more: it sent to Rome a special envoy in the person of Cardinal Rochechouart, offering to protect the Society if the constitutions were slightly altered to provide for the appointment of a Vicar-General who would be chosen by agreement between the General and the French Government and would control the Jesuits in France. But the General, Father Lorenzo Ricci, rejected outright this interference of a state in the affairs of St Ignatius's Society. 'Sint ut sunt, aut non sint,' he said of the constitutions; 'Let them be as they are, or let them not be.'

They were destined not to be. Despite renewed efforts on the part of Choiseul, the Parlement took the offensive. An enormous work appeared, containing 'all sorts of dangerous and pernicious statements made by the so-called Jesuits'. Many bishops protested, led by Mgr Christophe de Beaumont, Archbishop of Paris. A judgment given on 6th August 1762 decreed the suppression of the Society within the jurisdiction of the Parlement de Paris. The year 1763 was a year of defeat, during which the humiliating Treaty of Paris was signed. It was necessary to increase taxation, but this could not be done without the *parlements*. One after another the provincial courts, excepting those of Flanders, Franche-Comté, Alsace and Artois, adopted the judgment of 1762. The king yielded. On 18th November 1764 the Society was declared abolished in France, and the members were forbidden to live any longer as religious.[9] In vain Clement XIII pulled himself together and issued an Encyclical protesting against that decision; the latter was approved by a large majority of the bishops, but its text, which was not registered by the *parlements*, was unknown to the people of France. The leading Christian kingdom thus rejected the Society of Jesus,[10] and its example was immediately followed by others.

The Family Compact (1761), which linked the Bourbons of France with those of Spain and Italy, operated in this matter, and Catholic Spain, the land of St Ignatius, expelled the Jesuits from her soil. The fact seems hardly credible, especially as twenty years earlier, when an initial offensive was launched against the Society, King Philip V had set up a commission of inquiry which resulted in the Edict of Madrid (1743), altogether favourable to the sons of St Ignatius. Why did his son Carlos III reopen the affair? Though a pious and upright prince, he was extremely authoritarian by temperament and jealous of his power. Moreover it is beyond doubt that in the kingdom of the Catholic Sovereign the Society had incurred a great deal of hostility through its power and influence, as well as through the criticism directed by some of its members against the state of the clergy. A novel by Father de Isla, which was really a merciless satire on the monks, had aroused furious indignation. At least three-quarters of the hierarchy found the Jesuits a nuisance. And so when Count d'Aranda, a friend of Voltaire and a determined anticlerical, took office as president of the Council of Castile (1766) he found no difficulty in staging an all-out offensive against the Society. He warned the king that the Jesuits were hatching a plot to drive him from the throne and replace him with one of his brothers; and a search of Jesuit houses furnished easy proof of the conspiracy, since it had been planted there by the minister's secret agents. At the same time Aranda had his master informed that public opinion was unanimously hostile to the Fathers, and it would therefore be dangerous to oppose it. Carlos III signed the Pragmatic Sanction of 1767, decreeing the dissolution of the Society; the Fathers were arrested at dead of night and put on board ship for Civitavecchia. Unable to land there, they were eventually stranded in Corsica.[11] Voltaire wrote to congratulate Aranda.

At Naples, under little Ferdinand IV, second son of Carlos III, the administration was reminiscent of a comedy, full of theatrical intrigue, clownish disputes and unexpected turns of fortune. The minister Tanucci, completely subservient to orders from Madrid, handled the affair like a very Figaro. The Jesuits were actually accused of having settled in the Kingdom of the Two Sicilies (in 1549!) without written authority, of having poisoned the king's fiancée, and even of having caused the reawakening of Vesuvius! Finally, when news arrived of the suppression of the Jesuits in Spain, four proud Neapolitan regiments (not one less) marched out of barracks as if on the way to manœuvres. Then, about turn—a consummate piece of strategy! They surrounded the buildings which housed a few hundred Jesuits, took them into custody and embarked them for Terracina in the Papal States.

Events took a different course in the grand duchy of Parma-Piacenza, and involved more serious consequences. The domains of the Farnesi, theoretically a fief of the Apostolic See, had been assigned by the treaty of Aix-la-Chapelle (1748) to Philip de Bourbon of Spain, younger son of Philip V and Elizabeth Farnese, who was succeeded in 1765 by young Ferdinand. Rome had not recognized that assignment, upon which she had not been consulted. When the Frenchman Guillaume du Tillot, a friend of Voltaire and Condillac, became prime minister of the grand duchy and decided to

conduct a policy of arrogant independence towards the Holy
See, one of his first acts, with a view to pleasing Versailles
and Madrid, was to arrest and expel one hundred and seventy
Jesuits, most of whom were foreigners teaching in the schools
and the university. At the same time he adopted a number of
anticlerical measures, and the Holy See was at long last
aroused. Clement XIII had taken no steps against Pombal,
Aranda or Tanucci; his Encyclical of 1765 had been a mere
posy laid upon the tomb of the Society. This time he protested, possibly because there was a question of a papal fief
which he hoped to recover. A pontifical edict declared that
the authority of the Bourbons was invalid in the grand duchy.
'The Pope's an idiot,' murmured Choiseul. At all events the
pontifical thunderbolt failed to save the Jesuits, all of whom
were expelled from Parma-Piacenza; but it had even graver
repercussions. Ferdinand, invoking the Family Pact, invited
his relatives at Versailles, Madrid and Naples to help him
break the Pope's resistance. French troops occupied Avignon,
the Neapolitans Benevento; and the four governments agreed
to compel Rome to suppress the Society, which was falsely
accused of having, in the person of its General, instigated the
vexatious declaration.

A further stage in the affair was reached with the death of
Clement XIII, which enabled the Bourbon powers to accomplish their designs. We do not know exactly what occurred
during the long Conclave of more than three months, which
ended on 18th May 1769 with the election of Clement XIV;
but many factors suggest that Cardinal Ganganelli, an aged
and insignificant Franciscan, was not put forward by the
Spanish Cardinal de Solis and the French Cardinal de Bernis
without serious reasons. Both indeed prided themselves upon
having exacted from the future Pope a formal undertaking
to suppress the Society of Jesus before securing his election;
and it must be admitted that the behaviour of the Sovereign
Pontiff renders their claim more than probable.

As soon as he had been crowned, Clement XIV showed
himself remarkably well disposed towards those states which
had persecuted the Society: Pombal's brother received the
red hat, and the decree against Parma-Piacenza was repealed.
The Franciscan Pope's anti-Jesuit sentiments were also re-

flected in a series of small discourtesies—searching of colleges
and suppression of a few, as well as some hints addressed in
public to the General. Nevertheless Clement hesitated, temporized, cavilled. A conference of canonists explained that he
could use his sole authority to suppress the Society; but he
told the ambassadors of Spain, Portugal, Naples, Parma and
France that he would have to humour those states which opposed the suppression, notably Austria, Poland, Genoa and
Venice. Month by month the atmosphere grew heavier at
Rome. Battle was joined between the friends and enemies of
the Society. Bernardina Baruzzi, the visionary of Viterbo who
was consulted by visitors from far-distant parts, declared that
Clement XIV was going to die, punished by Heaven for his
impious project, and that he would be damned. It was asserted that Father Lorenzo Ricci had interviewed the seer.

The arrival in Rome of Moniño (later Count of Florida-
Blanca) as Spanish ambassador brought matters to a head.
Cold, sharp and determined, he won Cardinal de Bernis to his
side and bribed the Pope's *entourage*. At the same moment
the King of Poland lost all his prestige in consequence of the
first partition,[12] while Joseph II, co-regent of Austria, had a
strong influence over his mother, Maria Theresa. Dismayed
by Bernardina Baruzzi's prophecies, scared also by the more
mundane threats of Moniño, the miserable Clement knew
not which way to turn. At last he yielded, and on 8th June
1773 the Brief *Dominus ac Redemptor* suppressed the Society of Jesus. Many people remarked that the text omitted
the traditional words *motu proprio*, and it was rumoured in
the Eternal City that the Pope, stricken with remorse, had
tried to recover his document, but that Moniño had lost no
time in dispatching it to Madrid. At all events measures were
duly taken to give it effect. Bishops were ordered to see that
Jesuit houses were closed; the church of the Gesù at Rome
was confiscated; and the Fathers were everywhere expelled.

'Poor Pope,' exclaimed St Alphonsus de Liguori; 'what
could he do in such difficult circumstances, when all the
Powers were demanding suppression?' Truly a man would
have needed a character of steel to resist that coalition, and
Clement XIV possessed nothing of the kind. There can be
no doubt that he bitterly regretted the decision to which he

had been hounded. Many said that his death in the following
year was due rather to his terrible remorse than to the hideous eczema which invaded his body, or to pneumonia, which
he caught while riding in the rain to the church of the Minerva. The friends of the Jesuits insisted that before dying
he revoked his Brief;[13] but their enemies spread a story that
he had been poisoned by the Jesuits themselves.

Voltaire, on learning of the suppression, laughed loudly
and declared: 'In twenty years there will be nothing left of
the Church.' History would not confirm his prediction, but
none can doubt that the lamentable decision of Clement XIV
struck a fearful blow at the Catholic cause. The unhappy
Pope had doubtless thought thereby to disarm the hostility of
the Powers; but his error was quickly apparent, for it was in
fact the signal for a general offensive against papal authority.
Surely he must have realized the appalling damage his action
would entail: Christian education deprived of eight hundred
colleges and fifteen thousand teachers; the Missions to pagan
lands beheaded at a single stroke; a whole vast army of
Catholic thinkers—that very force which had resisted the errors of Jansenism—become suspect and as it were condemned.
We know that scarcely two years after the death of Clement
XIV Cardinal Antonelli submitted to Pius VI a memoran-
dum condemning the Brief *Dominus ac Redemptor*. But it
was too late; Giovanni Angelo Braschi was not the man to
reopen so difficult a question. The Society of Jesus, the
Pope's finest troops, would no longer be at his side when the
cyclone burst upon his throne and on the Universal Church.
We are told that just before his death Clement XIV uttered
these words: 'I have cut off my right hand.' It was sadly true.

The Society continued to exist only in Russia,[14] where it
was sheltered by Catherine II, and in Prussia, where Frederick II, who had thought of declaring himself its protector,
entrusted the Jesuits with a number of schools. The decree
of suppression was applied differently in different countries:
in Austria with considerable indulgence, in the Catholic cantons of Switzerland scarcely at all. In France, where certain
pious ladies of the royal family dreamed of restoration, a
measure of tolerance prevailed; quite a large number of Jesuits continued to teach. Fifty were destined to mount the

revolutionary scaffold, and when they were beatified Rome was careful to refer to each of them as 'a former member of the Society of Jesus'. In Italy, from 1797 onwards we find a number of 'Fathers of the Faith' who closely resembled the Jesuits.

4. ASSAULTS UPON ROME

The Papacy had become so feeble that it was inevitably exposed to the danger of attack by the Powers, especially in an age when fashionable ideas were urging governments to increase their own authority by curtailing the rights—even the spiritual rights—of Holy Church. During the eighteenth century there was perhaps not one Catholic state that did not quarrel with Rome over matters great or small. André Latreille[15] has done well to point out how mistaken it would be 'to suppose that the Revolution unexpectedly let loose a storm upon a Church that enjoyed peace under the protection of the old dynasties'. The remarkable memoirs of Cardinal Pacca show, on the contrary, that there existed 'a current of militant hostility towards the Papacy (living centre of the Universal Church), which originated in the intellectual and moral crisis of the sixteenth century and whose waters steadily increased throughout the old Europe of monarchies and feudalism before breaking their banks during the Revolution'.

Under Louis XIV, France had overfed that stream, and she continued to swim with it under his successors. Gallicanism, which had provoked the crisis of 1682, had been officially dormant since the end of the Great Reign. Among the bishops it seemed to be disappearing altogether; since 1693 theological schools had not been obliged to teach the Declaration in Four Articles. But it remained vigorous in the *parlements*, where its aggressiveness was fostered by the Jansenist ferment. There were also still some exponents of the doctrine: Honoré de Tournely, Chancellor d'Aguesseau, the great Flemish jurist Z. B. Van Espen and the Oratorian Vivien de la Borde (a manifest disciple of Richer), whose *Témoignage de la vérité* was widely read and applied. The whole century was thus marked by a series of incidents differing as regards their significance but all proclaiming an attitude of mind.

In 1729 Benedict XIII canonized Gregory VII, that great Pope who had subjected the Emperor Henry IV to the humiliation of Canossa. The Parlement de Paris branded the office composed in honour of the new saint as 'prejudicial to the royal authority', and forbade its celebration in France. Cardinal de Fleury, the prime minister, remained silent. The example set by France was followed by the Netherlands and even by Austria.

Enforcement of the Bull *Unigenitus* and, more generally, the whole story of Jansenism in the eighteenth century,[16] enabled the Gallicans or the Parlement to intervene in religious affairs. When the royal ordinance of 1730 enjoined unqualified acceptance of the Bull, Abbé d'Albert, a councillor of the Parlement and evidently more royalist than the king, declared that such a measure 'removed the crown from the monarch's head, and the sceptre from his hand'. One of the most surprising spectacles during the subsequent affair of the *Billets de Confession* was that of secular tribunals—in which moreover a number of clerics sat—declaring themselves, with government approval, competent in such clearly spiritual a matter as refusal of the sacraments.

Ten years later, in 1765, the Assembly of the Clergy, alarmed by the steady encroachment of the secular authority, promulgated the official doctrine of the rights and duties of the State in its relations with the Church; but the Parlement condemned the Acts of the Assembly as tainted with error. The King's Council reversed that decision, only to propound in the following year a theory remarkably like that of the Parlement. The Church, it maintained, was certainly entitled 'to decide by itself what was to be believed and practised', but the State was empowered to authorize or forbid publication of those decisions and to inquire 'whether they conformed to the maxims of the realm'. That was Gallicanism pure and simple, foreshadowing the Civil Constitution of the Clergy and Napoleon's Organic Articles.

The same year witnessed the beginning of an episode which threw into strong relief the French Government's lack of consideration in its dealings with the Church and the Holy

See. A group of Benedictines had requested various alterations in their statutes, and the Assembly of the Clergy resolved to ask the Pope to appoint a committee, the so-called Commission des Réguliers, to decide the matter and others concerning the reorganization of regular orders and institutes.[17] Rome was in no hurry to comply; meanwhile the French Government seized upon this request and determined to set up a committee of its own accord, under the presidency of Loménie de Brienne, Archbishop of Toulouse, a philosopher and Gallican prelate. The bishops as a whole sided with the government, urged by the desire for stricter control over convents where laxity prevailed. An edict of 24th March 1768 settled not only the Benedictine dispute, but many other questions besides. Vows might no longer be taken at the age of sixteen, but at twenty-one by men and at eighteen by women—an excellent means, said d'Alembert, of drying up the flow of vocations. Congregations were forbidden to have more than two establishments at Paris, or more than one in provincial cities. Every house that did not contain a minimum number of religious, varying from nine to fifteen, was to close. Clement XIII protested in vain. Within a period of fifteen years four hundred religious houses were suppressed in France; nine congregations, including the Servites, Antonines and Celestines, disappeared. In 1784, when the bishops, disturbed by these results, asked for and obtained the suppression of the Commission des Réguliers, the number of religious had decreased by one-third. 'Philosophy', already victorious over the Jesuits, had won yet another victory.

It was not, however, from France that the most violent attacks were launched. 'In Germany', says Georges Goyau, 'the dream of all sovereigns, even of those who were Catholics, was to make themselves popes in their own dominions.' Erastus, it will be remembered, was a German, and it was on German soil that Erastianism spread, attempting to justify domination of the spiritual by the temporal. Moreover, despite the concordat of 1648, relations between the Holy See and the German Church were not invariably good. The episcopate frequently complained of interference by the Roman Curia; the one hundred and two grievances formulated by the German nation at the Diet of Nuremberg (1523) had not been forgotten. Weakened in the seventeenth century by the menace of Protestantism, the Church in Germany suffered further through the animosity against Rome which reappeared in the eighteenth. Again the prince-archbishops, more anxious than ever to be local popes, favoured the growth of Febronianism, an astonishing doctrine rather like that of Marsilio,[18] which if it had triumphed would have made the State sole guarantor of dogma, reducing priests to the status of mere moralists and the Pope to that of a master of ceremonies.

Justinius Febronius was the pseudonym of Nicholas von Hontheim (1701–90), a brilliant prelate who had studied first under Van Espen at the University of Louvain, then at the German College in Rome, and had finally been appointed coadjutor to the Prince-Archbishop Elector of Trier. Incidentally, he had adopted the pseudonym out of affection for his cousin, a canoness whose names in religion were Justinia Febronia. In 1763 there was published at Frankfurt his *De Statu Ecclesiae*, of which one may say that it was Rousseau's *Contrat Social* applied to the Church. According to Febronius, authority within the Church belongs primarily to the community of the faithful (*ecclesia*), which possesses the power of the keys conferred by Christ. The Pope therefore has no right of jurisdiction, but only a primacy of honour. The bishops are delegates of the community; they have the use and usufruct of spiritual power; together they constitute the episcopal body and exercise true sovereignty. The princes, as depositaries of temporal authority, enjoy extensive rights, notably that of reforming the Church and of defending national Churches against immoderate exercise of his authority by the Pope. Febronius considered that the termination of papal abuses would restore Christianity to its original purity and enable dissenters to return to the bosom of the Church. Princes and bishops were ready to welcome such ideas, whether or not they were likely to solve religious differences. Nor was this true of Germany alone; *De Statu Ecclesiae* was translated without delay into French, Italian, Spanish and Portuguese.

Meanwhile there was some lively reaction to this singular book, as the subtitle declared it to be. Numerous treatises and pamphlets were written to refute it—in Germany by Amort, Kleiner and Trautwein; in Italy by Pietro Ballerini, St Alphonsus de Liguori and the Jesuit Francesco Antonio Zaccaria; in France by the learned Abbé Bergier. The Assembly of the French Clergy, learning that Febronius invoked Gallicanism in support of his views, protested indignantly. Though placed on the Index in 1764 by Clement XIII, Febronius's work remained the handbook of all who were hostile to the Papacy; and its author defended himself energetically, knowing that he had plenty of support. When the Pope called upon the German bishops to implement the decision of the Index, they set up a committee at Koblenz with Hontheim himself as president; and its final agenda consisted of thirty grievances against Rome, all of which were taken word for word from the offending book. However, at the earnest request of Pius VI and the insistence of his archbishop, Febronius agreed to publish a retraction of his theories, perhaps more formal than sincere; and he ended his long life at peace with the Church.

But his ideas continued to prosper none the less. Twenty years after the condemnation of *De Statu Ecclesiae* they provoked a serious crisis in the three famous archiepiscopal electorates of Cologne, Trier and Mainz, which had caused the Rhine to be nicknamed 'street of priests'. The three archbishops, princes rather of the Empire than of the Church, were extremely jealous of their authority and behaved cavalierly towards the Pope. They thoroughly approved the theories of Febronius—who, it will be remembered, was coadjutor to one of them, the Archbishop of Trier—and in order to propagate those theories they had founded the University of Bonn, hoping thereby to counteract the ultramontane teaching of Cologne University. Next, Duke Charles Theodore of Bavaria, anxious to remove a number of his subjects from dependence upon foreign bishops, persuaded Rome to establish at Munich a nunciature with which he would be able to discuss ecclesiastical affairs without recourse to the Nuncio at Vienna or Cologne. The three lords of the Rhineland considered themselves affronted and raised howls of indignation, in which they were joined by the Archbishop of Salzburg; but Pius VI refused to abolish the new nunciature. Accordingly, in 1786, the archiepiscopal quartet held a meeting at Ems for the purpose of organizing an out-and-out rebellion. They drew up an elaborate memorial which pretended not only to limit the rights of nuncios to the purely diplomatic field and legally to establish the independence of bishops, but also to introduce reforms touching divine worship, popular devotion, recruitment of the religious orders and so on. This caused a good deal of resistance in their own dioceses. The situation soon became hopelessly confused: nuncio's prelates against bishops' prelates, 'Roman' clergy against 'episcopal' clergy. When the armies of the French Revolution invaded their territories, in 1792, they found these extraordinary princes of the Church in open conflict with the Apostolic See.

5. JOSEPHISM

Such convulsions amounted to very little when compared with the crisis in Austria. It seems incredible that in a state governed by the Catholic dynasty of Hapsburg there should have occurred a religious revolution, a systematic overthrow of all that the Church believed inviolable. But that is exactly what happened. Caesaropapism indeed had been making constant progress there; by the end of the seventeenth century it yielded nothing to the absolutism of Louis XIV. The Emperor Charles VI even had the bishops watched by his police; and he quarrelled so violently with the Archbishop of Prague about measures to be taken against Protestant dissenters that he even spoke of having him arrested.

The situation deteriorated during the eighteenth century for two reasons. First because it was quite clear that the Austrian Church stood in need of reform, administrative as well as moral and spiritual; it was necessary to restore order in badly governed dioceses and in decadent religious houses. On the other hand that necessity furnished a pretext for permanent State intervention, and the State was all too willing to seize its opportunity. Erastian, Gallican, Jansenist and Febronian ideas made rapid progress in the ancient empire of the two-headed eagle.

During the reign of Maria Theresa (1740–80) the remarkable effort to confront the terrible crisis which threatened the Crown, and to reorganize the State, involved some conflict with the Church. The empress was extremely pious, but inclined to Jansenism; so were her confessors and Van Swieten, one of her advisers. Her *entourage* also included such Voltaireans as Kaunitz and such avowed atheists as Cobenzl. Despite the opposition of Cardinal Migazzi, Archbishop of Vienna, certain steps were taken whose significance was clear. Control of the censorship of books was taken from the Jesuits; works condemned by Rome (e.g. Febronius and some Jansenist material) were authorized; the new Council of State prepared to secularize ecclesiastical property and to organize the clergy as a body of civil servants; imperial decrees restricted the foundation of convents and the accretion of goods in mortmain, altered diocesan boundaries, reorganized the programme of religious instruction and limited the rights of bishops over the seminaries; nor might any Bull be published in Austria unless and until it had been endorsed by the government. Behind all these measures there was undoubtedly an overall plan to subject all ecclesiastical affairs to State control. Raustenbrauch, the Benedictine rector of Vienna University, and the learned canonist Valentin Eybel were among the theorists who supported it.

The affair took an even more serious turn with the accession of Maria Theresa's son, Joseph II (1741–90). From his youth a great admirer of Frederick II of Prussia, he had enthusiastically embraced theories which were beginning to be described as 'enlightened despotism'. Those who rallied to these theories were sovereign rulers, or prime ministers acting in their name, who claimed to place the 'lights' of the age, in other words the methods of absolutism, at the service of the new ideas. Decisions taken in high places for the benefit of the various peoples, and without reference to them, would be irresistibly carried out. Frederick II of Prussia, Catherine II of Russia, the ministers Pombal in Portugal, Aranda in Spain, Tillot at Parma and Tanucci at Naples, together with Joseph II himself, were to be the principal representatives of this new tendency. Religious matters would naturally not lie beyond the reach of such zealous despots. 'There is no question',

wrote Voltaire, 'of effecting a revolution as in the days of
Luther and Calvin, but of doing so in the minds of those who
have been born to govern.' Won over to the new ideas, ministers and sovereigns would reform religion as they would
reform everything else—without reference to the Pope.

So long as Maria Theresa lived she managed with great
skill to avoid a conflict with Rome, and her measures, though
they disturbed the Curia, provoked no reaction. But her son
possessed no such skill. Joseph belonged to a class of men at
once muddle-headed and stubborn, dreamy yet intransigent,
from whom one may expect the most surprising decisions. As
a young man, endowed with tireless energy and limitless ambition, he was strongly attracted by 'philosophical' ideas, to
the intense grief of his mother. She nearly fainted when he
told her that he refused to have an official confessor, and
when he declared he would make Philosophy the legislator of
his empire she almost died of apoplexy. A journey to Rome
in the pontificate of Clement XIV completed the ruin of his
respect for Roman ways. 'The cardinals', he used to say, 'surrounded me with the vulgar curiosity we apply to an elephant
or a rhinoceros.' That, however, did not prevent him from
being a sincere and even a devout Catholic. The man was full
of contradictions. Immediately after his accession he began to
fulfil his dream, which was just as contradictory in its notions
as he was in himself.

Josephism, as his system came to be known throughout
Europe, arose from two ideas, one political and the other
spiritual. Rightly preoccupied with the condition of his empire and with the growing menace of his much admired
neighbour, the King of Prussia, Joseph II wished to centralize
his dominions, to create a unified Austrian state, more stable
and more efficiently organized. This led him to regard the
Church as a mere cog in the State machine, and to seek to
eliminate from its institutions and customs all that he considered an impediment to the creation of a modern state. On
the other hand, his 'refurbished Church', emancipated from
Rome and completely subject to the monarch, seemed to
offer a highly effective means of transforming society in accordance with that new 'insight' which Philosophy had conferred upon his believing soul.

This twofold purpose led Joseph II to take certain steps, not all of which were bad, but whose general tendency was to limit as far as possible, and even to abolish, the rights of the Pope. Assisted by such counsellors as Kaunitz and Heinke, as well as by the canonists Raustenbrauch and Eybel, he strove for ten years to create a truly national Church of Austria in which the Pope would retain nothing but remote authority in matters of dogma, without the right to intervene in any matter of discipline or administration. Baron von Heinke actually studied a plan to erect a 'Central Synod' consisting of the Patriarchs of Bohemia and Hungary, the Archbishop of Vienna (who would be advanced to the dignity of patriarch) and a lay official to administer the national Church, manage its property and exercise supreme jurisdiction. Peter the Great's example had not been forgotten.[19] All means of action possessed by the Pope were taken from him: no document from the Holy See might enter Austria without having been endorsed by the government; ecclesiastics were obliged under severe penalties 'to abandon the foolish idea that ministers of religion are subject only to the Pope and not to the civil power'; bishops had to take a special oath to the sovereign, promising to observe all the laws of the State 'without reserve or exception'. A point was ultimately reached when the ecclesiastical authorities could no longer communicate with Rome to obtain a dispensation for marriage, nor a religious superior with his General.

Master of his Church, or believing himself so, Joseph II undertook at the same time to reform it. There followed a series of measures in which we can recognize a curious mingling of clearly 'philosophical' influences with a determination (wholesome in itself) to organize the Austrian Church on more satisfactory lines and to improve its conduct. Austria contained a very large number of religious houses—probably between two and three thousand. But Joseph II had a horror of monks, 'shaven-headed creatures whom the common people worship on bended knee', because, as he said, following Voltaire, 'being useless to the world they cannot be pleasing to God'. A single decree suppressed no fewer than six hundred monasteries, and then another one hundred and sixty-three, not to mention hermitages. Only those monks and nuns were left in peace who were engaged in education and charitable works. Existing dioceses were divided in such a way as to render their administration difficult. The reform already undertaken in this field had proved insufficient, and a number of imperial decrees were not functioning at all; so Joseph used the property confiscated from the suppressed houses to found five General Seminaries, staffed with reliable teachers, where candidates for the priesthood would do their studies. Far in advance of his time, the enlightened despot made residence in the seminaries obligatory, but he also subjected the training of future priests to State control.

Not every feature of this somewhat chaotic task was reprehensible; many of them indeed might deserve admiration but for the fact that they were manifestly and primarily intended to hamstring the Church. When, for example, on one occasion he appointed fifteen hundred carefully chosen priests to found parishes where there were none, or when he struggled against superstitious practices and the sale of indulgences, which had again become widespread, Joseph II was behaving as a good servant of the Church. But his zeal carried him too far; it led him to regulate the calendar of pilgrimages, the number of candles that might be burned before each altar, the sale of pious statues and even the use of certain liturgical formulae. 'My dear brother the Sacristan,' laughed Frederick II. His Majesty's subjects were none the less a little surprised when an imperial ordinance forbade them the use of coffins, which were to be replaced by funeral bags!

It was not, however, this macabre affair that resulted in conflict. Even within the ranks of his own episcopate Joseph II met with strong resistance, especially from Cardinal Migazzi, although some quite worthy bishops, e.g. Mgr Colloredo of Salzburg, sided with the imperial party because of the useful reforms which enlightened despotism was accomplishing. Needless to say, Rome could not accept this calculated dismemberment of her authority. As Pius VI learned of the new 'reformation' decrees, he sent protest after protest; and his Nuncio Garampi spent much of his time delivering them at the Chancellery. In Rome the Austrian ambassador, Cardinal Herzan, who was completely devoted to his master, calmly brushed aside the indignation of the Pope, while Kaunitz, imperturbable, did just as he pleased. After repeated objurgations and threats the Pontiff resolved to go in person, to admonish his beloved son of Austria, and accordingly set out in February 1782. Joseph II, though somewhat uneasy at heart, declared himself highly flattered, and honoured the Pope with every mark of an exterior respect which laid him under no obligation. His legal advisers, with Kaunitz at their head, convinced him that this unwonted visit from the Vicar of Christ proved only that he, the emperor, was the stronger. During an official reception at Vienna the Pope turned upon Kaunitz with these words: 'Prince, you are a very old man, and you have little time in which to alter your ways.' Next day the celebrated minister distributed a spiteful pamphlet by Eybel entitled *What is the Pope?* and purporting to show that the successor of St Peter was merely one bishop among many. At the end of a month Pius VI took his departure, profoundly humiliated and having been compelled to make extensive concessions to the emperor and the Austrian bishops for fear of a schism. 'He has a black eye,' sneered Kaunitz.[20]

Nevertheless the enlightened despot met with fierce resistance from the Catholics of Belgium, who were impatient of Austrian tutelage and strongly objected to Josephism with its system of political centralization, which was hostile to regional liberties. When the despot sought to apply his measures to the Low Countries by nationalizing the seminaries, suppressing the convents and regulating the details of the Mass, Cardinal Frankenberg, Archbishop of Malines, published an energetic *Doctrinal Declaration*, to which the people responded with a veritable insurrection. Josephism therefore entered the year 1789 with dark prospects; at Vienna, Gran and Trier the archbishops were preparing to resist. Joseph II died in 1790 after composing this melancholy epitaph for his tomb: 'Here lies a prince whose intentions were pure, but who had the misfortune to see all his projects fail.' He was, of course, exaggerating; he had succeeded in many respects, even, in a sense, on the religious plane. For the Austrian Church benefited by his reforms, and his system remained in force, almost unaltered, until 1918. But that crisis between the ancient Catholic family of Hapsburg and the Pope was an unhappy augury. It was yet another fissure in the Christian edifice.

Unfortunately it was not the only one of its kind. If a man were to pass in review all the Catholic states on the eve of that cyclone that was to shake the world to its foundations, he would discover many more. Everywhere enlightened despotism took sides against the Papacy, often against the Church, and struck grievous blows at Christianity. In Portugal, Pombal was not only hostile to the Jesuits; he strove to discredit the religious orders in general, to domesticate the clergy and to meddle continuously in matters far removed from civil jurisdiction. He has been said to have held his country for ten years in a state of 'masked schism'. In Spain there had been disputes between the government and Rome ever since the advent of the Bourbon dynasty; tension between Madrid and the Holy See over Cardinal Alberoni, a compatriot and protégé of the queen, had almost resulted in open rupture. The two concordats of 1737 and 1753 had in principle re-established harmony; but Spaniards still complained that Rome exerted too much influence among them. The rise to power of highly 'enlightened' ministers led to a veritable crisis. The entire work of Aranda and Florida-Blanca tended to subject the Church to royal authority. Their policy, in which Gallicanism imported from France intermingled with the new ideas, was to increase the number of benefices at the disposal of the Crown, to limit the jurisdiction of ecclesiastical courts, to abolish the right of asylum, to lay hands on the Church's revenues, to exercise an even stricter control over the Inquisition and to get rid of the Jesuits.

The same tendencies prevailed in the small Italian states. The dynasty of Piedmont-Sardinia, and especially Radicati, one of its most devoted servants, had shown themselves from the beginning of the century upholders of more or less enlightened caesaropapism, claiming the right to nominate bishops and abbots, and resisting the Pope in the management of purely ecclesiastical affairs. At Parma, somewhat later, the minister du Tillot was a zealous partisan of Josephism; he penalized property held in mortmain, with a view to lessening the influence of the clergy, and subjected priests to the authority of a special tribunal. For similar reasons Genoa temporarily broke off relations with the Holy See. At Naples, Tanucci followed a similar plan, which was carried even further in Tuscany under the Grand Duke Leopold, brother of Joseph II. Leopold, an even more enlightened despot, aspired to create a Tuscan Church, independent of Rome, with his friend Scipio Ricci, Bishop of Pistoia, as its spiritual head, but subject to his own supreme authority. In his *Pastoral Instruction*, Ricci allowed to the sovereign thirty-one rights in the religious sphere. The same steps were taken in Tuscany as in Austria, and even more thoroughly. The Synod of Pistoia (1768) did not confine itself to passing measures that bore the stamp of Gallicanism and Febronianism; its members, many of whom were friendly to the Jansenists, moved on to the field of dogma. Here they adopted the theories of Baius, Jansenius and Quesnel; they authorized the use of vernacular in the liturgy; they altered the discipline of the sacraments, including that of marriage, and decided that all religious orders should follow the Rule of St Benedict 'adapted to the way of life followed by the Gentlemen of Port-Royal'. Delighted with what he had achieved, Leopold summoned a Council at Florence to ratify these decisions; but the very first meeting provoked such opposition from the bishops that he had to abandon his purpose. The people too were exasperated by a series of unwelcome decrees whereby the government sought to regulate the smallest details of public worship and private devotion. It was forbidden, for example, to light more than fourteen candles before an altar; all in excess of that number were to be extinguished by the police! It was forbidden to expose relics which the enlightened authorities considered false—among them the Blessed Virgin's girdle, a great favourite with the populace. When an order was given that statues of Our Lady must no longer be adorned with the customary veils, except on solemn feast days, there was an explosion. Riots occurred, particularly in Ricci's diocese of Pistoia-Prato. When Leopold left Florence on his accession to the imperial throne in 1790, his son and successor, Ferdinand III, wisely put an end to the experiment. Four years

later Pius VI resolved at long last to condemn the acts
of Pistoia, and Scipio Ricci himself submitted. Indeed at
that date there was more concern with the presence of French
sans-culottes in Italy than with the number of candles to
be lit.

Assailed thus on all sides in its most indisputable rights,
the Papacy appeared to be mortally wounded. Just then a
curious but most irreverent booklet, entitled *Pape en chemise*,
was going the rounds of Europe. 'Christendom will be happier', it said, 'when the Pope is reduced to the status of
plain Abbé de Saint-Pierre.' That stage had not been reached,
but it was serious enough that such thoughts had found a pen.
As for believing that Christendom would be happier without
a ruler or a guide, that was another matter. Experience allowed room for doubt.

6. EUROPE IN SHREDS

Was the Pope in truth the moral head of Christian peoples
and the guide of nations? The question allowed of only one
answer. Ever since the treaties of Westphalia, the seventeenth
century had shown how little influence was wielded by the
Vicar of Christ in disputes arising from the claims of nation-
states. The eighteenth century completed that eclipse. Rome
was conspicuous by her repeated absence from congresses,
negotiations and treaties. She protested, but in vain. As a
temporal power she could not be compared with those that
led the western world; she counted for nothing in the struggle
for balance of power. As a spiritual force she was no longer
capable of recalling men to the principles which Christianity
should impose on international relations. A great voice had
been silenced, one might have thought, for ever.

In order to judge the contempt with which the Powers
treated the Holy See, it is enough to follow stage by stage the
affairs of Naples, Sicily, Parma and Piacenza. The outbreak
of the War of the Spanish Succession (1700) had placed
Clement XI in an extremely delicate situation. As overlord of
the Two Sicilies, a Spanish possession, he found himself un-
willingly involved in the conflict, and both sides owed him a

grudge. Accordingly, when the treaties of Utrecht and Rad-stadt were negotiated, two papal fiefs were disposed of without even consulting him: the Kingdom of Naples was assigned to the Emperor Charles VI, and Sicily to the new King of Sardinia. Innocent XIII needed all his skill to obtain recognition of his right of investiture. A few years later the question of Parma and Piacenza arose. These were also papal fiefs; but without the least regard for the suzerainty of St Peter, the emperor promised the grand duchy to Don Carlos, son of Elizabeth Farnese. At the Congress of Cambrai, Innocent XIII protested vigorously but in vain; he had to bow to the wishes of the Austrian court. Ten years afterwards, on the death of the last Farnese duke, the transfer to the house of Spain was made without reference to the Holy See. Clement XII refused to recognize the new sovereign, but at the end of another three years he was obliged to give way. During the negotiations at Aix-la-Chapelle, Benedict XIV vainly demanded recognition of his rights; he received no reply. In 1787 even the external sign of the Holy See's overlordship of Naples was abolished: the King of the Two Sicilies notified Rome that he would no longer send the famous white mule with its load of seven thousand golden *scudi*. Pius VI protested, but once more in vain.

Those events were significant. It is of course possible to argue that the question was one of mere archaic survivals and that it was natural for modern states to desire freedom from a suzerainty that had ceased to have any foundation. But this methodical eviction of the Papacy betrayed an attitude of mind. It was not only in order to dispose of papal property that the Powers behaved with such insolence; it was in order to show that they no longer accepted the Pope's advice, still less his arbitration. Monarchs were ready enough to have recourse to him whenever they desired support for their ambitions, as when the ruler of Prussia humbly begged Benedict XIV to recognize his kingly title. But as soon as there was a conflict of interests no one dreamt of appealing to the Pope. If he offered his services—away with him! Thus in 1730, when the Corsican affair began, Clement XII approached Genoa with an offer of mediation only to meet with a humiliating refusal.

Such was the final result of that gradual laicization of politics, whose course we have followed from the fifteenth century onwards. It need hardly be said that the idea of Christendom, of Christian brotherhood, no longer had any meaning. Equally anachronistic was the idea of a crusade. The Turks were now hopelessly decadent; even the Russians were more than a match for them—'one-eyed men fighting the blind', said Frederick II. Indeed the Ottoman Empire already showed signs of breaking up. And so the crusade, that one last means by which the baptized might have been given some semblance of unity, was a thing of the past.

The only link, therefore, between states was the famous policy of equilibrium, which was inaugurated by the treaties of Westphalia and had told against Louis XIV with his bid for European hegemony. France had suffered defeat, but that was no guarantee of peace. As new ambitions emerged, difficulties quickly arose among the victorious allies. While the emperor turned from the crumbling Holy Roman Empire and laboured to strengthen his power in Austria, the Hohenzollern dynasty in northern Germany created a kingdom whose ambition was to unify the whole Germanic world under its own leadership. England, having discovered her maritime and colonial vocation, adopted a policy of shifting continental alliances, which enabled her to outstrip France in Asia and Africa. Russia, still mysterious in the immensity of her plains, already foresaw that she would one day loom large in western affairs.

Nationalism was rampant on all sides and made rapid progress in the second half of the eighteenth century, when the various national literatures rejected the tutelage of France. Herder, Grimm, Winckelmann and soon afterwards Goethe helped the Germanic soul to become conscious of itself, and Frederick II extolled 'the beloved German Fatherland'. The English, through jealousy of the French and the spirit of strife, tended to hold aloof in their singularity and insularity. In order to repel all foreign influences they declared: 'Our trade and manufactures are at stake.' Spaniards lauded the beauty of their tongue, and cried up all things Spanish; even the Jesuit exiles proudly proclaimed their country's right to glory. In Italy itself—Italy, a mere geographical expression—the

national sentiment was voiced by Muratori, Denina and Al-
fieri. 'Italy waits and hopes,' wrote Catherine II. The spirit of
the nineteenth century was everywhere abroad.

A glance at the chronological table will show that war was
endemic throughout that century which is commonly represented as pleasant and easy-going, preoccupied with *fêtes galantes* and intellectual recreation. War broke out over the
Italian question raised by Alberoni, minister of the Parmesan
Farnesi, with Queen Elizabeth Farnese in Spain. It broke out
once more over the Polish succession. It became more widespread when the Austrian succession was disputed, lasting
eight years (1740–8) and ending with a short truce of three
years before starting again as the Seven Years War (1756–
63). There was fighting in France, Germany, Italy and the
Low Countries; there was fighting at sea and in far-distant
colonies. The game of alliances made, unmade, thrown over
and then renewed is sufficient evidence that cynicism was
universal. The major powers played it with profitable audacity; but smaller states began to ask themselves how long their
right to existence would be guaranteed and whether they
were not destined to be swallowed up by their more powerful
neighbours.

Europe as Christendom was dead. What remained of the
grandiose schemes evolved by noble minds for the reconstruction of western unity, the projects of Dubois, Crucé, Sully and
Grotius?[21] There were still men who cherished them and
formed similar designs, but those men recognized the chimerical nature of their ideas. In order to limit the rights of
sovereignty it would have been necessary to impose the sovereignty of law; and who was capable of doing that? Towards the
end of the seventeenth century Leibniz was intoxicated with
the mystic vision of 'catholicity' restored, of a reconciliation
between Protestants and Romans, after which Europe would
undertake to unify the world by raising all peoples to the
standards of her civilization; but in his closing years he realized that his impatient ardour was premature, that his lofty
idealism was powerless against the sottish ambition of vested
interests, and he murmured sadly: 'There are fatalities which
prevent mankind from being happy.' After him, in 1713, the

Abbé de Saint-Pierre's *Projet pour rendre la paix perpetuelle en Europe* suggested a union of all sovereigns in a collective pact, the application of which would be controlled by a 'European Senate' of forty members, a real federal government with headquarters in 'The City of Peace'; but Saint-Pierre failed to state who would guarantee the powers of that Senate and how it would provide for the execution of its orders, as Jean-Jacques Rousseau pointed out when he revived the plan.[22] Wesley and Mably devised equally grandiose schemes, but they too met with the same insurmountable difficulty: upon what was the law to be based? How were personal interests and passions to be brought within the rule of principles? There was no one like St Bernard, Gregory VII or Innocent III to remind the Powers of their weakness and dependence. Human strength, as Leibniz and after him Wesley realized, is inadequate to a task whose fulfilment belongs to God, that God to whom the Abbé de Saint-Pierre allowed no place in his scheme, and whom Bentham and Kant likewise ignored.

What could be substituted for a Christian concept of the world? During the eighteenth century, which saw the triumph of cosmopolitanism, Europe was full of keen intellects, the philosophers and encyclopaedists were in constant correspondence;[23] French was the universal language and a certain identity of views created a harmony of feeling. But only a few men were involved, and Europe as conceived by the philosophers was theoretical, abstract, without influence on international politics. The only man who took a serious interest in the lofty ideas of the Abbé de Saint-Pierre was Rousseau, whom the others ridiculed and opposed. 'Enlightened despots' professed themselves disciples of the philosophers, but they were the first to practice a policy of falsehood and compulsion. Frederick II, after reading the project for universal peace, wrote to Voltaire: 'The thing is most practicable; it lacks nothing but the consent of Europe and a few other such trifles.' *Faustrecht* seemed to him a surer method. Alberoni, another advanced spirit, had already formulated the highly realistic principle of 'cutting up and slicing states and kingdoms as if they were Dutch cheeses'. That rule was soon to be applied.

7. THE FIRST PARTITION OF POLAND

The last quarter of the eighteenth century witnessed one of the most appalling tragedies of European history. In thirty years a very great state was rubbed from the map and divided among its three neighbours. With it there disappeared one of the countries in which Roman Catholicism had its deepest roots, a bastion of the Church in northern Europe. The partition of Poland was perhaps the most sinister crack in an ancient edifice doomed to destruction.

Poland, under the presidency of its kings, had been steadily declining since the death of Sobieski.[24] Lying amid vast plains, without natural frontiers and including large foreign minorities among her population of 17,000,000, Poland more than any other state had need of stability; in fact, however, she was in the grip of anarchy. She had no exchequer and no standing army; her political system was altogether crazy, what with an elective monarchy dependent on the Diet, every member of which was entitled to veto a decision taken by the rest.

Her neighbours, too, especially Prussia and Russia, had often dreamed, as the Sergeant-King put it, of 'cutting the cake'. Preparatory to the execution of that design, Peter the Great and subsequent czars had done all they could to foster disorder and impotence in that unhappy land while their ambassadors behaved almost as 'protectors'. Furthermore the Russians could rely for support on the 'dissenting' Orthodox and Protestants, to whom Catholicism denied all political rights. That dangerous situation lasted until about 1760, despite the efforts of a few far-sighted patriots, among whom was Prince Czartoryski, a zealous advocate of political reform, and Father Ponarski, whose work in the field of morality and education heralded a revival of the national consciousness.

King Augustus III died in 1763. Catherine II had just ascended the throne of Russia; Frederick II was master of Prussia; and France, the traditional ally of Poland, had been defeated in the Seven Years War and was unable to intervene. Prussia and Russia agreed to secure the election of Stanislaus Poniatowski, a young Polish noble and a favourite of Catherine II. He was not lacking in patriotism or intelligence; but he was weak, and, being neck-deep in debt, he depended too much on the Czarina. In order to assure the success of her candidate, Russian troops advanced almost to the gates of Warsaw. That brutal intervention caused a patriotic reaction, and the Diet considered Czartoryski's proposal to abolish the free veto. Repnine, the Russian ambassador, countered by demanding equal rights for the Protestants and members of the Orthodox Church—a move which caused serious dissension among them. As soon as the matter came to the vote, 'arguments were supported by cannon and bayonets', as Frederick II observed, and the Diet deliberated under the supervision of Russian soldiers.

In spite of the prevailing slackness, resistance was organized. A few members of the episcopate were among the most ardent of those who protested; Repnine had the Bishop of Cracow arrested by the grenadiers and escorted into exile at Smolensk. Terrorized, the deputies voted to retain the free veto—that 'jewel of the Constitution' as Repnine described it —and to suppress the laws against Protestants and Orthodox. Russia declared herself Protectress of the laws and guarantor of the liberties of Poland.

The insult was resented by a very large majority of the people. Civil war broke out, led by magnates and bishops, in the name of liberty and the faith. But in those tragic circumstances the Poles were unable to unite. The Jesuits and indeed most of the regular clergy advised their people to rally round King Poniatowski. Some of the nobles and a few bishops supported the confederation formed at Bar, in Podolia, which had no leaders, no effective organization, and which foolishly proclaimed that Poland, once liberated, would re-enact the laws against religious dissenters. Repnine promptly incited the Orthodox to insurrection. That terrible rising is said to have claimed 200,000 victims, and Russian troops went into action against the 'rebel' confederates of Bar.

The tragic turning point was reached. In vain Choiseul sent a French military mission which included Dumouriez, counsellor of the free Poles. In vain he launched a Turkish counter-attack, which was rendered ineffective by the naval defeat of Tchesme. In 1770 Frederick II began the partition of

Poland, for fear of seeing Russia and Austria become too powerful in the event of their agreeing to swallow up pieces of the Turkish Empire. He was clever enough to place Maria Theresa at his mercy by offering her a share in the operation. Two years of diplomatic negotiations were necessary to overcome the scruples of the empress.

At this point a Catholic historian is obliged to ask himself one grave question. Why did the Pope say nothing? Why did he stand mute and impotent, watching the preparations for an act of political butchery? Maria Theresa had scruples: she was horrified by the proposals of the 'two monsters'. 'I do not understand a policy', she wrote, 'which assumes that if two men use their superiority to oppress an innocent party, a third may and ought to perpetrate the same injustice.' She feared 'to lose the honour and respect of Europe'. Could not the Pope, then, have protested loudly against the infamous plot and reminded Maria Theresa of her duties as a Christian queen? A threat of Hapsburg intervention backed by France might have driven off the wild beasts. But the Pope was poor Clement XIV, and he was too busy wondering whether or not to suppress the Society of Jesus. He spoke no word.

At Maria Theresa's side was her son Joseph II, who was not a man to entertain scruples. 'Enough of these jeremiads!' he told his mother. She gave way, and a mere political consideration drew from her these almost incredible words: 'One must know how to submit and not lose one's reputation and integrity before God for a small profit.' A small profit! In other words scruples of conscience must bow before a large profit.

On 25th July 1772 the First Partition of Poland was signed at St Petersburg. The treaty began with an invocation of the Holy Trinity. Catherine II took the larger part of Lithuania, with 1,600,000 subjects. Frederick was satisfied with 700,000 from Polish Prussia, minus Danzig and Thorn. Maria Theresa, for all her wretched scruples received Galicia and the county of Zips with 2,600,000 souls. A year of occupation was needed before the Diet could be persuaded to acquiesce in that dismemberment of the fatherland. As for the deplorable constitution, the victors demanded that it should never be altered, which enabled them twenty years later (1792) to complete their work. The realistic policy had triumphed, the policy devoid of faith and conscience; but Europe would soon discover that 'the system of partition' provided a formidable example.

The partition left Poland proper, the most Catholic part of the country, theoretically intact but in fact uncertain of itself, worried about its future, tormented by the insolence of the Age of Enlightenment and baffled by the ensuing suppression of the Jesuits. An effort to re-awaken the national and Catholic soul of the Polish people was made by a few courageous souls, among them Mgr Grabowski, Prince-Bishop of Varmia, and the Basilian Fathers.

In the regions annexed by Prussia and Austria there was little change; Frederick II was too much a sceptic, Maria Theresa and Joseph II after her too Catholic, to indulge in persecution. But things were very different in the territories assigned to Russia. Despite written promises given by Catherine II, the Russianization of Catholics went on apace. True, the Empress was willing to shelter the Jesuits, but she was resolved to stamp out Catholicism in the Ukraine. The Uniates in particular were subjected to repeated vexation, and the Uniate Church of the Ukraine was gradually disorganized, with the approval of certain bishops, including Mallo of Mohilev. That, however, was a minor consequence of a tragedy whose two decisive acts concluded with Poland's erasure from the map for more than one hundred years.[25]

8. EVERYTHING POINTS TO A GREAT REVOLUTION[26]

It may be asked whether there was no other great Catholic country that afforded disquieting evidence of collapse. One such was France; yes, France, which in the preceding era had embodied in its plenitude the ideal of order, discipline and harmony—France of the neo-classical age. That cannot be denied; France was in the throes of an internal crisis which became more and more grave as the century proceeded. The crisis seemed wholly political; but it involved religion also, despite the evidence of events in Poland. The gravity of the situation was quite plain to a number of clear-sighted minds. In 1753, less than forty years after the death of Louis XIV, these words were written by d'Argenson, Secretary of State for Foreign Affairs: 'Everything points to a great revolution in the fields of religion and government.' Thirty years later, in 1785, the catastrophe appeared so inevitable, and the hour of destiny so close at hand, that the aged Cardinal de Bernis longed to die before the tragedy he predicted could begin.

In the closing years of the Great Reign, it will be remembered,[27] there were some alarming symptoms of disaster, fissures apparent in the mighty edifice. Principles were not at stake; they were still part and parcel of the civil regime, but their application was already disputed. The privileges of certain classes of society were no longer recognized without reserve. Men were troubled by the constant recurrence of war, by governmental extravagance and by the crushing weight of taxation. A few brave and far-sighted people—Vauban, Fénelon and Boisguilbert—had dared to proclaim that some radical reforms were indispensable. But no one had listened to them; attempts had even been made to silence them. New ideas, however, were spreading little by little, undermining the spiritual and moral foundations of the regime. A crisis of conscience stealthily mingled its effects with the latent crisis in political and social life.[28]

After the death of Louis XIV that twofold crisis rapidly became more acute; throughout the eighteenth century its gravity increased until it erupted in the revolution foreseen by d'Argenson. At first glance that result may seem surprising; it is not easy to detect material reasons for the explosion that took place in 1789. France was prosperous as she had seldom been in the course of her history. Between 1715 and 1792 she never once suffered foreign invasion. Once only, in 1720, she experienced the horrors of a great epidemic and even then the plague was confined to Marseilles and its neighbourhood. Her agriculture never ceased to thrive: fallow and waste land steadily gave place to arable. Her industry and commerce, too, were flourishing. It was at this period that her engineers laid down the splendid network of roads which have lasted until today, while many cities benefited by extensive planning of which they still have reason to be proud. A further shining proof of that prosperity is provided by statistics: the population, which had slowly dwindled during the sixteenth century, increased by leaps and bounds, rising from 18,000,000 in 1715 to nearly 27,000,000 in 1789—more than Britain (15,-000,000) and Prussia (9,000,000) combined. As Mathiez rightly observed: 'It was in a highly flourishing, not an exhausted country, that the Revolution broke out.'[29]

But, as the history of other periods shows, it is quite possible for a vigorous and prosperous country to have a weak government and a hopeless political system. France at that time was in the throes of a triple crisis (political, financial and social), the three elements being closely intermingled. Royal power was on the decline; except during the seven years 1726-43, when Cardinal Fleury guided the ship of state, the king's authority was unequal to his duties. The Regency (1715-23) was a time of amiable folly, when it was thought that all problems could be solved by expedients. The personal rule of Louis XV (1743-74), in whom there was no lack of intelligence, gave way to indolence and sceptical indifference; that of Louis XVI (1774-89) lapsed into feebleness. But it is impossible to justify autocrats who could no longer discharge the duties of their position and who no longer had the public good at heart. When the supreme authority was weak, those who enjoyed the privileges of ancient nobility or of new-found wealth became more arrogant; they were far more insufferable towards the end of the regime than in the days of Versailles. Louis XIV would never have allowed the nobles to dominate the throne, or the *parlements* (mere law-courts) to withstand the government. His successors were content to do so, and thereby precluded those reforms which might have remedied the situation by putting an end, for example, to the catastrophic financial deficit.

As always happens under a weak regime, eighteenth-century France had become a tourney-ground of castes and vested interests. This fact assumed increasing gravity with the mounting tide of new ideas. Doctrines were spreading which no longer had anything in common with those upon which the system was based. New principles were proclaimed in such works as Montesquieu's *Esprit des lois* and Rousseau's *Le Contrat social*. Year by year, as the century rolled on, public opinion embraced the new theories with a degree of enthusiasm which by 1770 had become irresistible. Men were less and less ready to obey without dispute any authority that was not founded upon its own merits; less and less willing to tolerate social and financial inequalities which nothing could justify. The situation became tragic: on one side a fossilized regime of unyielding habit and narrow prerogative; on the other, a nation desiring change but wishing to effect it without appeal to violence. The Revolution then was no furious outburst of an unhappy people, but the almost accidental result of a series of errors and misunderstandings imposed on a weak government by stupidity and private interest.

The history of France in the eighteenth century, which it would be useless to rehearse in the present context; is the history of lost opportunities and voluntary surrender. There were plenty of intelligent men who saw clearly what ought to be done, but those who held the reins of power lacked the energy to support them. Thus Machault d'Arnouville failed in his attempt to introduce a fairer system of taxation; thus the triumvirate of Mapeou, Terray and d'Argenson failed in its effort to curtail privileges, especially those of the *parlements*; thus, under Louis XVI, Turgot failed in his vast undertaking to reorganize both the finances and the economy of France. The country remained on its feet as long as it did because it possessed great vitality, because its administrative framework was still reliable, and because an ancient people respectful of tradition does not quickly challenge the established order. Meanwhile, however, the machinery of government was slowly running down; the men responsible for its working knew that if they opposed those in power they would be disowned, and therefore made no attempt to do so. A revolutionary situation was created at a moment when the revolutionary doctrine had just been formulated and when circumstances had produced a body of revolutionary spirits who desired to share power and put an end to privilege. The three factors necessary for a revolution were present together at the end of the reign of Louis XIV, and an explosion was bound to follow.

Observers who prophesied the forthcoming revolution were convinced that it would affect the Church. We have already quoted some words of d'Argenson. Those of Cardinal de Bernis, to which they alluded, are even more significant: 'I am an old man, and I would like to die without witnessing the revolution that threatens the clergy and religion itself.' Notice, he makes no reference to the disaster threatening the social order and the State. In fact the Revolution, which was initially far from hostile to the Church, quickly assumed a markedly anti-religious character under the influence of certain minds and under pressure of events.

A moment's reflection will show that it could not have been otherwise. The Church, let us recall,[30] was part and parcel of the regime, closely linked with monarchical institutions, her pulpit 'back to back with the throne', her bishops nominated by the king and treated too often as senior civil servants, her Gallican clergy more attached no doubt to their temporal lord than to their respected but distant spiritual leader. The Christian faith itself was intimately associated with the absolute monarchy, whose security she guaranteed by recognizing the 'divine right of kings'. It was therefore inevitable that the fissures which occurred in the regime should have repercussions in the Church. Of that the philosophers were well aware, directing their attacks simultaneously against the political and social system and against Catholicism, its doctrine and its institutions. Daniel Mornet[31] does not separate the propagation of 'anti-religious philosophy and that of revolutionary ideas'; he shows that they went hand in hand. What were the philosophers criticizing when they denounced 'fanaticism'? The 'intolerance' of the Church, her claim to impose belief by force and to chastise the body in order to save the soul, or the intervention of the secular arm, which punished spiritual offences with temporal pains? Both together. And in that association the Church was at a disadvantage, for the civil authority gave no effective support to the bastions of faith; on the contrary, it often caused the Church to be blamed for a genuine act of fanaticism which she had not intended. For example, in the painful affair of the Chevalier de La Barre. This young nobleman, aged twenty-one and living at Abbeville, allowed himself to be led astray, says Voltaire, by 'some young madcaps whose wild debauchery ended in public profanation'. A crucifix was desecrated, and an inquiry, conducted in somewhat irregular fashion, led to La Barre's arrest. After a trial in which the partisan passions of a small town enjoyed free play, he was condemned to death by a *secular* tribunal and decapitated. Responsibility for the sentence and execution lay therefore entirely with the magistrates. A number of ecclesiastics actually intervened to save the young fool: his aunt, the Abbess of Willancourt, who gave evidence at the trial, and Mgr de la Motte, Bishop of Amiens, who asked the king for a reprieve. The Nuncio publicly censured the extreme severity of the sentence. On the other hand, La Barre's accomplice Etallonde, who was the real author of the desecration, managed to escape and reach England, thanks to some priests who hid him and enabled him to get away. Nevertheless, the 'La Barre affair' is still cited as evidence of the Church's fanaticism. It is the subject of an exhaustive study by Marc Chassaigne,[32] who shows that Voltaire, so far from taking steps on behalf of the condemned, was terrified when he learned that a copy of his *Dictionnaire philosophique* had been found among the young man's belongings. He referred to the Chevalier as a 'poor fool' and (supreme insult) as 'Polyeucte'. He refrained from writing a word about the affair until long afterwards, when the danger had passed.

The approaching Revolution, then, considered religion and the government, the Church and the monarchy, Christianity and the regime as interdependent. In the eyes of the masses the clergy too often appeared 'as an instrument of royal government, a subservient spiritual police force, while the magistrates posed as friends of the people'. Even matters of faith had assumed a political disguise, and Gallicanism had succeeded in uniting the two disciplines of Church and State, each of which shared the fate of the other. History has shown time and again that the Church gains nothing from too close an association with the established order and temporal institutions. It was not the Church that precipitated the fall of the old regime, which was doomed by its own faults to ultimate destruction; but she was involved in that fall and was seriously wounded, although she managed to survive the disaster.

But how could she have severed her links with a regime from which she derived so many advantages? Men are men, and even when dedicated to the service of God they find it

hard to free themselves from Mammon's yoke. The Church of
France, as first Order of the State, was enormously rich, because she was the largest landowner.[33] Though relatively poor
in certain areas, in others, e.g. Velay, Alsace and Franche-
Comté, she possessed very large tracts of the soil. The sum
total of her realty in the shape of farmland and forest, together with her rents and other income, represented a capital
of about 3,000,000,000 *livres*, to the annual revenues from
which must be added some 250,000,000 *livres*, the fruits of
ecclesiastical taxation, the tithe, which was badly balanced
and seemed oppressive. It is true that the tithe, despite its
name, never rose to a tenth of the payer's income; and it is
also true that the Church had in practice to meet the whole
cost of her charitable and educational undertakings. But the
fact remains that her enormous wealth, constantly increasing,
disquieted and provoked the nation at large, all the more so
because it was free from any sort of control. The clergy in
fact enjoyed the unique privilege of deciding for itself how
much of its revenues it would set aside for the benefit of the
State. That amount was very small—about 417,000 *livres* of
ordinary tithes, and 6,000,000 as a so-called free gift. The
undeniable generosity of many priests did not compensate,
in the public eye, for that immunity, which seemed all the
more unjust because the impecunious State was for ever
pleading poverty and increasing taxation. The obstinacy with
which the Assembly of the Clergy defended the fiscal exemption of clerics, as if it were proof of their sacred character,
helped to create an impression that the Church was unwilling
to see the end of a regime of privilege and that she was one
of its most resolute champions.

Moreover, so far from disowning that regime, the Church
in the eighteenth century fostered it within herself. There
was a highly significant development as regards the choice
of bishops, not only in France but also in Austria and the
whole Germanic world. From the Regency onwards the episcopate was drawn exclusively from the ranks of the nobility,
and even of the higher nobility.[34] Bossuet and Bourdaloue
had argued in vain that membership of a noble family was
not sufficient to make a good shepherd of souls; plebeians no
longer had access to the mitre. D'Aviau, Vicar-General of

Poitiers, was respected by the whole diocese; but when his bishop, Mgr de Saint-Aulaire, suggested his elevation to the episcopate, M. de Marbœuf, minister of benefices, refused on the mistaken grounds that he belonged to nothing better than the gentry. On the eve of the Revolution only one French bishop out of one hundred and thirty-five was a commoner, whereas the greatest families occupied the principal sees—Montmorency at Metz; Rohan at Strasbourg and Cambrai; La Rochefoucauld at Rouen, Beauvais and Saintes; Talleyrand-Périgord at Rheims and Autun; Polignac at Meaux, and Clermont-Tonnerre at Châlons-sur-Marne. Public opinion inevitably associated the ecclesiastical hierarchy with the worst aspects of social inequality. The revolutionaries inevitably obtained a hearing when they declared that it was necessary to overthrow the Church in order to get rid of the old regime. Therein lay one of the most obvious reasons for the disaster expected by Cardinal de Bernis.

9. A REVOLUTIONARY CLERGY?

It may even be asked whether there were not within the Church itself some elements sympathetic to the idea of change, of a revolution perhaps, whose effect would be to destroy the established order. Here we must note the importance of a fact which is too frequently neglected by historians who study the origins of the Revolution, but which was to prove decisive from the religious point of view. I refer to a movement known as Catholic Presbyterianism, which, though it had long existed, first became manifest in the reign of Louis XIV;[35] it was powerfully assisted by Jansenism,[36] but did not vanish when the latter disintegrated. Catholic Presbyterianism showed itself in a latent antagonism between the lower clergy, consisting of rectors, vicars and curates, and the higher clergy, which was too rich and too often full of arrogance and disdain.

This movement arose from two sets of causes. One of them belonged to the practical and wholly temporal order, arising from the material condition of the lower clergy. That condition, however, was variable; we must not think of all French priests of the old regime as akin to those poor creatures whose unhappy lot was deplored by that zealous apostle, Voltaire, 'fighting their wretched parishioners over a sheaf of corn'. The system was the same as it had been at the beginning of the seventeenth century. Generally speaking the parish priest and his curate (whom he paid from his own purse) had to live on the parochial revenues, collecting tithes on the products of field, poultry yard, garden and piggery; and even that was a source of much anxiety and frequent dispute. In a great many cases, too, the revenues were taken by the *curé primitif*,[37] who might even be a bishop, an abbey or a cathedral chapter, with no apostolic duties to fulfil. In that case the acting parish priest was supposed to receive a fixed salary, sufficient upon which to live; it was known as the *portion congrue* ('proper allowance') and amounted (*c.* 1789) to 700 *livres* a year, which would have been adequate.[38] Too often, however, parish priests were not provided with this necessary minimum; it was sometimes reduced to 300, i.e. to near-starvation level, and in such cases the words 'proper allowance' deserved the meaning of 'short commons' customarily assigned to them. Yet that was nothing to the plight of many non-beneficed priests. One figure will indicate the enormity of the abuse: from a total income of 250,000,000 *livres* received by the French Church, only 40,000,000 were assigned to the lower clergy as a whole.

Those material circumstances embittered the characters of many priests in an age when the idea of equality was making progress. But what annoyed the sacerdotal proletariat still more was the contempt in which they were held by the higher clergy and the nobility. The ostentation of prelates added insult to injury. Traditions and customs of unknown origin withheld from clergymen in receipt of the 'proper allowance' those small sops to vanity and marks of esteem which flatter self-respect. If there was to be a ceremonial visit from His Lordship the Bishop the *curé primitif* took precedence, and the *congruiste* sometimes lacked the right even to a seat in the choir. The memoirs of one Norman parish priest describe Monsigneur rattling by in his dandy carriage while he, the poor vicar, 'in order to avoid the horses' hoofs and the insolent coachman's whip', has to flatten himself against the bank,

hat in hand and spattered with mud. The squires were no
more agreeable; many a parish priest was invited to the
manor-house only to be offered dinner in the kitchen. All
these humiliations created a bitterness of feeling worse than
that provoked by financial inequality.

The ground was therefore well prepared for the spread of
doctrines which encouraged the lower clergy to claim their
rights and oppose the hierarchy. About the year 1700, under
the influence of Richer's theories, it was publicly maintained
that originally there was no difference between bishops and
priests; side by side with the Twelve Apostles were there not
seventy-two Disciples upon whom Our Lord Himself had conferred power? The tenth chapter of St Luke and the twentieth
of Acts were there to prove as much. As early as 1700 the
cathedral chapter of Chartres had invited their bishop to
declare the soundness of that theory. Similar ideas were propounded and argued by the sarcastic Abbé Boileau; by Guy
Drapier, parish priest of Saint-Sauveur at Beauvais; by the
two Nicolas Petitpied, uncle and nephew; by the jurist Duguet
and the canonist Nicolas Travers. The Jansenists, after their
separation from the Gallican episcopate by the Bull *Unigenitus* resolutely supported the Presbyterian movement. On the
eve of the Revolution it had an eloquent champion in the
advocate Nicolas Maultrot, a learned canonist who reaffirmed
the divine origin of the jurisdiction belonging to parish priests,
and suggested the establishment of diocesan synods with
which the bishops would have to share their rights. Two of
his works, *Défense des droits du second ordre* and *Juridiction
ordinaire immédiate,* caused a great sensation. Even more
audacious was Adrien le Paige, Bailiff of the Temple, who
spoke of 'a necessary revolution'.

Thus the clergy was profoundly unsettled by a crisis that
could have the most alarming consequences. Throughout the
century there were numerous outbreaks of hostility between
bishops and their priests. In Dauphiné, the Abbé Reymond's
influential *Défense des droits des curés* skilfully combined
the practical demands of the lower clergy for an increase in
the 'proper allowance' with the claims of the spiritual. The
movement passed beyond the borders of France, and 'presbyterian' theses were officially adopted by the Synod of Pis-

toia.[39] In Lorraine, shortly before the Revolution, the Abbé
Grégoire incited clerical opinion; in Provence the parish
priests organized themselves into a kind of trade union, and
their example was followed by their neighbours in Dauphiné.

The symptoms were indeed grave, a proof that the edifice
of the Church was cracking and splitting asunder. The result
became clear when the 'Civil Constitution of the Clergy',
directly inspired by Maultrot's Presbyterian theories, precipitated the schism of the clergy who accepted it.

10. THE CHRISTIAN SOUL IN PERIL

These were dire portents in the Christian sky; but they
were not the only ones, nor even the most serious. It was not
so much the outward structure of the Church that stood in
danger as her soul, the Christian people's soul. When Pius VI
turned his back for a few hours upon those stately ceremonies
he loved so well, and devoted himself to examining the conscience of Christendom, for whose fate he was answerable to
God, his intelligence and clear-sightedness immediately filled
his heart with anguish. On Christmas Eve 1775 he published
the Encyclical *Inscrutabile divinae sapientiae consilium*, certainly the most lucid analysis yet made of the perils to which
the Church was exposed, a document whose only fault lay in
its not being followed by practical decisions. The Pope was
not mistaken: faith had been shaken and irreligion was making rapid strides; morality, and with it the foundations of
Christian society, had become unstable.

It is well at this point to remind ourselves of the crises
which had shaken the Catholic soul for nearly two hundred
years. We have already traced their history, and must now
consider their results. Jansenism was supposed to have been
defeated, but it remained a leaven of discord; even in Italy, as
was clear at the Synod of Pistoia, it not only led many Catholics to disobey and contemn the hierarchical authorities, but
it also drove souls to discouragement or to mockery of religion
by its excessive demands and the violent extremes to which it
often had recourse. The practice of infrequent communion
and the convulsions in the cemetery of Saint-Médard had

been equally, though in different ways, disastrous for the faith.[40] Quietism, less violent and less prolonged, was none the less harmful; as a result of the scandals to which it gave rise, but more so because of the aridity to which it led by way of reaction, the living faith became too often a body of recipes and regulations. It was largely due to those two doctrinal crises that the strong religious current which had watered the Age of Spiritual Grandeur dried up almost completely. Only an intense stirring of pure, ardent and enthusiastic faith could have availed at that moment when every vital truth had been breached and all but overwhelmed.

The satanic revolt of the intellect had steadily progressed for more than two centuries. The stage of mere anticlericalism had been passed; it was against Christianity itself that Voltaire had struggled with such brilliant success. Worse still, after the period 1760–70, his successors went further, regarding his Deism as outmoded and declaring themselves atheists. That age of unrest and hidden peril gives us the impression that the ancient bastion of faith was under attack from all sides. The popes took steps to counter the ideas of the philosophers. Clement XII, Benedict XIV, Clement XIII and Pius VI were not lacking in courage. But their coercive measures were unable to prevent the spread of dangerous theories; the poison proved irresistible—even in Spain, where a regular *cordon sanitaire* was drawn around the frontiers, and even in the Papal States. The rank and file were not deeply affected, but the upper classes were more or less contaminated in every land. Subscribers to the *Encyclopaedia* were potential agnostics, even though they continued to hear Mass as a matter of convention or routine. Unbelief was perhaps less serious inasmuch as it was not always shouted from the roof-tops. But when Prince de Conti, feeling the approach of death, had his door closed against the Archbishop of Paris, who had come to give him the last sacraments, the whole Catholic Church was appalled. It was a sign of the times, a catastrophic sign, especially as that great lord was not alone in his behaviour.

Was Christianity, then, so near to destruction that none talked of its restoration? The eighteenth century was a strange period, full of unrest and anxious seeking disguised as elegant scepticism. Many embraced humanitarian Deism, derived from the teaching of Rousseau, in place of a declining faith. The religion of the Supreme Being, favoured some while later by Maximilien de Robespierre, became a veritable bogus substitute for faith. There were others. That age, in which Illuminism, esotericism and occultism of all kinds were rife, presented an amazing and highly significant spectacle. There was a revival of old doctrines which had lingered in the depths of the western soul for hundreds of years, a new interest in Gnosis and the gnostics, and new thoughts on the bases of scientism; all were present in those strange movements where the charlatan rubbed shoulders with the artless or dissolute thinker. Langlet-Dufresnoy's *Histoire de la philosophie hermétique* (1744) unleashed a wave of such doctrines. Balsamo, who called himself Cagliostro, declared himself immortal and preached the mysteries of Isis. Lavater of Zürich and Weishaupt of Ingolstadt claimed to reveal the secret teaching of Israel and of the true Church: the former proclaimed that he was a reincarnation of Jesus, the second went back to Noah! What was so attractive in the teaching of a Swiss priest named Gassner, who seemed to offer a curious mixture of exorcism and hypnotism, and whom crowds of half-witted people flocked to consult in his presbytery at Coire in Grisons? Swedenborg claimed to have been sent by God in order to reveal the spiritual meaning of the Holy Scripture. His doctrine found favour in certain Protestant circles and also in a number of masonic lodges; in 1787 there were two Swedenborgian lodges at Paris and two at Toulouse. It was likewise in certain German lodges, notably in Bavaria, that Illuminism developed; but the 'magi of Copenhagen' soon came to the rescue. Initiates declared themselves believers and raged against the Encyclopaedists and Voltaire, 'that scribe from the Abyss'; but they taught the doctrine of reincarnation. In Bavaria the more intelligent organized themselves on the lines of a religious order, which actually found its way into the Church. Martinès de Pasqually, the wandering prophet of Montpellier, Toulouse and San Domingo, followed by his disciple Claude de Saint-Martin, introduced similar ideas. 'Martinism' posed as the supreme revelation, the authentic religion of which Christianity is only a caricature. Then there was Friedrich Mesmer (1734–1815),

who in 1773 proposed the use of electromagnetism in order
to cure nervous diseases; he went beyond his role as a healer
and developed theories akin to Illuminism. It may be that
such eccentric pursuits expressed a longing for God, but they
did a great deal of harm to the Church and to Christian faith
itself. Charles Emmanuel Dahlberg, Prince of Erfurt, was
another sign of the times. He welcomed to his court all the
most suspect thinkers, was the friend of visionaries and illu-
minists, as well as of rationalist philosophers, and was also
a freemason. Yet he was appointed Coadjutor of Mainz,
which meant that he would ultimately become archbishop of
the most important see in Germany.

Thus the foundations of Christianity were undermined at
many points, and the results were only too apparent. The
most obvious symptom was a moral crisis so manifest that it
will always be associated with the eighteenth century. That
crisis, however, revealed itself not only in sexual licence; more
serious in a way, and less familiar, than *fêtes galantes* and
'Embarkations for Cythera' was the return to brutishness of
manners. Popular risings were common coin everywhere,
caused by social conditions and the decline of authority; between 1715 and 1781 there were more than thirty in France
alone. Begging, which the seventeenth century had struggled
to suppress, now reappeared; in a country as rich as France,
the Abbé Baudeau estimated in 1765 that there were no fewer
than 3,000,000 destitute men and women. Proof of the low
ebb to which Christian vitality had sunk is provided by the
slowing down of charitable work for the remedy of such evils;
only half as many hospices and hospitals were founded in the
eighteenth century as in the seventeenth, which did not prevent the Encyclopaedists from declaring that the age of charity had given place to the age of humanitarian benevolence.

Another disquieting symptom was the increase of crime.
At Rome, for example, during the pontificate of Clement
XIV, four thousand murders were committed in twelve years
among a population of 160,000 souls, not to mention another
six thousand in the Papal States. Brigandage reappeared in all
countries, particularly in southern Italy, Bohemia, Germany
and France. Organized bands terrorized whole districts, com-
manded often by renegade aristocrats who found hospitality

in the most unlikely places. Mandrin, for example, a bandit from Dauphiné, was arrested in the country house of a counsellor of the Grenoble *parlement*. In 1783 an official in Maine declared that no one dared go out after dark; and at Gaillac in 1789, long before the famous 'Great Fear', a special guard was formed to deal with the brigands.[41] In Swabia and Franconia no road was safe. In Sicily the police recorded, without much surprise, two hundred and thirty-two acts of aggression in a single year.

Less disagreeable, but equally serious as symptoms of moral decline, insincerity and lewdness were rife in high society. The atmosphere of one French aristocrat's house was such that ladies had often to leave the room, while the Duc d'Orléans appeared on the stage and sang songs so ribald that they cannot be printed. The Bishop of Bruges was obliged to issue a pastoral letter denouncing women who bathed stark naked. At Vienna 'street nymphs' crowded the Graben or enlivened with their frolics the shrubberies of the Prater, just as at Paris they enlivened the galleries of the Palais-Royal. At Naples prostitution of both sexes was rampant, and at Venice the Carnival became an orgy. In Spain, Valencia had an evil reputation, and the *hidalgos* liked to call themselves 'good Catholics and bad Christians'.

A study of contemporary art and literature also provides evidence of the abasement of western society. Erotic literature, not always in the shape of a masterpiece, was more than plentiful, from Crébillon the Younger to Diderot's *La Religieuse*, from Voltaire's odious *Pucelle* to the unspeakable romances of the Marquis de Sade, not forgetting the German Lyser and his *Encomium of Polygamy*. Among the most popular artists were Boucher, Greuze and Fragonard. Even in churches the choice of biblical subjects was suggestive—'Lot and his Daughters', 'Bathsheba Bathing', 'Susannah and the Elders'. A glance at Santerre's 'Susannah' in the Louvre makes one think that the sinuous curves of that charming figure were not intended to awaken mystical sentiments. And when Lemoine lay dying he had one of his pictures of the Blessed Virgin burned, considering it no less an obstacle than sin to his salvation.

Still more serious was the break-up of family life. The fact
that comedy depicted so many husbands and wives tolerant
of one another's adulteries was doubtless a reflection of contemporary manners. Conjugal faithfulness and jealousy were
considered bad taste. The learned Father Kolb, a professor at
the seminary of Rottenberg in the Tyrol, found many excuses
for *fornicatio simplex*. In France, as in Austria, jurists laboured to prove that marriage is simply a contract and, like all
contracts, can be broken; Joseph II's legists, and in France,
Talon, Launoy and Le Ridant, all reached this conclusion.
The necessity of regularizing Protestant marriages[42] deprived
the Church of the exclusive control over such matters. Divorce was round the corner.

There we may leave the picture. In every country and on
all sides the ancient edifice of Christian society was falling to
pieces. The neo-classical era at its greatest had witnessed the
success of a determination to hold in check the forces that
were disrupting society; but that era was now manifestly
ended. The neo-classical spirit had become sterile and exhausted, and not in the literary field alone. The entire *ancien
régime*, in the widest sense of that phrase, was called in question—the social and political system which it supported, as
well as the concept of man and of the world which underlay
it. Christianity, so clearly associated with the regime, was
doomed to share in its collapse; would she have the strength
to survive the terrible crisis that impended, and to create a
new order from the ruins of a dead world? That was the question which called for an answer as the first salvoes of the Revolution thundered.

11. EVER-OPEN WOUNDS

The answer to that question was by no means certain, for
all was not well within the bosom of the Church. In order to
confront the danger, she would need to be strong—steadfast in
support of the Holy See and completely faithful to her ideal.
Such, alas, was not the spectacle she afforded. Torn with doctrinal disputes and secular interference and corroded by irreligious philosophies, she was passing through one of those

periods of relapse when the leaven of Christ seems incapable of raising the heavy human lump.

Without wishing to exaggerate their extent, we must recognize that old abuses had returned at every level of the sacerdotal hierarchy. History repeats itself endlessly; the errors we noted about the year 1500, on the eve of the Protestant revolution, recurred now in almost identical form. The old wounds reopened; perhaps they had never really healed.

There were some defects at the very top, on the throne of St Peter, where one might have hoped to find none. Those popes, personally respectable and often edifying, were not always attended by men worthy of themselves. Under Benedict XIII the Carmelite Coscia was believed to put up everything for sale—titles, appointments, influence. The Venetian family Rezzonico had an unsavoury reputation under Clement XIII. Certain nuncios were severely criticized: Bentivoglio at Paris, Acquaviva at Madrid. Under Pius VI there was even a return to the worst form of nepotism, reminiscent of Alexander VI. No sooner was Gian Carlo Braschi elected than the tribe invaded the Sacred Palace. His uncle Bandi received the red hat, so did his nephew Romuald Onesti; his brother Luigi, who became a papal official and married a wealthy heiress, proceeded to speculate on the liquidation of Jesuit property and was thereby enabled to acquire the duchy of Nemi. There was also the rather shady episode of an inheritance, which does little credit to the Pope. Pius VI conferred a favour upon a notorious liar in exchange for a will making him sole legatee; but the man's niece disputed the deed, and the tribunal of the Rota was compelled to decide against the Pope.

The Sacred College, which the seventeenth-century popes had tried to improve, was again the victim of unworthy appointments. One fact deserves special notice: the cardinalate became confined almost exclusively to Italians; they eventually numbered fifty out of seventy, twenty of them born in the Papal States. That, of course, does not explain the lowering of quality, but it does show beyond doubt that the popes, instead of making the Senate of the Church a body representative of her universality, were concerned only with their own *entourage*. Hence the appointment of nephews, uncles and undesirable friends. Coscia was particularly scandalous, but he was not the only one to engage in barefaced trafficking. Many non-Italian creations, too, were equally unsatisfactory. Dubois was given the red hat for purely political reasons. The Abbé de Bernis, who wrote such charming ditties in honour of the ladies, was a friend of Mme de Pompadour; consequently, despite his ordination to the diaconate at the age of forty, he had less than three years to wait for the purple, and as French ambassador at Rome he was the subject of much talk on account of his devotion to a young woman. Again, what persuaded Clement XII to displease Fleury by creating the hardly respectable Tencin cardinal? Even children were once more appointed to the Sacred College: Luis Antonio Jaime de Bourbon Farnese, son of Philip V, received the hat at the age of eight. It is hardly surprising that such princes of the Church were not greatly attached to their dignity; Luis Antonio Jaime abandoned it in order to marry, as a Medici and an Este had done before, and as several others did afterwards. Nor is it surprising that the voice of scandal soon defiled the purple robes so ill deserved. Under pressure of opinion the successors of Benedict XIII sent Cardinal Coscia to languish for years in the Castle of Sant' Angelo, while in France the celebrated 'Affair of the Necklace' placed the ridiculous Cardinal de Rohan in a most awkward situation. Those, it may be said, were exceptions. No doubt; the majority of cardinals did not conform to Saint-Simon's famous portrait of one who 'spent his life in gambling, in good living and in company with the youngest and prettiest women'. But however few there may have been of those scabby sheep, they were far too many.

The episcopate was passing through a similar crisis. Temporal sovereigns reserved to themselves practically all appointments; and if a ruler were not careful in his choice, a diocese might well find an unworthy man at its head. It is indeed remarkable that mediocre bishops formed a minority, but that minority was heavily criticized. The plague of the episcopate was love of worldly goods. The very rich dioceses were objects of shameless competition; the lamentable practice of pluralism was insolently paraded. Thus the Duke of Saxony agreed to become Prince-Bishop of Ratisbon on condition of being at the same time Coadjutor of Liège with right of succession. In France,[43] Cardinal de Polignac collected five abbeys and two priories, while Cardinal de Rohan held four monasteries in addition to his wealthy diocese of Strasbourg. Some bishops lived in almost unbelievable luxury: Rohan kept one hundred and eighty horses in his stables, could lodge seven hundred visitors in his palace and enjoyed an income of 800,000 *livres*, more than a thousand times that received by one of his 'congruist' clergy.

It is understandable that such ostentatious persons were men rather of the world than of the Church. They lived surrounded by a host of young 'vicars-general', all members of distinguished families and with an eye to higher things. Their conduct too often justified the raillery of Saint-Simon. Visiting Germany in the middle of the century, the Abbé de Pradt said of those pastors: 'they behave more like princes than bishops'. And in 1781 a papal legate in the Empire thought the fact that bishops no longer danced a notable improvement in regularity. It need hardly be said that such prelates could not be persuaded to reside in their dioceses; 'they regard the land which God has given them as disagreeable and tedious', observed the sorrowful Archbishop of Vienne, Lefranc de Pompignan. At the court of Louis XV, certainly no home of piety, there were never less than about thirty bishops, and as many at that of Maria Theresa of Austria. They contented themselves with brief sojourns in the cities of their sees, where they nevertheless built splendid mansions; eighteenth-century bishops seem to have had a mania for building. The virtuoso of absenteeism was Cardinal de Polignac. He died in 1741 without ever having set foot in the diocese of Auch, of which he had held the title for twenty years. Worldly bishops, politician-bishops (Loménie de Brienne was their model) and even warrior-bishops, such as Mgr von Gallen, Archbishop of Münster, who fought with distinction against the Dutch—all these types,[44] which were thought to have disappeared, were once more rampant.[45] There was an even worse and hitherto unknown type of irreligious and even atheistic bishop: Jarente of Orléans, whose misconduct was notorious; Talleyrand of Autun, who had kept a mistress ever since his days as a seminarian; Loménie de

Brienne, 'surrounded by a licentious and brilliant court', and so openly 'philosophical' that when he tried to obtain the See of Paris, Louis XVI rejected his application with the remark that 'the Archbishop of Paris must at least believe in God'.

Another scandal was that of the 'courtier-abbés'. Here we have the very root of the evil that was corroding the Church: the lack of true vocation among a large part of the clergy. The custom among noble families of placing in the Church their younger sons, who could not inherit their father's property and had no taste for the army, still prevailed; the Tridentine decrees had proved incapable of preventing it. A boy was marked out for an ecclesiastical title, a girl was for the cloister, without the least attempt to learn whether or not the divine call had echoed in their souls. For some this forced vocation was a tragedy. Thus Charles-Maurice Talleyrand, obliged by his family to take Holy Orders because he was a younger son and lame, confided to one of his fellow students in the seminary: 'They compel me to become an ecclesiastic; they'll regret it.' Happy those who, like Turgot, had the courage to leave. One such was Chateaubriand; provided at the age of twenty with a commandery of the Knights of Malta and duly tonsured, he waited to regain his liberty no longer than it took his hair to grow. Others, 'victims of a state of affairs which drove them into the priesthood, and subject to social pressure which the better among them were ready to endure, were vowed at once to sacrilege and unhappiness'.[46] Those of them who were resigned to their fate or merely cynical used the priesthood to further their careers, for the episcopate could lead to high office in the State. In the seminaries ambitious young men prepared themselves 'not so much to administer the sacraments as to administer provinces'. Numerous also were those who, immediately after ordination, arranged to live at court or to join the *entourage* of some great personage, often moving in disreputable circles. The Abbés Chateauneuf and Chaulieu wrote licentious verses in honour of Lisette and Phyllis, who were certainly not frequent visitors to the confessional, and the Italian Galiani was regarded as 'a champion clown'. Moreover, as we have seen, the 'philosophical' tribe produced another type of abbé, which unscrupulously paraded its irreligion. Such was the Abbé de Boufflers, who publicly declared himself an atheist and was unfrocked.

Priests without a vocation were to be found elsewhere than at court and in intellectual circles. At a lower level there were swarms of rectors, chaplains and non-beneficed clergymen, not to mention sacristans, churchwardens and vergers who wore ecclesiastical dress (to which not all were entitled) and whose behaviour was often reprehensible. Rome was full of such people, more so than Paris, Madrid and Vienna. They idled about town, frequented the antechambers of the rich, looking for employment as tutors, almoners and even less exalted situations. It is significant that on four occasions during the eighteenth century the Pope was obliged to remind tonsured clerics that certain livelihoods were barred to them, including those of lackey and barber.

The parochial clergy were no more deserving of praise.[47] In the first place their numbers were decreasing noticeably, even in Austria, Italy and Spain. We read in the memoirs of a Breton parish priest these words, which might have been written today: 'People are always complaining about the scarcity of priests, and lamenting the fate of parishes almost deserted and abandoned.'[48] The material conditions we have described did not help to solve this problem. Priests were indeed much better trained than at the beginning of the seventeenth century; in France the parochial clergy formed the most reliable element of the Church. Wherever seminaries had been founded their influence had been decisive. But there were not seminaries everywhere; even in France, which was far ahead of other countries in that respect, thirty-one dioceses were without a seminary in 1789, as were more than half those of Italy, where thirty-two were opened in a hundred years. In Spain it was not until the last third of the century that any serious effort was made. Furthermore, it should be noted that attendance at a seminary was not yet obligatory for ordination, and the period of study was extremely varied, ranging from a few weeks to three years. Worse still, the seminaries themselves were passing through a crisis. Those houses, established for the training of first-rate priests, were themselves too frequently prey to worldly seductions. When M. Emery was elected Superior-General of Saint-Sulpice in 1782 he found the seminary in a state that would have caused M. Olier to turn in his grave. Worldliness had reigned in the house ever since 1750, when Cardinal Fleury took rooms at Issy-les-Moulineaux, in the precincts of the seminary, and ministers, great lords and noble ladies made a habit of visiting the place. The young clerics, recruited mainly from the nobility and professional classes, had valets to wait upon them, wore the soutane with a train and had their hair curled. When the new superior undertook to restore discipline he met with resistance that was almost a riot. One night the seminarists let off fireworks at the four corners of the building; one of them (walking in his sleep, it was declared) drove a knife into M. Emery's bed, but he was fortunately not there.[49]

On leaving the seminary, those priests who had a true vocation and wished to devote themselves to souls were faced with another difficulty: how obtain a parish? In most cases that could not be achieved by applying to their own bishops, who usually lacked the right to appoint parish priests. In the diocese of Mans, for example, this was true of 348 out of 443 parishes, and of 217 out of 286 in the diocese of Boulogne. Appointments were in the hands of cathedral chapters, administrators of hospitals, mitred abbots and even laymen;[50] it is easy to imagine the intrigues and even the financial negotiations upon which they depended. The custom moreover was almost universal; it caused utter stagnation and even worse. In Portugal, for instance, concubinage of priests was widespread. In Italy the clergy lived much as did their people, and were equally superstitious; nor did familiarity with ecclesiastical affairs always encourage respect for religion. In Austria and indeed throughout the Empire the parochial clergy clung so resolutely to their creature comforts that they seemed hardly qualified to teach Christian renunciation.

Furthermore, even had those priests been worthy of their calling, they were so numerous that not all could give useful service; the majority were not engaged in pastoral work. The wastage of clerical personnel was perhaps the greatest defect of the Church under the old regime. It would be a serious mistake to think of the clergy at that period in terms of our own day. Priests in the twentieth century, though their zeal no doubt varies from one individual or country to another, do try to fulfil the duties of a pastor, guiding, edifying and instructing their parishioners. Under the old regime, of course, there were in every parish one or two priests whose work was truly pastoral; but side by side with them there existed a whole host of priests who, though attached to the parish, took no part whatever in what we mean by 'parochial ministry'. Out of three hundred priests belonging to the parish of Saint-Sulpice at Paris, only three or four corresponded to our idea of parochial clergy. The rest were concerned exclusively with divine worship, and discharged the duties attaching to the very numerous foundations bequeathed for the souls of the dead. Moreover the celebration of the liturgy required a large body of choristers. High masses, solemn vespers and solemn receptions were everyday occurrences in the wealthy parishes; they were all very well in themselves, but they barred innumerable clerics from parochial work. Among these choral priests were the 'host-bearer', the 'canopy-bearer', the 'bell-bearer', the parish priest's clerk, who attended him during services, and the preacher's clerk. On great feast days, such as Easter and Christmas, they did not even hear confessions, but left the whole work to the parish priest and his curate. Thus an army of clergymen, so impressive when we consider their numbers alone, did not mean that the spiritual life of the faithful derived the least benefit from their presence.

Among the regular clergy the situation was distinctly alarming. No doubt there were exceptions, and we must not speak, as many historians have done, of a general decline of the orders and congregations. The Carthusians, Trappists and Capuchins, for example, and most of the female communities, were unaffected; but even so, far too many religious houses afforded the spectacle of a life far from exemplary and sometimes scandalous. Would all the work done by the reformers over a period of two hundred years, then, prove to have been in vain? The trouble was that the regular institutes still suffered from Commendam and Exemption, two wounds which it had never been possible to heal and which secular governments had taken care to foster. Commendam, whose origins we have already described,[51] continued to increase. A single figure will suffice to show the extent of the evil: in France, just before the drastic reform undertaken by the Commission des Réguliers, which suppressed many houses,[52] seven hundred and eighty out of eight hundred and twenty houses of men were held *in commendam*. The custom had spread to all countries, for kings and princes found it a useful means of paying for services received. Commendatory abbots deprived their communities of at least one-third of their revenues, and M. Emery did not hesitate to call them 'titled thieves'.[53] That, however, was of secondary importance; much more serious was the fact that those alien abbots took no interest in the spiritual life of their monks, let them behave as they liked, would not allow canonical visitations and took no part in the canonical chapters. Nor could any authority intervene, for most communities had long since obtained from the Holy See the privilege of 'exemption', which prevented the bishop from exercising the slightest control and thereby left them with no ruler at all.

The regulars were consequently in a state of partial but disturbing instability. The contrast is striking between the sumptuous exteriors of those eighteenth-century abbeys and the disorderly life within. At Cîteaux, for example, there was built a monumental façade which may still be seen; it is a hundred yards long, and would probably have measured six hundred had it been completed. Magnificent! But the Cistercian Order of the Common Observance was in full decline; its monasteries were empty and its loyalties forgotten. In many other abbeys, too, we find the same sort of 'abbatial palaces', which retain so much charm but were evidently not intended for the practice of asceticism.

Behind these outward appearances the spectacle was distressing. The decrease of vocations was even more marked among the regulars than among the secular clergy. Even allowing for the destructive work of the Commission, that decrease is impressive: between 1770 and 1789 the number of choir monks fell from twenty-six thousand to sixteen thousand two hundred. In the space of one hundred years the number of Benedictines in Europe as a whole was nearly halved. Even in such countries as Spain and Austria, where monastic vocations were still plentiful, the figures show a reduction of 7 per cent in the former and 6 per cent in the latter. Many houses had only a few religious; in 1789, sixty-nine Cistercian communities of the Common Observance consisted of no more than three monks. In many houses, too, the bell continued to ring for Matins, but no one came to church. Enclosure was no longer observed: the monks were free to go out, and laymen free to visit them. Some mitred abbots are said to have entertained dancing girls in the place of honour at their tables. Anarchy was rife. One monk, whose abbot had given him an order, replied: 'Sir, I do not recognize you as my superior.' And it was the twenty-eight Benedictines of Saint-Germain-des-Prés who, by asking for some relaxation of their rule, brought about the Commission des Réguliers. Between the Abbot General of Cîteaux and other abbots of the Order there were countless lawsuits, submitted to the King's Council in defiance of all canonical rules. Even in the mendicant orders, which were free from the ravages of commendam, observance was remarkably poor. Reports of Dominican provincials disclose grave abuses: not all members of the Order lived in its monasteries; friars were becoming less and less obedient to their superiors, and some were downright ill-behaved. It is highly significant that no general chapters of the Order were held between 1700 and 1721, between 1725 and 1746, or between 1747 and 1789. As for the Dominican nuns, their conduct is agreed to have been on the whole somewhat better, but there were unedifying exceptions. One community danced and played cards; others, more numerous, were satisfied with leading indolent lives, without scandal but also without true piety.

It is not surprising in the circumstances that there was little chance of keeping the people's faith alive, that missions were declining in both quantity and quality, that education, which had already been hard hit by the suppression of the Jesuits, sank to a low ebb, and that works of charity, even in Monsieur Vincent's homeland, were enervated. 'If the salt of the earth loses its savour,' said Christ, 'wherewith shall it be salted?'

12. IN THE LIGHT OF THE SCAFFOLD

The picture was dark indeed. The appearance of Christian society and of the Church in the eighteenth century left little room for hope. There seemed only one answer to the question outstanding at the end of Louis XIV's reign. Would Christianity be capable of pervading the world that was striving to be born, of giving shape to the mysterious future that would emerge from the approaching cataclysm? Would the Church have sufficient vitality not only to survive the forthcoming trials, but also to renew herself, re-create herself and effect a new synthesis between her eternal principles and the new form of society? First thoughts suggest a categorical No.

Such, however, was not the reply of history. Hard facts would give the lie to those pessimistic forecasts; the collapse predicted by some did not occur. That Church, so many of whose members we have found untrue to their vocation, underwent the most terrible of ordeals; but, so far from capitulating, she endured with a degree of heroism worthy of her past. Less than twenty years after the death of Voltaire she counted two thousand five hundred martyrs who had truly died for the faith. In 1789 there were too many worldly bishops. There were also those, some of them the very same men, who between 1792 and 1795 perished rather than desert their flocks. There were too many priests without vocation, too many more concerned with augmenting their meagre salaries than with saving souls; but there were also those who, during the Terror, celebrated thousands of clandestine Masses, the two hundred 'chaplains of the guillotine' who dared to minister to the condemned, the priests who refused the oath knowing the risk they ran. In 1789 there were too many religious unfaithful to their vows, too many thoughtless nuns; but there were communities such as that of the Carmelites at Compiègne, who went to execution all together, without a single apostasy. The fierce light of the scaffold permitted no pretence or secret compromise.

Nor was the splendid testimony borne by Holy Church confined to the several grades of her hierarchy. The Christian people, at least in certain of its elements, seemed far removed from the spirit of the Gospel. Nevertheless, when it had to choose between God and the denial of Him, between the Church and her persecutors, they chose without hesitation and not in the way expected by the wiseacres. In vain they were offered a Church without the Pope, founded on the Revolution; in vain the authorities tried to dechristianize manners, customs and even the calendar; in vain it was sought to establish absurd cults of the Goddess Reason or of the Supreme Being. What of those who succumbed to such propaganda: were they numerous? So many men and women remained loyal to the ancient faith that their influence ultimately proved decisive. 'Our revolution has failed in the sphere of religion,' wrote Clarke in 1796; 'France has returned to Roman Catholicism.' And when Bonaparte sought to restore order in the country he was obliged to reconcile the Revolution with the Church, to 'kiss the shoes of an aged soothsayer', as an anonymous lampoon declared. It would have been impossible for him to do otherwise.

The evidence of vitality provided by the Church in France is specially deserving of our notice, because it was hallowed in blood; but France was no solitary witness. The great revolutionary wave engulfed almost the whole of Catholic Europe: the *sans-culottes* made their way into Italy as into Belgium; Napoleon's Old Guard overran both Spain and Austria; but nowhere was the ancient edifice destroyed. On the contrary, at many points it was the Catholics that organized resistance: in Belgium, for example, and above all in Spain, where the clergy rallied their people in defence of national liberty. When the storm had passed, the Church, still firmly on her feet, was seen throughout Europe not only to have survived the ordeal, but even to have benefited, being now less attached to the temporal institutions of the old order and more capable of confronting the future.

This manifold witness of history is significant. It proves that, although certain aspects of the Christian world on the eve of the Revolution were disquieting, they had no foundation in reality. There is always a danger, when considering the state of the Church in a given period, of allowing more importance to the conduct of the wayward sheep, who attract notice, than to the solid worth of all those unnamed men and women whose deeds are unrecorded. The Church in the eighteenth century was not without her faults, and Christian society was indubitably tainted; but what the harsh light of the scaffold showed beyond all denying was that side by side with many faults, with many shortcomings, Christians preserved their loyalties intact.

CHAPTER V

THE REMNANT

1. GOD'S BEGGAR

In one of his reports addressed to the minister Vergennes, the French ambassador, Cardinal de Bernis, thought it worth while to mention a trifling incident that had just occurred in Rome. 'We have had here', he wrote on 30th April 1783, 'since the 16th of this month, in one of the city's churches, a spectacle which edifies some and shocks others. . . .' He himself appears to have been among those who were shocked. The cardinal went on to explain that he was referring to the way in which people were flocking to the grave of a French-born beggar, a louse-ridden wretch who until quite recently could have been seen holding out his battered bowl outside churches and even on the doorstep of the embassy. His Eminence had never thought of him as a kind of saint in a niche. Was it a manœuvre on the part of the Jesuits, anxious for the restoration of their Society; or was it perhaps a show staged by the Jansenists? The ambassador could not make up his mind, but of three things he was certain: the whole affair reeked of fanaticism, it was ridiculous, and it was greatly to be deplored.

The man whose body now lay in the church of Santa Maria del Monte had for several years been a familiar figure in Rome. Some had seen him lying in a hole under a stairway on the Quirinal, curled up like a large dog. Others had come across him in the Colosseum at night, when he left his den and went to sing litanies at the foot of that cross which commemorated the martyrs in the huge arena. Sometimes he had lodged in a lowly hostel for down-and-outs run by a good priest; more often he fed himself on what he could get from dustbins. Who in fact was this beggar, and where did he come from? Some declared that he was one of those Jesuits who had been made destitute by the suppression of their

Society; others thought he had an aristocratic look and must
be the black sheep of his family doing penance. He was commonly said to be a Frenchman, but some put him down as
a Pole.

His appearance was more than remarkable—at first sight
repulsive. No one would have thought his rags had once been
clothes; he stank to heaven, and it was unnecessary to go
close to him in order to see that his chest was covered with
lice. A careful observer, none the less, could detect a strange
and mysterious nobility in his countenance, as if the spirit
of childhood, to which the Kingdom has been promised,
looked forth from those haggard features, from those sunken
eyes, from those restless, half-opened lips. What supernatural
power flowed from him? Many priests had seen him praying
for hours just inside or on the threshold of their churches,
lost in ineffable meditation. Many a layman too, after throwing a few coins into his bowl, had received from him, together
with his thanks, such words as had moved their hearts. Young
people and a number of religious declared that they had
seen him in ecstasy before the Blessed Sacrament, raised
above the ground in defiance of the laws of gravity. Children, it was said, had been cured simply because he took
them by the hand; and he was rumoured to have uttered
strange, prophetic words, foretelling that a terrible fire would
soon devour his homeland, that the abbeys in which he had
once lodged would go up in flames, that the sacred hosts
would be profaned and the priests persecuted.

The hermit of the Colosseum, the beggar of the Forty
Hours, the ecstatic of the Roman churches, bore an ancient
French name: Benedict Joseph Labre. He was born in 1748
at Amettes-en-Artois, in the diocese of Boulogne, son of a
numerous, indeed too numerous, family of poor peasants who,
in order to make ends meet, also ran a small shop selling
groceries and haberdashery. Although he was the eldest,
Benedict was destined for the priesthood under the guidance
of his worthy uncle, the rector of Erin. But even while he
seemed marked out for an untroubled career, in which his
intelligence and application guaranteed his success, his road
took a sudden turn on the threshold of adolescence. Had some
mental illness come upon him? No, his malady was deeper

still: the great hunger that torments predestined souls, hunger for God. He was in the throes of doubt, anguish and self-aversion. In the library of his uncle's presbytery young Benedict read the overwhelming sermons of Father Lejeune,[1] the famous blind Oratorian, in which he discovered the unfathomable misery of man's heart and his own need of a more austere life. He applied for admission first to the Carthusians, then to the Cistercians of the Strict Observance at La Trappe and Sept-Fonts, but without success. Perhaps it was his rustic manner or his sickly looks that worried the priors. At all events he received the same answer in each case: 'My son, it is not to our Order that God is calling you.'

To what, then, was he summoned? The truth at length shone through his unhappiness: God was calling him to a life of utter self-abandonment modelled upon that of Christ, who had not so much as a stone whereon to lay His head; a life of absolute poverty, complete humility and entire self-sacrifice. To be nothing, to possess nothing, to feed on alms, to sleep in any convenient church-porch or cave—that was still not enough; there had always been pilgrims on the roads of Christendom, who led lives of that sort and won respect thereby. Benedict wished for more: to be scorned and rejected by the world, disdained and ill-treated by the very tramps. He gradually reached a state of complete indifference to his outward appearance and even to his personal cleanliness, which disgusted men of nicer sensibilities and earned him nothing but insult and contempt. Only there, in that state of abjection, could he find peace and an end to the anguish which consumed his heart when he thought of his condition as a sinner, never sure of having been forgiven, never certain that he would not fall into the abyss. There seemed no better way of saving his soul than to deliver his body while yet alive to the vermin that would soon devour it in the grave. And so for fifteen years he wandered from one sanctuary or one relic to another: from the Black Virgin of Einsiedeln to the Holy Shroud at Chambéry, from Compostella to Assisi and the Holy House of Loreto. A large rosary around his neck, and on his shoulder a wallet containing a few crusts, a well-thumbed copy of the *Imitation* and two or three equally tattered works on prayer, he trav-

elled on and on, with swollen legs and bleeding feet, often
so exhausted that some kind soul would take pity and give
him shelter in an outhouse. Those years of journeying witnessed many a cruel or touching episode. On one occasion
a priest had him imprisoned, suspecting him of having stolen
a chalice; on another he stopped to help a man who had been
wounded by brigands, and was accused of attempted murder.
Often he was stoned.[2] But he received all those insults with
a smile, as the most precious gift that Christ crucified can
confer upon those whom He loves; and when someone hurled
a flint that struck him and drew blood, he picked it up and
kissed it with love.

Such was the strange personality who died at Rome in
Holy Week, 1783, in a shop whither he had been carried after collapsing in the street. Such was the fascinating figure to
whose tomb at Santa Maria del Monte crowds of people were
now flocking, patricians and plebeians together. A saint?
Once when he chanced to overhear the word—*il santo! il
santo!*—Benedict Labre fled in horror. He a saint? Why, he
knew only too well that he was the most miserable of sinners.
Yet we recognize him as a saint: the most extraordinary saint
of his time, and the most significant as well. This man, who
rejected all that his contemporaries loved most—material comfort, worldly pleasure and intellectual pursuits—must surely
be said to have been raised up by God for the express purpose of teaching the world a lesson. There is a logic of sanctity
of which the history of the Church affords numerous examples; it is as if, at the very moment when humanity betrays its soul, God takes care to appoint a few of His chosen
witnesses to stand as a solemn warning. Sanctity is the antidote to the poisons that are killing us. Thus the Poverello
of Assisi came forward to protest against the tyranny of gold,
as did Monsieur Vincent against the uncontrolled forms of
violence. So too, later on, did Benedict Labre, the Curé d'Ars
and Thérèse of Lisieux against the satanic pride of men. In
the mid eighteenth century, an age of godlessness and self-
indulgence, the beggar of the Colosseum fulfilled this duty
to perfection; in the days of Voltaire and the *Encyclopaedia*
his constant prayer was equivalent to a protest.

No doubt this was not altogether clear to all those who, day and night, swarmed into the church where his body lay, struggling to obtain relics and asking the dead man to work miracles—which he did. But the tempestuous manifestations of popular fervour bore eloquent witness to a mystery ever renewed, the presence of sanctity on earth. During those four holy days in 1783 no service could be held in Santa Maria del Monte, and Christ Himself in the Eucharist gave place to the lowliest of His servants. But that was not only, as Cardinal de Bernis thought, a mere exhibition of fanaticism. It may be that God, by raising up the most paradoxical of saints, the least characteristic of his age, wished to prove that that age was not so lost as it seemed, and that it would once again find itself faithful amid trial and tribulation. 'One supposes that this pious comedy will not quickly end,' concluded the irritable ambassador. It is still in progress.[3]

2. FAITHFUL FRANCE

It is significant that Benedict Labre, the saint who challenged his age, was born in the land of decadent elegance, of irreligious philosophies and dashing romances, in the bosom of a Church whose numerous enemies were conspiring to destroy her and foretelling her early collapse. The mere presence of the saintly beggar was doubtless insufficient to invalidate the distressing evidence of degradation that was plain for all to see; but his existence was one sign, among others, of a different state of affairs. A closer look shows clearly that while the Church in France lay gravely wounded, she was by no means in her last agony, and that on the whole the weight of her errors was less heavy in the scales of destiny than that of her honour.

Officially France was still 'the eldest daughter of the Church'; no Frenchman, from the king to the humblest of his subjects, doubted that. The heir of Louis XIV was still considered, and considered himself, as 'God's Viceroy', whose duty it was to defend the interests of the faith; Louis XV, whose private life was certainly not governed by his religion, took that duty very seriously, and Louis XVI was ready to

assume all the obligations it imposed. Catholicism remained
the religion of the State; other confessions had a *de facto*
but no *de jure* existence; nor was that principle affected even
by the tolerant edict of 1787, which regulated the civil status
of Protestants.

Moreover it was enough to set foot in France to realize that
one was in a Catholic country. The Church there was omnipresent. The traveller was struck by the number of places of
worship that met his eyes wherever he went. As he looked
down from the hill of Montmartre, Paris seemed to bristle
with belfries, as did Lyons from the height of Fourvière.
In small cities the impression was even more startling. At
Tréguier, in Brittany, there were nearly as many religious
edifices as dwelling houses; Gray, in Burgundy, with a population of four thousand, had no fewer than fourteen churches
and twenty-two chapels. Parishes were on average from four
to seven times more numerous than today. For a population
of about 600,000 souls Paris had fifty-two, i.e. three times
as many, proportionately, as in 1900; the city also contained
eleven collegiate churches and thirty-eight convents. In small
provincial cities the parochial situation was even more remarkable: Douai was thought to be in a bad way because it
had only six parishes for twenty thousand faithful, whereas
Cambrai prided itself upon possessing twelve for fifteen thousand. Very few French villages were without their parish
priest, even when they contained only a hundred or so inhabitants.[4]

Everywhere—at street-corners, in public squares and on
bridges—there were crucifixes or statues of saints. At night
flickering lamps kept vigil in their niches at the feet of Our
Lady carved in wood or stone. In the country innumerable
crosses were to be seen wherever four roads met; for missionaries of every order and congregation had adopted the
habit of planting one at the end of their stay in the parish,
as earnest of the good resolutions made. Many of them can
still be seen. There were also numerous oratories, particularly
in the south; their popularity was of Italian and Spanish origin. New laws were read from them. The crucifix was obligatory in every courtroom,[5] as well as in the debating cham-
ber at the city hall; and the aldermen and council had their

bench of honour in the church, which they never failed to occupy on Sundays and solemn festivals.

As it had always been since France was France, the whole individual and social life of Frenchmen was still dominated and controlled by the rules, customs and traditions of the Catholic Church. Nothing in this respect had altered since the Middle Ages. The ordinances of Villers-Cotterêts (1539) and Blois (1579), which entrusted the clergy with the task of registering births, marriages and deaths, were still in force; the Code Louis of 1667 obliged incumbents to deposit a copy of their parish registers at the offices of the bailiwick, but the original remained in the presbytery. The famous edict of 1788, which was intended to decide the thorny problem of the civil status of Protestants,[6] and was stoutly opposed by certain bishops, created an exception to the rule, but did not abolish it. So far as Catholics were concerned the only legal enactments were those registered by the Church.

Again as in the Middle Ages, daily life followed the rhythm of the liturgical calendar, which determined the periods of labour and days of rest; the workers' only days of respite were the Church's holidays of obligation, and some, e.g. the cobbler La Fontaine, complained that they were rather too frequent. Professional organization, even though the guild system had become outmoded, retained its traditionally religious characteristics; the confraternities of craftsmen remained very much alive, and wilful absence from Mass and procession on the holy patron's feast was considered a disgrace. Moreover every ceremony and every important date were obligatory occasions of solemn processions.[7] On 4th May 1789, before the meeting of the States-General, one of the grandest of all passed through the streets of Versailles. The Archbishop of Paris carried the Blessed Sacrament; behind him came the king in his splendid robes, with the queen and all the princes of the blood, followed by the interminable ranks of those representing the three Estates. Once again, on 15th August 1793, the Convention interrupted its labours in order to allow members to walk in the procession in honour of Our Lady's Assumption; so firmly were these customs anchored in French life.

Two great public services were still more or less completely in the hands of the Church and chargeable to her, although there was already a certain tendency to laicize them. I refer to public assistance and education. The philanthropic societies founded towards the end of the eighteenth century, as a reaction against the very idea of Christian 'charity', did not in fact amount to much; and the plans for 'national education' drawn up by La Chalotais, Turgot and Condorcet had not yet emerged from their dusty files in 1789. The truth is that in France under the old regime all children were educated by the Church; the sick, the aged and the orphans who needed care were tended by her alone.

Today, when social security and the various forms of state assistance have developed on so vast a scale, it is hard for us westerners to imagine a system in which no such things existed, in which the whole work of alleviating misery, distress and suffering depended upon charity alone. In proportion to the population there were not many fewer hospitals, hospices and orphanages in the France of 1789 than there are in our day. Religious orders devoted themselves to these tasks with unlimited devotion: Brothers of St John of God, Camillans, Lazarists, Sisters of Charity, Augustinian nuns and other more recent institutions. To go out and provide for the needs of the poor was considered in the most elegant circles an absolute duty for young ladies brought up as Christians. Mme Elisabeth, for example, the saintly sister of Louis XVI, took a regular course of nursing, in order to devote herself more efficiently to the sick. We must also remark that the Church was in large measure responsible for a number of social works and enterprises of public utility. Among these were the relief of unemployment, the opening of extensive building sites, the provision of fire insurance[8] and reserves of food in case of famine. We shall find numerous instances when we come to deal with the bishops of this period, many of whom showed themselves true fathers towards their people, no less generous than capable. It is difficult to say how much of the Church's enormous income was earmarked for such charitable purposes. Certainly one-sixth or one-fifth; to which must be added the still heavier cost of education.

Since the beginning of the seventeenth century much effort

had been expended on the development of education, a most important means of forming Catholics, and it had borne good fruit. The slowing down observable during the eighteenth century had not as yet seriously affected the extraordinary vitality of that work. Primary schools were extremely numerous—twenty-five thousand for thirty-seven thousand parishes, says Taine, and recent studies have proved his figure too small by at least a quarter. Many bishops had taken care that every parish in their dioceses should have a school. Since the death of St John Baptist de la Salle the Little Schools of the good Brothers had multiplied and their methods had been adopted almost everywhere. Girls were provided for by a whole host of teaching orders, many of which were confined to a single diocese, while the Sisters of Charity and St Grignion de Montfort's Daughters of Wisdom had made steady progress. The colleges that we should describe as secondary schools were likewise very numerous (more than nine hundred on the eve of the Revolution), not to mention the junior seminaries. In all these most of the teaching staff were clerics—Jesuits, Oratorians, Piarists or secular priests; and when the Society of Jesus was suppressed one of the main preoccupations of the bishops was to replace the vanished teachers as quickly as possible in order to avoid closing their colleges. The student population too was very large; the figures are in some cases quite remarkable. The college at Billom, in Auvergne, had no fewer than two thousand pupils. Two colleges in the diocese of Coutances, one at Coutances itself and another at Valognes, had fifteen hundred between them. Some parish folk complained that the Church set too much store by intellectual training; agriculture, they said, had need of hands.[9] Voltaire thought much the same: the 'torrent of education' must cease. The same situation prevailed in the sphere of female education. The Ursulines above all, the Visitandines, the Dames de Saint-Maur and many others devoted themselves to the training of young ladies. Some local congregations, too, enjoyed notable success, among them the Sisters of Ernemont, founded at Rouen, who eventually had one hundred houses.[10] As regards higher education, it need hardly be said that the universities providing it remained under strict control by the Church. The Sorbonne still posed as guardian of the faith, as was evident from the Jansenist affair, and in 1789 half the number of its teachers were still clerics. At every level, then, the youth of France was educated by the Church, and even those who afterwards fought against her (Robespierre, for instance) would pay tribute to their former teachers. We may add that adult Frenchmen who retained a taste for culture continued to depend upon the Church; public libraries and reading rooms, which became more and more popular throughout the century, were often episcopal or religious foundations,[11] a fact which, it must be admitted, did not prevent all of them from keeping suspect books on their shelves.

It may be argued that all we have been describing was merely part of the institutional framework within which the French people lived, and had nothing to do with the inner life of souls. It is nevertheless of the highest importance that men led their lives in a Christian setting and were officially obedient to Christian precepts. Fashion, routine, human respect, none of which is praiseworthy in itself, can all help to support the edifice of religion, just as today in proletarian circles they help to undermine it. But one need only read the accounts written by travellers in France during the eighteenth century to realize that it was not simply a question of conformity, but that here was a people whose roots were still profoundly Christian, who practised their religion with genuine fervour and never dreamed of throwing off its yoke. Mrs Cradock, an English Protestant who journeyed about France from 1783 to 1786, afterwards paid tribute to the vitality of the Catholic Church. Everywhere she saw churches full to overflowing, the faithful listening to sermons that lasted much longer than an hour, and gladly attending interminable services whose majesty and splendour delighted her.

Mrs Cradock's testimony was true in all respects. Under the influence of the great neo-classical century the Catholic religion remained purposely solemn and somewhat pompous in appearance. Kneeling before altars overloaded with gilded ornament, men and women loved to watch the progress of splendid liturgical ceremonies. Mrs Cradock attended one such in Notre-Dame, celebrated by the cardinal in presence of sixteen bishops, sixty priests and a vast congregation. It

was also true that those same men and women had a taste
for pulpit-oratory which our contemporaries seem not to experience to the same degree. In 1755, at Aubais in Languedoc,
there was a minor riot because the Lenten preacher delivered
only three sermons a week.[12]

These external aspects, however, do not enable us to pre-
judge the inner life of souls. It was no doubt still full of
vitality. Let us recall the observations of Gabriel Le Bras on
the practice of religion under the old regime.[13] According to
the founder of religious sociology, 'it was never more widespread' in France than between 1660 and the Revolution.
Available statistics confirm that opinion, and none of them
are startling. In the parish of Saint-Nicolas at Coutances,
Easter confessions were so numerous that some people, to
quote the rector, had to wait 'several days outside the con-
fessionals'. At Belley, in Bugey, which had a total population of about four thousand souls, Easter communions exceeded three thousand five hundred. In Brittany one could
have counted those who did not fulfil the Paschal obligation.
At the college of Molsheim, in Alsace, which had about a
thousand pupils, the annual number of communions, which
was seven thousand in 1650, rose to sixty thousand in 1738.
Attendance at Mass on Sundays, if not quite universal, was
extremely general. At the hour of death very few declined
the consolations of religion; those who did so were remembered with a degree of horror that bore eloquent witness to
the common attitude; and indeed the art of dying well, which
we saw to have been so well established at the height of the
neo-classical era, was still widely practised. From this point
of view Louis XV himself might serve as an example. On
the eve of the Revolution, therefore, France appeared from
every point of view to be fundamentally Christian. The sceptical Abbé de Véri recognized as much when he wrote: 'In
the eyes of the common people, not to believe in religion is
to have all the vices and a total lack of honesty.'[14]

The common people? Not alone, but certainly first and
foremost. In order to realize what France was in the eighteenth century, and how deep her Christian roots remained,
it is necessary to conjure up in detail that popular piety, so
humble of heart and so impervious to 'philosophical' argu-

ment, of which many contemporary documents give an account and which still has power to move us. Certain districts remind one of huge monoliths, especially those in which the great seventeenth-century missionaries had laboured—Michel le Nobletz and Father Maunoir in Brittany, St John Eudes and after him St Grignion de Montfort in Normandy, Pierre Fourier in Lorraine, St Francis Régis in Velay and Vivarais. In all those territories the faith was particularly ardent. But one might consider many other provinces and find with Conradt 'that multitude of practices, rites, festivals and fasts' which wove the web of French life; that devotion, and also that Christian solidity of manners, of which so many contemporary memoirs and so much private correspondence furnish the proof. Rétif de la Bretonne, whose *Vie de mon père* describes village ways, emphasizes the great respect in which a family of peasants held the practice of religion. They did not confine themselves to hearing Mass and performing their Easter duties; every evening the father of the family read from Holy Scripture, pausing occasionally to make some brief comment. Prayers followed, and then the children had to recite a page from the diocesan catechism; after which all retired to bed in silence, games and laughter being forbidden after prayers. Next day, at work, the previous night's reading often provided topics of conversation. We cannot venture to guarantee that all French peasants resembled that virtuous paterfamilias, that stern guardian of sound morals, who did not hesitate to thrash his eldest son, grown up though he was, for the least peccadillo; but the Rétif family was not the only one of its kind.

Other ranks of society were very similar. The middle classes, who, as we have seen, were deeply affected by 'philosophical' propaganda, furnished countless examples quite as remarkable. The *livres de raison*, use of which had become widespread during the seventeenth century,[15] are full of notices which prove that Voltaire and his friends had not been at work everywhere. Even in the 'Memorials of Complaint', drawn up by the Third Estate (i.e. chiefly by members of the middle classes) for the meeting of the States-General, we find such words as these: 'If you want to be happy have a clear conscience', or 'Happiness on earth is to be had at the price of fearing God and serving Him'. Some of these good Christian *bourgeois* are better known to us than others through their published memoirs, or their private papers which have been discovered and published. Among them is the saintly jeweller Paul de Halde, who, 'having made a pact with God', bequeathed his entire fortune to the poor. Such also is Antoinette Briselle of Aramon, near Nîmes, who spent all her property in providing dowries for poor girls. Such yet again are the Chaminade family, lower middle-class people from Perigueux, who were careful to record in their *livre de raison* that they closed their shop on Sundays and holidays of obligation, and that they had given four of their thirteen children to the Church.[16] But many others, lost in anonymity and oblivion, led no less virtuous lives.

One of the most notable features of the Church in France on the eve of the Revolution was the vitality of parochial communities. Our own age, which has merely rediscovered the communal link represented by the parish, is far from having forged it. Under the direction of a parish priest, who long remained at its head and was often its very life and soul, the little flock stood together in a brotherhood and intimacy of which we, in the enormous parishes of our great cities, have no idea. The priest knew everything, good and bad, about his parishioners, and he never hesitated when occasion demanded to rebuke one or other of them from the pulpit. He took part in their day-to-day existence, and gave them advice on all sorts of matters which had nothing to do with theology. Laymen, on the other hand, played a part in parochial affairs, in which they were no doubt quite as influential as our Catholic Action movements. What we observed at Saint-Didier-sur-Rochefort about 1640[17] must certainly have been repeated in countless French parishes a hundred years later: laymen had much more say in running the parish than they have now. In many places they formed the *général de la paroisse*, which, like the Peiraeus, was not a man but the entire parochial community. The *général* met in the church or in the cemetery and made important decisions. In some places it elected the curate, and a *général* consisting of women met to choose the midwife. The *général* was summoned by the great bell. As for the church-wardens, who formed the Vestry, they had duties that were not confined to the administration of temporal goods, for it was they who chose the preachers for Advent and Lent. Pious confraternities,[18] which were very numerous and became even more so during the Age of Enlightenment, also played a part in parochial life, arranging for the celebration of Masses, organizing ceremonies and processions.

Thus neither the lower nor the middle classes, in the age of 'King Voltaire', appeared to have deserted the Church. Nor did the nobility, despite its reputation for shameful immorality due to the example given by a few of its members. Here again we need only consult the memoirs of many great lords and the correspondence of many noble ladies. The Duc de Croy, the Prince de Montbarcy, the Marquis de Saint-Chamans, are irrefutable witnesses of a simple, solid and active faith. Mme de Montbarcy was another beautiful soul; she lived in the world like a religious, never forgetting her rank but practising a meticulous asceticism. The Duc de Penthièvre, too, was a profound believer, recording in his diary each occasion on which he received Holy Communion, which was usually once a fortnight. But the Marquis de Castellane, a devotee of the Sacred Heart, was equally fervent; so was the Comte de Ferronays, on whose body a hair shirt was found. The greatest French families included some exemplary Christians: the Aguesseaus, the Aiguillons, the Montyons and countless others. As regards the provincial nobility, whose poverty generally excluded them from the temptations of court life, they showed on the whole an even firmer adherence to Christian principles. Never separating their loyalty to the throne from their Catholic faith, they proved themselves capable of defending both by providing officers for the armies of Vendée.

Surely, moreover, it is in the first of all French families that we find the most outstanding proof of France's continued loyalty. When the race of St Louis was about to vanish after a thousand years into bloody darkness, did it not retain, more fully than a conceited people thinks, the sense of what it owed to the anointing at Rheims? Louis XV's life was often an offence against the Commandments; but when he came to die he repented publicly, confessed his sins and abandoned himself to God like a true Christian. His queen, Maria Leczinska, was so devout that her daughters used to say: 'Mama spends her days even more piously than we were taught to do at the convent.' The king's cousin, the Duc d'Orléans, so different in this respect from his father the regent, always went at least once a year to make a penitential retreat at Sainte-Geneviève. And the first Dauphin, a man of great capacity, whose premature death was to prove disastrous for the regime, brought up his children to love their neighbour and all mankind, gave an unfailing example of true Christian living and died peacefully, declaring that he had 'never been dazzled by the brilliance of the throne' and had always felt himself detached from life and dedicated to God.

From that family of sincere believers there stand out some radiant figures whom the Church has raised to her altars. Great was the astonishment at Versailles when Madame Louise de France (1737–87), seventh and youngest daughter of Louis XV, announced her decision to enter the convent of Saint-Denis, so austere that it was known as the Carmelite La Trappe. But the young princess stood firm. She had been forming her resolution for several years, reading each day the works of St Teresa, studying the Rule and thinking with heartfelt longing of her dearest friends who had been widowed and had taken that same road. The king was overwhelmed when asked for his permission, but declared that he claimed no right to challenge the will of God. Becoming Mother Teresa of St Augustine, Louise begged to be treated on a level with the most obscure of her companions; she accepted the humblest tasks (that of 'third sacristan', for instance), and refused point-blank to have more warmth or better food than the others. And when the king came to see her, as he often did, and used his privilege to enter the enclosure, Mother Teresa made him sit on the straw mattress in her cell, then took him off to divine office and placed him in the stalls. Thus did Blessed Louise of France redeem the sins of her father, and he was well aware of it.

On that mournful day in January 1793 when the Capetian dynasty went to mount the scaffold erected by its subjects, yet another profound believer, the weak though kindly Louis

XVI, showed that if he had not managed to grapple with the forces of history he knew how to face death and God. There were also the charming figures of his two sisters, living proofs of what great and noble things the Catholic faith could still accomplish. Madame Clotilde, queen-consort of Piedmont-Sardinia, set an unfailing example of goodness, charity and self-discipline which the Church has recognized. Madame Elisabeth (1764–1794) agile as a sylph, brisk as a little fairy, but as generous and devout as her sister, enlivened the court of Versailles with her merry graces. Later she wished to join her aunt Louise at Carmel, but could not obtain her brother's permission; she therefore devoted herself to charitable works, founding a body of wet-nurses and a dispensary in her delightful château at Montreuil. We shall find Madame Elisabeth undaunted in peril: she refused to emigrate, and died by guillotine at the age of thirty years.

3. THE CLERGY WILL NOT YIELD

What now of the clergy? It is quite clear that the spiritual vitality manifested by the Church in France would not have been possible unless her official grades also had been reliable —far more reliable than the deplorable features we have described might lead us to think. It is here above all that we must shade the picture and not take as a general rule those aspects which, however numerous and alarming, were none the less exceptional. There is nothing to justify the belief that the French clergy consisted for the most part of worldly bishops, courtier-abbés, immoral parish-priests and religious neglectful of their vows. The unworthy were a small though too clamorous minority.

The episcopate, whose recruitment from among the upper classes has been severely criticized, was by no means bad. The *feuille des bénéfices*, i.e. the list of appointments to episcopal sees, was nearly always in the hands of responsible men anxious to choose well. It is true that Jarente, Bishop of Orleans, an abandoned prelate assisted by a still worse nephew, allowed the royal mistresses a say in such appointments between 1757 and 1771; but Cardinal de Fleury, who was helped in his choice by the superior of Saint-Sulpice, as well as Boyer, who was advised by his friend the saintly Abbé Léger. Lefranc de Pompignan, La Roche-Aymon and Marbœuf all had the highest sense of their duties. Louis XVI took a personal interest in these matters; it was he who had Mgr de Juigné placed at the head of the archdiocese of Paris, a man renowned for his priestly virtues. It has been estimated that of one hundred and thirty-five bishops possessed by France on the eve of the Revolution more than one hundred were beyond reproach. Voltaire himself paid them tribute. 'The body of bishops', he wrote, 'was composed almost entirely of virtuous men who thought and acted in a manner worthy of their birth.'

Those bishops observed the law of residence and never dreamed of deserting their diocese in order to live at Versailles. We know of several who remained in the same see until death, refusing to leave a poor diocese for one more wealthy. Such were Mgr de Galard at Puy, Mgr de Cugnac at Lectoure and Mgr de Quincey at Belley. Others remained faithful to a see for about half a century: Levis, forty-six years at Pamiers; La Rochefoucauld, fifty-three years at Rouen. Nor can we forget the example of Mgr Le Franc de Pompignan, Archbishop of Vienne. Summoned by the king to Paris as Minister of the *Feuille*, he refused to keep his episcopal title or to touch the revenues of his see, since he could no longer administer it effectively.

Episcopal activity in the eighteenth century often achieved social and intellectual results the memory of which still lingers in many dioceses. Some bishops founded colleges or strove to keep open those of the Jesuits when the suppression of the Society jeopardized their existence. Others laid the foundations of what are now municipal libraries. Even more surprising, we find the Bishop of Castres introducing vaccine (it was called inoculation) in order to combat smallpox; the Bishop of Langres establishing among his flock a system of fire insurance; the Bishop of Bayeux, moved by the distress occasioned by unemployment, reviving the lace-making industry in order to provide work for his people; and the Bishop of Arles starting courses in midwifery and child welfare. As for Mgr de La Marche, Bishop of Saint-Pol-de-Léon in Brittany, he took so much trouble to encourage the growing of potatoes that his people's gratitude conferred upon him, in the rugged dialect of Armorica, the title 'Eskop ar patates'.[19] At the time of the great scarcities which ravaged France on several occasions during the years preceding the Revolution, in many dioceses it was the bishops who, more efficient than the secular authorities, grappled with the problem of food control and sometimes quietened the unrest due to famine.

Their efforts were not dictated only by some vague humanitarian 'social sense'; many were animated by the most genuine charity, and of that there are countless proofs. Mgr Christophe de Beaumont of Paris retained no more than 100,-000 *livres* out of an income amounting to 600,000; all the remainder was spent upon charitable and educational works. At Albi, during the floods of 1766, Bernis, who was far from a saint, gave away all that he had and incurred debts of 150,000 *livres* in order to succour the homeless. Nor has Marseilles forgotten the heroism and kindness of Mgr de Belsunce during the great plague that devastated the city; his palace remained open to the sick throughout the epidemic, and his treasury was emptied for the purchase of drugs and other medical supplies. On major festival days Mgr d'Arches of Bayonne used to invite all the city's paupers to his table, and sometimes housed his guests for three successive days. When the good bishop died, his whole fortune consisted of only 90 *livres*. Finally, at Auch, men still talk of Mgr d'Apchon, who rushed into a burning house where no one else dared venture, in order to save a woman and her child.[20]

The personal virtues of many bishops were thus undeniable; some are remembered as downright ascetics. Among the latter were Mgr de Royère, who when alone ate nothing but bread dipped in water, and Mgr de Trémines who lived like a monk. Mgr Berger de Malissoles, Bishop of Gap from 1706 to 1738, was nicknamed 'the saint of the Alps'; but one of his successors, Broue de Vareilles, was his rival and almost his equal. Mgr de la Motte of Amiens, who recited the office daily with his canons, declared in public that he would have loved above all things to have been a Trappist.

All those bishops had the loftiest conception of their duties, as is clear from the writings of Mgr Le Franc de Pompi-

gnan, as well as of the dignity attaching to their state. It must
not be believed that they were all mere courtiers, ready to
do the bidding of authority. Mgr de Beauvais[21] and Mgr
Fumel denounced the misconduct of Louis XV; and one
day when Mgr Christophe de Beaumont, on a visit to Versailles, was invited by the king to go and pay his respects
to Madame de Pompadour, he walked to the window,
pointed to his carriage in the courtyard, and said quietly that
he was ready to start for home at once. Nor can we forget
the generous attitude adopted by Mgr de la Motte in the
terrible affair of the Chevalier de La Barre.[22]

The prelates of the eighteenth century, therefore, were
not mere worldly bishops or mere administrators of dioceses.
A great many of them were actively concerned with the moral
and spiritual life of their flocks, particularly of their priests.
Regular visitations, ecclesiastical conferences, retreats for
priests and diocesan synods had all been perfected in the
seventeenth century, and they continued to be employed as
a means of fostering the spirit of reform. We shall see that
many bishops interested themselves in the layman's missal;
nearly all of them took steps to revise the breviary intended
for the use of the faithful. All this, it must be acknowledged,
affords an image of the episcopate under the old regime very
different from the one now current. As we come to know
them better, we understand more clearly why most of those
blue-blooded bishops showed such courage in face of revolutionary persecution.

If the commonly accepted view of the French episcopate
under the old regime is ill-considered and unjustified, so also
is that of the French priesthood. Side by side with clerics
devoid of vocation, priestlings in search of prebends, and
non-beneficed priests anxious for nothing but Mass stipends,
there were many who fulfilled their sacerdotal task quietly,
honestly and piously. They are little known; there was none
to preserve their memory as Joseph Grandet had done for
their predecessors.[23] And yet what we do know of them at
second hand, through chronicles, memoirs and correspondence, is worthy of admiration.

Let us go back to Rétif de la Bretonne. His pen is usually
considered more suited to scenes of gallantry than to portraits

of holy priests, but with what emotion he speaks to us of those he knew. There was the Abbé Pinard of Nitri in Burgundy, 'indulgent, carrying his soul on his lips, goodness in his eyes, and all his parishioners in his heart'. Another was the writer's own brother, the Abbé Edme Rétif de la Bretonne, parish priest of Courgis, 'helper of the sick, father of all his parishioners'; far from being a 'presbyterianist', he claimed to love his bishop 'as a friend and father', and refused the offer of a wealthy parish in order to remain united with the one he had espoused. Yet another, at Saint-Sulpice in Paris, was Jean-Baptiste Languet de Gergy (cousin of Jean-Joseph, the bishop), to whom Frederick II wrote: 'I know that what distinguishes you is prayer, charity and your tremendous zeal in the conduct of your church.'

We could name many more of such holy French priests, whose solid virtues formed the Church's armour in the sombre hours of the Revolution. In Franche-Comté we find the Venerable Antoine Receveur: moved by the thought of so many souls, even priestly souls, ravaged by 'philosophical' doubt, he organized a centre of spiritual help, from which arose the small Congregation of La Retraite. At Mussidan, Pierre Dubarail and Henri Moze, assisted by Mgr de Prémeaux and the Duc de La Force, embarked on an undertaking similar to that of Receveur and formed a large number of priests in Périgord into the Confraternity of St Charles. In Lorraine, Galland, parish priest of Charmes, worked in the public kitchens he had established; while Blessed Jean-Martin Moye, whose Poor Sisters did untold good, spoke with such vehemence of the people's misery that his bishop was persuaded to allow him to go to China. At Anglet, between Biarritz and Bayonne, Pierre Duhalde was not only a parish priest utterly devoted to his flock and a tireless missionary, but also the founder of a major seminary. His pupil and curate, Daguerre, continued and extended his work, became the bishop's close collaborator and laboured for fifty years not only to revive the fervour of priests, but also to found schools, open houses of retreat and establish a body of diocesan missionaries. He left behind him a host of disciples whose influence was felt far into the nineteenth century. There was indeed hardly a district of France that did not produce one or more of such exemplary priests. A glance at the western parts of the kingdom will discover Father Cormaux, a highly successful missionary who ended his life on the scaffold;[24] the amazing rector of Paramé, who was none other than Father Clorivière, a former Jesuit and one of the leading mystics of his age;[25] René Bérault, parish priest of Baugé, who made a foundation during the Terror;[26] and lastly, among many others, Louis-Marie Baudouin,[27] who was curate of Luçon at the outbreak of the Revolution, and was already laying plans for the foundation of an institute that was afterwards known as the Fathers of Chavagnes. At Paris itself, on the eve of the Revolution, there were numerous holy priests who in the days ahead were to celebrate clandestine Masses and serve as chaplains at the foot of the guillotine. While remembering these little-known priests, we cannot refrain from quoting the tribute paid to them by Tocqueville: 'All things considered and notwithstanding the vices of some of its members, I do not know whether the world has ever seen a body of clergy more remarkable than the Catholic clergy of France at the outbreak of the Revolution, more enlightened or better equipped with public virtues.[28] I began this study of the old society full of prejudice against them; I end it full of respect.'[29]

The above facts were due to a mighty effort on the part of the Church in France during a period of one hundred years, an effort embodied chiefly in the foundation of seminaries. Those generations of priests, better instructed and more deeply spiritual, had been trained in houses established by many dioceses under the influence of Bérulle, St Vincent de Paul, St John Eudes, M. Olier and others. There were now one hundred and thirty dioceses and one hundred and thirty seminaries—a world record. This, of course, does not mean that there was one in each diocese; some dioceses, e.g. Paris, had three, while thirty had none at all. Nor does it mean that the situation was all that could have been desired; recruitment was often linked with money and was therefore not always beyond criticism. An admixture of worldly elements—as we have seen at Saint-Sulpice[30]—sometimes resulted in disorderly behaviour; moreover, since residence in a seminary was not as yet everywhere a *sine qua non* of ordination, its happy effects were by no means universal. Nevertheless there were still men who devoted themselves to the erection of new seminaries, as well as to the reform and reorganization of less fervent establishments, with a degree of courage and magnanimity that would have delighted Jean-Jacques Olier and his rivals. One such was Antoine de Calvet, son of the Treasurer-General of Toulouse. First he established a seminary in the attics of his father's house; then he managed to buy ten houses, one after another, in the neighbourhood of Saint-Germain, and founded the Seminary of St Charles which housed sixty students. Next there was Jean Bonnet, a missionary upon whom Bossuet had conferred the tonsure. Becoming Superior-General of the Lazarists in 1711, he laboured unceasingly to found three seminaries in France, five in Italy and seven in Poland, and even thought of founding one in the Île de Bourbon (now Réunion). Above all there was Monsieur Emery, Jacques-André Emery (1732–1811), whom we have already encountered in the field of apologetics,[31] and whom we shall later find associated with the revival of mysticism,[32] a splendid figure embodying the purest spirit of Saint-Sulpice. Elected Superior-General in 1782, and finding the great Parisian seminary in a worse than sorry state, he managed by his firmness and ability to restore discipline and deepen its spiritual life. During the Revolution, when the Church had been deprived of her leaders on the scaffold or through emigration, he was destined to play a most important part as her 'living conscience', and later, under Napoleon, who respected him, to prepare her re-establishment. It is impossible to praise too highly the work of the French seminaries in the eighteenth century. As late as 1775 the Assembly of the Clergy drew up an admirable monitory on the role of the seminaries and the urgent need of still further foundations. An indirect but well advised and unqualified tribute was paid to the French seminaries by Pope Benedict XIV. Praising the intellectual and moral soundness of the priests of France, he said: 'They are so well trained that when they lay aside their studies and enter the ministry they are able to hold their ground in debate, to write and speak upon the most vital questions.'

We turn now to an aspect of the French clergy under the old regime which official history appears to overlook. It is necessary likewise to reconsider the view commonly taken of the regulars. 'There is scarcely a monastery', wrote Voltaire, 'which is not the home of worthy souls who do honour to our human nature. Too many writers have chosen to look only for the vices and disorders with which those refuges of piety have sometimes been defiled.' A fair judgment, and one for which we may be grateful to its author. The monks and nuns of France may have included a number of black sheep, but the latter were not the majority.

As we have seen,[33] that statement is undeniable in relation to the orders and congregations of women. Among them good behaviour and fervour were the rule; worldliness and frivolity appear only as exceptions. Diderot's shameful work entitled *La Religieuse* has helped posterity to believe calumnies which objective study reduces to nothing. Even in houses recruited from among the nobility and disposing of considerable revenues, it is remarkable to find the religious practising the virtues of renunciation, poverty and humility in their most authentic forms. Think of the Carmel at Saint-Denis in the days of Madame Louise. Mme de Genlis, after spending some months with the Benedictine nuns at Origny-Sainte-Benoîte, wrote: 'In this abbey I have seen nothing but perfect innocence, sincere piety and virtuous example.' Helen Massalska, the future Princesse de Ligne, after a stay at the Abbaye aux Bois, bore identical witness. How many of the eight thousand French enclosed nuns—Carmelites, Poor Clares, Visitandines, Dominicans, Cistercians—were dubious or unfaithful? Certainly very few indeed. The Poor Clares, who were extremely numerous, made a whole series of foundations. New institutes sprang up, among them a group of humble peasant women of Lamastre in the Vivarais, whom Father Vigne formed into a contemplative order to be known as the Sisters of the Most Holy Sacrament. Again, to anticipate a little, one cannot but recognize the lofty merits of the nuns of France in the attachment they showed to their convents and their habit during the revolutionary persecution. Out of two thousand Carmelites there were fewer than ten defections. Even among the Benedictines, whose conduct may sometimes have appeared to fall short of perfection, we find the same exemplary loyalty: in certain provinces not a single religious chose to accept the freedom offered by the law.

The spectacle was no less edifying in those institutes and congregations which for two hundred years had dedicated themselves to the necessary tasks of charity and education. The ten thousand sisters who worked in the hospitals and those fifteen thousand whose duty lay in the schools were doubtless not all saints; but the vast majority of them were women of irreproachable morality, simple and solid faith, and admirable devotion. The daughters of Monsieur Vincent covered themselves with glory in the eighteenth century: their mother house numbered a thousand religious; they spread to the remotest provinces of France, bringing with them the lessons of charity as they had vowed to do; and their ranks included such outstanding figures as the Sisters Rutan at Dax or Sister Elizabeth Baudet at Lyons. At that time too the Ursulines in France numbered more than eight thousand. First-rate teachers and also models of the spiritual life in the tradition of Marie de l'Incarnation, they have continued ever since to exert a decisive influence upon the womanhood of France. Much virtue lay hidden behind their great achievements. But there was no less virtue in the many less numerous and even very small orders. Whether we consider St Grignion de Montfort's Daughters of Wisdom, the Sisters of Charity of Nevers or the more recently formed Congregations of the Good Shepherd and Divine Providence, in each and every one of them some noble and saintly figure emerges from the shadows. For a just judgment upon the female religious of France we may turn once more to Voltaire: 'Perhaps there is nothing greater on earth than the sacrifice of youth and beauty, often of high birth, made by the gentle sex in order to work in the hospitals for the relief of human misery, the sight of which is so revolting to our delicacy. Peoples separated from the Roman religion have imitated but imperfectly so generous a charity.'

Decadence was certainly advanced among the men; but here again we must be on our guard against exaggeration. Taine, in his *Origines de la France contemporaine*, estimates that 'half the monastic orders were worthy of all respect'. It is indeed possible to find in every one of the great orders examples of perfect lives utterly dedicated to God, and there were certainly many others whose merits are known only to the Supreme Judge. Among the Trappists, for example, Father Gervaise, author of an *apologia* for de Rancé, died a voluntary recluse; among the Carthusians three great Generals, Fathers Le Masson, Montgeffond and Biclet, were not unworthy of their Order's traditions. Towards the end of the century there were even a number of reformers: Father Flamain among the Premonstratensians; at Cîteaux, Father Trouvé, Father Antonine and the famous Dom Guérin who later rebuilt Morimond.

It is also worth noting that the regularity and spiritual radiance of many religious houses is confirmed by such documentary evidence as the later Memorials of Complaint and even the reports of the revolutionary committees charged with inspecting the monasteries. At Thionville the population declared unanimously: 'The Charterhouse is for us the Ark of the Lord.' The inspectors sent to La Trappe paid magnificent tribute to those monks 'who, with the exception of five or six, are men of strong character and well balanced, whose piety reaches the heights of rapture and who appear to love their state with all their heart'. Even the Benedictine abbeys, about which there was rather more to say, continued to serve as centres of charity and spiritual life in many provinces. The people loved them, and were grateful to them for having opened their storehouses to all and sundry during the hard winters of 1784 and 1786; and when the revolutionaries suppressed them there were many protests.

Conditions were similar among the mendicants. The Capuchins appeared to be quite uncontaminated. The Cordeliers, who in 1771 made a determined effort to reorganize themselves, included a number of devout and earnest men, while the Recollects remained observant and influential. In Dominican circles the anti-Roman leanings of the convent of Saint-Jacques at Paris led to some degree of laxity, but the rule was followed strictly at Saint-Honoré. Father Cloche, master-general until 1720, left behind him an inspiring memory. Fifty years later when Loménie de Brienne and Bernis invited the Dominicans to modify their constitutions in a way that would render them more independent of ecclesiastical authority, the chapter refused outright. The above facts are hardly suggestive of decadence. And of course in those institutes of more recent origin, where fervour was still in full flood, the scene was yet more encouraging—among the Brothers of St John of God, for instance, and the Lazarists.

The conclusion is inevitable. The French clergy of the eighteenth century was not without merit, any more than was the Church in France as a whole. It is true that the Church manifested grave shortcomings in her recruitment, in her administration and in her attitude to contemporary dangers; but she had plenty of reserve strength, both in her clergy and in the mass of her faithful children. Far from finding the French people, as some believe, rotten to the core, uprooted from their traditions, given over to impiety and dissension, the Revolution found them still firm upon the age-old foundations of their faith and well able to defend it.

4. SIGNS OF REVIVAL

It found them indeed more resolute, more truly Christian than fifty years earlier. For a more attentive study reveals this surprising fact, that as the century advanced there was an increasing and clearly defined movement towards revival, towards a reawakening of the spirit of reform, even towards a quickening of mystical life. It was as if the Catholic faith, threatened on so many sides, felt the need for a return to its sources. The phenomenon was not exclusive to France, but it was particularly marked in that country.

The principal means of ploughing and re-sowing the Christian field in the age of spiritual grandeur had been the Mission. It had continued to be employed, though rather less, in the reign of Louis XIV.[34] Only one man of outstanding quality had devoted himself to that apostolate—St Grignion de Montfort. After him there had been a slowing down. Nevertheless, the system had not been wholly abandoned; in many dioceses teams of religious were still invited at regular intervals to come for a few weeks and strengthen the efforts of the parochial clergy. Bishops took an interest in the work, and generous layfolk made foundations to finance missions.

Among these latter was the widow Cabizolle of Aimargues, near Nîmes; she left all her goods in perpetuity for the payment of four Recollects, who were to come every year and stir up her village. But on the whole there was a definite slackening of impetus.

About the middle of the century, however, we begin to observe a recovery corresponding to that taking place in other lands—particularly in Italy, the home of St Leonard of Port Maurice, St Paul of the Cross and St Alphonsus de Liguori.[35] The missionary orders resumed work in earnest: Lazarists in Brie and Beauce; Eudists in Normandy, Brittany and Maine; Spiritans in Poitou and Anjou; Jesuits and Capuchins in the central southern and Alpine districts; and, mainly in the west, the sons of St Grignion de Montfort, called 'Mulotins' after his successor Father Mulot.

The most striking figure of that motley throng, and one of the most forceful in all Christian history, was Jacques Bridaine (1701–67). Unceasingly by hill and dale, chiefly in the south of France, he preached no fewer than two hundred and fifty-six missions in thirty-five years, addressing crowds not only in the churches but also in the public squares and market places; he was a great orator, loud of voice, by turns vehement and gentle, purposely proletarian in manner, full of wit and memorable sayings. One day, when speaking about the four last things, he paused suddenly, came down from the pulpit and cried out: 'Follow me! I'm going to take you home!' Then he led his audience to the cemetery, where unfilled graves showed each man what would be his last resting place. Bridaine had no use for refined moral counsels or academic graces. Yet it was he that paved the way for a whole army of popular preachers who, without going to his lengths, were no less capable of touching the masses, and who in those final years before the Revolution thundered courageously against the moral corruptions and impiety of the philosophers. Such a one was Father Pierre Humbert in Franche-Comté, whose sermons were a racy mixture of patois and French. Others were the Abbé Régnis, parish priest of Gap, whose missionary services were in demand throughout the Alps; or again, in the diocese of Bayonne, the Abbé Daguerre, who formed groups of missionaries that did excellent work throughout the district. The missions continued long after the outbreak of the Revolution, and were held in some places as late as 1793.

Another sign of increasing religous activity was a spate of pious books. Spiritual works of the previous century were republished, even those of Arnauld and the great Jansenists. Bossuet had the honour of many reprints as well as a complete edition. Letourneur's *Année chrétienne*, which ran to no fewer than nine hundred pages, was extremely popular. Between 1735 and the Revolution, the *Imitation of Christ* was reprinted nineteen times in France alone. Other successful works were Father Pichon's *Ésprit de Jésus-Christ*, Father Girardeau's *Évangile médité*, and the Abbé Clément's *Méditations sur la Passion*. All classes of society had their own pious literature, adapted to their state. While the *Journée du Chrétien*, dedicated to 'Mesdames de France', was widely read in cultured circles, quite as many lesser folk pored over a work entitled *Instructions et Prières à l'usage des domestiques et des personnes qui travaillent en ville*. In 1772 the parish priest of Pontarlier, in Haut-Jura, published his *Méthode pour la direction des âmes* for the benefit of his peasant congregation; but this excellent little book soon penetrated far beyond the humble fields in which its author had set it. Some of these spiritual treatises fell into the sentimental category, among them Father Fidèle's *Chrétien sensible*, and the *Délices de la religion* by that gentle soul Lamourette, who, after a famous kiss, died upon the scaffold. Others even ventured into the humorous category. One such was entitled *La Tabatière mystique* ('The Mystical Snuff Box') and another *La Purge spirituelle* ('The Spiritual Laxative'). It is more important to note that during the twenty-five years preceding the Revolution it became customary to use elaborate Mass books which enabled readers to follow the liturgy in detail and even to consult scriptural or patristic texts. The best was acknowledged to be that of the diocese of Lodève, *Encologe ou livre d'Église*, which contained the whole office in Latin and French; but Mgr de Vintimille, Archbishop of Paris, issued one very similar, and before long a large number of dioceses began to follow the example of the capital. There again our age is no pioneer.

It is even more remarkable that as the years went by an

unexpected phenomenon occurred in the reappearance of the mystic stream. It will be remembered that in consequence of attacks by the Jansenists and their friends, as well as of the errors of the Quietists, with whom they were unjustly confused, the mystics had been thoroughly discredited. It seemed no longer possible to approach God through 'pure love', and all the great preachers, Massillon at their head, taught only the moral demands of Christianity. Spiritual works suspected of mysticism were placed on the Index by Rome, and the Dominican Schramm, in a preface to his *Mystical Theology* (1774), declared that the very word mystic aroused nausea and fear in many believers. A large field of religious experience, the whole spiritual tradition of St Bernard, of Tauler and Suso, of St Teresa and St John of the Cross, of Marie de l'Incarnation and others—was suddenly abandoned. And that loss was not without harmful effects upon the vitality of the faith.

Until about 1750 very few dared to say that mystical experience is necessary to the fullness of Christianity, and that, when properly used, it leads the soul to God. Father Judde implied as much in his *Instructions sur l'Oraison*; so did Father Gallifet, though without much skill. The last representative of the great seventeenth-century mystical school (that of Father Louis Lallemant) seems to have been Father de Caussade (1675–1751), whose *Instructions spirituelles en forme de dialogues* (1741) made clever use of Bossuet's authority to defend true against false mysticism; but the great Jesuit's fundamental work, *Abandon à la Providence*, in which he taught that 'the whole Gospel consists in leaving God to do His work, and in doing what He requires of us', a phrase that sums up the famous doctrine of adherence, was still in the form of manuscript notebooks that passed secretly from hand to hand.[36]

At the time of Caussade's death it seemed there was no one left to bear the mystical torch; but in that same hour a new host appeared which would prove not unworthy of its predecessors. It must, however, be admitted that the eighteenth-century mystics are by no means familiar figures; indeed they are almost completely unknown to Catholics. Death prevented Henri Bremond from studying them in such detail as he had intended. But three of them occupy special places of honour in the noble gallery of the *Histoire littéraire de sentiment religieux:* Fathers Lombez, Grou and Clorivière.

The first, Jean Lapeyrie (1703–78)—in religion, Ambroise de Lombez—was a Capuchin, one of the glories of his Order at that time, an exquisitely gentle and delicate soul in whom there seemed to live again St Francis's spirit of charity and renunciation. A popular preacher, chiefly in south-western France but also in Paris, as well as a director of souls in whom Queen Maria Leczinska chose to confide, he published two treatises, *Paix intérieure* and *Joie de l'âme,* in which he countered Jansenist rigorism and proclaimed the inner experience in the serenity of divine love. He used to tell those who sought his direction: 'Give God your heart, which is what He wants, and be at rest.'

Father Grou, S.J. (1741–1803), was a disciple of the mysterious Father Surin, but also of St Francis de Sales and of Cardinal de Bérulle. A distinguished humanist, an expert on Plato and Cicero, he was the very type of those teachers so many of whom were found in the Society's schools, erudite but strict disciplinarians; and he himself practised the stern asceticism laid down in the *Exercises.* In consequence of the Society's suppression, which was a terrible blow to all the sons of St Ignatius, he underwent a spiritual crisis. He felt himself more than ever in the hands of God, and was converted at the end of a retreat during which he read St Jeanne de Chantal. It was not enough that he should sanctify himself. 'The blow must come from without.' The essential duty is to give oneself to Christ, to deliver oneself into the hands of that Spirit who despoils us of ourselves, to love, to wait for the gift of God, to offer oneself and to contemplate. This wholly mystical doctrine was set forth by Father Grou principally in two works which appeared on the eve of the Revolution: *Caractères de la vraie dévotion* (1788) and *Maximes spirituelles* (1789).[37]

Another Jesuit, however, whose talent was not much inferior to that of Father Grou, and who afterwards proved himself a brilliant man of action, was already teaching a similar doctrine. This was Father de Clorivière (1735–1819). The mystical life, he wrote, is nothing else but sanctifying grace, welling up in all its fullness in the heart of man. Why refuse it? When the soul withdraws into herself the light of God shines forth in her darkness. It is therefore useless to busy oneself with sanctification through asceticism, unless we have within us this sense of the divine, the will to meet God and lose ourselves in Him. All these truths Father de Clorivière proclaimed with such vehemence that his brethren sometimes thought him a fanatic. Later he embodied his teaching in *Considérations sur l'esprit d'oraison* and *Pratique de l'oraison devenue facile* (1818); but his influence as preacher, spiritual director, head of several colleges, and even for a time as parish priest, had enabled him to spread it long before.

Thus on the eve of the Revolution the mystical current had regained some of its vigour in the sphere of French Catholicism. It received a strong impulse when M. Emery, most renowned of contemporary Sulpicians, whose decisive role in the reform of seminaries we have already noticed, published his *Esprit de Sainte Thérèse*. Saint-Sulpice had links with Carmel through M. Olier and Bérulle; and M. Emery discovered there what he thought could restore energy to Christian life, which had become hardened and fossilized by Jansenism. His modesty led him, instead of expounding a doctrine of his own, to select and publish carefully chosen extracts from the great Spanish mystic in accordance with a method he had, as an apologist, already applied to the philosophers.[38] But that simple anthology, familiar to all who had heard the great superior at Saint-Sulpice, was carried far and wide by innumerable priests; it exerted a profound influence, whose traces may be followed into the nineteenth century.

Such then was the spectacle (surprising in view of official accounts) presented by French Catholicism at the moment it was about to face a terrible ordeal. The mystical revival corresponded to a reawakening of souls. Of this reawakening there were many different signs. New houses of retreat were established, while others reopened their doors. When the suppression of the Jesuits seemed likely to close those belonging to the Society, an appeal was made to other orders, to secular priests, and even to former Jesuits now disguised, with a view to keeping them open, for they were much frequented. Pious confraternities also witnessed an amazing increase in their number: between 1750 and the Revolution, seven hundred and forty-three new ones came into existence, and many more have escaped notice. Following Benedict XIV's Brief of 1751, which not only authorized but actually recommended them, feminine congregations sprang up, secular institutes in which pious laywomen undertook to live a fully Christian life. It was in these fervent circles that Marian devotion regained its vigour after having been ridiculed by the philosophers and seriously damaged. The practice of 'Mary's Month' had numerous supporters, thanks to the work of Father Doré at Nancy and Mme Louise at Carmel. Taking his cue from St John Eudes and St Grignion de Montfort, the Jesuit Father de Gallifet laboured to spread devotion to the Immaculate Heart of Mary, a task which was continued later by Father de Clorivière. The Way of the Cross reached France from Italy, where it had been started by St Leonard of Port Maurice, and soon became popular. It was under the influence of the Marian revival that there grew up the custom of clothing very young children in blue and white, the two colours symbolic of Our Lady.

If we had to choose one from among all the signs of spiritual reawakening, it would surely be the spread of devotion to the Sacred Heart. As we have seen,[39] it began with the teaching of St John Eudes and St Margaret Mary Alacoque, but at once encountered strong resistance from all the enemies of mysticism, who looked upon it with grave suspicion. At the beginning of the eighteenth century it was still sporadic: some Visitandines and Jesuits, for example, dedicated chapels to the Heart of Jesus (the first were at Coutances and Grenoble), but they did so without official authority.

Little by little, however, the movement gained ground. In 1711 Canon Simon Gourdan, the priest in charge of the underground chapel of Saint-Victor at Paris, published a letter to show that the Heart of Jesus is truly the symbol of Christ's soul consumed with love and adoration. In 1722 he developed his ideas in a book entitled *Cœur chrétien formé sur la Cœur de Jésus-Christ*. Jean-Joseph Languet de Gergy, vicar-general of Autun, later Bishop of Soissons and finally Archbishop of Paris, perceiving in devotion to the Sacred

Heart an antidote to Jansenism,[40] published a successful Life of St Margaret Mary. At Marseilles, Anne-Madeleine Rémuzat, a younger sister of the mystic of Paray-le-Monial, was also directed by interior voices to dedicate herself to the new devotion. And when the city fell victim to a terrible plague (1720) the bishop, Mgr de Belsunce, torn from his apathy by the Visitandine's appeal and becoming at once a hero and a saint, instituted in his diocese, by way of expiation and intercession, an annual feast of the Sacred Heart, which the city fathers undertook to celebrate.

Year by year the devotion went from strength to strength. Its official approval by the Church was sought by St Veronica Giuliani in Italy, by Dom Bede Sommerberger in Germany and by Bernardo de Hoyos in Spain. In France it was supported by the influential Capuchins, and by 1740 there were no fewer than seven hundred and two confraternities of the Sacred Heart. From Poland, where the new feast had been authorized, the cult received some powerful backing in the person of the queen, Maria Leczinska; she did all she could to spread it, providing for novenas of votive Masses, writing to Clement XII, Clement XIII and Benedict XIV for its official recognition, and asking the same favour from the Assembly of the Clergy.

Nevertheless resistance was not wanting. Certain theologians accused the new cult of in some way splitting the Divine Person. Why, they asked, adore the Heart of Christ rather than His wounds, or His side pierced by the lance, or His eyes wet with tears? Nor was it without good cause that powerful Jansenist elements saw in devotion to the Sacred Heart the antithesis of their own doctrines. Opposition went even to the extent of violence, and preachers advocating the cult were sometimes openly denounced in church. At Notre-Dame in Paris, on the day when Mgr Christophe de Beaumont inaugurated the feast, a Jansenist verger hid the archbishop's liturgical vestments.

The current, however, proved irresistible. In 1765 Rome, after much hesitation, authorized the feast of the Sacred Heart and the composition of a special office, though she waited until 1816 before adopting it herself and imposing it on the universal Church. Propaganda in favour of the new devotion continued to flow, especially in France. Under Louis XVI, Fathers Lenfant and Hébert were its heralds; Clorivière and Cormaux gave the name 'Priests of the Sacred Heart' to their small foundation, which was in fact a clandestine revival of the Society of Jesus. At Nantes, Marie-Anne Galipaud, another visionary, continued the tradition of her Visitandine predecessors. The Revolution itself could not halt the movement, and even during those tragic years new congregations, institutes and confraternities sprang up, named after the Sacred Heart of Christ.[41] In 1788, the very year before the storm broke, Mme Elisabeth went and asked her brother to repeat in his turn, though in a different way, the illustrious deed of his ancestor[42] by dedicating his kingdom to the Sacred Heart. The indolent Louis XVI, good Christian though he was, had none of the mystical leanings of Louis XIII. He therefore declined the invitation. Later, however, in the Tuileries, after it had been sacked by the revolutionary mob, there was found, enclosed in a portfolio of blue morocco, the text of the dedication prepared by Mme Elisabeth. Re-read in the light of history, her words assume prophetic significance: 'O Jesus Christ, all hearts in this kingdom, from that of our august monarch to that of his lowliest subject, unite in the ardour of charity to offer themselves to thee. Yes, Heart of Jesus, we offer thee our whole country and the hearts of all thy children. O Blessed Virgin, they are now in thy hands; we have delivered them to thee by dedicating ourselves to thee as our protectress and our mother. Today, we beseech thee, offer them to the Heart of Jesus. Presented by thee, He will accept them, pardon them, bless them and sanctify them; He will save all France and give new life to religion on her soil.'

It is surely not untrue to say that the country from which such utterance could spring was still profoundly Christian.

5. THE VOICE OF THE POPES

It was no doubt useful to show in some detail how much spiritual strength remained to the Church in France during the eighteenth century, to that Church which has so often been misunderstood and calumniated, and which was about to confront the full fury of the Revolution. But what we have been saying about her applies *mutatis mutandis* to the Church in almost every country of the West. Despite shortcomings and mistakes which have been laid at her door, it is quite certain that souls steeped in the fire of Christ continued to labour everywhere for God's kingdom, and that the great principles that had more than once enabled the Church to recover and renovate herself were far from decrepit.

That was what really mattered. The history of the Church, though man-made, is not mere human history. Political events, which mark its stages and of which alone secular history takes account, are not the only ones demanding our attention; nor indeed are they the most important. The true history of Christianity is that of souls. However much the Church may be vilified by her adversaries, and even defiled by some of her members, her fortune really depends on the degree to which she preserves in her own bosom the cardinal virtues of faith, hope and charity. She loses them if she betrays her soul, if those to whom Christ's message has been entrusted no longer hear its call, if (to anticipate a little and use a phrase soon to be written by a prophet of the abyss) 'God is dead'.

To say that the Catholic and Roman Church in the eighteenth century still occupied a considerable place in the western world is a statement of prime importance in the political sphere. It is true that on the eve of the Revolution Catholicism still covered nearly two-thirds of Europe; that it continued to hold those positions which it had held or recovered in the sixteenth century; that it had hardly been affected by the alarming progress of Protestantism. But to estimate the life of a religion by the area it covers, by the millions of adherents it can claim, amounts to very little. Statistics are always worthless when they reckon baptized persons as Catholics, without showing how many of them are truly faithful; and in the eighteenth century there was small chance of the figures themselves being exact. Much more important than these geographical and statistical calculations is the work of discovering signs of deep vitality in the Catholic soul, proofs that God still dwelt within her.

Now these signs are many and manifest. It has been considered that the Papacy in the eighteenth century was too weak, too inefficient, too little in touch with the new world then coming to birth, sometimes even losing its prestige through the insolence of secular powers or through its own mistakes; but it would be unfair to maintain that it was in every respect unequal to its task. There is at least one field in which the eighteenth-century popes proved themselves faithful to the demands of their high office, one in which it is of the utmost importance that the Vicar of Christ should make his voice loud and clear since integrity of faith, enforcement of discipline and the increase of fervour in man's soul are all at stake. No, we are not entitled to say that those popes hid their light under a bushel.

We must not forget that in the great doctrinal crises which caused such terrible upheavals in the Church, particularly that of Jansenism, it was to the Papacy that men turned in order to know what road they ought to follow, and it was the decisions of the Papacy that finally settled the dispute. It may be thought that in the intellectual and moral crisis, arising from the progress of new ideas, mere censures were not enough; but we cannot deny that the popes were gifted with farsightedness and firmness to an extent not always characteristic of their Renaissance predecessors. Even upon matters where the danger was not evident to their contemporaries, the popes saw clearly. For example, the Bull *In eminenti* (1738) of Clement XII and *Providas Romanorum* (1751) of Benedict XIV condemned Freemasonry, to which good Catholics had thought they could safely belong. The same doctrinal vigour belonged even to those popes who in other respects seemed rather weak. If Pius VI bravely resisted Joseph II[43] and ultimately obtained the submission of Febronius,[44] it was not only because he was resolved to defend the temporal rights of the Apostolic See, but also because he understood clearly that the whole spiritual authority of Christ's vicar was at stake.

Every one of those popes sought to help maintain or reanimate the spirit of reform. Even those who yielded too readily to their advisers—Benedict XIII is an example, and Pius VI still more so—never looked upon the principles of Trent as a dead letter. The famous decision against nepotism in the Bull

Romanum decet pontificem,[45] of Innocent XII, so far from being abrogated, were several times repeated, notably by Benedict XIV. Clement XII actually took steps to prevent certain cardinals from placing themselves at the service of secular powers in the Conclave. His Constitution *Apostolatus officium* (1732) dealing with papal elections contained a number of clauses that are still in force.

Reform of the clergy remained one of the major preoccupations of the popes throughout the eighteenth century, as is clear from an unbroken stream of Bulls, Briefs and Encyclicals. One of the most important documents of Benedict XIV was the *De Synodo dioecesano*, which reorganized the dioceses of Italy and reminded all bishops throughout the world of their duty to keep residence and set a good example. It even went into details, forbidding bishops to remain longer than three months outside their dioceses and firmly declaring that the shepherd must regularly visit all his flock. But Benedict XIII had already given similar counsel, and Clement XIII, formerly Bishop of Padua, afterwards reiterated the admonitions of his predecessor with admirable firmness, not hesitating to write personally to the bishops of Germany to rebuke them for their scandalous accumulation of benefices.

Many of the eighteenth-century popes took an active interest likewise in the welfare of seminaries. Particularly remarkable are the two letters addressed by Benedict XIII to the bishops in order to remind them that it was their duty to found seminaries in accordance with the decrees of Trent; and the same Pontiff founded the Congregation of Seminaries, which was intended to facilitate the work. Every one of those popes has to his credit either the establishment of a seminary, or help given to a bishop (e.g. St Alphonsus de Liguori) who was trying to reform his clergy; the Franciscan Pope Clement XIV even dreamed of restoring to the Church the simplicity of Apostolic times, and he more than once suggested to priests that they should follow the ideal of monastic poverty and renunciation. Every one of them, too, concerned himself with religious observance, suppressing some small lax communities, giving others energetic superiors, and smoothing the path of such new institutes as the Passionists,[46] whose extreme austerity could serve as an example to older orders.

Side by side with this work of reform, and indeed inseparable from it, we must notice also the doctrinal achievements of those pontificates. As we have seen,[47] Benedict XIV occupies pride of place from this point of view; he was the forerunner of some nineteenth- and twentieth-century popes whose encyclicals were destined to provide the Church with answers to all the great contemporary problems. But Pius VI also understood the importance of his role in this domain, as is shown by his instruction of Christmas 1775. Instructions on the Holy Mass issued by Benedict XIV, and repeated by Clement XIV, are still worthy of admiration: 'Parish priests should lead their people in acts of faith, hope and charity, explain to them the gospel, the commandments of God and the sacraments, and not hesitate to question them in order to learn whether they have properly understood.' Certain pious practices, e.g. the commemoration of Our Lord's death each Friday at three o'clock and the Stations of the Cross, date from this period and were propagated with support from the sovereign pontiffs. We have already seen that the cult of the Sacred Heart was authorized in 1765. It should also be noted that in upholding the custom of solemn canonizations these popes did more than yield to the rather pompous and gaudy taste of the period. Their choice of saints was in almost every case significant. Among the men and women whom they raised to the altars were such great ascetics and penitents as Margaret of Cortona, Elizabeth of Aragon, Laurence of Brindisi; religious and educational reformers of the previous century, such as Jerome Aemilian, Jeanne de Chantal, Joseph Calasanctius and Angela Merici; witnesses of the Gospel who had risked and even sacrificed their lives for God's cause, such as Toribio Mogrobejo, Francis Solano and Fidelis of Sigmaringen. We have already noted[48] the significance attaching to the canonization by Benedict XIII of Gregory VII, Stanislaus Kostka and John Nepomucene, heroic defenders of the rights of the Church in face of secular ambitions. Let it not be said that all that pious activity counted for little in the great disputes which involved the future of the Church. To reanimate the inmost forces of the Christian soul was to labour for the most fundamental needs of the Church. Looking closely at the popes of the eighteenth century one obtains a glimpse of what the Papacy might become, once rejuvenated by the approaching ordeal and resolved to meet its obligations.

6. CATHOLIC BASTIONS: SPAIN

Spiritual reality must likewise be set against appearances when considering the great Catholic countries and asking to what extent they remained loyal to the Catholic cause. In Spain and in the Hapsburg Empire appearances indicated tension between the civil power and the Church—'a sort of *Kulturkampf*', as Latreille says. But it would be wrong to conclude that Spain under Aranda, who expelled the Jesuits, and Austria under Joseph II, were about to lapse into irreligion. The truth is quite otherwise: 'The crisis of regalism took place almost on the surface of the national life.' Neither Spain nor Austria had abandoned their positions as Christian bastions, which, as we have seen,[49] they had held at the beginning of the seventeenth century.

This was true particularly of Spain. The Church's place in the Most Catholic Kingdom was remarked by all travellers. Everywhere there were churches, monasteries and chapels; everywhere there were religious of all orders. 'More habits than men,' some whispered sneeringly. With a population of 10,000,000 (less by more than a half than that of France), Spain had more clerics than France—seventy thousand seculars and eight thousand regulars, excluding women. And her territory, little if at all larger, included one hundred and sixty dioceses as against one hundred and thirty in France. All was far from perfect in those tonsured ranks, where beneficed clergymen were three times more numerous than those who served parishes; but the Spanish clergy were none the less respected and obeyed by the people. 'The nation's lifeblood resided in the clergy,' writes Desdevises du Dézert, a great authority on Spain; and this was soon proved true in the conflict with Napoleon.

Catholicism therefore was not only the state religion; it was the religion without which neither the State nor the Spanish people could have imagined itself. 'The Spanish soul', writes the same author, 'is quite impregnated with it, and that faith has become its necessary attribute.' Ten centuries of tradition, struggle and hardship had effected the fusion; in all the glorious episodes of their history, from the battles of the Reconquista to the great adventures in America and the Indies, Spaniards found proof of their Catholic vocation. And towards the end of the eighteenth century they felt all the more attached to it as they began to ask themselves sadly whether their greatness was not a thing of the past.

Faith then remained the armour of the Hispanic soul, a faith austere, stern, meticulous in its observances, not perhaps devoid of superstition, but forming a barrier well-nigh impervious to all dangers. There were practically no Protestants in Spain; there were practically no Philosophers or Libertines. The intellectual and moral crisis which troubled France was non-existent beyond the Pyrenees; only a few intellectuals read Voltaire and *The Encyclopaedia*, which they had to procure clandestinely. The middle classes, moreover, which provided the main forces of freethinking, counted for very little, while the nobility were too badly educated to be much influenced by harmful ideas.

The kings were still believers, even when, as in the case of the last Hapsburgs, their moral conduct was not in accord with the commandments of God; and even when (as did the Bourbons, worthy descendants of Louis XIV) they showed scant respect for the Apostolic See. Personally pious and zealous, those Bourbons were undoubtedly sincere in the practice of their holy religion. Carlos III himself, whose minister Aranda so detested the Church that his friend Voltaire congratulated him as 'a new Heracles who had cleansed the Augean stables', belonged to the Third Order of St Francis, heard Mass daily, communicated frequently, made an annual retreat, and dedicated his kingdom to Our Lady of the Immaculate Conception. The quarrels which those sovereigns had with the Holy See[50] arose from the view they took of their own role; like Philip II and Louis XIV they looked upon themselves as viceroys of God and never imagined there was anything wrong with the authority they wielded over the Church for the greater glory of God. The concordat of 1753, which Ferdinand VI obtained from Benedict XIV, had considerably increased the rights of the Crown over the Church: the king made appointments to all benefices, and in most cases papal confirmation was not required. Most lawsuits involving clerics or matters of religion were decided at Madrid by the tribunal of the Spanish Rota, in which the influence of the government often made itself felt, and the Roman Rota was powerless to intervene. All the ancient orders of chivalry, which were reviving at that time—Santiago, Calatrava and the Holy Sepulchre—had the king as grand master or lieutenant.

As for the Inquisition, the formidable tribunal which had done so much to preserve unity of faith in Spain and to set public opinion against all suspected of heterodoxy, its importance was declining. Under Philip V it had executed seventy-nine persons; throughout the century its toll of heretics, quietists, blasphemers, bigamists and sorcerers declined year by year. But State influence upon it, which had always been considerable, steadily increased. In 1768 Madrid obtained from Rome an undertaking that no inquisitorial decision should be carried out, even if it were Roman, without consent of the Grand Council of Castile. On the eve of 1789 there was talk in Spain of reforming the Inquisition, but not of making it independent of government authority.

Eighteenth-century Spain, then, was Spain as she had always been. That, however, does not mean that she remained supine in the contemplation of her past, or that the Spanish Church was such as the philosophers liked to represent her —a monster of intolerance and routine, doomed to unavoidable decadence and dragging the whole country after her. A careful study of the facts reveals a very different situation. The Spanish episcopate, unlike those of France and the Hapsburg dominions, was not recruited mainly from the higher nobility; many bishops were of lowly extraction, which prevented them from lapsing into worldliness and kept them in closer touch with their priests. Some proved themselves men of the highest quality—perhaps not in the intellectual sphere, with the exception of Mgr Armanya at Tarragona and Mgr Juan Diaz de la Guerra at Siguezza, who concerned themselves with the foundation of libraries, the development of schools, and with art and literature in general. But in the field of the apostolate, of spiritual revival and reform of morals many of them were quite outstanding. Mgr Armanya himself, a former hermit of St Augustine, made numerous episcopal visitations, revived the tradition of diocesan synods and took a personal interest in his priests. Mgr Diego de Rivera at Barbasto, Mgr Cenarro at Valladolid, Mgr Jose Clement at Barcelona, Mgr Valero y Losa (son of a charcoal burner, who rose from the position of a humble parish priest to become Archbishop of Toledo) and many others provided similar examples. One had to fight furious opposition from his chapter in order to regularize the distribution of prebends. Another, Mgr Bastero at Gerona, worked himself to death visiting his diocese and looking after his priests; he left behind him the reputation of a saint.[51]

It was due to those bishops that a strong reforming movement set in, particularly during the second half of the eighteenth century. The creation of seminaries had been a slow process in Spain, but now more interest was shown. At Pampeluna, Mgr Lorenzo Irigoyen invited the help of François Daguerre, the famous apostle of the Basques, in reorganizing his senior seminary and founding a junior. The decadent seminary at Barcelona was reinvigorated by Felipe de Aguendo. After the suppression of the Society of Jesus several bishops acquired property abandoned by the Fathers and used it for the enlargement or establishment of seminaries; no fewer than nine were opened between 1777 and 1789.

Missionary activity, which also had been making very little progress, began now to increase. There were few provinces of Spain that were not visited in the course of the century by ardent and vehement missionaries, Dominicans, Jesuits, Capuchins, Hieronymites or hermits, several of whom preached in penitential garb, discipline in hand and brow covered with ashes. The Jesuit Pedro de Catalayud left his mark upon Navarre, Castile and Aragon. His missions began and ended with a solemn procession; they lasted fifteen or twenty days, and their graces were continued through the Confraternity of the Sacred Heart which he founded, through the bodies of priests which he organized and through his *Practical Catechism* which he distributed. In the south of the peninsula, from Malaga to Seville and Cordoba, and as far as the Atlantic, a Capuchin named Diego de Cadix astonished the crowds; his eloquence was compared with that of St Vincent Ferrer, miracles were attributed to him and it was known that he wore next his skin a kind of doublet made of felt and studded on the inside with sharp spikes.

Thus the religious life of Spain in the Age of Enlightenment, though strictly in line with its age-old traditions, was by no means fossilized. Pilgrimages, especially those to Compostella, were still truly fervent. Such abbeys as Montserrat and Valladolid, which latter belonged to the Cassinese Congregation and worked for the reform of the Benedictine Order, were still active centres of spiritual life and in some cases of intellectual life also. The Order of the Penitence of Nazareth, one of the last orders to be founded before the French Revolution, originated in Spain. An austere, discalced society, it was approved by Pius VI in 1784; its members went about urging men to model their lives upon that of the Blessed Virgin and preaching devotion to her Immaculate Conception. When we think of the mighty work accomplished by the Spanish Church beyond the Atlantic;[52] when we recall that it provided most of the clergy in America, sending out more than four thousand five hundred priests and a host of religious (twelve hundred and fifty Brothers of St John of God alone) between 1730 and 1789; when we remind ourselves further that those who often set the most eloquent example of charity—e.g. the Bethlemites, founded by Father de Betancur of Guatemala specially to care for the sick and destitute—were Spaniards, we realize how false and unjust is the traditional image of Catholic Spain, derived from the sometimes questionable behaviour of its flagellants and the gaudy pomp of Holy Week at Seville. It was not only in externals, any more than in the political field, that the land of Ferdinand and Isabella remained a bastion of the Church.

7. CATHOLIC BASTIONS: FROM FLANDERS TO HUNGARY

There was another such bastion, less monolithic perhaps but still very firm. It stretched from Flanders to the middle Danube, and included what is now Belgium (at that time the Austrian Low Countries), Rhineland Germany and its vicinity, Bavaria and the Hapsburg dominions. Its core lay in south-west Germany, between the great religious centres of Mainz, Ratisbon and Vienna. There St Boniface had erected the earliest episcopal sees; there the monks had opened up the way for civilization; there finally, in the seventeenth century, the Hapsburgs, rulers of the Holy Roman and Germanic Empire and patrons of an important seignorial and ecclesiastical clientele, had launched the counter-offensive whose base the Jesuits had established at Innsbruck.[53] Thus Catholicism in those regions was on something comparable to a war footing. Heretics were quite close: in many places their territories interlocked with those of Catholics; Prussia and Holland, leaders of European Protestantism, exerted an influence which it was necessary to oppose. Consequently the spirit of counter-reformation was still active in Catholic *Mitteleuropa*; and while it sometimes led to deplorable acts of intolerance, one cannot deny that it helped to keep the faith alive and vigorous.

The Austrian Low Countries (modern Belgium) afforded a good example of that Catholic vitality. They had scarcely been affected by their Protestant neighbours to the north; the small Calvinist communities at Roulers, Turnhout, Ypres and Bruges radiated no farther. Even Jansenism, which had arisen there, had been stamped out. The University of Louvain with its forty-five colleges exerted an enormous influence on the upper classes and the clergy; its library, under the direction of the learned Van de Velde, became one of the finest in Europe. The 'philosophical' plague had contaminated only a few intellectual and middle-class circles. The common people, especially in Flanders, retained a faith of almost medieval fervour; they went in crowds on the great Marian pilgrimages to the Sablon at Brussels, to Foy Notre-Dame and to Montaigu, or on the famous penitential processions to Furnes and Bruges. The convents of Béguines were full. Agnes Berlique's 'Apostolines' opened numerous houses, where they received poor girls and taught them a trade. Devotion to the Sacred Heart spread in the southern Low Countries as quickly as in France. A vigorous and warm-hearted piety, not hesitating to combine the realities of life with spiritual demands, was the characteristic of Belgian Catholicism.

In other regions subject to Austria the situation was undoubtedly less peaceful, but faith was equally uncompromising. In Bohemia the restoration of Catholicism had been one of the principal episodes of the Counter-Reformation. The White Mountain remained a terrible memory,[54] and Catholicism seemed to be imposed from without by brutal foreigners. The truth, however, was quite different; it was not under police pressure alone that numerous Czechs had become fervent Romans. An apologetic at once national and Catholic, instigated by Pechria Czehorad, had found its way into many minds. Vogt, a Piarist, had recalled the historic greatness of the fatherland; many of the five hundred and seventy Jesuits who worked in Bohemia had striven to do likewise; the indefatigable Father Koniach, who for thirty-seven years preached as many as five sermons a day and spent up to eight hours in the confessional, exalted the national loyalty of Catholics. That loyalty was fostered among the common people by devotion to St John Nepomucene and to Our Lady of the Holy Mountain of Przibzam, as it was among the upper classes by new Czech versions of the Bible and Eleanor Sporck's translations of the great French doctrinal works. A Catholic Bohemia had arisen, perhaps more conscious of itself than in the days before the Thirty Years War. No less than Hussite Bohemia, so dear to secular historians, it was destined to bring about the nineteenth-century renascence.

In Hungary, after the many errors that had proved so costly,[55] official violence had given way to apostolic zeal. Ever since Father Stankowiz and Mgr Erdödy had inaugurated missions towards the end of the seventeenth century, there had been ceaseless labour among the Protestant population; and that labour had achieved better results than the old methods of Cardinal Pazmany, who sent heretics to the galleys. Some prelates proved themselves incomparable apostles; among them were Kereszt, a popular orator whose poignant sermons converted thousands of Calvinists, and Charles Esterhazy, a great church builder who founded more than a hundred parishes. One set of figures shows the result of all that work: between 1700 and 1789 the number of Hungarian seminarists rose from 114 to 296.

In Germany and in the Hapsburg states, Austria and its dependencies, the situation seemed complicated. Appearances were impressive. The Nuncio Pacca's memoirs reveal that the Church and her clergy in those parts were 'at the summit of human grandeur', that they wielded considerable authority in the Empire, that they owned 'vast areas of the fairest and most fertile land' (more than three-eighths, some said) and that millions of people were subject to their temporal power. He might have added that churches and convents were as numerous as in Spain, that in the Hapsburg states alone there were sixty-five thousand religious of both sexes in two thousand houses, and many other facts of the same kind.

What was the reality that underlay those externals to which baroque art lent its sumptuous adornment? One might, with absolute impartiality, draw a very different picture. Was not Catholic Germany the land also of Febronius and of those proud bishops who rebelled against the Pope? And did not Joseph II, Emperor of Austria, revive the old quarrel between priesthood and empire? Apart from human shortcomings, which they shared with priests everywhere, had not the Austro-German clergy, too comfortable and too affluent, lapsed into torpor and routine? Moreover it seemed—Pacca expressly tells us so—that 'philosophical' irreligion and the *Aufklärung* had made conspicuous progress, even among the clergy, and that there had been less resistance to those destructive forces than in France.

None of all this can be denied. But which of the two pictures is more accurate? The truth is that, as in France, notwithstanding the power and luxury of the Church, and in spite of real errors and shortcomings, Catholicism remained extremely vigorous in all the countries of west and south-west Germany, as in the hereditary dominions of the Hapsburgs, and that the Church there was by no means on the wane. Proof of this may be seen in fairly numerous conversions, not all of which were inspired by political considerations. Those of the house of Württemburg, of Princess Nassau-Saarbruck and of Amelia von Schettau (who became Princess Galitzin and made her drawing-room a centre of the apostolate) were perhaps of limited importance from a political point of view, but they were straws in the wind. It may be seen in the vitality of the great universities, fortresses not long since of the Counter-Reformation: Innsbruck, Mainz, Fulda, Vienna, Würzburg and Münster; their influence was hardly offset by the opposition of Bonn, which had been founded to serve the new ideas. It may be seen in the activity of the bishops, many of whom were quite outstanding—real leaders, true shepherds anxious to train their priests well, to win respect for the Gospel and to foster Christian living among their people. Among these prelates was Mgr Königsegg of Cologne; the two Schönbrons at Mainz and Würzburg; Count von Trautson, Archbishop of Vienna; and even some bishops who had embraced Josephism and Erastianism, e.g. Mgr Colloredo of Salzburg and Mgr Max Franz von Lorraine-Hapsburg, brother of Joseph II, whose pastoral gifts were none the less unquestionable. It was indeed this youngest son of Maria Theresa who, about 1775, gave fresh impulse to the flagging work of creating seminaries; on the eve of the French Revolution the seminaries of Germany and Austria were enjoying a second spring.

Yet another proof of the vitality of German-speaking Catholicism is afforded by the activity of many religious orders and congregations. A curious branch of the Benedictines, the Benedictines of the Guardian Angels, undertook a most interesting spiritual revival which resulted also in some reaction and some critical moments. The Bartholomites, founded by Bartholomew Holzhauser[56] for the reform of the clergy, achieved great success. Under the direction of the Baroness von Neuhaus and the Countess von Lemberg, two women of equal holiness and ability, the Ursulines put new life into the teaching of girls, while Franz von Furstenberg, then Bernard von Overberg, both of whom were supported by Princess Galitzin, devoted themselves to an apostolate for the education of boys. Nor must we overlook the growth of popular missions, in which Jesuits, Capuchins and Franciscans competed one with another. Father Christian Brez travelled all over Germany, Father Mersch distinguished himself in Bavaria, and Fathers Hoyer and Saint-Grembs in the Rhineland. There was scarcely a country in central Europe that was not thus reinvigorated between 1720 and the outbreak of the French Revolution.

On the whole, our view of German-speaking Catholicism is far from discouraging. Furthermore, there is abundant evidence of lively faith among the masses, of which we may quote a single instance. When the Nuncio Pacca visited Augsburg he was met by sixteen thousand Catholics of all ages, some of whom had travelled long distances; they had come to ask him for confirmation, which a negligent clergy had failed to administer—a fine example of sturdy faith. Devotional life made some progress even during the second half of the century under the influence of pious congregations which multiplied just as they were doing in France. Pilgrimages were so popular and devotions so numerous that Mgr von Trautson became uneasy, remarking with some wit that 'too much veneration for the channels of grace leads people to forget Christ, the source of grace'. The cult of the Sacred Heart, whose great exponent was Dom Bede Sommerberger, and that of the Immaculate Conception made steady progress. All these facts are representative of a religion firmly based and still very much alive, and that explains why the German and Austrian peoples, though swept by the revolutionary and Napoleonic cyclone, were able to survive without serious damage to their faith. As the storm approached, therefore, the Church possessed bastions capable of resistance.[57]

8. ITALY, LAND OF SAINTS

What now of Italy? Italy, where princes and republics were ever ready to flout the Pope's authority, where 'Pasquino' and the rabble scoffed without let or hindrance at the officials of the Curia, the cardinals and even the sovereign pontiffs themselves; Italy, where the morals of clergy and laity alike were no more edifying than elsewhere—how far, we may ask, was Italy a pillar of strength in Holy Church? It is of course evident that she did not form a massive bloc like Spain, Austria or even France. Still divided politically among six powers—the Papal States, the Republic of Venice, the kingdom of Piedmont-Sardinia, Genoa, and Tuscany with the Two Sicilies—she was suffering, even in the religious sphere, from that division and its resultant discord. It is, however, none the less true that Catholicism was omnipresent and powerful, linked with all her traditions and with all the lessons of her past, the only firm basis for a sense of unity which was not as yet formulated in political terms but which existed in many souls as a nostalgia of greatness.

The Catholic religion occupied a pre-eminent place in Italian life; there was indeed no domain in which it was not present. Every city and township was full of churches, bastioned with convents, swarming with clerics and religious of all habits. Rome, seen from the Pincio, looked like a forest of bell-towers, domes and cupolas rising from a sea of golden and rose-red roof-tops. Naples, which had a shady reputation, contained fifty churches, two hundred chapels and more than thirty convents. External signs? Not altogether. The Stations of the Cross in the Colosseum were visited by thousands, and every day one saw pious folk climbing the Scala Santa or the steep ascent of the Ara Coeli on their knees. The crowds hurrying to the bier on which lay Benedict Labre's corpse were drawn not by mere curiosity but by genuine faith.

Indeed the most outstanding feature of Italian Catholicism was the near unanimity and the vigour of popular faith. At Naples the 'miracle of St Januarius', when the martyr's blood liquefied in the ampulla shown by the archbishop to the public, drew masses of sincere believers. The pilgrimage to Our Lady of Loreto attracted many more throughout the year. The tomb of St Francis at Assisi and that of St Dominic at Bologna had their devotees; so had the mysterious face of the Holy Shroud at Turin. These popular devotions brought the faithful into picturesque and sometimes disconcerting intimacy with the things of religion. The names of God and the Blessed Virgin were introduced into every facet of day-to-day existence, often, so it seems, in the most unsuitable manner. Men swore by Christ and His Blessed Mother; nor was it only on the stage that women were heard praying the Madonna to guard them or their paramours. 'Means have been found', said the virtuous Benedict XIV, 'to combine attendance at Mass and at worldly gatherings, and frequentation of the sacraments and the company of women.' He was well informed.

But there was something more serious in Italian Catholicism. The custom of weekly communion was spreading; so was that of celebrating the first Friday of each month by hearing Mass. It was in Italy, at Parma, that the first book devoted to the Month of Mary was printed. The practice of the Forty Hours was general; so too, in many parishes, was that of perpetual adoration. It is impossible to exaggerate the importance of the fact that Protestantism had been practically eliminated from the whole of Italy, and that while Jansenism, which had a few adherents there, was decidedly anti-Roman, it took the form not so much of a doctrinal deviation as of an inclination towards exaggerated austerity.

The reforming movement, which had been so strong throughout Italy on the morrow of Trent, but had seemed to slow down in the seventeenth century, regained some of its vigour during the eighteenth. The number of good bishops devoted to their flocks and anxious, as worthy disciples of St Charles Borromeo, to improve their clergy, seems to have been considerable. Among them were Mgr Galiani, Archbishop of Taranto, who was constantly on the roads of his poor diocese, and whom the King of the Two Sicilies appointed as his senior chaplain. Mgr Borgia, Bishop of Aversa, was nicknamed by his people 'Monsignor Wallet', because he was never without that useful piece of baggage on the many journeys he undertook in search of alms for his poor. Mgr Gradenigo, a former Theatine, made Udine a model diocese. There were also Mgr Gioanetti, a former Camaldolese, whose asceticism edified Bologna; Mgr Lambertini, Archbishop of Bologna and afterwards Pope Benedict XIV; and lastly a true saint, Mgr Alfonso de Liguori in the tiny diocese of Sant' Agatha dei Gottici.

The reform of the clergy and the creation of seminaries also found zealous workers. Several men devoted themselves to the necessary tasks of opening new seminaries, reorganizing those that had gradually lapsed into decadence, and introducing the French system whereby seminarists were kept strictly apart from lay students. We may recall the part played by the French Lazarist Jean Bonnet, who established in Italy five seminaries of his congregation. Girolamo Andreucci, restorer of the seminary at Tivoli, was summoned to Rome to direct that of the Gesù. Others laboured to improve the existing clergy, a task to which the saintly Roman priest Giovanni Battista dei Rossi dedicated his life with excellent results; St Alphonsus de Liguori did likewise in the territory of Naples. Pope Benedict XIV, in his appeals for a better training of the clergy, drew upon the teaching of both. In various parts of Italy groups were formed with a view to uniting the best of the clergy and of the laity in the work of the apostolate. In northern Italy, for example, there was the Amicizia Cristiana, founded by Father Diesbach, a former Calvinist who had become a Jesuit; at Turin, Bruno Lanteri's Compagnia del Divino Amore; at Naples, the small groups of 'pious workmen', with whom Alphonsus de Liguori was for some time associated, and those Redemptorist detachments who were led by Vincenzo Mandarini in the struggle against irreligion by means of popular education. The same movement of reform and restoration manifested itself in the religious orders and congregations. Important events among the Dominicans at Rome were the reconstitution of the Congregation of San Marco and the formation of another called after Santa Sabina, of which latter Father Cloche, Father Pipia and Father (afterwards Cardinal) Orsi were distinguished members. Similar work was accomplished among the Benedictines and Franciscans.

A current of austerity, moreover, was flowing through Italy at that time, despite the country's reputation of gaiety and frivolity. Many souls dreamed of a mystic life and practised extraordinary asceticism. We shall find proof of that in St Leonard of Port Maurice, in St Paul of the Cross and in St Gerard Majella, who astounded his contemporaries with the rigour of his penances. The Baptistines, an order founded at Naples by Francesco Olivieri, offered a way of life no less austere than that of the Passionists; for women not satisfied with the rigours of Carmel, Battista Solimani and her niece Maria Vernazzo founded the Hermits of St John the Baptist, who were invited to live like the precursor in the desert.

One of the most significant features of what seemed much

like a second spring was the growth of missions throughout
the peninsula. That growth, starting from very little at the
beginning of the seventeenth century, went from strength to
strength until, in the eighteenth, missions became highly
fashionable. Whole districts, e.g. those of Padua, Naples,
the Roman Campagna and its surrounding hills, had been
stirred by the missions of St Francis Girolamo and St Antony Baldinucci. Certain bishops, among them Mgr Pignatelli
at Rome, undertook responsibility for the great apostolic task,
in which they themselves sometimes took a hand. The Congregation of Pious Workers, founded in 1607 by Dom
Carafa and of which Mgr Falcoza was General for some
time, laboured in southern Italy. Capuchin missions were innumerable and attracted enormous crowds; Oratorians and
Jesuits competed with them, and their rivalry was sometimes
acrimonious.

Those missions, too, were purposely spectacular. A huge
platform was erected in the body of the church (or in front
of the main door), in the centre of which a crucifix was set
up. There the missioners spoke for hours on end, relieving
one another and sitting down from time to time in order to
recover breath, after which they began all over again. It was
not unusual, as we shall find St Paul of the Cross doing, for
a missioner to scourge himself to blood before starting to
preach. When St Alphonsus de Liguori, skull in hand, spoke
of the four last things he had a terrifying picture of a man
burning in hell carried up and down among his audience
amid the light of torches. Such ways, perhaps, are far removed from ours, but it is beyond doubt that the growth of
the missions corresponded in Italy with real progress in the
fields of evangelization and moral conduct.

Pious and violent Italy with its colourful religion and full
of contrasts! It is impossible not to recognize the striking
testimony she bore to the Church in that age of 'enlightenment' and unbelief. Italy, who in the preceding epoch had
appeared to leave to France the privilege of producing saints,
became once more the birthplace of men who were destined
above all others to leave a mark upon their age and, at least
in the case of one among them, to work with an eye to the
future—saints, all of whom were to prove themselves great

missioners and great rousers of souls, as though Providence desired to show thereby that it awaited a great reawakening of the Christian conscience.

9. ST LEONARD OF PORT MAURICE

There we have a fact whose importance cannot be overestimated. The 'Age of Enlightenment', an age in which we have seen unbelief make such alarming progress, was also an age of sanctity. Reacting against the degradation of religion which they observed,[58] and assuming the double role of protest and example, which has always been the function of sanctity, a large number of men strove at once to restore to the Church her true character and to defend her against her enemies.

In the first quarter of the eighteenth century it might have appeared that sanctity had suffered an eclipse. The last survivors of the preceding epoch were now dead: Grignion de Montfort in 1716, John Baptist de la Salle in 1719. In 1716 also Naples lost Francesco de Girolamo, the apostle whose voice had for long years summoned her to penance. The Capuchin nun Veronica Giuliani, a stigmatic, was now gazing upon another light with eyes that had been dazzled in ecstasy. It seemed that there was no one left to continue the good work. Soon, however, as if in obedience to some mysterious dialectical law, as the century appeared more and more hostile to the faith, new figures arose not unworthy of the past.

All the great Catholic countries had one or more of them. In France, we have already met Mme Louise, Queen Clotilde, Mme Elisabeth and the verminous St Benedict Joseph Labre, men and women born into the most widely different classes of society. In Spain the great penitent Juan Varella y Losada, though never raised to the altar, might well deserve that honour. Towards the end of the century Austria had one apostle of outstanding merit in Clement Hofbauer. But Italy above all had the good fortune to produce men devoured by love of God, men who would work themselves to death tilling her soil with a view to fresh harvests. They were to be found in every province, from the Ligurian mountains to the Campanian plains, from Rome to Corsica, which at that time was linked with the neighbouring peninsula rather than with France, who was about to annex it.

In Corsica there was St Theophilus of Corte (1676–1740), a Franciscan consumed with mystical longing. He would have liked to shut himself away in some *retiro* among the mountains of his native land, there to lead a stern ascetic life and meditate upon 'the one thing necessary'; but in fact the call of the apostolate led him to renounce solitude and preach in the towns and villages of his island or, later, in nearby Tuscany. At Rome there was St John Baptist dei Rossi (1698–1764), a priest of Santa Maria in Cosmedin, who devoted himself exclusively to the evangelization of the poor of Trinità dei Pellegrini and to the spiritual direction of the clergy. Like the Curé d'Ars, he was a slave of the confessional, sometimes spending there twelve hours on end, and like him, too, did battle with the powers of darkness.

Three Italian saints, who resemble each other in certain respects and whose work drove yet deeper into the furrows whence the future was to spring, deserve particular attention: St Leonard of Port Maurice, St Paul of the Cross and St Alphonsus de Liguori.

One cold winter morning in 1716, when snow covered the hills of Tuscany, a party of Franciscans, walking in procession and singing hymns, set out from their convent at Florence for a solitary retreat where they intended to settle. The townsfolk, who knew them well, were amazed and pitied them as they went barefoot in the snow. But the friars appeared to feel nothing, no more, says the chronicle, than if they had been walking on a carpet of flowers. Soon the little band disappeared on the mountainous road and their voices died away. But Florence did not forget them.

They were Franciscans of a reformed observance named after St Bonaventure on the Palatine, an observance which had some time previously returned to the austerity and renunciation dear to the Poverello's heart. Had not St Francis himself left the world and gone to draw in the absolute solitude of a hermitage the spiritual strength with which he was destined to rekindle the Christian flame? Were not Alverno and the Carceri among the high places of Franciscan tradition? So thought the leader of that little band. He was called Paolo Girolamo Casanova, but as he had been born at Port Maurice, near Genoa, his name in religion was Leonard of Port Maurice. He was a tall lean man with majestic face beneath a lofty brow and with piercing eyes. As a youth he had attended the Jesuit college at Rome, and St Vincent Ferrer was one of his models. He had pondered the lives and teaching of the Fathers of the desert.

At Incontro he ended his journey, not far from the exquisite little church of San Salvatore del Monte[59] which Michelangelo used to call 'my pretty little peasant girl'. There eight cells were built and their furniture reduced to an absolute minimum: a block of wood to serve as a pillow, two blankets, a small lamp and a skull. The food problem was no cause of worry to the hermits, for the leader of this arduous undertaking had laid down a regime of nine annual fasts, which, taken together, allowed exactly five days on which the friars might exceed a minimal diet. Some years later Leonard wrote to Pope Clement XI: 'The world is crumbling beneath the weight of its crimes. The honour of God, trodden underfoot by the malice of men, demands reparation, which only the penance of religious can provide.' And he, with his seven brethren, was making reparation.

That austere life, that terrible mortification, soon became known in Florence and began to exert some influence. Penitents were seen climbing the slopes of Monte Croce to make the Stations of the Cross, which the Fathers had erected. Cosimo III de' Medici, whose heart was frequently burdened with grave problems, often visited the solitaries and accorded them his patronage. For fourteen years Leonard of Port Maurice did nothing but pray, mortify himself and meditate, evolving in secret the spiritual doctrine he would later expound in his sermons and books. In 1730, being then in his middle forties, he decided that he had remained long enough in the desert. Yielding to the call of an increasing number of souls at Florence and elsewhere who desired his presence, he came down from Monte Croce.

There now began a second period of his life, which was destined to continue until death. Throughout the peninsula men soon began to speak of him as an outstanding preacher. After attending one of his sermons a member of the ducal court exclaimed: 'I thought I was listening to the trumpets of the Holy Ghost.' 'Dust!' cried the orator to huge crowds. 'Life is but dust! Young man, where is your childhood? Gone, vanished into dust! Grown man, where is your youth? Gone, vanished into dust!' Thus sounded what the saint called 'the knell of sinners', to which echo replied: 'Penance!' The thought was by no means original, but Friar Leonard's eloquence drew from that treasury of eternal truth accents that wrung the heart.

More original in a way was the practice of which he made himself the herald, the spokesman, and which he linked with devotion to the Sacred Heart of which he was a zealous propagandist—the practice of the *Via Crucis*, the Way of the Cross. Like Paul of the Cross, his young rival in apostleship and penance, with whom a petty monkish quarrel once brought him into conflict, he had made this great discovery, that the only effective weapon with which to combat the intellectual pride and the sins of a world given over to pleasure is the 'folly of the Cross'. Crosses, therefore, he planted everywhere, introducing Stations of the Cross wherever he preached. A list, drawn up by himself and believed to be incomplete, enumerates no fewer than five hundred and seventy-six. The most celebrated were those he set up at Christmas 1750 in the Colosseum, where so many martyrs had shed their blood for Christ; they have ever since remained one of the most popular centres of piety in Rome, and near them St Benedict Labre chose to live and die.

Settling at Rome in 1730, in the convent of St Bonaventure on the Palatine, which preserves an impressive portrait of him, Friar Leonard of Port Maurice was looked upon for the next twenty years as the living embodiment of the ideal of reform that was now more than ever necessary. The highest dignitaries came to knock at the door of his cell, and he was visited more than once by Pope Benedict XIV himself. His authority was such that bishops asked him to solve difficult cases, as for example when he was called upon to advise whether the work of St Paul of the Cross and his Passionists should be accepted or rejected. But from time to time he left his hill and went to do missionary work in Tuscany, Liguria, Romagna, and even in Corsica, where he preached twelve missions in six months, erected Stations of the Cross in a hundred churches and converted the notorious bandit Lupo d'Isolaccio (1744).[60] Above all, however, it was at Rome that he preached, filling the churches to overflowing until he was obliged to take over the entire Piazza Navona. There the people stood packed like sardines to hear him announce the Holy Year of 1750. He became a legend in his own lifetime: at San Germano, when he had once more finished sounding his 'knell of sinners', the church bells started to swing of their own accord and kept tolling mournfully for twelve hours without anyone pulling the ropes—a fact authenticated by several notaries. A number of societies founded by him, e.g. the Coroncina and the Lovers of Jesus and Mary, were ready to continue his labours. The voice of the people had canonized him long before the Vicar of Christ raised him to the altar.[61]

10. ST PAUL OF THE CROSS, APOSTLE OF THE PASSION

Friar Leonard had devoted himself tirelessly and almost exclusively to teaching the world the lesson of the Cross, that the essence of Christianity consists in Jesus crucified. Another great spiritual guide was about to take up that lesson and to repeat it even more emphatically in an even louder and more moving voice. Paul Danei, who wished to be known simply as Paul of the Cross (1694–1776), is a strange and somewhat mysterious figure, at once a lofty mystic, familiar with ineffable reality, and a resolute fighter of earthly battles, possessed of a tender and sensitive heart as well as of an exacting conscience that demanded much both of himself and of others. Combining the characteristics of St Francis of Assisi and of St Francis de Sales, his was a nature of apparent contradictions which only the love of Christ could reconcile.

Few men, few saints even, give such an impression of having been led by a unique necessity towards a single goal. At the age of ten, when he began to meditate upon the sufferings of Christ in His Passion, young Danei had drunk gall like

the victim of Calvary and never went to sleep without a crucifix in his hand. At sixteen the parochial confraternity of St
Antony, which he had joined, elected him prior, so eloquent
were his words and so remarkable his austerity. At eighteen
he was the centre of a group of veritable disciples, twelve of
whom entered religion. None who came in contact with that
tall, thin, pale-faced lad could escape his spell; gladly or
grudgingly they yielded to his will. Soon he would encounter
the first of those obstacles which for years on end made his
life one long battle, and which at the same time would show
him his vocation.

His spiritual experiences were so strange that his parish
priest held him in suspicion. Another confessor, feeling himself outstripped by a penitent so advanced in the mystic way,
resolved to have no more to do with him. Some bitter jeal-
ousies began to rear their heads, but he derived from insults
nothing but an increased longing for humiliation, thanks to
which he would more closely resemble the Master scourged
and covered with spittle. In any case, what were his difficulties here below in comparison with the splendid and terrible
realities with which he enjoyed direct contact? In 1713, after
hearing a sermon, he had a vision of hell yawning before him,
and he never afterwards forgot the intolerable anguish with
which his soul was then filled. This experience of the Invisible, however, was about to be enlarged through the medium of ineffable ecstasies in which the heavens were opened
to reveal the glory of the Most Holy Trinity and associate
him with the unutterable happiness of the blessed. On Good
Friday 1715, while lost in contemplation, he experienced in
his flesh the sufferings of the Crucified and in his soul the
nameless joy of union with God, and he understood with a
certitude beyond human imagining that to suffer in Christ
and to be united with His joy are one and the same. He was
barely twenty years old, and he had already determined on
his vocation as apostle of the Passion.

For four years he continued, in one ecstasy after another, to
experience the divine approaches which would lead him to
the supreme grace of mystical marriage. This he received in
1722 or 1723, in his beloved solitude at Arpentaro. It was the

Passion of Christ alone then that he set himself henceforth to meditate, to teach and, above all, to live. He has been called 'the greatest spiritual figure of his age'; certainly in none more than in him does the mystical experience seem to have become part and parcel of life. If ever the famous saying of St Thomas Aquinas were true, that we transmit to others only what we have ourselves contemplated—*contemplata tradere aliis*—it applies perfectly to Paul Danei. Nourished not only upon Scripture, of which he had a profound knowledge, but also upon Tauler, his favourite author, upon St Teresa and St John of the Cross, as well as upon St Francis de Sales, he had no need to learn the great precept of what Bremond calls 'the metaphysic of the saints', which is to adhere to Christ; he had discovered it through vital experience. Like the Apostle whose name he bore, he could have said: 'It is no longer I that live but Christ who liveth in me.' Who lives and who dies . . . The whole of his life then, all his thought and all his activity, were devoted to proclaiming the Passion of Jesus. His writings (few in number and consisting for the most part of wonderful letters) and his sermons would never cease to do just that. It is difficult not to see therein a sign; this apostle of the Passion of Jesus was born in exactly the same year as Voltaire, and died at about the same time.

Nevertheless, despite his fixed determination, Paul Danei did not immediately discover in what way God would enable him to fulfil it. First there was a period of irresolution, during which he served in the Venetian army against the Turks. In 1720 the Bishop of Alexandria, after subjecting him to a long examination, authorized him to preach the burning truths with which he overflowed and clothed him in the coarse black tunic adorned with a white heart surmounted by a cross, which afterwards became the badge of the Passionists; yet even then the way ahead was far from straight and easy for the man who was to be known henceforward as Paul of the Cross. An idea took shape in his mind that he was called to found a congregation vowed exclusively to teach the Passion of Christ; and in order to remove his doubt, after years of struggle and anxiety, Our Lady of the Dolours appeared to him and confirmed him in his belief. But what kind of a congregation, and how? Should he go with some companions (if so, who were they to be?) and live as a hermit in a wild spot to contemplate the five wounds of the Crucified? Or should he take the road and proclaim to the world the truths he had learned? Many years passed before all this was made clear.

Twenty-six years, indeed, rolled by from that November day when the Bishop of Alexandria authorized him to preach, and granted him a hermitage, until the moment when his Congregation of the Passion was canonically approved. And that congregation existed on paper before it had any members—a rare occurrence in the history of the Church. If he had remained in his hermitage on Monte Arpentaro, above the seaside mere of Ortobello, he might have been left in peace. But his wish to found a new order, and the fact that he permitted enormous crowds to attend his sermons, was less acceptable. Existing orders and congregations looked upon him with a jaundiced eye, and this sort of apostolic rivalry so often turns, alas, to bitterness. The Franciscans in particular showed themselves hostile, doing their level best to prevent his access to Rome and even for a time opposing him with the undisputed authority of Brother Leonard of Port Maurice. This preacher, they grumbled, was not a priest. He was eventually ordained, but the attack was sustained with unrelenting fury; Pope Clement XII regarded Paul Danei as an adventurer and declined to receive him. The first friends to join the saint subsequently left him. The clergy of Ortobello sided against him and led him a hard life. He had to await the accession of Benedict XIV to the Apostolic throne before everything was settled; solemn approbation of the new institute was not proclaimed until 1746. 'A congregation that should have been the first in Christendom, but which appeared to be the last,' said the holy Pope when blessing its founder. But Paul of the Cross had certainly learnt the meaning of that phrase 'carrying one's cross'.

It may be asked what enabled the saint to fight on for a quarter of a century and at last to triumph. Nothing other than a burning conviction which emanated from him and imposed itself on others. Bishops who had heard tell of him asked him to come and preach missions in their dioceses, usually in the poorest districts such as the desolate regions of Maremma. Wherever he went he spoke only of the Passion. His friend and biographer, St Vincent Mary Strambi, has left moving accounts of those enormous gatherings, at which Paul mimed the scenes of the Passion, scourging himself in public the more vividly to recall the Scourging at the Pillar, weeping in such a way as to wring sobs from many throats and tears from many eyes. When at last he dragged himself[62] to the foot of the great cross standing in the centre of the platform, and when he intoned the sequence *Ecce lignum crucis*, there was hardly a member of the audience who could restrain his emotion. 'He seemed', says the narrator, 'to be dying and laying his soul in the Saviour's wounds.'

It was thus, at the cost of so much effort and suffering, that the Passionists came into being, that they rode out many a storm and that they ended victorious. From 1746 onwards, although not yet immune from redoubled assault and calumny, the new institute went from strength to strength. It began to establish regular houses of retreat. Vocations flowed in. After a delay of thirty years, patiently endured, a congregation of women was founded, inspired by the same ideal; and two spiritual friendships, beautiful as those which had united St Clare to St Francis of Assisi and St Jeanne de Chantal to St Francis de Sales, brought to the saint the consolation of joys that had been so rare in his life. In 1769 Clement XIV, who had long been Paul's friend, once more confirmed his work and made him a royal gift, the Roman basilica of SS. John and Paul, to serve as the mother house of the Congregation. In 1775 the Passionists numbered two hundred and possessed twelve houses.[63]

The founder was ready to die. He was now a very old man, broken and deformed by rheumatism, literally exhausted in the service of God. To the many visitors who crowded his door he continued to murmur of Our Lord's Passion and of His redemptive sufferings; and when he could no longer speak he distributed little crosses of black wood. He died in 1776, having never ceased to cry to the world a message that was always the same but none the less essential.[64]

11. ST ALPHONSUS DE LIGUORI. THE RELIGION OF THE NEW AGE

At about the same time, in Italy which had become once more the homeland of saints, another witness of Christ was at work, one whose achievement proved even more considerable. About 1750 the steep lanes in the poorest quarters of Naples saw him pass with unkempt beard and patched soutane, astride a jaded donkey no more handsome than himself. As he went along, with limbs already a little misshapen by the ailment which afflicted him, he was greeted with tender familiarity by a crowd of fishermen and fishmongers. For each he had a kindly word and a smile. If a stranger asked: 'Who is that curious priest?' the good folk replied in no uncertain terms that he was a rich nobleman who had become a beggar for the love of beggars, nothing less than the heir of one of the city's leading families. His name was Don Alphonso de Liguori. Some said he was a saint.

His youth had certainly been passed in surroundings very different from the voluntary poverty in which he was now seen. In the house of his father, Captain-General of the King's Galleys, where he was born in 1696, he had been a brilliantly gifted child, secretly admired and specially favoured by his parents. He had distinguished himself in literature, mathematics, philosophy, music and painting. At the age of twelve he joined the Faculty of Canon and Civil Law, and four years later emerged with a doctorate *in utroque jure*. An elegant horseman and a perfect dancer, he could not but have enjoyed a splendid career. At twenty-five he was one of the glories of the Neapolitan Bar and one of the most fashionable members of society. It was then that the Lord took hold upon him.

The well-known incident which brought about his 'conversion' appears so trifling that one can hardly give it all the credit for so radical a change. One day when he was conducting a case for the Duke of Gravina against the Duke of Tuscany, his opponent took him up on a point of procedure with such skill that he found himself completely baffled. The invincible young counsel stood silent, abashed and looking silly! Straightforwardly he at once acknowledged his error, and the whole of Naples roared with mirth. Was it this bitter humiliation alone that persuaded him to tear himself from earthly vanities? Surely God had long been at work within him, brought up as he had been by a devout father and a more than pious mother among brothers and sisters who gave to the Church a priest, a Benedictine monk and two nuns. The incident was doubtless the mere occasion of a spiritual crystallization.

Decisive at all events it proved. A few weeks after the defeat in court he had made his decision. His father learned of it one day when, to his grave displeasure, he failed to persuade his brilliant son to accompany him to the royal palace, where the Cardinal Viceroy was giving a great banquet in honour of the Empress Elizabeth, Queen of Naples. Alphonsus was no longer concerned with temporal ambitions. He had thrown his gentleman's sword at the foot of a statue of Our Lady of Mercy and served for a time as a male nurse in the hospital for incurables. Then he met the man who first directed him to the right road, Father Cutica, superior of the Lazarists who were preaching a mission in the poorest quarter of the city, and he listened to him speaking of Monsieur Vincent.

It was a meeting of capital importance, one that one can scarcely refrain from describing as providential in the deepest sense of the word. On the threshold of the neo-classical period, this remarkable being, the saint who embodied the aspirations of the Christian conscience in all their fullness, was a little peasant from the Landes whom Christ had led slowly, step by step, to take upon himself all the anguish of his age.[65] Towards the very end of that stage in the Church's history, behold a new saint had arisen, mysteriously bound to Vincent de Paul by secret links, as if he had been chosen expressly to succeed him.

The young barrister who had lost his case through having confused Neapolitan with Lombard law, learned from his meeting with Father Cutica the great Vincentian principle: 'Christ's charity compelleth us.' At Naples, more than anywhere else, there was need of charity. The city swarmed with a population of artisans and stevedores, coachmen and sailors, more or less unemployed, as well as of thieves and prostitutes who were never out of work. It was among such folk that the Lazarists were toiling and that the young man saw them at work. Ordained priest in 1721, he devoted himself to the apostolate with the same ardour that he had lately expended in other forms of activity. In fact he was still feeling his way. He had joined the Congregation of Apostolic Missions, a group of priests who, like the Oratorians, sought to promote the ideal of priestly sanctity among its members; and he was also interested in a missionary society whose purpose was to prepare men for China. Together with other members of his Congregation he visited the small ports around the Bay of Naples, where misery was equally rife. The taste for popular preaching seemed in him to dominate all others. His voice, at once penetrating and persuasive, was able to reach vast audiences. Leaving Neapolitan territory, he made himself heard in the provinces of Lecce, Capodimonte and as far as Bari. He also went on pilgrimage to Monte Gargano. At the age of thirty-five he had established his reputation as a great missioner and a commanding orator.

At this point Providence led him a stage further. Quite by chance Don Alphonso made the same discovery that Monsieur Vincent had made at Folleville in Picardy when he saw the distress of the French countryside on Mme de Gondi's estates. In certain circles, despite the best of intentions—those, for example, of the Apostolic Missions—his independent attitude was not unanimously approved. He was still impetuous and had a ready tongue, faults which he afterwards firmly corrected. Disagreements about which little or nothing is known led him to withdraw from those circles in which he had won his spurs. Very tired, he went with a few companions to meditate in solitude among the wild mountains which overlook the sea near Amalfi. There he found a state of spiritual ruin far worse than that of the Neapolitan proletariat, who were at least within reach of churches and had priests around every corner; that of the tatterdemalion goatherds and herdsmen in the mountains was nobody's concern. This discovery wrung his heart. Was the distress of the poor so great? Worse than any he had ever before seen. And there were no labourers to tend and gather that harvest of souls.

Everything combined to determine his course. Mgr Falcoza, Bishop of Castellamare, whom Alphonsus had known at Naples in the Congregation of Pious Workers and whom he had informed of his harrowing observations, replied with an urgent appeal. Since God had brought him face to face with that distress, why should he not endeavour to relieve it? Since he thought there was as much to do for the poor mountaineers as for the fishermen of the coast and the stevedores of the ports, why should he not form fresh teams of men expressly for that purpose? Father Cutica, the Dominican Fiorillo and the Jesuit Manulis encouraged him to accept the suggestion. Heaven itself appeared to have taken a hand. Mother Crostarosa, a Visitandine nun, swore she had heard in ecstasy the Lord speaking of him and of the congregation he was to found. How resist so much pressure? Mother Crostarosa's community took the initiative of preaching by example, of forming themselves into a new institute[66] which, in total renunciation and the strictest enclosure, would pray the Redeemer of the world to ransom the poorest of His poor and inspire those who would undertake to bring them light. On Sunday, 9th November 1732, Alphonsus with five companions of like mind knelt in the cathedral at Scala to vow the foundation of a new body of apostles. It was formally approved seventeen years later by the saintly Pope Benedict XIV, who gave it the name under which it became famous—the Congregation of the Most Holy Redeemer.

Alphonsus was now head of a very young congregation. As yet it had only a few members (about twenty, perhaps) and made no great noise in the world. But the influence of the Redemptorists increased rapidly. Mgr Pignatelli, Cardinal Archbishop of Naples, gave them his official support. All the small neighbouring dioceses invited them to preach their resounding and spectacular missions. Houses of the new institute were opened—four in the Kingdom of Naples, one at Girgenti in Sicily, four in the Papal States. It was soon learned that Benedict XIV held the apostle of Scala in very high esteem, and when in 1746 he published his great Encyclical on the need for a new apostolate it was said that he was referring to the thought and example of Don Alphonso without naming him.

Was it this very success that provoked opposition? At all events the founder quickly met with difficulties. Those whom his vehement tongue touched on the raw, public adulterers and thieves of every rank, waged a ceaseless campaign of calumny against him. Mother Crostarosa was expelled from the community at Scala. The authoritarianism of Mgr Falcoza did not ease Alphonsus's task. Because they held differing ideas regarding the right method to pursue, his very dear friend Mandarini, one of the five founders at Scala, left the new congregation to found the Congregation of the Blessed Sacrament, which intended to reach the masses through the schools. The civil authorities themselves intervened. Naples was then on the way to that 'enlightened despotism' of which the minister Tanucci was to be the typical representative. The palace did not approve of religious having friends at Rome, and it was even more disturbed by the fact that their public teaching, which was strictly moral, ignored the rights of states. Consequently the Redemptorists were pestered by regalist officialdom, even to the extent of police searches and threats of expulsion.

In 1762, no doubt in order to give the young institute firmer bases and its founder more authority, Clement XIII ordered Don Alphonso to accept an episcopal title and a diocese; not much of a diocese, in all truth—thirty-four thousand souls in thirty parishes. By virtue of obedience, though much against his inclination, Alphonsus agreed. Appointed Bishop of Sant' Agatha dei Gottici, between Benevento and Capua, he gave himself to his very poor diocese with characteristic zeal, striving hard to reform his clergy, establishing a kind of permanent mission in his parishes and doing all he could to organize charitable work on behalf of his flock, among whom there was a great deal of want. This of course was not exactly the work of which he had dreamed, and there was a risk that his Congregation might develop without him; for he was now far away in his remote little diocese, and before long he was virtually confined to his room by the terrible progress of articular rheumatism to which he had long been subject. This withdrawal, however, had at least one notable advantage: it enabled him to set down in writing all the fruits of his long spiritual life, all that he had said in his sermons. And from that life, entirely devoted as it seemed to outward activity, there flowed a written work of considerable dimensions, a body of spiritual teaching equal in breadth and richness.

For—and here undoubtedly is a mark of true genius—this man whom we have seen occupied entirely with the apostolate, spending his days on the mission, preaching and hearing confessions, proved himself at the same time an astonishing thinker, theorist and spiritual writer. Even during the most active period of his life he found means of committing to paper a number of treatises that formed both the foundation and the prolongation of his preaching. Later, imprisoned by sickness, he revised and enlarged them; until the end of his life, when he became almost blind, he continued to serve with his pen that truth which he could no longer teach by word of mouth. His writings consist of more than two hundred works, belonging to every category: apologetic and dogmatic in the *Admirable Guidance of Divine Providence* and *The Triumph of the Church*; moral and casuistical in his great *Moral Theory* (three large folio volumes), the *Practical Guide for Confessors* and similar manuals; spiritual and mystical in *The Glories of Mary, Visits to the Blessed Sacrament*, the splendid *Great Means to Prayer* and the *Practice of the Love of Jesus Christ* (1759); philosophical and polemical in the *Defence of Dogma*. Translated almost at once into all European languages, his books exerted a considerable influence. One of his contemporaries said of his treatise entitled *Preparation for Death*: 'It has had more effect upon the whole of Naples than a mission.'

His doctrine was not perhaps entirely original, any more indeed than was that of Monsieur Vincent. Many of its elements were borrowed directly from his predecessors, Lorenzo Scupoli, Philip Neri, the French school with which St Vincent de Paul brought him into contact, St Francis de Sales and, above all, the great Spaniards, notably St Teresa, but more particularly St Ignatius, whose influence upon him, both direct and indirect, was considerable. It has even been said that his work is a mere synthesis of all the thought and devotion of the faithful over a period of two hundred years. But that very synthesis is original, that wonderful way in which St Alphonsus was able to extract, from experience acquired in the course of two centuries of discussion, what would in practice help Christian souls and enable them to advance in the way of sanctity. We must leave it to theologians to decide whether he was a 'tutiorist', a 'probabilist' or a 'probabiliorist', if not an 'equiprobabilist'. His teaching, though fiercely attacked, especially by the Dominicans, has been officially approved by the Church; its principal features are a degree of prudence and a sense of the happy medium which stamp him as the most useful Christian thinker of his age and one also who pointed the road into the future.

The religion he teaches is profoundly human, without extravagance of any kind, austere but with restraint, mystical but in moderation. It is as far removed from Jansenism as it is from laxism and Quietism. He is not out—despite some theatrical sermons—to terrorize souls with threats of inevitable damnation. But nor is he out to spread too soft a carpet beneath the sinner's feet. What the missioner must rouse above all in the souls of his hearers is confidence in God. Why refuse absolution or impose extravagant penances? Why debar souls from the Eucharist, the very food that nourishes them? He is quite sure that without this divine support the human will is helpless in face of temptation. Liguori's system envelops the Christian in a whole network of devotions and sacramentals which hallow his entire life. There were those who railed against such pious practices as the rosary, litanies and the wearing of the scapular, all of which are dear to the people. But these things have their rightful place in Christian life. We may likewise ignore those who poured ridicule on the cult of the Blessed Virgin and the new devotion to the Sacred Heart; the logical end of their protests is an arid religion, in which God is no longer present to the heart. Looking back across two centuries at the thought of St Alphonsus de Liguori, we shall inevitably find that it covered all the main factors of post-revolutionary Catholicism. There are very few elements of religious life, as practised during the nineteenth century, whose roots are not found in that doctrine. Whether there is question of participation in the sacraments, of the Marian cult, of moral conduct or of the place to be allowed to contemplation, this wise and prudent man, who fought so well for Christ, has something to say about them all. When refuting Hobbes or Locke, the pantheism of Spinoza or the scepticism of Voltaire, he realized, as did very few apologists of that age, the necessity of opposing hostile philosophies with a living religion, a faith that vivifies the whole of man's being. At a time when apologetics seemed at a low ebb, he alone foresaw that in order to give back to the Church her full strength it was not enough to defend her as an institution, but that it was necessary to feed her from the true sources of life, to present her once again as the Mystical Body of Christ, long before papal teaching reminded the faithful of that truth. It is not commonly recognized how much the Catholic soul in the new age owed to the spiritual teaching of St Alphonsus.

That teaching appears today so fully and straightforwardly Catholic that one is surprised to learn how much resistance it provoked. In fact it was opposed to all those trends which at that time were harrying the world: 'philosophy', Jansenism and state authoritarianism, all of which had adherents sufficiently intelligent to realize the inconvenience of St Alphonsus de Liguori. Thus towards the end of his life, when he might have expected to be gathering the fruits of his labour, he found himself exposed to renewed and yet more violent attack. It was a curious situation. His written work was in everybody's hands; his influence was increasing; the sacerdotal retreats he conducted in his remote little diocese were attended by numerous priests; and yet at the same time certain impetuous Dominicans suspected him of heresy, and some of his adversaries denounced him to Rome. The old man, with body warped and head hanging down upon his chest, who could not rise unaided from his chair, was greatly upset. The secular authorities made things hard for the Redemptorists, especially after Tanucci took over the government of Naples. It became necessary to close the house at Girgenti. And when the Society of Jesus had been suppressed, the Neapolitan police accused the young congregation of being a clandestine revival thereof and watched it closely.

The life of St Alphonsus de Liguori ended amid trial and tribulation. Having obtained from Pope Clement XIV permission to lay aside the episcopal duties he was no longer able to fulfil, and having taken up residence in 1775 at the Redemptorist house at Nocera, he was obliged to look on helplessly as his work was demolished. The saint's immediate collaborators were circumvented by threats and cunning. One of them, Father Majone, in hope of securing from the Neapolitan government recognition for the institute, modified the rule as conceived by the saint; the spirit of the Age of Enlightenment had indeed passed that way. Suddenly Rome, alarmed by hostile reports, became angry, Pius VI cried treason, and condemnation followed. The Redemptorist houses in the Papal States were henceforth the sole authentic members of the Congregation of the Most Holy Redeemer, under the presidency of Father Francesco de Paula, the very man who had denounced his leader to the Roman authorities. 'The Pope's will is God's will,' murmured the saint on receiving the dreadful news; 'Lord, I wish all that you wish, I desire only what you desire.' It was in the peace of a supernatural hope that he died on 1st August 1787.

The disastrous break, however, was not to last. In 1793, thanks to the resolute efforts of Father Blasucci, an admirable religious, unity was restored. Father Francesco was shown the door, and the Redemptorists, having survived the storms of their early years, went rapidly from strength to strength, until, a century later, they numbered about five thousand and had nearly four hundred houses.[67] Saintly figures sprang from their ranks even during the saint's lifetime. Among them was St Gerard Majella (1726–45); son of a Neapolitan workman, he experienced the heights of ecstasy, inflicted terrible penances upon himself, preached to enormous crowds of the Redeemer's infinite goodness and died at the age of nineteen with the smile of Paradise on his lips. Later comes St Clement Hofbauer (1751–1820), a young Moravian who joined the Redemptorists after hearing Mass in one of their Italian houses. Beginning his career in the Church as an opponent of Josephism, he ministered tirelessly to the poor at Vienna and Warsaw throughout the revolutionary and Napoleonic periods. Was it perhaps the founder's long years of trial that won for the Congregation of the Most Holy Redeemer its glorious future?

History has ignored the testimony of the saints, being more concerned with the destructive influence of the Encyclopaedists and Voltaire than with this hidden and ceaselessly thwarted work. There is no more striking symptom of the Church's vitality than the presence of sanctity among her ranks at that decisive hour—sanctity which has always been her consolation and her hope.

12. MEETING THE CHALLENGE

The powers of sanctity, however, and its courage to meet the forces of death were already translating themselves into deeds. Wherever Catholics had been the victims of heavy blows, we find them inflexible under persecution and discovering in their faith reasons for hope and perseverance. Moreover, in those lands where the Catholic Church appeared to have lost the day, the last third of the eighteenth century found it making progress, having scored points off its enemies and in some cases even having won decisive positions. That impressive reawakening was full of promise. It was reasonable to hope that when, a little later, Catholicism was persecuted elsewhere, e.g. in France, it would be able to confront the storm and to re-establish itself after a bitter ordeal.

In hapless Poland, doomed to a tragic destiny, it seems to have been around the Catholic faith that there gathered those forces which would attempt to stave off disaster. Despite the numerous crises that had troubled her, she remained as profoundly Catholic as she had been at the end of the sixteenth century. Some of her priests and bishops, some even of her primates, may have been open to criticism, some of her monasteries unruly and defiant of authority, some of her kings notorious Erastians resolved upon domesticating the Church; but it is none the less certain that the vast majority of her people were imbued with Catholicism and never thought of the nation's destiny within any but a Catholic framework. Socinianism had been practically stamped out; Protestantism had made very little headway; 'philosophical' ideas had reached only a very small minority of nobles. The masses lived in an atmosphere of simple piety, medieval as that of Spain. During the forty years of relative calm that followed the Peace of Neustadt a number of great religious manifestations had increased their fervour, such as the crown-

ing of the Virgin of Czestochowa. Devotion to the Sacred
Heart was making rapid progress; Poland actually was the
first country in which it received official recognition. The
Lazarists, the Sisters of St Vincent de Paul, and in other
sectors the Ursulines, had gone from strength to strength.

When the first act of the drama ended there was a brief
period of uncertainty, the more so because partition almost
coincided with the suppression of the Society of Jesus. The
Polish Church found herself deprived of five hundred and
ninety-nine Jesuit priests, who had exerted a good influence
through their sixty-six colleges, their twenty-seven seminaries
and their sixty missions. It was necessary to provide for their
immediate replacement, and to this task of reviving the educational system Poland devoted herself first. Canon Kollentaj,
apostle of the national language, showed the way, followed
by Father Gregory Piramovicz. The Piarists and their recent
offshoot, the Marians, as well as the Basilians of the oriental
rite, shared in this work. A number of bishops lent it their
support, and an effort for the reform of Catholicism began
among the Poles themselves, among the Lithuanians (where
the Mariavites, founded by Turczynowicz, parish priest of
Vilna, did much good in the poorest circles) and among the
German settlers in Poland, who were visited in 1784 by the
great Redemptorist missionary St Clement Hofbauer. The reorganization of Basilian monasteries, accomplished between
1780 and 1788, was another indication of the effort at reform.
And that effort was inseparable from another in which certain
Catholics and even some bishops were then engaged, with a
view to giving their people a national soul which might stand
firm when the storm broke once again. An *Address to the
Fatherland* by Mgr Krasicki, Prince-Bishop of Warsaw, shook
the indifferent and those who had lost heart. Bishops Zaluski
and Naruszewicz were other great protagonists of Catholic
and national loyalties. Many priests took a hand in the movement which, in 1791, attempted to save the country. This
endeavour proved fruitless. Poland was not to escape her
sorrowful destiny. But when she had been erased from the
map of Europe, it was due to the vigour of their faith that the
chlopi, rallied around their clergy, resisted for more than a
hundred years the 'apostolate of the knout'.[68]

What the resistance of a whole people can achieve when it is defending its faith and freedom is proved by the case of Ireland. Though subjected to cruel oppression for more than a century,[69] the people of St Patrick had not given way. Their tenacity and their hope remained unbroken. All attempts by the occupying power to smash the national opposition had failed. Those who informed against priests had had to abandon their trade, for fear of being discovered lying in some remote place with a dagger between their shoulders. In 1725 the English had increased the penalties upon priests found celebrating Mass, but all in vain. They had opened English schools, Protestant, of course, but again to no effect; the Irish children attended them grudgingly in time of famine, because meals were provided, but the classrooms emptied as soon as there was something to eat elsewhere. The authorities had even offered dignities and high office to any who were prepared to collaborate; less than two hundred agreed to do so. In the span of one hundred years Ireland counted fewer than four thousand apostates. While hundreds of young men left each year to fight against the English in those famous Irish Brigades known as the Wild Geese, priests who had been trained abroad—especially in France, where there was a celebrated Irish Seminary at Paris—bravely returned to carry out their apostolic task in their own country. An official report in 1732 claimed that they numbered fourteen hundred and forty-five, but there were certainly at least four times as many. Officially, too, there were eight hundred and ninety-two 'prayer houses', where Mass was celebrated clandestinely, and there must have been many more. The British authorities dared not even forbid the great pilgrimages to St Patrick's Purgatory on the Island of Lough Derg, to Glendalough, or to the hermitage of St Finbar.

Such unshakable resistance led a few more reasonable and more statesmanlike Englishmen to ask themselves whether a change of attitude were not desirable. After all, the bishops were surely the best guarantors of public order. Moreover, as the century advanced, the British Crown met with increasing difficulties, in Europe as in America; might it not be wiser to settle the Irish question and close that open wound? After the rising of the 'Whiteboys' in 1767 the partisans of forceful methods carried the day, and the Whiteboys Act increased the severity of anti-Catholic laws. But the other trend was henceforth the stronger, especially as a party was formed among the Irish themselves resolved to profit by events without recourse to violence.

In 1756 Dr Curry and Mgr O'Keefe founded the Catholic Association, whose influence quickly spread. Their declared purpose was to make the English realize that it was in their own interest to reach agreement with Ireland and abandon persecution. They obtained reforms in exchange for absolute loyalty, which went so far as to prevent an attempted landing by the French in 1759, and even to the point of allowing Irish volunteers to serve in British regiments. Clearly such a policy was workable only because it rested upon a hundred years of obstinate resistance and thousands of heroic sacrifices. But it was clever: it succeeded. Gradually the occupation became less burdensome, less exasperating. Mass could be celebrated without interference from the English authorities, and some Dominican convents were actually re-established in the island. The Knights of St Patrick held their club meetings openly. In 1778, threatened with another French landing, Ireland organized her own defence. World opinion, moreover, began to concern itself with the lot of the Irish. Franklin spoke of it with emotion, and Lucas, founder of *Freeman's Journal*, criticized the 'Turkish despotism' of the English. In 1792 Henry Grattan, although a Protestant, secured the franchise for Catholics in Ireland.

Still more amazing, a similar success was obtained in England itself. If there was one country in which there seemed no longer any hope for Catholics, it was certainly the United Kingdom. Excluded from office, deprived of practically all rights, treated as outcasts, and even obliged by a law of 1753 to marry before an Anglican parson if they wished their union to be recognized by the State, they were a wretched little flock of some thirty thousand souls about the year 1730, 'not even a sect,' said Cardinal Newman, 'but a handful of individuals who might be numbered like the survivors of the Deluge'. But their resistance too was admirable. Among them too there were 'prayer houses' and clandestine Masses. At the head of a clergy working in secret, a number of vicars-apostolic proved themselves the bravest and most intelligent of leaders: Petre until 1758, Challoner until 1781 and Talbot until 1790. In their seminary at Douai, the Jesuits of the English Province trained the heroic members of the London Mission, while in the convent of the Holy Sepulchre at Liège, Mother Christina Dennett, niece of the Father Provincial and a great mystic, promised them victory. Mgr Capsara, Nuncio at Cologne, kept that Church of silence in touch with Rome. There was no violence, no sensational activity, but slow, patient work in order to convince Anglicans and Nonconformists that there would be no end to that resistance, and in order to seize every opportunity of proclaiming the sacred rights which the very principles of England should guarantee to Catholics. Despite the attitude of some more violent elements (e.g. Bishop Milne), Lord Petre and the two brothers Berington won general acceptance for this policy of firm flexibility, whose aim was the abolition of the Test Act. A Catholic Committee was formed to carry out the policy—sometimes with excessive daring. The government preferred to ignore it than to take action against it. Would Catholics, in exchange for new guarantees, agree to take an oath of loyalty to the British Crown? William Pitt called upon them to do so, having already been secretly assured by eminent Catholic theologians on the Continent that such an oath would be quite permissible. The great minister was anxious to settle the Catholic question and to unify the country with a view to the struggles that he foresaw in the near future. In 1778, notwithstanding the fury of the populace, the Catholic Relief Act repealed a number of penal laws; and in 1791 the Public Worship Act finally put an end to the old regime of exclusion, if not to the contempt in which Anglicans and Nonconformists held the papists. On the eve of the French Revolution there were not more than seventy thousand English Catholics. By 1815 they had more than doubled. That, it may be said, was due to political skill. But, as in Ireland and everywhere else, such skill would have been useless had it not been supported by the firmness and courage of loyal Catholics.

In the Prussian kingdom properly so called, Catholics formed an insignificant minority, but they were more numerous in the Hohenzollern dominions of south-west Germany.

There were many, too, among the soldiers whom the kings at Berlin recruited for their armies, as well as among the labourers and craftsmen whom they brought into the country, not to mention the populations of annexed territories such as Silesia. Moreover the Hohenzollern sovereigns, as a whole, were not exactly rampant Protestants, and Frederick II even spread abroad a highly 'philosophical' scepticism. The Catholic Church made use of all these factors to re-establish herself in the Prussian states. As early as 1723 the Dominicans succeeded in creating a number of missions to Catholic workers; one of them, Father Bruno, distinguished himself by his holiness and intellectual gifts. Soon afterwards chaplains were admitted to the Royal Guard, in which numerous foreigners had enlisted. In 1747 a Catholic church was built at Berlin; in 1773 it became the nucleus of a parish, and its influence was increased by the addition of an orphanage and a hospital. The Ursulines opened boarding-schools, notably at Breslau. In Silesia, recently conquered, Frederick II assured the Jesuits of his sympathy and invited them to create a Silesian Province. He remained faithful to his promise even when the Society had been suppressed.[70] Finally, in 1788, an edict granted the Catholics of Prussia the same rights as were enjoyed by the Lutherans.

In the northern Low Countries (modern Holland), though they had been badly shaken by the Jansenist schism of Utrecht,[71] the Catholic Church managed likewise to recover something of its old position. Her most remarkable leader was Andreas Aerts, Vicar-General of Bois-le-Duc, a great converter of Protestants and a tireless missionary. The Capuchins of the southern Low Countries, particularly those of Brussels and Namur, lent vigorous help to this revival. Also at Bois-le-Duc a mystic known as John the Evangelist exercised considerable influence. On the eve of the French Revolution, by which time the schism of Utrecht had largely diminished in importance, the Catholic Church had recovered sufficient strength in the Low Countries to be able to demand equality of rights with the Protestants; and she obtained it in 1798 when the new constitution was proclaimed.

Towards the end of the eighteenth century Catholicism was replanted even in Sweden, that most resolute bastion of Prot-

estantism. This was the work of Vicar-Apostolic Oster, a Lor-
rainer who had been headmaster of a college at Sarre, and was
sent to Sweden by Propaganda in 1783. The little Catholic
flock numbered only a few thousands; at Stockholm it consisted of fewer than two thousand souls. Circumstances, however, appeared favourable; Gustav III, a philosopher-king, had
recently abrogated the law excluding Jesuits from his realm,
because he wanted schools run by those excellent teachers.
Nevertheless difficulties were not lacking: Swedish law still
regarded conversion as a misdemeanour. Attacked by Protestant pastors, hindered in his work by the chaplains to Catholic
embassies, who supported the policy of 'no history', and even
denounced to Rome, the vicar-apostolic struggled on for five
years until the Revolution,[72] in order to increase his faithful
flock, whose very existence in the land of Gustavus Adolfus
was something like a miracle.

Thus in all countries the Catholic Church, so far from
being weakened and undermined by the forces of decadence,
as she is so often represented, gives an impression of extraordinary vitality at those points where her safety appeared
most gravely imperilled. The fire of Christ was by no means
extinct; it needed only to be fanned.

13. BIRTH OF A CHURCH DESTINED TO GREATNESS

At the other side of the world, beyond the Atlantic, the
Catholic Church provided another and striking proof that she
was still very much alive—in that young power that was soon
to be called the United States of America. And yet, God
knows, on the threshold of the eighteenth century the position
of the Catholics in the Thirteen Colonies was wretched. Lord
Baltimore's noble endeavour during the seventeenth century
to found a Catholic colony in Maryland came to nothing after
his death.[73] The English revolution of 1688 and the accession of William III had resulted directly in the protestantiza-
tion of Maryland. Whereas Lord Baltimore had generously
thrown open his domains to all Christian creeds, emissaries of
the Archbishop of Canterbury applied the anti-papist laws in
full. In 1704 the parliament of Baltimore forbade Catholics

to celebrate Mass in public or to educate children. 'Thus',
says the Protestant historian Bancroft, 'the Catholics found
themselves treated as helots in the country which, in their
truly *catholic* liberalism, they had made an asylum not only
for themselves but also for all persecuted sects.'[74]

That situation was destined to last without change for
nearly a hundred years. In order to justify their hostility towards Catholics, the Protestant masters of the colonies used
to say there was every reason to believe that the Papists were
secret agents of France and Spain, great Catholic powers
whose greed awaited nothing but an opportunity to swallow
the free territories of His Majesty. However, in spite of near-
persecution the Catholics stood their ground. Though virtually deprived of clergy, churches and schools, they managed
to survive. One Catholic historian finds the reasons for that
survival 'in the family spirit, tradition, education, catechism,
and also in the customs of hospitality, in relations with the
"manors" (a kind of seigniorial possessions which fostered a
more humane spirit and a greater sense of responsibility in
the slave trade), and lastly in the presence of Jesuits, who
stood fast and, by dint of energy and ability, thus maintained
the country under the direct influence of the Church'.[75]

That resistance had, as everywhere else, the results that
always flow from firmness and heroism. In 1755 a parish was
created at Baltimore, the very first in what were to be the
United States. Fourteen Jesuit Fathers and half a dozen secular priests re-settled in the Colonies—which admittedly did
not amount to much. But in 1770 there were certainly no
more than twenty-five thousand Catholics, most of them in
Maryland and the rest chiefly in Pennsylvania, where the
Quaker regime had allowed the settlement of a few thousand
German Catholics.

The situation changed soon afterwards, mainly because
the Catholic Church in America had the good fortune to
produce a man of outstanding quality, John Carroll (1735–
1815). He was of Irish descent, steadfast and fearless like all
his race. Born in Maryland, he did his studies at Saint-Omer
in France; then he joined the Society of Jesus, and made his
profession two years before it was suppressed. While exercising his ministry in the countryside where Washington, the

American capital, was soon to rise, he watched with excitement the grave events that led to the War of Independence. One of his close relations, Charles Carroll, was among the secret leaders of the approaching rebellion; and the ex-Jesuit even agreed to accompany him, along with Benjamin Franklin and Samuel Chase, on a mission whose purpose was to ask the Canadians for benevolent neutrality.

The War of Independence broke out. While the Anglican clergy remained, more or less secretly, loyal at heart to the British Crown, and while many Protestants fought the English with guilty consciences, the little Catholic Church, a despised minority, rallied boldly to the national cause. John Carroll employed all his authority to urge the Catholics in that direction, and received the thanks of Washington himself. The influence of France, that generous ally whose armed intervention on behalf of the cause of Independence was to prove decisive, was likewise of benefit to the Catholics: the Assembly of the French Clergy in 1780 voted a gratuitous gift of 30,000,000 *livres* to support the insurgents.

The result was all that John Carroll could have hoped. On 17th September 1784 the constitution proposed by George Washington and adopted by all the states included the following clause: 'Congress shall pass no law establishing any religion or prohibiting the free exercise of any religion; no law restraining freedom of speech or of the press, the right to assemble peacefully and to address petitions to the government seeking redress of any grievance.' It was the end of intolerance. Among the fifty-five signatories of that document were four Catholics (one of them Charles Carroll) and such great figures as Washington, Franklin, Madison and Hamilton. In 1789 the proclamation of liberty of conscience marked its logical conclusion.

The Catholic Church, then, had won her freedom, and there was nothing to prevent her growth. But she could not remain dependent on a foreign authority (in this case the Vicar-Apostolic at London), nor could she be considered as a mere missionary land. Pope Pius VI—and this was surely one of his happiest decisions—found exceptional means of dealing with an exceptional situation. He began by conferring upon John Carroll, whom all knew to have been the architect of success, the somewhat unusual title of Superior of Missions in the Thirteen States. Then, in 1784, he directed all priests exercising a ministry in the United States to assemble in what was virtually a national synod, and to choose whomsoever they considered best qualified to govern the American Church. John Carroll was elected by twenty-four out of twenty-six votes. Leaving his farm on the Potomac, where he had controlled the missions, he took up residence at Baltimore with the title of prefect apostolic, which he exchanged five years later for that of bishop. Thus was founded the first diocese in the United States.

Difficulties however, psychological and otherwise, were not yet at an end. Though officially free and enjoying equal rights, Catholics were none the less still despised and treated as second-rate citizens. A few rays of glory fell upon them when the French minister invited the members of Congress to attend a *Te Deum* in the Catholic chapel at Philadelphia, and Washington knelt in the front row side by side with La Fayette. But there was still a long way to go, and it required all the steadfast ability of Mgr Carroll to bring about a gradual change by means of his personal contacts and his prestige.

His most serious problem was lack of priests. The Catholic communities of Maryland had just sufficient for their survival, and Pennsylvania was not much better off. How was it possible to enlarge the Church's field without clergy? The situation was all the more delicate in that the clergy came from almost every European country, and ministered to Catholics who were immigrants likewise. At the first United States Synod twenty-five nations would be represented. It was at this juncture that Providence intervened through the agency of two men of genius. The French Revolution had just broken out when Mgr Carroll arrived in England for his consecration, and M. Emery saw there an opportunity of escape for a few of his students at Saint-Sulpice. He offered them to the new bishop, and in the spring of 1791 five young Frenchmen set out to serve as the nucleus of the first American seminary. On board ship with them was a thoughtful young man named Chateaubriand, who dreamed of great discoveries and of boundless spaces for his imaginary characters.

A new page was opening in the history of the Church in

America. Soon an autochthonous clergy would develop, trained on Sulpician lines and strengthened by priests and religious driven from France by the Revolution. Great devotion was shown towards that young Church, e.g. by Elizabeth Seton, a convert from Protestantism and foundress of the Charity of Emmitsburg, in whom there lived once more the radiant generosity of the first Grey Sisters. Mgr Carroll was grieved by the failure, through lack of support, of his Indian missions, which would doubtless have saved the redskins from extermination. But he could die content: the Church to whose being he had contributed so much was sure of its future. By 1800 it included 100,000 members, and 1,600,000 by 1850: the Church in America was henceforth destined to the glory it enjoys today.

14. A LIVING ART

If one last proof be sought that the sap of faith was still alive throughout the vast body of Catholic society in the eighteenth century, that proof will be found in art. The whole history of the Church shows that periods of solid faith or spiritual reawakening run parallel with flourishing periods of art. The age of philosophical irreligion was certainly not marked by any decline of artistic production; indeed, as the century advanced there was a noticeable increase of vitality, one might almost say a new flowering. Shortly before the outbreak of the French Revolution, on a hill that had been for centuries one of the holy places of Paris, a new church was completed, one whose dome was the loftiest in the capital— the church of Sainte-Geneviève which Soufflet had planned in 1757 and which was completed by his pupil Rondelet. That fact was not without significance.

In all Catholic countries the eighteenth century, especially its second half, witnessed the construction of innumerable churches, chapels and monasteries—proof that there was sufficient money to pay for them and consequently that the generosity of the faithful had not dried up. Not that there were no difficulties; here and there work was frequently interrupted and resumed. At Saint-Sulpice, for example, this happened seven times; but even in the Middle Ages such occurrences were not unknown. Of course there was not the same prodigious efflorescence of religious edifices as had followed the Council of Trent and continued into the early part of the seventeenth century; but the results achieved in the eighteenth were far from negligible, and it is not always realized that many churches which are now the pride of French cities are contemporary with Diderot and Voltaire.

We find the same activity in Rome. There Clement XII gave St John Lateran its monumental façade; Pius VI built the sacristy of St Peter's; the architect Fuga made additions to many churches, and adorned Santa Maria Maggiore with its gracefully ornamented front. We find it also at Venice and Milan, as well as at Naples, where Vanvitelli constructed the lovely Annunziata, and at Turin, where, on the noble hill of Sperga, Juvara raised the magnificent dome of his basilica, one hundred and sixty-five feet high. In Belgium, Mathys completed St Peter's at Ghent. In the Germanic countries and those subject to the Hapsburgs, Neumann built the church of the Fourteen Saints at Würzburg—a masterpiece. In Bavaria, Swabia and Franconia the Azams were responsible for numerous exquisite churches in which baroque gave free vent to fantasy and display. At Vienna the Karlskirche, the church of St Peter and that of the Piarists were triumphantly finished, while vast and splendid works were carried out in many other cities. Even in the Swiss cantons it was the period in which the cathedral of St Gall was completed, in which Kuen built the beautiful church of St Mary at Bregenz. As for France, the completion of Sainte-Geneviève was far from an exception. On the contrary. At Paris, Saint-Louis-du-Louvre and Saint-Philippe-du-Roule rose from the earth; Saint-Sulpice was nearing completion under Servandoni, who gave it its celebrated façade; Saint-Roch, Saint-Louis-en-l'Isle, Notre-Dame-des-Victoires and Saint-Thomas d'Aquin were restored or transformed. Travelling through the French provinces one might draw up a long list of churches, many of them of great importance, dating from this period: at Versailles, Cambrai, Lille, Arras, Metz, Lyons, Besançon with its famous Madeleine, as well as towns in Brittany, Aquitaine, Provence and Comte-Venaissin—more than fifty in all. To this evidence of vitality furnished by religious architecture must be added the countless and frequently enormous undertakings carried out in the monasteries, many of which were rebuilt or altered at that time. In France we have the great façade of Cîteaux, the imposing architectural range of Mondaye, the Abbaye-aux-Dames and the Abbaye-aux-Hommes at Caen, Fleury-sur-Loire and Montmajour near Arles. In Belgium, Orval was restored; in Austria and Germany, Melk, Mariazell, Klosterneuberg and St Florian; in Switzerland, the incomparable monastic church at Einsiedeln.

The religious architecture of the eighteenth century, full of vitality though it was, nevertheless reveals somehow the troubled spirit of its age. To what style does it belong? That is hard to say. Really, it belongs to none: all were accepted according to taste and temperament, even the old medieval style (Gothic) which had come to be described as barbarian. It appears that, in order to follow fashion and improve upon what were considered regrettable vestiges of the past, many parish priests and chapters demolished rood-screens, concealed ogival arcades behind plain arches of stucco, and even plastered whole façades, as at Saint-Lazare at Autun. In many cathedrals the canons, in order to screen their stalls and caring nothing for the fact that they were destroying noble vistas, built cumbrous choir towers in which the wood often ramified into the slender strands of 'spider-leg' style. Nevertheless a few venturesome minds were beginning to oppose that contempt of medieval art. Among them were the Abbés Lebœuf and Cochin, who admired the charming delicacy and wonderful lightness of Gothic churches; they derived inspiration from the old craftsmen, whose lessons they applied in many works of reconstruction as well as in building the towers of Sainte-Croix at Orleans and of the cathedrals at La Rochelle and Versailles.

Baroque still had many devotees, at any rate in a clearly defined field which included Italy, Austria, southern Germany and Bohemia, together with a few districts in Spain and Portugal. Becoming more and more unrestrained, and abandoning itself to all the charming frenzies of decorative inventiveness, it developed into *rocaille* and thence into rococo. Many churches and chapels looked like boudoirs of the Blessed Sacrament! Many too resembled pieces of finely wrought goldsmith's work. Austria was as it were the National Gallery of that art; but Einsiedeln in Switzerland, together with certain churches in Spain and southern Portugal, might have disputed the prize with her, not forgetting the American Indies, where baroque inspiration mingled with native influences and distant memories of the autochthonous past. So many streams of gold! So many angels gambolling on masses of painted wood! So many sunbursts springing from petrified clouds of incense! France, however, remaining strictly 'classical' in this domain, resisted the supreme offensive of baroque, allowing it nothing but the ornamentation of Saint-Merry, of Saint-Louis-du-Louvre, of the Visitation at Le Mans and of the Oratory at Avignon.

There was some reaction against the excesses of baroque, but nothing equivalent to an organized counter-offensive. What could one oppose to such extravagance? The great art of the Renaissance, from which baroque had emerged but which it had disfigured? Or that which the Jesuits had recently made fashionable, with their broken triangular pediments and their façade upon which ranges of pillars climbed one above another? Or, since there was a growing interest in ancient ruins, the art of Athens or of Paestum? Three Parisian churches admirably represent the three tendencies. Taking as his model the Graeco-Roman temple, Chalgrin, after a preliminary trial at Saint-Philippe-du-Roule, embarked upon that radical imitation which he accomplished in La Madeleine. At Saint-Sulpice, Servandoni erected a façade with two superposed porticoes, one Doric and the other Ionic, supporting a balcony reminiscent of the one at St Peter's from which the Pope gives his blessing. And at Sainte-Geneviève, now known as the Panthéon, the majestic cupola, 250 feet high and resting on an imposing colonnade, showed how strong the taste for imitation had become in that neo-classicism. Eighteenth-century religious architecture was the art of a Christian society which, though it still believed, was not quite certain how to map its course; it hesitated between several currents, and finally lapsed into mere copying, mere pastiche; and that, as we know too well, was to be its worst misfortune in the following century.

Was the situation very different in the plastic arts? Neither painting nor sculpture disdained religious inspiration. If one had the least doubt on this point, the presence of Tiepolo (1696–1770) would suffice to remove it. The Venetian master worked far into the century, to the end of his life a magician of large surfaces, covering the walls and ceilings of many churches and bishops' palaces with his glistening compositions. The Finding of the Holy Cross, the Ascent to Calvary, the Holy Family, the Adoration of the Magi and the sufferings of the martyrs afforded him his noblest and profoundly Christian subjects. But he was by no means alone. At Naples, Solimeni was his rival. In France, Jean-François de Troy, the great decorator of Besançon and author of the beautiful 'History of Esther', might also have been; so too might François Lemoyne, whose lady chapel at Saint-Sulpice is a gem. In Germany the Günthers were no less eminent. It should also be added that numerous painters on canvas, whose playful or sentimental pictures adorned many a drawing-room, devoted almost as much time to less frivolous themes. Greuze moved sensitive hearts with his 'Father explaining the Bible'; Chardin with his 'Grace'. All the same, one cannot help noticing in eighteenth-century religious painting a sort of internal discord, of duality. Was it necessary, in order to rouse emotion, to follow the grand baroque tradition of Rubens and Bernini, or rather to shun extravagant gestures, to hedge the truth with reserve—in a word, to follow in the footsteps of the Carrachi? The problem remains unsolved.

Likewise in sculpture: one need only compare two eighteenth-century statues of St Bruno. The one by Slodtz at St Peter's in Rome (1730) is all curves and violent emotion. Houdon's, at Santa Maria degli Angeli (1766), is lost in meditation altogether interior and spiritual. The two trends are discovered in all the sculpture of that period, which seems to have been groping its way. Like architecture and painting, it did not ignore the religious aspect of life; most sculptors produced many works inspired by religion, but can it be said that all those works were masterpieces? No. It was the period in which Catholic sculpture began its horrible descent into triviality. Consider J. B. Lemoine's 'Baptism of Christ' in the church of St Roch at Paris; there, someone has rightly said, the Messiah looks like 'a sweet-faced client taking treatment at a perfumer's'. It must, however, be added that in numerous churches there are eighteenth-century crucifixes that bear witness to genuine religious inspiration. Only a few yards from Lemoine's 'Baptism', Falconet's 'Christ in Agony' is a thing of very different quality. The works produced by Pajou for Saint-Louis-de-Versailles and the figures of Our Lady by Pigalle and Bouchardon speak directly to the soul. In Italy the Venetians Marchiori, Miliza and Scafurotto were far from negligible. Just as the period was about to close, a strange artist came upon the scene, a man of sure but cold talent, whom some recognized as a genius while others saw him merely as a skilful copyist—Canova (1757–1822), whom Pius VI appreciated and patronized.

15. ET NON IMPEDIAS MUSICAM

It is true that art always holds up to society the mirror in which it desires to recognize itself; it is perhaps from music that we should seek the most faithful image of that contradictory and passionate century. Even more than the plastic arts it was associated with all that seems characteristic of the age, its amusements and frivolities, its sports and *fêtes galantes*. But were those features of a pleasure-loving world the only things it reflected? To answer that question one need only peruse the catalogue of works produced at that time by the great musicians. There one finds a great deal more than comic operas and pastorals, or those pieces for the harpsichord and quartets which delighted contemporary drawing-rooms. Religious music occupied a considerable place in the list, and often seems to prevail over its rival.

All the leading Catholic countries had their master musicians. In Italy, where Scarlatti, author of numerous Masses and oratorios, died in 1725, there was Jomelli, whose *Miserere* overwhelmed huge audiences; there was Pergolesi, whose *Stabat Mater* still has power to move us. In France the classical continuity was assured by Lalande, Clérambault, the illustrious Couperin and Jean-Philippe Rameau. A great artist, endowed with admirably proportioned gifts yet devoured by an interior fire, Rameau sometimes allowed his music, ordinarily measured and reserved, to speak with heart-rending violence; so true it was that for him 'true music is the language of the heart'. Though he earned his living as an organist, it was not so much through the organ as through the human voice that he sought to reveal the secret depths of his faith. This he did in his motets—the *Laboravi* for five voices, the great choruses of *Quam dilecta* and *In convertendo*.

Germany, however, and the lands governed by the Hapsburgs, possessed the richest promise for the future. At this time they had just awakened to that musical vocation of which they were destined to provide much splendid evidence during the Romantic nineteenth century. Among them religious music had recently enjoyed a second spring, in surroundings that were strictly speaking Protestant, but in such a way that its message spread far beyond the framework of obedience and sects, and became part of the common heritage of all Christians.[76] The Lutheran Johann Sebastian Bach wrote five Masses, including the *Mass in B Minor*. In Germany, too, partitioned among rival confessions, and subsequently in England, where religious differences were even more acrimonious, Frederick Handel conceived his great biblical works, his charming *Ode to St Cecilia* and that stupendous oratorio *Messiah*, in which no Catholic can fail to hear proclaimed the message of a faith and of a hope that are wholly fraternal.

With Handel and Bach religious music seemed to have recovered its true voice. Nevertheless it was in danger. Gregorian chant, the most genuinely liturgical music, had become debased and was very little used. As in the domain of plastic arts, the lure of the profane was everywhere. The peril lay not so much in the fact that Christian musicians were ready to ally themselves with the worldly inspiration of librettists, as when Rameau set to music the obscenities of Gentil-Bernard; no, it lay in the unhealthy state of religious music itself. 'A cancer was ravaging the music of the Church,' says Colling. After the deaths, in 1750 and 1759 respectively, of Bach and Handel, it might have been asked whether any man of genius would arise to carry on the torch. The answer, in the shape of Haydn and Mozart, was not long delayed.

With Haydn and Mozart, both of whom were Catholics, religious music set out upon new roads. Four large volumes of the complete edition of Mozart consist of religious music, as does a good third of Haydn's output.

Despite their preoccupation with secular music they gave religious music a fresh impetus. Haydn, who served as organist to the Benedictines at Salzburg and who used to meet a word of praise with the assurance that he was paying homage to God, wrote numerous versions of the *Te Deum* and *Stabat Mater*; but the summit of his religious music is represented by three great works—the moving oratorio *Return of Tobias*; the strange and pathetic series of *adagios* entitled *The Seven Last Words of Christ*, intended for performance during the intervals in a sermon on the Passion; and the vast poem *The Creation*. Haydn's music proceeded from unquestioning faith; it reveals with absolute sincerity confidence in God and peaceful assurance.

Just as the century of unbelief and rebellion was about to be engulfed in a terrible tragedy, Europe was astounded by music so pure, so full of mysterious certitude, that it seemed to be nothing less than the music of angels. Mozart triumphed in the realm of sound at an age when most men are still prattling. At twelve he was an infant prodigy for whose services princely courts bid one against another, whom foreign academies were proud to welcome and whom the Pope created a Knight of the Golden Spur. Yet when he died at the age of thirty-five, having given to mankind some of the greatest masterpieces of music, he passed from the scene in sorrow, loneliness, penury; and his body was laid in a common grave where none would ever find it. A sad fate that has not ceased to move our hearts; but also a perfectly Christian fate, if it be true that the faithful Christian's greatest privilege is to imitate Christ, in death and dereliction.

Wolfgang Amadeus Mozart, though a sincere believer, was yet a tortured soul, searching desperately for truth. He appears as a typical representative of that eighteenth-century religion which, though not without secret stresses, painful questionings and some anguish, still contained unbroken loyalties far stronger than is commonly believed. His was truly an interior voice, the voice of a soul full of divine grace, which moved him to write the unsurpassable *Ave verum* or those solemn *Credos*, which in his Masses assumed extraordinary significance as marks of personal involvement and indisputable affirmation.

16. REQUIEM OF HOPE

In the month of July 1791, in his modest apartment at Vienna, Mozart received a remarkable visitor. There entered an unknown man, thin and dressed in grey, who would not disclose his name. Handing the composer an unsigned letter, he asked for a speedy reply. It was an urgent request, but accepted in advance any conditions that the recipient might choose to make. Mozart considered the messenger for a long time, his heart beating in his throat. For him, who was so attentive to all that the physical senses are insufficient to perceive, the visit must have seemed a portent. The anonymous patron wanted a Requiem Mass.[77]

Mozart was sick, restless and discouraged. He had long felt within himself 'a certain truly painful void, a nostalgia that never ceased', and from which music alone could rescue him. He accepted the order. How indeed could he have refused it? He stood in such grave need of money to provide for his family and care for his beloved wife, who was pregnant and in ill health. And then, can a man escape his destiny? With a break of only eighteen days in order to write an opera, he devoted the remainder of his failing energy to the *Requiem*.

Seated with Constance on a bench in the Prater, watching the yellow leaves of autumn fall, he may have had before his eyes the image of the mysterious visitor who bade him make haste. When the first snow of December fell he had no longer the strength to rise, and it was upon his deathbed that he tried to complete the work. 'I have no right', he murmured, 'to leave it unfinished.'

Few works of Mozart are so perfect as this last labour accomplished in the shadow of death. Perhaps, however, that sublime work is more in the nature of a prophetic sign than of a testimony. The mysterious privilege of some geniuses is to be secretly 'tuned in' to events, even when those events appear not to concern them, and to provide a very profound and very exact impression of contemporary hopes and fears. For as Mozart lay dying in his lonely room the world also was entering into darkness. The French Revolution had begun two years earlier, alarming the whole of Europe. The first waves of refugees were arriving in the cities of Germany, bringing with them tragic news. The king had been overtaken in his attempted flight, and, being now at the mercy of an enraged mob, was likely to suffer the fate of Charles I of England. The European capitals were talking of war. A conflict had just broken out between the new masters of France and the Church, a conflict which some believed to herald a great schism. This was the most fearful knell that had been heard for two hundred years.

It is symbolical that Mozart's *Requiem* was written during the year 1791, when the fate of Europe and of western civilization was being decided far from Vienna.

From beginning to end of the *Requiem* two kinds of themes alternate and answer one another: those of terror and those of appeasement. Anguish is present in the 'Dies Irae'; but there are far more numerous passages that express confidence, gentleness and consolation. It is not the anguish of death that Mozart's *Requiem* leaves in the hearer's memory, but rather an invincible hope, a transcendent certainty that is anchored in the heart of man by faith.

The faith that inspired Mozart on his deathbed and confirmed him in his supernatural confidence had not vanished from the Christian soul. Eighteen centuries of history had caused Christianity to strike such deep roots in western society that despite mistakes and shortcomings it could not disappear. Mozart's *Requiem* seems to answer in some mysterious manner to another voice which rose from innumerable cloisters, from wild retreats and random shelters where saints atoned with penance for the follies of their age, from missionary stations in the heart of China and Africa, where heroes of self-sacrifice continued to do battle for Christ. And it was that faith, still firm, that guaranteed the future.

The Christian West was about to live through some tragic hours. So many errors had been committed, so much infidelity had been perpetrated, that they could be redeemed only by suffering and bloodshed. The Church herself would have much to endure, for she too had been unequal to the charge laid upon her by her Master, and had failed to guide her children along their difficult road. But the ordeal would not last for ever. That 'tenderness of Christ for man', evoked in such poignant phrases by the *Recordare* of the *Requiem*, would not be in vain. After a period of anguish and uncertainty would come the years of hope. A regenerate Church was to emerge from the revolutionary whirlwind, a Church cleansed in large measure from the errors that had constituted her weakness, and ready to purify herself still further. In a difficult world, where the forces of death would become ever more menacing, she would indeed have to wage a sterner struggle than ever before. But it was already certain that, redeemed by the sacrifice of her martyrs and enlightened by the example of her saints, she would enter the nineteenth century with faith and hope intact, prepared to face whatever destiny awaited her.

CHRONOLOGICAL TABLE

Date	History of the Church	Political and Social History	Arts, Literature and Science
1701		War of the Spanish Succession (1701–14). Birth of Prussian royalty.	
1702	Protestant revolt in France: the *Camisards*. Jansenist schism of Utrecht. Foundation of the Seminary of the Holy Ghost.	Anne of England (1702–14).	
1704	Condemnation of the 'Malabar rites'.		Death of Bossuet and Bourdaloue.
1705	Bull *Vineam Domini* condemning the 'respectful silence' of the Jansenists.	Joseph I, emperor (1705–11).	
1707			Vivaldi, composer (1675–1741).
1708	Condemnation of Quesnel.		Death of Mansart.
1709	Dispersion of Port-Royal des Champs.	Victory of Peter the Great at Poltava.	
1710	Destruction of the monastery of Port-Royal.		
1711		Charles VI of Austria (1711–1740).	

	Religion	Politics	Culture
1713	Bull *Unigenitus*.	The 'Sergeant-King' in Prussia (1713–40).	Collins's *Discourse on Freethinking*.
1714		George I of England (1714–1727).	Watteau (1684–1721). The thermometer.
1715	Bull *Ex illa die* condemning the Chinese rites.	Death of Louis XIV. Beginning of the Regency (1715–1723) and of the reign of Louis XV.	Death of Fénelon and Malebranche. Johann Sebastian Bach (1685–1750). Handel (1685–1759).
1716			Death of Leibniz.
1717	Edict of Kang-Hsi barring the missions from China.	Foundation of the London masonic lodge.	Swedenborg (1688–1772).
1718			Voltaire's *Oedipe*.
1719			Wolf's *Philosophical Thoughts on God*. Montesquieu's *Lettres Persanes*.
1720	'Accommodation' in the Jansenist affair. Consecration of Marseilles to the Sacred Heart. Innocent XIII (1721–4)		Lancret (1690–1743).
1721		Anderson organizes the Grand Lodge of England. Peter the Great suppresses the patriarchate of Moscow.	
1722	Zinzendorf founds Herrnhut.		
1723			Tiepolo (1693–1770). The Fahrenheit thermometer.
1724	Benedict XIII (1724–30).		

Date	History of the Church	Political and Social History	Arts, Literature and Science
1725		Death of Peter the Great.	
1726		Minister Fleury (1726-43).	
1727		George II of England (1727-1760).	Foundation of the *Nouvelles ecclésiastiques*. Hogarth, painter (1697-1764).
1728	Submission of Cardinal de Noailles.		Voltaire's *Henriade. Chambers's Encyclopaedia*.
1729			In Germany, Wolff. Chardin (1699-1779).
1730	Clement XII (1730-40). St Alphonsus de Liguori founds the Redemptorists (1730-2).		Tindal's *Christianity Old as the World*.
1731	The Convulsionists of Saint-Médard.		Linnaeus.
1732		The first masonic lodge in France.	
1733	Activity of Wesley (1703-91), founder of the Methodists.	War of the Polish Succession (1733-5).	Pope's *Essay on Man*. Boucher (1703-70).
1734			Voltaire's *Lettres philosophiques*. Quentin La Tour, painter (1704-88).
1736			Death of Pergolesi (1710-1736). Calculation of the terrestrial meridian.

	Religious	Political / Military	Cultural / Scientific
1737	St Paul of the Cross founds the Passionists.		
1738	Bull *In eminenti* condemning freemasonry.		
1739			
1740	Benedict XIV (1740–58).	France renews 'Capitulations' with Turks. Frederick II of Prussia (1740–86). Maria Theresa of Austria (1740–1780). War of the Austrian Succession (1740–80).	Soufflot, architect (1709–80). Apogee of the *Aufklärung*.
1742		Charles VII, emperor (1742–1745).	
1744	Benedict XIV encourages the 'pariah' missions in India.		
1745		Battle of Fontenoy. Francis I, emperor (1745–65).	Pigalle (1714–87). Gluck (1714–85). The Leyden jar.
1748			Toussaint's *Les Mœurs*. Montesquieu's *L'Esprit des lois*. Hume's *Essay on Human Understanding*. Franklin's works on electricity.
1749		Dupleix in India (1749–54).	Diderot's *Lettre sur les Aveugles*. Buffon's *Natural History* (publication lasted fifty-five years).
1750			Death of Bach.

Date	History of the Church	Political and Social History	Arts, Literature and Science
1751			Thesis of the Abbé de Prades. First volume of the *Encyclopaedia*. Voltaire's *Siècle de Louis XIV*.
1752	Affair of the 'Billets de Confessions'.		
1753			Voltaire placed on the Index.
1754			Publication of *Roma Sotterranea*. Greuze
1755			Death of Montesquieu. Greuze (1725–1805). Voltaire's *Essai sur les Mœurs*.
1756		Deportation of the French Academians.	
1757		Seven Years War (1756–63). Damien's attempted assassination of Louis XV.	
1758	Clement XIII (1758–69). Suppression of the Jesuits in Portugal.		
1759		Battle of the Heights of Abraham (Quebec) and death of Montcalm; France loses Canada.	Death of Handel.
1760	Father Junipero Serra in California.	George III of England (1760–1820). The affair of La Valette. End of French India.	The steam engine. The lightning conductor. Rousseau's *Nouvelle Héloïse*.
1761	Execution of Father Malagrida in Portugal.		
1762		Catherine II of Russia (1762–1796).	Rousseau's *Émile* and *Contrat Social*.

1763	Febronius publishes his book on 'The State of the Church'.	Treaty of Paris, France loses Canada and India.	Death of Rameau. Lagrange's studies of the moon.
1764	Suppression of the Jesuits in France.		
1765	Institution of the feast of the Sacred Heart.	Joseph II, emperor (1765–90).	
1766		Execution of the Chevalier de la Barre.	Bougainville's voyage. Priestley's studies in chemistry.
1767	Mgr Pigneau de Béhaine in Indo-China.		
1768	The Commission des Réguliers in France.		Cook's voyages (1768–79).
1769	Clement XIV (1769–74).		
1770			Rousseau's *Confessions*. Birth of Beethoven.
1771			Cugnot's first automobile.
1772		First Partition of Poland	Last volume of the *Encyclopaedia*. Lavoisier's studies in chemistry (synthesis of water).
1773	Rome suppresses the Society of Jesus.	The Grand Orient of France.	
1774		Louis XVI.	
1775	Pius VI (1775–99).	Revolt of the thirteen English colonies in America and foundation of the United States.	

Date	History of the Church	Political and Social History	Arts, Literature and Science
1776		Defeat of Turgot.	
1778			Death of Rousseau and Voltaire. Goya (1746–1828). Lessing's *Divine Education of Humanity*.
1780	The Relief Act in England (toleration for Catholics).	Joseph II of Austria rules alone after death of his mother, Maria Theresa.	
1781	Beginning of Josephism in Austria.		Kant's *Critique of Pure Reason*. Herschel discovers Uranus.
1782	Pius VI at Vienna.		
1783	Death of St Benedict Labre.	Treaty of Versailles hallowing the birth of the United States.	Montgolfier's first balloon. Death of d'Alembert. Death of Diderot. Beaumarchais's *Marriage of Figaro*.
1785		The Affair of the Necklace.	Voyage of La Pérouse.
1786			Mozart (1756–91).
1787	Synod of Pistoia.		Bernardin de Saint-Pierre's *Paul et Virginie*.
1788		Protestants win civil status in France.	
1789		Beginning of the French Revolution. Insurrection of the Low Countries against Joseph II.	

SELECT BIBLIOGRAPHY

GENERAL WORKS

A. PRIMARILY SECULAR

Peuples et civilisations: vol. xi, by P. Muret; vol. xii, by Ph. Sagnac.
The Cambridge Modern History.
Histoire générale des civilisations, vol. viii, by R. Mousnier.
J. PIRENNE: *Les grands courants de l'Histoire universelle*.
P. RENOUVIN (ed.): *Histoire des relations internationales*, vols. ii and iii.
CH. SEIGNOBOS: *Essai d'une histoire comparée des peuples de l'Europe*, Paris, 1938.
R. GROUSSET: *Histoire de la Chine*, 47th edition, 1942; *Histoire de l'Extrême-Orient*, 1929.
G. LE GENTIL: *La découverte du monde*, Paris, 1952.
The Cambridge History of the British Empire, Cambridge, 1929.
LANNOY and VAN DER LINDEN: *Histoire de l'expansion coloniale des peuples européens*, Brussels, 1907–11.
A. MICHEL: *Grande Histoire de l'Art*, vol. vii.

B. PRIMARILY RELIGIOUS

E. PRECLIN and E. JARRY: *Les luttes politiques et doctrinales aux XVIIe et XVIIIe siècles*, Paris, 1955–6.
L. F. A. VON PASTOR: *History of the Popes since the end of the Middle Ages* (Eng. trans., 1891–1938).
M. CREIGHTON: *A History of the Papacy*, 1897.
J. B. BOSSUET: *L'Histoire des variations des églises protestantes*, 1688.
FATHER P. HUGHES: *A History of the Church*, 2nd edition, 1948.
G. LE BRAS: *Histoire du droit et des institutions de l'Église en Occident*, 1956.
The Catholic Encyclopaedia.

CHAPTER I. THE INTELLECTUAL REVOLT

P. HAZARD: *La Crise de la conscience européenne*, Paris, 1935; *La Pensée européene au XVIIIe siècle*, Paris, 1946.

D. MORNET: *Les Origines intellectuelles de la Revolution*, Paris, 1933.

J.-M. BELIN: *Le Mouvement philosophique de 1748 à 1799*, Paris, 1913.

M. ROUSTAN: *Les Philosophes et la Société française au XVIIIe siècle*, Paris, 1911.

A. MOND: *De Pascal à Chateaubriand . . .*, Paris, 1916.

E. VACANDAR: *Études de critique et d'histoire religieuse* (Galileo), Paris, 1905.

J. MARITAIN: *Trois Réformateurs* (for Descartes), Paris, 1927.

M. L. HUBERT: *Pascal's Unfinished Apology*, Oxford, 1932.

J. BARUZI: *Leibniz et l'organisation religieuse de la Terre*, Paris, 1909.

H. GOUHIER: *La philosophie de Malebranche et son expérience religieuse*, Paris, 1926.

L. BRUNSCHWICG: *Spinoza et ses contemporains*, Paris, 1925.

P. SIWCK: *Spinoza et le panthéisme religieux*, Paris, 1927.

P.-M. MASSON: *La religion de Rousseau*, Paris, 1916.

L. STEPHEN: *History of English Thought in the Eighteenth Century*, London, 1876.

J. N. FIGGIS: *The Divine Right of Kings*, Cambridge, 1914.

M. COLINON: *L'Église en face de la Franc-Maçonnerie*, Paris, 1954.

C. LEDRÉ: *La Franc-Maçonnerie*, Paris, 1956.

CHAPTER II. SUCCESS AND FAILURE IN THE MISSION FIELD

R. STREIT: *Bibliotheca Missionum*, vols. iv–vi, Münster, 1939.

MGR DELACROIX (ed.): *Histoire universelle des Missions catholiques*, vol. ii, Monaco-Paris, 1957.

G. GOYAU: *La France Missionnaire dans les cinq parties du monde*, Paris, 1948.

B. DE VAULX: *Églises de couleur*, Paris, 1957.

F. A. PLATTNER: *Quand l'Europe cherchait l'Asie*, Tournai-Paris, 1954.

G. SOULIÉ: *Epopée des Jesuites en Chine*, Paris, 1928.

P. LÉOPOLD DELPLACE: *Le Catholicisme au Japon*, Brussels, 1909–10.

J. MONSTERLEET: *L'Église du Japon*, Toulouse, 1958.

K. SCOTT LATOURETTE: *A History of Christian Missions in China*, New York, 1929.

R. MACLAGAN: *The Jesuits and the Great Mogul*, London, 1932.

P. BESSIÈRES: *S. Jean de Britto*, Paris, 1945.

G. GOYAU: *Les origines religeuses du Canada*, Paris, 1924.

E. LAUVRIÈRE: *La Tragédie d'un peuple* (on Acadia), Paris, 1923.

J. DESCOLA: *Quand les Jesuites sont au pouvoir* (on Reductions), Paris, 1956.

O. ENGLEBERT: *Le dernier des Conquistadors* (on Father Junipero Serra), Paris, 1956.

CHAPTER III. CHURCHES OUTSIDE THE CHURCH

J. COURVOISIER: *Brève Histoire de protestanisme*, Neuchatel, 1952.

J. DEDIEU: *Instabilité du protestanisme*, Paris, 1928.

E. G. LÉONARD: *Le Protestant français*, Paris, 1953.

H. VAN ETTEN: *George Fox et les Quakers*, Paris, 1957.

G. GOYAU: *Allemagne religieuse*, Paris, 1898.

AGNES DE LA GORCE: *Wesley, maître d'un peuple*, Paris, 1940.

M. PIETTE: *La Réaction de Wesley dans l'évolution du protestanisme*, Paris, 1925.

A. B. BASS: *Protestantism in the United States*, New York, 1929.

W. L. SPERRY: *Religion in America*, New York, 1946.

L. H. MONSATIER: *William Penn, aventurier de la Paix*, Geneva, 1944.

MGR DUMONT: *Églises orientales unies et dissidentes*, Paris, 1937.

H. MUSSET: *Histoire du Christianisme specialement en Orient*, Jerusalem, 1948.

G. DE REYNOLD: *Monde Russe*, Paris, 1950.

P. PASCAL: *Arrakum et le début du Raskol*, Paris, 1938.

I. KOLOGRINOV: *Essai sur la Sainteté en Russie*, Bruges, 1953.

N. ARSENIER: *La Sainte Moscou*, Paris, 1948.

CHAPTER IV. (STORM AND STRESS) AND CHAPTER V (THE REMNANT)

L. LATREILLE: *L'Église catholique et la Révolution*, Paris, 1946.

CANON SICARD: *Les Évêques avant la Révolution*, 2nd edition, Paris, 1930.

F. MASSON: *Cardinal de Bernis*, Paris, 1884.

E. SEVESTRE: *L'Organisation du clergé paroissale à la veille de la Révolution*, Paris, 1911.

S. LEMAIRE: *La Commission des Réguliers*, Paris, 1926.

On the suppression of the Jesuits see articles by Sydney Smith in *The Month*, 1902–3; on Febronianism those by G. Goyau in *Quinzaine*, 1905.

AGNES DE LA GORCE: *Le Pauvre qui trouva la joie* (St Benedict Labre), 2nd edition, Paris, 1952.

A. PARRAUD-CHARMANTIER: *Le Général de paroisse en Bretagne*, Rennes, 1926.

A. Desprairies: 'Les assemblées du Général de la Paroisse dans le Cotentin', in *Bulletin de la Société des Antiques de Normandie*, vol. xiv, 1888.

J. Bremond: *Le Courant mystique au XVIIIᵉ siècle*, Paris, 1943.

G. de Grandmaison: *Madame Louise*, Paris, 1922.

Canon Leflon: *Monsieur Emery*, 2 vols., Paris, 1944–6.

C. Almeras: *Saint Paul de la Croix*, Paris, 1957.

P. Berthe: *Saint Alphonse de Liguori*, Paris, 1900.

M. de Meulemuster: *Origines de la Congrégation du T. S. Rédempteur*, Louvain, 1953, 1957.

T. Maynard: *The Story of American Catholicism*.

P. Guilday: *The Life and Times of John Carroll*.

R. Schneider: *L'Art français au XVIIIᵉ siècle*.

Suzanne Clercx: *Le Baroque et la musique*, Brussels, 1948.

E. M. Dosta: *Historia del arte hispano-americano*, vol. i, Buenos Aires, 1945.

R. Rolland: *Handel*.

H. Gheon: *Mozart*.

NOTES

CHAPTER I

1. That of Anne Gonzaga of Cleves, Princess Palatine, delivered in the church of Val de Grace, 9th August 1685.
2. See the index to *The Protestant Reformation*.
3. *The Church in the Seventeenth Century*, Chapter V.
4. In France it no longer had any power.
5. He is supposed, after his abjuration, to have struck the ground and exclaimed 'Nevertheless it moves!' But the story has no foundation. It is impossible to believe that after having shown so little courage during his trial he would have had the audacity to utter words which might have sent him to the stake as a perjurer and relapsed. It is, however, true that later on and in the presence of friends, but privately, he gave way to rebellious feelings: 'To allow persons completely ignorant of an art or science to be called upon to judge those who know is the way to ruin a state. . . .'
6. At Amsterdam, Uriel da Costa, a Christian who had embraced Judaism because he did not believe in the divinity of Christ, disputed the historical truth of the Mosaic revelation. He was condemned to receive the thirty-nine ritual strokes of flagellation, tied half naked to a post, and to be trampled on by the congregation. Later, Spinoza's criticism of the Bible won him innumerable enemies, and he was obliged on more than one occasion to flee from the sanctions of vigilant rabbinical authorities.
7. Not to mention Ninon de Lenclos.
8. After his death his library was purchased by Mazarin, and became the nucleus of the Bibliothèque Mazarine.
9. Descartes took the *Summa* on all his travels.
10. For biographical details see *The Church in the Seventeenth Century*, Chapter VI, section 3.
11. *The Church in the Seventeenth Century*, Vol. II, p. 230.
12. In 1842 Victor Cousin made a careful study of the file and both copies, and he notified the Académie Française of the discrepancies between them and the published text. A new edition of the *Pensées*, faithful to the original documents, was prepared. It was followed by many others, that of Brunschvicg (1897) being the most widely used. The first editors arranged the fragments in an arbitrary order, as also have nearly all their successors.
13. The Protestant apologists will be studied in Chapter III, section 5.

14. *The Church in the Seventeenth Century*, Chapter V.

15. His life and work have been studied in the previous volume.

16. Cf. Sainte-Beuve, *Lundis*, ii. 157–77.

17. When a visitor called at the bishop's palace he was told 'His Lordship is at his books', with the result that his people used to ask when they would have 'a bishop who had completed his studies'.

18. See p. 44.

19. H. Busson, *La Religion des classiques*.

20. See *The Church in the Seventeenth Century*, Chapter V, p. 13.

21. This is the title of Paul Hazard's famous book (see Select Bibliography). The beginnings of that crisis must be dated about 1680; in fact it was a direct continuation of the crisis we have noticed in the preceding period.

22. See P. Hazard, *La Crise de la conscience européenne*, and his article on the Quarrel of Ancients and Moderns in Grente's *Dictionnaire*. See also H. Rigault (1856) and H. Gillot (1914), *La Querelle des anciens et des modernes*.

23. See Chapter III, section 6.

24. Ibid.

25. The words addressed by Don Juan to the pauper: 'I give it to you for the love of mankind', express the new spirit, the heresy of the intellect. A Christian would have said 'in God's name'.

26. *Les Origines intellectuelles de la révolution*, p. 23.

27. See Chapter III, section 8.

28. See *The Church in the Seventeenth Century*, p. 306, footnote 2.

29. He was a cousin, on his mother's side, of the celebrated Carmelite, Mme Acarie, Marie de l'Incarnation, memories of whom had been impressed upon him during his formative years.

30. After the suppression of the Society of Jesus it was continued by the Premonstratensians of Tongerloo. King Leopold I of Belgium (1831–5) invited the Jesuits to take it over again, and it has proceeded steadily ever since. At present it has reached the month of November.

31. Le Nain de Tillemont, a Jansenist, used the same sound methods in his *Vie de Saint Louis* and *Histoire ecclésiastique des six premiers siècles*. Launoy earned the questionable nickname 'Denicheur des Saints' [one who removes saints from their niches].

32. After a long and bitter exchange of lampoons and arguments the two men were reconciled in brotherly fashion.

33. 'This conflict', writes Jean Dagens, 'brought Richard Simon, who was deaf to spiritual resources, into collision with Bossuet, who was blind to critical evidence' (*Le XVIIᵉ siècle, siècle de Saint Augustin*, p. 37).

34. Paul Hazard, *La Crise de la conscience européenne*, Introduction.

35. *Lettres persanes*.

36. *La Révolution française*.

37. These quickly became popular after the Italian Procopio opened his in 1665; in 1789 Paris contained more than eighteen hundred.

38. We must not, of course, see in every *société de pensée* a fore-runner of the Jacobin Club. Some of them had altogether peaceful ends in view, literary and scientific culture. Many academies belonged to a movement which can be traced back to the Italian Renaissance and which was continued in France by the foundation of the Acad-émie Française and the Académie des Sciences. But it remains none the less certain that a number of these groups were very soon pene-trated by the new ideas.

39. See Chapter IV, section 8.

40. Not for all of it, however. Daniel Mornet (op. cit.) has searched the library catalogues of 500 of Louis XV's contemporaries. The *Contrat social* appears only once, and Diderot's *Lettre sur les aveugles* seven times. On the other hand, *La Nouvelle Héloïse* is mentioned 165 times, and Bayle's *Dictionnaire* 288.

41. *Les Origines de la France contemporaine: l'Ancien Régime.*

42. This was the breach through which unbelief entered the soul of Mme Roland. Cf. E. Bernardin, *Les Idées religieuses de Mme Roland*, Paris, 1933, p. 106.

43. See *The Church in the Seventeenth Century*, Chapter V.

44. René Pomeau: *La Religion de Voltaire*, Paris, 1954.

45. That, however, scarcely justifies a recent Catholic historian in ranking Voltaire among the 'saints that might have been'.

46. But not unanimously. Marat, in *Ami du peuple*, described him as 'a scandalous writer whose heart was the seat of envy, ava-rice, treacherous revenge'.

47. In August 1954 the *Figaro littéraire* published what purports to be a facsimile of a retraction by Voltaire, declaring that he had confessed to the Abbé Gaultier and wished to die in the Catholic religion (see *Ecclesia*, Paris, March and June 1955, and *Revue d'his-toire littéraire de France*, 1955, pp. 291–318); the question remains undecided.

48. On 18th November 1750, at the Sorbonne, Prades upheld a thesis on 'The Heavenly Jerusalem', in which he claimed that Our Lord's miracles were doubtful if considered apart from the prophe-cies. It was pretended that Diderot was the real author of this thesis. Prades, censured, banished and deprived of his licence to teach, fled to Holland and thence to Prussia, where he was protected by Fred-erick II. He ultimately retracted and died in 1782 as archdeacon of Glogau in Silesia.

49. Maurice Masson. See Select Bibliography.

50. See Henri Guillemin, *Cette affaire infernale*, Paris, 1942.

51. On the evolution of Anglicanism see Chapter III.

52. The word *Aufklärung* has often been translated as 'illumina-tion', but this appears to be not quite correct. Sachs-Willgate's dic-tionary suggests 'enlightenment', 'classification', 'progress of knowl-

edge'. At all events, the term is comparable with the well-known phrase 'enlightened despotism'.

53. Aldous Huxley's *perennis philosophia*.

54. This, at a stretch, might be described as the logical conclusion of Édouard Le Roy's thought, and perhaps even of Père Teilhard de Chardin's.

55. The evidence of the papal nuncio, Pacca, is significant. 'During this period modern philosophy, in other words unbelief, made greater progress in the Protestant countries of the north than in France herself. . . . For many years everything favoured the advance of irreligion in Germany' (quoted by Latreille in *L'Église catholique et la Révolution*, vol. i, p. 50). We may therefore dispute the following statement taken from a religious history of Alsace: 'The linguistic situation in that province had saved it to some extent from the poison of Encyclopaedism.' The extent to which it did so was extremely small; for if there was a linguistic barrier in the west, the sluice gates were open in the east and southeast, where books and pamphlets crammed with philosophism poured in without let or hindrance.

56. The Abbé Lefranc, superior of the seminary at Coutances, had already denounced the 'masonic conspiracy'. He was among the victims of the Carmel massacres and has since been beatified.

57. See Chapter IV.

58. R. Priouret, *La Franc-Maçonnerie sous les lys*, Paris, 1953.

59. Anyone who does believe in a masonic conspiracy must refrain from associating the Jews with it. To say, as has been said in a recent French manual of Church history, that 'the Jews employed the solvent spirit of their race within the bosom of secret societies' is to circulate a lie. The Jews were self-centred and held themselves aloof from all such propaganda, as Leroy-Beaulieu has shown in his articles on the destiny of Israel.

60. A. Monod, *De Pascal à Chateaubriand, ou les Défenseurs du Christianisme de 1670 à 1802*, Paris, 1916.

61. Ibid.

62. In the catalogues of 500 libraries examined by Daniel Mornet, Pluche's *Spectacle de la nature* occurs 206 times, proof that the philosophical ideas were not the only ones to spread.

63. They have been studied in great detail, notably by Daniel Mornet in his remarkable work *Les Origines intellectuelles de la Révolution française*. See the Select Bibliography.

64. See Chapter V.

65. The rupture between the Revolution and religion was brought about by the Constitution Civil du Clergé, desired by Gallican jurists, partisans of state socialism and irreligious intellectuals, and supported by a section of the lower clergy hostile to privilege. At the time it was even regarded as a mistake by revolutionaries such as Grégoire. Nor must we forget that on 15th August 1793 the Convention interrupted its work in order to take part in the procession.

CHAPTER II

1. See *The Catholic Reformation*, Chapter IV.

2. A treaty signed in 1694, the year after the Bull of Alexander VI partitioning the newly discovered territories between Spain and Portugal.

3. Compared with these majestic missionary achievements on the part of Spain and Portugal, the French work in the settlements in Newfoundland and Canada were as yet insignificant.

4. Mgr Ingoli held the office for more than twenty-seven years.

5. There were exceptions, e.g. the Dutchmen who helped Père Isaac Jogues to escape from the Iroquois prisons, and those Englishmen who welcomed Monsieur Pallu.

6. Modern Nova Scotia.

7. His name is sometimes written Valignani.

8. See *The Church in the Seventeenth Century*, Chapter I, section 10.

9. Published in 1644 by a member of the Company of the Blessed Sacrament.

10. He travelled by the overland route in order to avoid Goa.

11. See *The Church in the Seventeenth Century*, Vol. I, p. 177.

12. A scion of the Montmorencys, he is sometimes called Montmorency-Laval.

13. See *The Church in the Seventeenth Century*, Vol. I, p. 119.

14. The house still stands in the Rue de Babylone, which preserves the Carmelite bishop's memory.

15. See *The Church in the Seventeenth Century*, Vol. II, p. 67.

16. Mgr Marella was nuncio first in Japan and then at Paris. His words are from a speech addressed to the archdiocese of Tokyo on 31st December 1936 and reported in *Missions catholiques* (16th April 1937).

17. See the word 'Templars' in the index to *Cathedral and Crusade*.

18. *Rome et les missions d'Indochine au 17ᵉ siècle*, 1943–8.

19. The Brief provoked a serious quarrel with Louis XIV, who was indignant at the thought of a French priest taking an oath of obedience to any authority but his own. Months of negotiation were required for the settlement of this small Gallican problem.

20. See *The Catholic Reformation*, Vol. II, p. 72.

21. In 1626 Propaganda directed the Bishop of Japan, then a refugee at Macao, to ordain some Japanese exiles for service in their own country.

22. The last of the Mings and his wife took refuge in southern China, where they received baptism under the names Constantine and Helena.

23. He had been horrified to learn that the word *tal* was used both for the Mass and for superstitious rites in honour of the dead.

24. The quarrel had repercussions in Paris. Father Le Comte, S.J., who had written an intemperate and untimely book on the subject, was fiercely denounced by Bossuet. The Sorbonne condemned the Chinese rites.

25. The Holy See's attitude towards this question of the Chinese rites remained unaltered down to our own day. The oath of obedience to the decisions of 1715 and 1742 was required of all missionaries until 1914. The question was reopened in 1939 by Pius XII, who approached it in an altogether different spirit; he authorized missionaries to accept those Chinese ceremonies which were not manifestly superstitious, and in 1942, referring to the decree in 1615 of Paul V, he allowed priests in China to celebrate Mass (excepting the Canon) in literary Chinese. See Cardinal Constantine's lecture at the Collegio Urbano, 10th March 1956.

26. In Cochin China the quarrel between the priests of the Mission and a Barnabite who had been appointed vicar-general turned into a veritable melodrama.

27. Buddhism is divided into two main systems of observance: the Great and the Little Vehicle. This latter is distinguished from the other by its view of Buddha as a human sage rather than a god. It is also the more strict and possesses an extremely powerful monastic organization.

28. The above is a summary of Father de Nobili's achievement, which has been described at greater length in *The Catholic Reformation*.

29. These words represent a deplorable degree of ignorance; the coast of Malabar had no apparent connection with the high plateau of Madura.

30. A few episodes are recorded in Plattner's book (referred to in the Select Bibliography), but only such as concern the Jesuits. Those concerning the Society of the Foreign Missions are to be found in works dealing with its origins.

31. See *The Catholic Reformation*, Index.

32. See section 8 below.

33. It must be noted that in the diplomatic language of the time 'capitulations' had not the pejorative sense which it now bears in military parlance. On the beneficial results of this policy see Mgr Basile Homsy, *Les capitulations et la protection des chrétiens au Proche-Orient*, 1956.

34. In 1665 the court of Louis XIV was all of a flutter at the arrival, as Nuncio Extraordinary of Alexander VII, of Father Dominic Ottoman, a Moslem convert who had joined the Order of Preachers. The *Gazette de France* and the *Gazette rimée* declared him to be a son of the Grand Turk Ibrahim. (It was perhaps this event that gave Molière's *Bourgeois Gentilhomme* the idea of marrying his daughter to none but the Grand Turk's son.) Such episodes helped to arouse interest in the Levant and its missions.

35. See *The Protestant Reformation*, Vol. II, p. 285.

36. It had ceased to exist about the middle of the seventh century.

37. Between six and nine thousand pounds.

38. The Maronites (see *Cathedral and Crusade*, Index) had finally returned to the bosom of the Roman Church after the mission of Father Eliano, S.J. and the foundation of the Maronite seminary at Rome in 1584.

39. The Melchites gradually resumed some importance, especially under the influence first of Mgr Eftimios Sayfi, Metropolitan of Tyre and Sidon, and secondly of two monastic congregations founded at about that time—the Basilians of the Holy Redeemer and the Basilians of St John the Baptist. But they were often opposed, even to the point of bloodshed, by the Nestorian Jacobites.

40. See *The Catholic Reformation*, Vol. II, p. 91.

41. See *The Church in the Seventeenth Century*, Vol. I, p. 306, footnote 2.

42. The Historical Society of Wisconsin produced a monumental edition in seventy-six volumes (1897–1901).

43. See *The Church in the Seventeenth Century*, Vol. I, p. 86.

44. Their hostility was sometimes fostered by British or Dutch intrigue.

45. F. Parkman, *The Jesuits in North America*, Boston, 1895.

46. Louisiana was subsequently restored to France and was finally sold to the United States by Napoleon.

47. See Chapter IV, section 3.

48. The *Code Noir* is printed in Isambert's *Anciennes lois françaises*, vol. xix, p. 496 ff. Substantial extracts are given in Jean Imbert's *Textes et documents de l'histoire des institutions*, Paris, 1957.

49. *L'essor de l'Empire espagnol d'Amérique*, Paris, 1955. The conclusions of recent historians tend also to rehabilitate the Spanish colonial administration. 'One fact remains certain: no government, no colonial administration, at least in its higher grades, had ever had for the natives placed under its care a solicitude such as that of Spain.' (Pierre Channu, 'L'Amérique espagnole coloniale', in *Revue historique*, July 1950.)

50. The Austrian dramatist Höchwalder took it as the subject of his play *On Earth as it is in Heaven*.

51. But its shareholders included many good Catholics—Chateaubriand, for example!

52. See *The Church in the Seventeenth Century*, Vol. I, p. 71.

53. See the indexes to *The Church of Apostles and Martyrs*, *The Church in the Dark Ages* and *The Catholic Reformation*.

54. An infusion of mint in olive oil used as an embrocation.

55. See Charles Penz, *Les Captifs français du Maroc au XVII*[e] *siècle*, 1944.

56. See Chapter III, section 14.

57. See Chapter III, section 14.

58. They were later joined by a Carmelite and two or three secular priests.

59. See Chapter IV, section 3.

60. Great-uncle of Baudelaire.

61. It is worthy of note that Mgr Pigneau de Béhaine was the first member of the Society of the Foreign Missions to take a view of the problem of rites different from that of his predecessors. Arriving in Indo-China convinced that the decrees proscribing native rites were justified, he declared twenty years later that those measures appeared to him excessive and ill advised. For example, he said he could not understand what element of superstition could be found in the custom of carrying banners at the funeral of a mandarin commemorating his life and work. The closely reasoned report he submitted on this question certainly did much to bring about the altered attitude which prevails today. In this respect Mgr Pigneau de Béhaine must be considered a great precursor.

62. Father Krose (*Katholische Missionstatistik*, 1928) has attempted to calculate, on the basis of Stephen Borgia's report, the number of Catholic conversions obtained by missionaries during the seventeenth and eighteenth century. He puts it at about 2,000,000. He estimates that between sixteen and eighteen millions were converted by the missions before 1600.

CHAPTER III

1. The Elector of Saxony embraced the Catholic faith in 1697, the Duke of Holstein in 1705.

2. See *The Church in the Seventeenth Century*, Chapter V, section 13.

3. See *The Church in the Seventeenth Century*, Chapter III, section 1.

4. As late as 1762 the three brothers Grenier were executed at Toulouse.

5. See *The Church in the Seventeenth Century*, Chapter V, section 12.

6. It is impossible to calculate the exact number of religious sects or 'denominations' in the United States. Statistics vary from 263 to more than 350 among the white population alone. Figures are not available for the black Protestant sects.

7. See *The Catholic Reformation*, Vol. I, pp. 315–317.

8. See *The Church in the Seventeenth Century*, Vol. I, p. 219.

9. See *The Catholic Reformation*, Chapter III, section 11.

10. See *The Catholic Reformation*, Vol. I, p. 315.

11. There are 175,000 of them today.

12. Akin to the Quakers in their more excessive features, as well as in their form of worship, were the 'Shakers', founded in the middle of the eighteenth century by Anne Lee. Their doctrine was original, to say the least. According to them the world was created by a male-female duality, Jesus being the male element and Anne Lee the fe-

male. In order to return to the original state of purity it was necessary to renounce marriage and practise total continence. The Shakers lived in communities of one hundred men and women, known as 'families', whose numbers were sustained by the admission of widows burdened with children. In 1774 Anne Lee took the whole of her little sect to New England; it prospered there, but discarded most of its ideas and became a form of Puritanism. As for the 'Jumpers', established in Cornwall about 1760, they too were believers in interior illumination, which inspired them to leap, run and dance in a manner reminiscent of whirling Dervishes.

13. Courvoisier.

14. *Histoire générale des Civilisations*, vol. v.

15. See Chapter I above.

16. See *The Catholic Reformation*, Vol. I, p. 314.

17. See Chapter I above.

18. Ibid.

19. Abbadie was long read in Catholic circles. When Marie Philipon, the future Mme Roland, felt her faith weakening, her confessor made her read several apologetic works, among them Abbadie's. See E. Bernardin, *Les idées religieuses de Mme Roland*.

20. This tribute was rendered to Pietism by the Catholic historian Georges de Plinval.

21. See *The Protestant Reformation*, Chapter V.

22. See *The Church in the Seventeenth Century*, Vol. I, p. 134.

23. It was the Methodists that began the struggle for the abolition of black slavery in the United States.

24. E.g. the terrible episode of the Salem Witches, when twenty men and women were hanged, on the testimony of hysterical little girls, for having signed a pact with the Devil.

25. The following lines from a Camisard hymn provide evidence of the missionary vocation among Protestants after the revocation:

> *Faut bâtir des temples au Levant*
> *Et même dedans l'Occident,*
> *Et dans la Barbarie*
> *Et dedans la Turquie*
> *Prêcher dans les îles,*
> *Venez-y comme ambassadeurs.*

26. See *The Catholic Reformation*, Vol. I, p. 320.

27. See *Le Miroir des dames chrétiennes*, Paris, 1937.

28. The question of the relationship between Protestantism and capitalism is much debated. See Henri Sée, 'Dans quelle mesure protestants et juifs ont-ils contribué au progrés de capitalisme moderne' in *Revue historique*, May 1927; Henri Hauser, 'À propos des idées économiques de Calvin' in *Mélanges Pirenne*, I; Weber, *Die protestantische Ethik und der Geist der Kapitalismus*, 1923. The phrase 'spirituality of success' is used by Jacques Le Goff in *Marchands et banquiers au moyen âge*, 1956.

29. See Chapter II, section 11. See also Maxime Cléret, *Ethiopie fidèle à la Croix*, Paris, 1957.

30. See *The Catholic Reformation*, Vol. I, p. 329.

31. See *The Church in the Seventeenth Century*, Vol. II, p. 99.

32. See Chapter II, section 13.

33. Politically this idea is at the root of pan-Slavism, a notion first conceived by the Croat Krijanich. He explained to Czar Alexis (who made him his librarian) that Russia was destined to be the eldest sister and guide of all Slav nations. The concept did much to influence the policies of the nineteenth-century czars; its first concrete manifestation was the dispatch in 1810 of a Russian force to help Karageorge, the hero of Serbian independence, against the Turks.

CHAPTER IV

1. The Pasquino was an ancient mutilated statue at Rome, on the pedestal of which were posted epigrams (*pasquinades*) about distinguished men, many of whom were high officials of the Curia.

2. '*Tarquin was the sixth* [king of Rome], *Nero the sixth* [emperor], *this man too* [Alexander] *is the sixth* [pope of that name];

   Rome has always been ruined under sixths.'

To which Onorati, a canon of the Curia, replied with the following distich:

   '*Si fuit, ut jactant, sub sextis perdita Roma,*
   Roma est sub sexto reddita et aucta Pio.'

   ['*If, as they boast, Rome has suffered ruin under sixths,*
   Rome has been restored and enriched under the sixth Pius.']

3. See *The Church in the Seventeenth Century*, Vol. II, p. 116.

4. For the work of the eighteenth-century popes see Chapter V, section 5.

5. See Chapter II, p. 120.

6. In France alone the Society possessed (1761) 111 colleges, nine novitiates, twenty-one seminaries, four houses of professed, eight missions and thirteen residences. Forty-three of these establishments were situated within the jurisdiction of the Parlement de Paris. Father Poirot, professor of rhetoric at the Collège de Clermont (afterwards the Lycée Louis-le-Grand) for more than forty years, saw sixteen of his former pupils seated together in the Académie Française. In certain provinces Jesuit influence was reflected in the baptismal registers; for during the eighteenth century the Christian names Ignace and Xavier, hitherto unknown, became widespread among the middle classes.

7. P. 164.

8. The complicated proceedings against the Jesuits before the *par-*

lements have been admirably explained by Jean Egret in an article entitled 'Le Procès des Jésuites devant les Parlements de France' (*Revue historique*, July 1950).

9. The property of the Jesuits was confiscated and sold. Nor had the affair ended in 1789; for in the year VI the Council of Five Hundred appointed a committee which found that most of the patrimony had 'melted in the crucible of legal proceedings'. See Jacques Bonzon, *La Vente d'une congrégation sous Louis XV*, Paris, 1901. Some historians, including the Calvinist Sismondi, consider that the wealth of the Jesuits, like that of the Templars before them, was largely responsible for their ruin.

10. Curiously enough, it became fashionable to house a Jesuit. Voltaire had his own in the person of Father Annat.

11. It was the arrival in Corsica of these four thousand five hundred men, who would have to be fed, that persuaded Genoa to cede the island to France. See H. de Montbar, 'Les Jésuites à la Corse', *Revue de Paris*, August 1958.

12. See section 7 below.

13. He was supposed to have handed his confessor a letter for his successor; but Pius VI never admitted that he did. A document purporting to be the same was published at Zürich in 1789.

14. See p. 175 above.

15. *L'Église catholique et la Révolution française*, Paris, 1949.

16. See *The Church in the Seventeenth Century*, Vol. II, p. 134.

17. See S. Lemaire, *La Commission des Réguliers*, Paris, 1926.

18. See *The Protestant Reformation*, Vol. I, pp. 54, 69, 70.

19. See pp. 251 ff.

20. Following this uncivil behaviour, which was typical of his contradictory character, Joseph went to Rome for Christmas 1783. A new question had to be decided, that of the archbishopric of Milan, to which see the emperor claimed sole right of appointment. After long interviews with the Pope, Joseph II obtained a sort of 'Lombard Concordat', which authorized him to nominate bishops and abbots. Once again he had been successful, but to a limited degree; having thought fit to come and negotiate in person, he thereby recognized the rights of the Apostolic See.

21. See *The Church in the Seventeenth Century*, Vol. I, p. 202.

22. See Bernard Voyonne, *Petite histoire de l'idée européenne*, 1954.

23. See Chapter I, p. 82.

24. See *The Church in the Seventeenth Century*, Vol. II, pp. 110–11.

25. The second and third partitions of Poland will be studied in the next volume.

26. The title and contents of this section might suggest that the French Revolution was virtually inevitable. But such an idea needs some qualification. In the first place it is certain that while numerous

observers foretold the Revolution of 1789, none foresaw it take the shape it did. It must also be emphasized that while 'philosophical' ideas played an undeniable part in the Revolution, the philosophers themselves did not begin it; men did not rush into the streets because they had read *The Social Contract*. The immediate cause of the Revolution was financial. The middle classes were afraid of bankruptcy, 'hideous bankruptcy' as Mirabeau was to say; they were indignant at the State's extravagance. That was why they revolted. The social and anti-religious outburst did not occur until later. The Revolution can be described as inevitable only in proportion as the *ancien régime* proved incapable of financial reorganization.

27. See *The Church in the Seventeenth Century*, Chapter IV, section 8.

28. See Chapter I.

29. *La Révolution française*, Paris, 1923, vol. i, p. 13. He also remarks that under Louis XIV many banks and joint-stock companies were founded.

30. *The Church in the Seventeenth Century*, Chapter IV, section 1.

31. *Origines intellectuelles de la Révolution*, Paris, 1933.

32. *Procès du Chevalier de la Barre*, Paris, 1932.

33. But the importance of the clergy's wealth derived from land has been greatly exaggerated. Barbier, a barrister, said in his famous *Journal* that the Church owned one-third of the territory. Marcel Marion, a specialist in the history of finance, put the figure at one-fifth. That is still too high. The real estate belonging to the clergy should be estimated district by district, as the Abbé Girault has done in his exhaustive work *Les biens d'Église dans la Sarthe á la fin du XVIIIe siècle*, Laval, 1953. This author, commissioned by the Sorbonne, arrives at a mean percentage (the assessment varies from one district to another) of 10.47. He remarks that the *Cahiers des États Généraux* greatly overestimate the wealth of the clergy: where they say half, the correct amount is never more than 37 per cent. And G. Lefebvre, who writes the preface, explains that ecclesiastical property, though extensive in the north and east, becomes progressively less as one moves westward and, above all, southward.

34. This was part of a general tendency which proves the fossilization of the regime. An edict of 1781 required four generations of nobility in order to qualify for a commission in the army. In the navy, only 'red heels' (noblemen) could become officers.

35. See *The Church in the Seventeenth Century*, Chapter V, section 9.

36. Ibid., Vol. II, p. 134 ff.

37. It is difficult to form an idea of the *curé primitif*; the phrase had no reference to time or intellectual gifts. When a religious establishment—an abbey, for example—founded a parish, that establishment, in the person of its head, the abbot, was *ipso facto* its *curé primitif*, and the priest who actually performed his spiritual functions was his 'perpetual curate'. The *curé primitif* celebrated High Mass on

solemn festivals. There was a certain similarity between him and the patron, but he was much more than a patron. The term *curé primitif* was not used until the seventeenth century. See E. Altette, *Le livre des treize curés de Beauvais*, Beauvais, 1934.

38. The proportion of parish priests dependent on the 'proper allowance' (who were obliged to leave the revenues of their benefices in the hands of the *curé primitif*) and of beneficed incumbents (who had full enjoyment of those revenues) differed widely from the common estimate. M. de Vaissière (*Curés de Campagne de l'ancienne France*, Paris, 1933) shows that in 1760 the diocese of Paris numbered 342 beneficed incumbents against 137 in receipt of the 'proper allowance'; Langres, 313 against 157; Rheims, 418 against 90; Limoges, 659 against 209. As for the penury of country priests, it has been greatly exaggerated, as appears from numerous recent works, among them the Abbé Girault's *Les biens d'église dans la Sarthe à la fin du XVIIIᵉ siècle* (Laval, 1953). This work shows us many parish priests living at ease in well-stocked presbyteries. The *Souvenirs d'un nonagénaire* left by Yves Besnard, former parish priest of Nouans in the diocese of Mans, enable us to see clearly the gulf between the records of the States-General and the true condition of the parish priests.

39. See p. 298 above.

40. We are here recapitulating in a few lines the final pages of the previous volume, *The Church in the Seventeenth Century*.

41. At Paris, however, a succession of able chief constables, among whom were Sartini and Le Noir, ensured the maximum of security.

42. See above, p. 192.

43. France was not the only country where bishops were chosen almost exclusively from the reigning family or the highest nobility. Cologne, Mainz and Trier, for example, had the sons of kings or brothers of the emperor as archbishops.

44. The Spanish episcopate had a better reputation. Hence the proverb: 'A fine body of clergy could be formed from Spanish bishops and French priests' (quoted by Cardinal Mathieu in his *L'Ancien Régime en Lorraine*, 3rd edition, Paris, 1907). The absenteeism of bishops resulted in the sacrament of confirmation having fallen into complete desuetude on the eve of the Revolution. The constitutional bishops took pains to restore it. Grégoire, at the beginning of his episcopate at Blois, confirmed forty thousand persons. Cf. A. Gazier, *Études sur l'histoire religieuse de la Révolution*, Paris, 1887, p. 82.

45. It is worth noting that it was during the eighteenth century that the custom spread of calling bishops 'My Lord' and 'Your Grace', titles hitherto reserved to princes. Saint-Simon tells us that the bishops themselves first conferred those flattering designations upon one another, in order to encourage their subjects to make use of them—a clever manœuvre, which started about 1690.

46. Canon Leflon in his work on M. Emery.

47. It must be added that material organization left much to be desired. The limits of urban parishes were badly defined; there was

a certain amount of overlapping, and the people of some quarters did not know to what parish they belonged. This gave rise to difficulties, incidents and even lawsuits. Niort was a case in point: see Mlle Frarard's *La Fin de l'Ancien Régime à Niort, essai de sociologie religieuse*, Paris, 1956. The same confusion affected diocesan boundaries; there were 'exemptions', i.e. areas contained within the limits of one diocese but belonging to another. For example, in the diocese of Coutances five parishes, forming the exemption of Ste-Mère-Église, belonged to the diocese of Bayeux, while the diocese of Coutances owned a parish (the priory of St-Lo) in the heart of the city of Rouen. The fifty-five parishes of Paris were very badly partitioned: Saint-Gervais had 24,000 communicants and Saint-Eustache 80,000, whereas there were only 300 in Saint-Josse and a mere 120 in Saint-Opportune. See Pisani, *L'Église de Paris et la Révolution*, Paris, 1908, vol. i, p. 11.

48. The situation of course was relative. There were still plenty of priests; any lack was relative to a still larger number.

49. See page 127 of Canon Leflon's book mentioned above. In 1788 and 1789 serious incidents occurred at the seminary of Toul, where students twice attempted to fire the house. See L. Manet, *Histoire du séminaire de Toul et de Nancy*, 1936, p. 28.

50. It must be remembered that where some landlord had long ago founded or endowed a church, his generosity was recognized by allowing his descendants the right of patronage over that church. In addition to certain marks of respect (e.g. a seat in the choir and precedence at the incensation and at the reception of blessed bread), patronage included the right to 'present' the parish priest, a right known as advowson. The bishop could not appoint anyone but the candidate presented by the patron. The system gave rise to many difficulties. It was extremely complicated. There is an admirably clear account in the Abbé Sicard's little book *La Nomination aux bénéfices ecclésiastiques avant 1789*, Paris, 1896, which is unfortunately difficult to procure.

51. See *The Church in the Seventeenth Century*, Chapter II.

52. See above, p. 288.

53. Yet the custom was so firmly established that he himself accepted two small commendams.

CHAPTER V

1. See *The Church in the Seventeenth Century*, Vol. I, p. 120.

2. One man gave him a better welcome when he called at his cottage at Dardilly, near Lyons, in July 1770. Benedict Labre had just left the Trappist house of Sept-Fonts and was on his way to Rome. His host, who greeted him with open arms and treated him with the utmost kindness, was named Pierre Vianney. He was the grandfather of the Curé d'Ars, who was born in that same cottage sixty years later.

3. Beatified by Pius IX in 1860, Benedict Joseph Labre was canonized by Leo XIII in 1883. With him we may compare his contemporary Pierre-Joseph Formet (1724–84), known as Brother Joseph, the hermit of Ventron in Hautes-Vosges, an apostle of humility and poverty. His hermitage is still (as it was even during the Terror) a place of frequent pilgrimage. The existence of hermitages in the middle of the eighteenth century is a sign of perseverance in the faith that should not be forgotten.

4. Some villages had several churches: Colombey-les-Deux-Églises was not unique. Gouville-sur-Màer, in Lower Normandy, had three.

5. The president's judgment began with the words: 'All having been seen and considered, and the Holy Name of God invoked.'

6. See p. 192 above.

7. It may not be generally known that the ceremonies of Corpus Christi at Paris were the true origin of the Salon de Peinture. The tradesmen of the Place Dauphiné used to erect a magnificent chapel of repose, which was adorned with pictures; and young painters found it a useful opportunity for the display of their talents. See F. Boucher, *Le Pont-Neuf*, Paris, 1923, vol. ii, p. 128.

8. In many towns the Capuchins themselves acted as firemen.

9. See Abbé Sicard, *Les Études classiques avant la Révolution*.

10. On the whole subject of education and the various teaching orders see *The Church in the Seventeenth Century*, Vol. II, p. 18 ff.

11. Such was the origin of the Bibliothèque Sainte-Geneviève at Paris, and of the Bibliothèque Municipale at Toulouse.

12. Léonard, *Mon village sous Louis XV*, Paris, 1941.

13. See *The Church in the Seventeenth Century*, Vol. II, p. 21.

14. The French language has retained a trace of this feeling. A Frenchman will say of a commodity or a proposition which does not inspire confidence: 'Cela ne me paraît pas très catholique.'

15. Originally the *livre de raison* was a ledger (Lat. *ratio* = account), but it became customary to include a record of important family events.

16. Diderot, by no means a good Catholic, had twelve priests among his near relations, including a brother.

17. *The Church in the Seventeenth Century*, Vol. I, p. 149. On the *général de la paroisse*, which some historians have taken for a head of militia, superior to the 'parish captains', see A. Perraud-Charmantier, *Le Général de la Paroisse en Bretagne*, Rennes, 1926; A. Desprairies, 'Les assemblées du Général de la Paroisse dans le Cotentin', in *Bulletin de la Société des Antiquaires de Normandie*, vol. xiv, 1888, p. 69. It is from this latter that I have borrowed the example of the election of the curate and the midwife. In his little book *Les curés du Vieux Cherbourg*, Mgr Leroux shows us a meeting of the *général* in the Church of Holy Trinity (1748). The purpose was to appoint an organist; the meeting was noisy, and one has the feeling of being present at a political gathering.

18. Not to be confused with the confraternities of tradesmen. See

G. Le Bras, 'Esquisse d'une histoire des confréres', in *Études de sociologie religieuse,* vol. ii, 1946, p. 428.

19. L. Kerkiriou, *J. F. de la Marche,* Paris, 1924.

20. Mgr Juigné, Bishop of Châlons-sur-Marne and later Archbishop of Paris, behaved with the same courage during the terrible fire at Saint-Dizier.

21. It was he who, in the funeral oration on Louis XV, uttered the famous words: 'The silence of peoples is the lesson of kings.'

22. See p. 311 above.

23. See *The Church in the Seventeenth Century,* Vol. I, p. 118.

24. See J. Herissay, *M. Cormaux, saint de Bretagne,* Paris, 1937.

25. See p. 364 below.

26. See G. Bernoville, *René Bérault et Anne de la Brouardiére,* Paris, 1954.

27. See Lives by Father Michaud (Brussels, 1909) and Father Chaillé (Fontenay-le-Comte, 1955).

28. The phrase 'public virtues' is exact and fully justified. Many of the parish priests, well acquainted with the new ideas and contemporary progress, endeavoured to educate their people, to improve their conditions and to guide them in every way. That explains why the philosophers often spoke of them with sympathy. 'I know nothing finer than a parish priest,' wrote Jean-Jacques Rousseau. It also explains their influence in the editing of the Memorials of Complaint: having been 'ministers of goodness', they were expected to be 'good patriots'. At the end of the eighteenth century country priests were greatly admired.

29. *L'Ancien Régime et la Révolution,* i. 169.

30. See p. 328 above.

31. Chapter I, p. 93.

32. P. 365.

33. P. 329 above.

34. See *The Church in the Seventeenth Century,* Vol. II, p. 73.

35. See below, p. 386.

36. The work was first published by Father Ramière, as late as 1860.

37. Circumstances obliged him to write under the pseudonym Le Claire, under which he had also to live.

38. See p. 93.

39. *The Church in the Seventeenth Century,* Chapter V, section 3.

40. See *The Church in the Seventeenth Century,* Vol. II, p. 406.

41. Coudrin's confraternity at Poitiers, Bonnardel's at Semur; the Comtesse de la Chevalerie's Congregation of the Sacred Heart; Sophie Barat's Ladies of the Sacred Heart at Tufin; Fathers of the Sacred Heart, founded at Louvain by Tournely and Charles de Broglie.

42. See *The Church in the Seventeenth Century,* Vol. I, p. 150.

43. See p. 295.

44. See p. 290.

45. See *The Church in the Seventeenth Century*, Vol. II, p. 115.
46. See p. 394.
47. See p. 272.
48. P. 271.
49. *The Church in the Seventeenth Century*, Vol. I, p. 115.
50. See pp. 286 ff.
51. With the great bishops of Spain we may compare certain fine Portuguese figures, notably Mgr Miguel de Annunciação, another hermit of St Augustine and a fine preacher, who became Bishop of Coimbra. He resisted Pombal so courageously that he spent eight years in an underground dungeon to which light and air penetrated through a hole in the ceiling.
52. See Chapter II, pp. 160 ff.
53. Latreille, op. cit.
54. See *The Church in the Seventeenth Century*, Vol. I, p. 182.
55. One need only recall the Kurutz Wars; see *The Church in the Seventeenth Century*, Vol. II, p. 101.
56. See *The Church in the Seventeenth Century*, Vol. I, p. 155.
57. It is against this background of faith still deeply rooted in souls that we must place the reforms of Maria Theresa and Joseph II; otherwise it is impossible fully to understand them. The methods adopted by those sovereigns may have been more than reprehensible, especially their presumption to act alone and in contempt of the Pope; but it is beyond doubt that they were sincere believers, that they wished to serve the Church and work for her good by ridding her of the blemishes that defiled her in various ways. Nor, it need hardly be said, were their reforms useless; on the whole they advanced the cause of God.
58. It is only fair to recall the work of Zinzendorf, of the Pietists, of Wesley and the Methodists among Protestants during the same period. See Index.
59. Now San Salvatore al Monte.
60. During the second centenary of the saint, the French historian Mgr Cristiani (a native of Corsica) preached in all the villages where he had erected Stations of the Cross.
61. Beatified in 1796 and canonized in 1867, St Leonard of Port Maurice was in 1923 proclaimed by Pius XI patron of home missions.
62. Because rheumatism had crippled him when he was still quite a young man.
63. Today there are more than three thousand six hundred members, with one hundred and eighty-four houses, in thirty-five countries. Five congregations of women, inspired by the same ideal but dedicated to charitable and missionary work, are attached to the Passionists. The Order took root in France towards the middle of the nineteenth century. Twice driven out by anti-religious laws and severely tried by the ordeal of war, it is now on the flood-tide of revival. During the nineteenth century the Passionists included in their ranks St Gabriel of the Seven Dolours, Blessed Dominic Barberi, predestined

apostle of England, and the mystical St Gemma Galgani. Another of their disciples, though not a member, was St Maria Goretti.

64. Declared Venerable in 1784, and Blessed in 1853, Paul of the Cross was canonized in 1867.

65. See the first chapter of The Church in the Seventeenth Century.

66. The Redemptoristines, whose habit is the brightest and most decorative in the whole Church. It consists of a red tunic, azure blue scapular and mantle, two superimposed veils of white and black respectively, and an embroidered image of the divine Redeemer on the breast.

67. The sanctity of Don Alphonso manifested itself during his lifetime in a manner so striking that his canonization was effected with unusual speed. His cause was introduced without the long preliminary formalities required by law; despite the unsettled times, it was so well managed that he was beatified nine years after his death and canonized twenty-three years later. Finally, in 1871, his doctrine, especially his moral and spiritual teaching, was given the highest approbation when Pius IX declared him a Doctor of the Church, a title which St Alphonsus de Liguori was the nineteenth to receive, immediately after St Thomas and St Bonaventure, from whom he was separated in time by five centuries.

68. Chlopi (peasants) is the title of a great novel by Ladislas Reymont; The Apostolate of the Knout is that of another of his works.

69. See The Church in the Seventeenth Century, Vol. I, p. 210.

70. See p. 285.

71. See The Church in the Seventeenth Century, Vol. II, p. 250.

72. At the outbreak of the Revolution, Oster was in France, where he only just escaped the guillotine.

73. See Chapter III, pp. 229–30.

74. History of the United States.

75. John Lafarge in The Catholic Review, April 1935.

76. See on Bach and Handel, p. 244.

77. It is now known that he was a wealthy gentleman who, having lost his wife, wished to dedicate a Mass to her, but who, considering himself something of a musician, desired that it should pass as his own work.

INDEX

IMAGE BOOKS

Image Books constitute a quality library of Catholic writings, broad in human interest and deep in Christian insight. They will include classical Christian writings, devotion, philosophy, education and history; biographies, novels and poetry; and books on contemporary social problems. They represent a planned program of making available to the widest possible audience the finest Catholic literature in attractive, paper-bound, inexpensive editions. They have been selected with these criteria in mind: that they must in every instance be well written, inspiring to the spirit, and of lasting value to the general audience who will purchase them.

The majority of Image Books will consist of reprints made possible through the cooperation of the publishers of the original editions. Occasionally certain much-needed volumes which are not available will also be initiated for this series.

A descriptive catalogue of the Image Books already published may be obtained by writing directly to the publisher. Comments and suggestions from those interested in the series are welcomed by the publisher. I 3